Ryan

Sams Teach Yourself SQL

in 24 Hours

Seventh Edition

SAMS

Sams Teach Yourself SQL in 24 Hours, Seventh Edition

ISBN-13: 978-0-13-754312-0
ISBN-10: 0-13-754312-3

Library of Congress Control Number: 2021948117

1 2021

Trademarks

Warning and Disclaimer

Special Sales

For information about buying this title in bulk quantities, or for special sales opportunities (which may include electronic versions; custom cover designs; and content particular to your business, training goals, marketing focus, or branding interests), please contact our corporate sales department at corpsales@pearsoned.com or (800) 382-3419.

For government sales inquiries, please contact governmentsales@pearsoned.com.

For questions about sales outside the U.S., please contact intlcs@pearson.com.

Editor-in-Chief
Mark Taub

Acquisitions Editor
Malobika Chakraborty

Development Editor
Mark Renfrow

Managing Editor
Sandra Schroeder

Senior Project Editor
Tonya Simpson

Copy Editor
Krista Hansing Editorial Services

Indexer
Cheryl Lenser

Proofreader
Betty Pessagno

Cover Designer
Chuti Prasertsith

Compositor
codemantra

Pearson's Commitment to Diversity, Equity, and Inclusion

Pearson is dedicated to creating bias-free content that reflects the diversity of all learners. We embrace the many dimensions of diversity, including but not limited to race, ethnicity, gender, socioeconomic status, ability, age, sexual orientation, and religious or political beliefs.

Education is a powerful force for equity and change in our world. It has the potential to deliver opportunities that improve lives and enable economic mobility. As we work with authors to create content for every product and service, we acknowledge our responsibility to demonstrate inclusivity and incorporate diverse scholarship so that everyone can achieve their potential through learning. As the world's leading learning company, we have a duty to help drive change and live up to our purpose to help more people create a better life for themselves and to create a better world.

Our ambition is to purposefully contribute to a world where:

- Everyone has an equitable and lifelong opportunity to succeed through learning.
- Our educational products and services are inclusive and represent the rich diversity of learners.
- Our educational content accurately reflects the histories and experiences of the learners we serve.
- Our educational content prompts deeper discussions with learners and motivates them to expand their own learning (and worldview).

While we work hard to present unbiased content, we want to hear from you about any concerns or needs with this Pearson product so that we can investigate and address them.

- Please contact us with concerns about any potential bias at https://www.pearson.com/report-bias.html.

Contents at a Glance

Table of Contents

About the Author

Ryan Stephens is an entrepreneur who has built his career and multiple IT companies around SQL, data, and relational databases. He has shared his knowledge and experience with organizations, students, and IT professionals all over the world. Two of the companies he has co-founded, Perpetual Technologies, Inc. (PTI), and Indy Data Partners, have provided expert database and IT services to large-scale government and commercial clients for more than 25 years. Ryan has authored several books for Pearson, including *Sams Teach Yourself SQL in 24 Hours*, 6th Edition; some of his books have been translated and published internationally. Additionally, Ryan has worked for large organizations and has consulted within the areas of SQL, database design, database management, and project management. He designed and taught a database management program for Indiana University–Purdue University in Indianapolis and currently teaches online SQL and database classes for Pearson Education.

Dedication

This book is dedicated to my daughter,
Charlie Marie, named after my late adoptive mom,
Charlotte Anne Pritchett Stephens, who is the first person I remember
teaching me to write. I love you both.

Acknowledgments

First of all, I would like to thank the contributing authors to previous editions of this book, Ronald Plew and Arie D. Jones.

Ronald Plew is my retired co-founder of Perpetual Technologies and is a great friend. I could not have started my first successful business without him. Ron studied and consulted in the field of relational database technology for more than 20 years, is a published author, and helped me build a database training program at Indiana University–Purdue University (IUPUI) in Indianapolis. Ron taught SQL and database classes at IUPUI for 5 years.

Arie D. Jones is the vice president for Emerging Technologies for Indy Data Partners, Inc. (IDP), in Indianapolis and helped me get that company off to a successful start. Arie leads IDP's team of experts in planning, design, development, deployment, and management of database environments and applications to achieve the best combination of tools and services for each client. He is a regular speaker at technical events and has authored several books and articles on database-related topics.

Thank you also to Angie Gleim, Amy Reeves, Terri Klein, and all of my team members for doing such a professional job running our companies so that I have the freedom to take on projects like this. And as always, thanks to the staff at Pearson and Sams Publishing for your attention to detail and patience. It is always a pleasure working with you.

We Want to Hear from You!

As the reader of this book, *you* are our most important critic and commentator. We value your opinion and want to know what we're doing right, what we could do better, what areas you'd like to see us publish in, and any other words of wisdom you're willing to pass our way.

We welcome your comments. You can email or write to let us know what you did or didn't like about this book—as well as what we can do to make our books better.

Please note that we cannot help you with technical problems related to the topic of this book.

When you write, please be sure to include this book's title and author as well as your name and email address. We will carefully review your comments and share them with the author and editors who worked on the book.

Email: community@informit.com

Reader Services

Register your copy of *Sams Teach Yourself SQL in 24 Hours* at informit.com for convenient access to downloads, updates, and corrections as they become available. To start the registration process, go to informit.com/register and log in or create an account.* Enter the product ISBN, 9780137543120, and click Submit. Once the process is complete, you will find any available bonus content under Registered Products.

*Be sure to check the box that you would like to hear from us in order to receive exclusive discounts on future editions of this product.

What This Book Is About

This book is about the Structured Query Language (SQL), the standard language used to communicate with any relational database. Relational databases are one of the most popular data-management solutions, and many vendor software implementations of SQL are available for organizations and individuals. The text does not focus on a specific implementation of SQL, but Oracle is used for most of the examples because it is a leading database-management software product that adheres closely to the SQL standard. In the upcoming hours, you learn how to apply the SQL standard from a practical standpoint, using real-world examples and hands-on exercises. You can use almost any SQL implementation with this book, which attests to the portability of SQL and its popularity.

What You Need for This Book

This book has no prerequisites, other than a desire to learn about relational databases and SQL. The material is adapted from an approach that the author has used for more than 25 years in the consulting and information technology world to teach thousands of students both locally and globally. It starts with a basic approach to understanding databases and both defining and managing data. It also introduces SQL as the standard language for communicating with any relational database. The book is set up to show all the basic concepts and syntax of SQL while also providing real-world examples. Beginners can easily learn from simplified examples, while experienced information technology professionals can peruse the more advanced exercises.

For software, access to a relational database management system is recommended. This book uses Oracle, but many other options also adhere to the SQL standard (including Microsoft SQL Server, MySQL, IBM, and PostgreSQL). If you do not currently have access to a relational database management system, many options are available for free, either as online access or as a download for learning and development purposes. The author provides guidance on software options in the book as well. All the database creation scripts and data are provided to the reader for hands-on exercises and continued learning after completing this book.

Thank you, and enjoy.

SQL is a database language. It is the standard language used to communicate with any relational database, which is one of the most popular databases in use today (and, in fact, for decades). As you begin to understand the nuts and bolts of a relational database—and even database design, which later chapters cover—you can more easily grasp the concepts of SQL and more quickly apply SQL concepts and syntax to real-world situations in real databases. Hour 2, "Exploring the Components of the SQL Language," focuses on the standard components of the SQL language to provide a preview. Then Hours 3, "Getting to Know Your Data," and 4, "Setting Up Your Database," get you involved with the database used in this book so that you deeply understand both the data and how that data is related in the database. When you have this information, you will understand SQL more easily, the knowledge you gain will stick, and you will have the basic foundation to start applying SQL.

Thriving in a Data-Driven World

Data is all around you: You can see it every day in your personal life and the organizations you work for. Data is on your phone, on your computer, in online stores, inside the walls of physical stores, and in complex databases in organizations all over the world. Truly, the world cannot survive without data.

Data, or information, has been around since the beginning of time and people have used that data to make decisions. The modern world has evolved to better understand how data can be used in everyday life and how to make organizations more competitive.

As the world becomes more competitive, it is your responsibility to learn how to use data effectively. You must be able to understand the information and data you're working with and how to apply it to everyday situations. In today's world, you have access to mountains of information, especially on the Internet. However, information must become usable data: If the data is not usable, it is useless. If it is inaccurate, it is useless. If it contains inconsistencies, it is useless. Databases and other technologies have helped people better take advantage of data, but this has also created a new problem: The volume of data is growing quickly and must be managed carefully. The relational database and SQL, in particular, facilitate easy data management, if done right.

NOTE

Information Must Become Usable Data

Information is all around us. However, a lot of information in this world is incorrect or not consistent with other sources. Even in databases within some of the most respected organizations in the world, data can be inaccurate or difficult to understand. This can create business problems. You must understand how to turn information into useful data for you and your organization. Fortunately, you can use the relational database and SQL to protect data and present it to end users in a relevant manner. Data must be kept safe, clean, and consistent within the database, and SQL offers a primary way to control that.

Organizations, Data, and User Communities

You know by now that data is critical to the success of any organization or individual. Within an organization, many types of individuals depend on data—some of them every day:

- Organizational leaders
- Managers
- Technical users
- Administrators
- Functional and end users
- Stakeholders
- Customers

Figure 1.1 illustrates these individuals and also shows how data sits at the core of any organization. All sorts of users access data that is stored in a database of some sort. Applications are available to end users to manage data in a database and query the data in the database. This data is available to customers and other users to access the database in a limited manner, without jeopardizing the integrity of the data itself. Reports and other useful information can be generated from a database so that key personnel in an organization can use them to make high-level decisions; *business intelligence* is another term for this. Additionally, the administrators of the database are included in the general information technology environment, along with technical users that design, develop, and code the elements within a database and the applications surrounding the data. By looking at this simple diagram, you can easily see how important data is in an organization. SQL is the standard language that brings everything together so that all individuals, whether directly or indirectly, can interact with the database and get both accurate and available data to successfully perform their everyday duties.

Databases Defined

In simple terms, a *database* is a collection of data. You might like to think of a database as an organized mechanism that has the capability to store information that a user can retrieve in an effective and efficient manner.

As previously mentioned, people use databases every day without realizing it. For example, a contact list is a database of names, addresses, emails, telephone numbers, and other important information. The listings are alphabetized or indexed, which enables the user to easily look up a particular contact and quickly get in touch. Ultimately, this data is stored in a database somewhere on a computer.

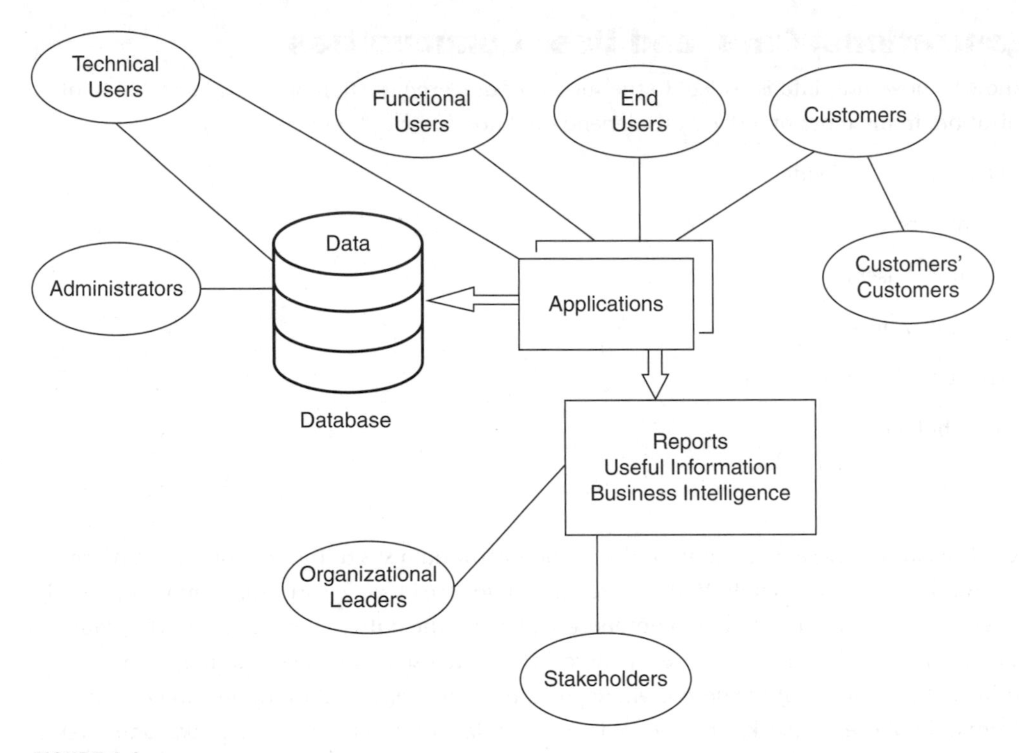

FIGURE 1.1
Data and user communities

Of course, databases must be maintained. As people move to different cities or states, entries have to be added or removed from the contact list. Likewise, entries need to be modified when people change names, addresses, telephone numbers, and so on. Figure 1.2 illustrates a simple database.

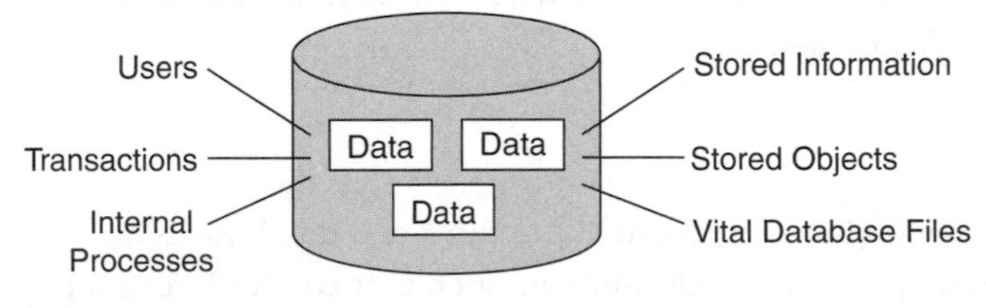

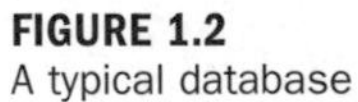

FIGURE 1.2
A typical database

Think of your mobile phone or any mobile device: It contains data and probably has many apps installed that access various databases. Additionally, your phone contains data in the form of contact lists and pictures.

Common Database Environments

In this section, you explore a couple of the most common database environments. A database environment contains all the key components to house a database and store data effectively, from the database itself, to the operating system, the network, and any applications that access the database via these key components. The following two major environments are briefly discussed in this hour:

- Client/server environments
- Web-based environments

Client/Server Environments

In the past, the computer industry was predominately ruled by mainframe computers—large, powerful systems capable of high storage capacity and high data processing capabilities. Users communicated with the mainframe through dumb terminals—terminals that did not think on their own but relied solely on the mainframe's CPU, storage, and memory. Each terminal had a data line attached to the mainframe. The mainframe environment definitely served its purpose and still does in many businesses, but a greater technology was soon introduced: the client/server model.

In the *client/server system*, the main computer, called the server, is accessible from a network—typically, a *local area network (LAN)* or a *wide area network (WAN)*. The server is normally accessed by personal computers (PCs) or other servers instead of dumb terminals. Each PC, called a *client*, is granted access to the network, allowing communication between the client and the server. The main difference between client/server and mainframe environments is that the user's PC in a client/server environment can think on its own and run its own processes using its own CPU and memory, but it is readily accessible to a server computer through a network. In most cases, a client/server system is much more flexible for today's overall business needs.

Modern database systems reside on various types of computer systems with various operating systems. The most common types of operating systems are Windows-based systems, Linux, and command-line systems such as UNIX. Databases reside mainly in client/server and web environments.

Lack of training and experience is the main reason for failed implementations of database systems. Today's businesses need personnel who can work within the client/server model and web-based systems (explained in the next section), can address the rising (and sometimes unreasonable) demands placed on modern organizations, and understand Internet technologies and network computing. Figure 1.3 illustrates the concept of client/server technology.

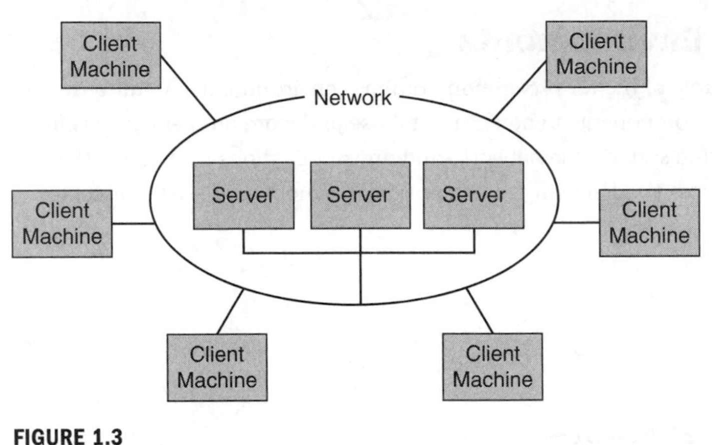

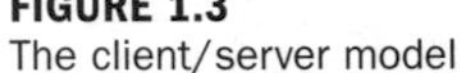

FIGURE 1.3
The client/server model

Web-Based Environments

Business information systems have largely moved toward web integration. Databases have been accessible through the Internet for years, meaning that customers access an organization's information through an Internet browser such as Chrome, Microsoft Edge, or Firefox. Customers (users of data) can order merchandise, check inventories, check the status of their orders, make administrative changes to accounts, transfer money from one account to another, and so on.

A customer simply invokes an Internet browser, goes to the organization's website, logs in (if required by the organization), and uses an application built into the organization's web page to access data. Most organizations first require users to register and then issue them a login and password.

Of course, many actions happen behind the scenes when a database is accessed through a web browser. For instance, the web application can execute SQL that accesses the organization's database, returns data to the web server, and then returns that data to the customer's Internet browser.

From the user's standpoint, the basic structure of a web-based database system is similar to that of a client/server system (refer to Figure 1.3). Each user has a client machine that is connected to the Internet and contains a web browser. The network in Figure 1.3 (for a web-based database) just happens to be the Internet instead of a local network. For the most part, a client is still accessing a server for information; it doesn't matter that the server might exist in another state or even another country. The main point of web-based database systems is to expand the potential customer base of a database system that knows no physical location bounds, thus increasing data availability and an organization's customer base.

NOTE

Data Integration Across Multiple Environments

These days, organizations and individuals alike use a variety of databases and applications to access data that is often spread among multiple environments. With modern technology, data located in a variety of environments, vendor implementations, and even types of databases can be seamlessly integrated.

Understanding the Relational Database

A *relational database* is a database that is divided into logical units called tables. These tables are related to one another within the database. A relational database allows data to be broken down into logical, smaller, manageable units, facilitating easier maintenance and providing more optimal database performance according to the level of organization. In Figure 1.4, you can see that tables are related to one another through a common key (data value) in a relational database.

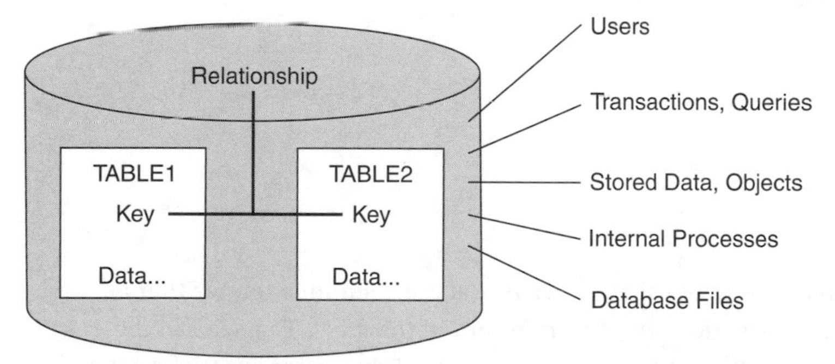

FIGURE 1.4
The relational database

Again, tables are related in a relational database so that adequate data can be retrieved in a single query (although the desired data might exist in more than one table). Having common *keys*, or *fields*, among relational database tables allows data from multiple tables to be joined to form one large set of data. As you venture deeper into this book, you see more of a relational database's advantages, including overall performance and easy data access.

NOTE

Relationships Within a Relational Database

The following sections provide an overview of relationships between data in a RDBMS. Sample data illustrates how data can be related to one another and how easy it is to bring common data together. Future hours expand upon this through numerous examples and hands-on exercises. You will even get the opportunity to design a portion of the sample database in this book and define relationships of your own.

Taking a Glimpse into a Sample Database

All databases have a simple reason for existing: They store and maintain valuable data. In this section, you look at a simplified example data set that illustrates how data might look in a relational database and also shows how data is related through key relationships. These relationships, which are also rules for how data is stored, hold the key to the value of a relational database.

Figure 1.5 shows a table called EMPLOYEES. A table is the most basic type of object where data is stored within a relational database. A database object is a defined structure that physically contains data or has an association to data stored in the database.

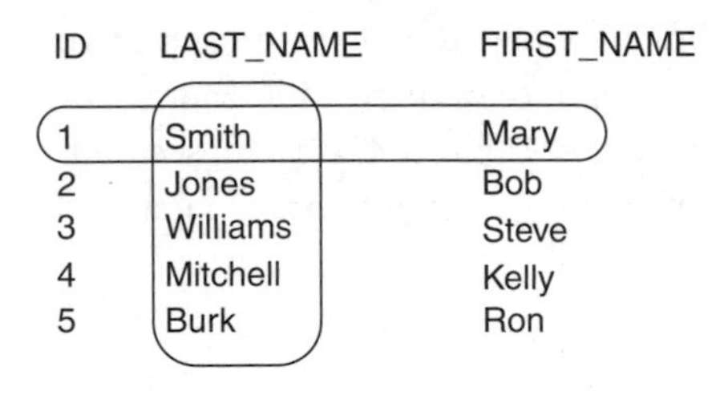

Table: EMPLOYEES

ID	LAST_NAME	FIRST_NAME
1	Smith	Mary
2	Jones	Bob
3	Williams	Steve
4	Mitchell	Kelly
5	Burk	Ron

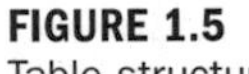

FIGURE 1.5
Table structure

Fields

Every table is divided into smaller entities called fields. A *field* is a column in a table that is designed to maintain specific information about every record in the table. The fields in the EMPLOYEES table consist of ID, LAST_NAME, and FIRST_NAME. They categorize the specific information that is maintained in a given table. Obviously, this is a simplistic example of the data that might be stored in a table such as EMPLOYEES.

Records, or Rows of Data

A *record*, also called a *row* of data, is a horizontal entry in a table. Looking at the last table, EMPLOYEES, consider the following first record in that table:

```
1        Smith       Mary
```

The record consists of an employee identification, employee last name, and employee first name. For every distinct employee, there should be a corresponding record in the EMPLOYEES table.

A *row of data* is an entire record in a relational database table.

Columns

A *column* is a vertical entity in a table that contains all the information associated with a specific field in a table. For example, a column in the EMPLOYEES table for the employee's last name consists of the following:

```
Smith
Jones
William
Mitchell
Burk
```

This column is based on the field LAST_NAME, the employee's last name. A column pulls information about a certain field from every record within a table.

Referential Integrity

Referential integrity is the hallmark of any relational database. Figure 1.6 shows two tables, EMPLOYEES and DEPENDENTS, that are related to one another in our imaginary database. The DEPENDENTS table is simply a table that contains information about dependents of each employee in the database, such as spouses and children. As in the EMPLOYEES table, the DEPENDENTS table has an ID. The ID in the DEPENDENTS table references, or is related to, the ID in the EMPLOYEES table. Again, this is a simplistic example to show how relationships work in a database and to help you understand referential integrity.

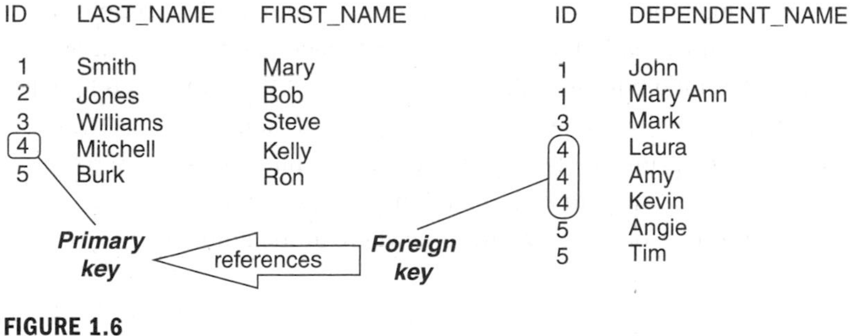

FIGURE 1.6
Table relationships

The key point to note in Figure 1.6 is that there is a relationship between the two tables through the ID field. The ID field in EMPLOYEES is related to the ID field in DEPENDENTS. The ID field in EMPLOYEES is a primary key, whereas the ID field in DEPENDENTS is a foreign key. These types of keys are critical to any relational database structure and to referential integrity.

For example, logical elements might include the following elements during conception:

- Entities
- Attributes
- Relationships
- Information/data

Those logical elements later become the following physical elements during database creation:

- Tables
- Fields/columns
- Primary and foreign key constraints (built-in database rules)
- Usable data

Database Schemas

A *schema* is a group of related objects in a database. A schema is owned by a single database user, and objects in the schema can be shared with other database users. Multiple schemas can exist in a database. Figure 1.7 illustrates a database schema.

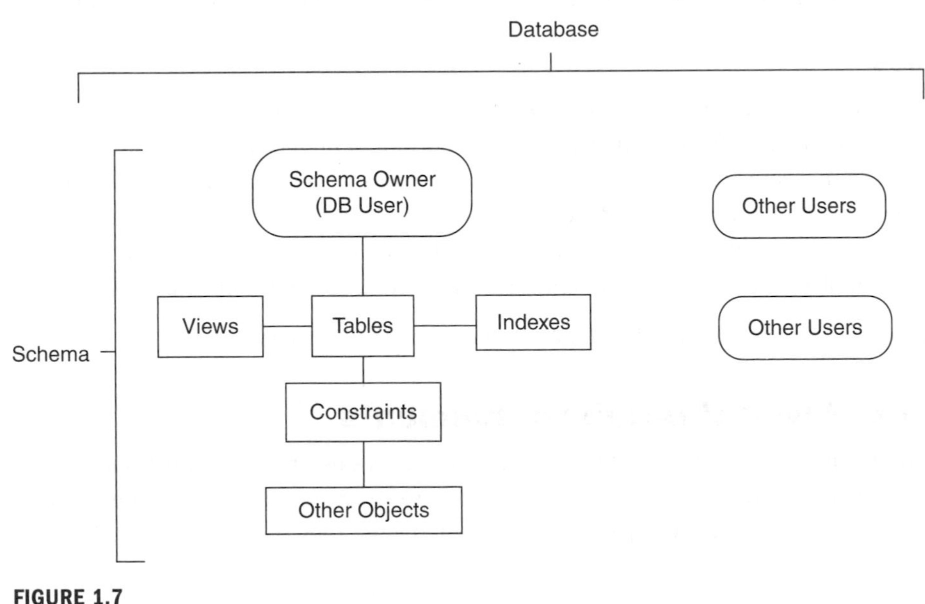

FIGURE 1.7
A schema

The Relational Database Continues to Lead the Way

The relational database has been the superior database choice for effectively managing data for several decades, and it continues to dominate the market share. This is true for many reasons:

- A well-designed relational database provides a simple, organized, easy-to-manage mechanism for data.
- A relational database is scalable as data grows and objects are added to the database.
- Linking data in multiple tables is easy.
- Maintaining the integrity of data is simple using built-in features such as referential integrity (primary and foreign key constraints).
- The overall management of data and use of SQL to communicate with the database is simplified.
- Relevant and useful data is easy to retrieve.

SQL and the relational database management system go hand in hand; you cannot have one without the other. SQL is an English-like language that enables you to create and manage a relational database and to then easily and effectively retrieve data from the database for a specific purpose.

Examples and Exercises

Most of the exercises that you encounter in this book use Oracle, a dominant leader in the market that adheres closely to the SQL standard but also offers many enhancements.

Oracle (as well as many implementations of SQL, or the relational database), make freely distributed versions of its database available. You can then select an implementation of your choice, install it, and follow along with the exercises in the book. Note that because these databases are not 100% compliant with SQL:2016, the exercises might have slight variations of the exact syntax suggested in the ANSI standard. However, if you learn the basics of the ANSI standard, you can generally translate your skills between different database implementations.

Summary

In this hour, you got a brief introduction to the SQL language and the relational database. SQL is the standard language for communicating with any relational database. It is important to first understand what comprises the relational database, identify the key elements, know what data looks like, and understand how the data in the relational database is related to other data within the database. When you fully grasp these concepts, your journey into the SQL language will take flight sooner and the concepts in this book will make more sense. The goal of this hour was to introduce some basic database concepts and give you a foundation for thinking about data at a higher level.

Simply put, a relational database is a database that is logically organized into multiple tables that might or might not be related to one another. A table consists of one or more columns, or fields, and one or more rows of data. A table can have just a few rows of data or millions upon millions of rows of data. Tables are related through common columns, or fields, that are defined in a relational database using constraints such as primary keys and foreign keys. These keys are built-in features of a relational database that maintain referential integrity within the database. This is the key to the relational database and one of the main components of SQL. Subsequent chapters cover all these concepts in examples and hands-on exercises.

Q&A

Q. If I learn SQL, can I use any of the implementations that use SQL?

A. Yes, you can communicate with a database whose implementation is compliant with ANSI SQL. If an implementation is not completely compliant, you likely will pick it up quickly with some adjustments.

Q. In a client/server environment, is the personal computer the client or the server?

A. The personal computer is the client in a client/server environment, although a server can also serve as a client.

Q. In the context of a database, how do information and usable data differ?

A. Information and data are conceptually the same. However, when you are creating a database, it is important to gather all required information and work to form that information into usable data. Usable data comes from reliable sources and is accurate, consistent, clean, and up-to-date. Usable data is critical for business operations and when making critical decisions. Data that is derived from inaccurate sources or that has not properly been entered or evolved with the database is not usable.

Q. Can SQL be used to integrate databases among multiple environments, platforms, or types of databases?

A. When working with a relational database, SQL is the primary language and tool for working with data, including integrating data among multiple sources. SQL is also necessary when migrating data between sources. Medium to large organizations commonly have many different sources of data, only some of which are SQL based. SQL is an important component for pulling everything together.

Workshop

The following workshop consists of a series of quiz questions and practical exercises. The quiz questions are designed to test your overall understanding of the current material. The practical exercises give you the opportunity to apply the concepts discussed during the current hour, as well as build on the knowledge you acquired in previous hours of study. Be sure to complete the quiz questions and exercises before continuing to the next hour. Refer to Appendix C, “Answers to Quizzes and Exercises,” for answers.

Quiz

1. What does the acronym SQL stand for?
2. What is a schema? Give an example.
3. How do logical and physical components within a relational database differ? How are they related?
4. What keys are used to define and enforce referential integrity in a relational database?
5. What is the most basic type of object in a relational database?
6. What elements comprise this object?
7. Must primary key column values be unique?
8. Must foreign key column values be unique?

Exercises

For the following exercises, refer to Figure 1.6, earlier in this hour.

1. Who are Mary Smith's dependents?
2. How many employees do not have dependents?
3. How many duplicate foreign key values exist in the `DEPENDENTS` table?
4. Who is Tim's parent or guardian?
5. Which employee can be deleted without first having to delete any dependent records?

HOUR 2
Exploring the Components of the SQL Language

What You'll Learn in This Hour:

- An introduction to and brief history of SQL
- An overview of the SQL standard
- An introduction to some vendor implementations of SQL
- The basic components, or sublanguages, that comprise the SQL language

SQL has many components that are simple yet offer flexibility and power for any user communicating with a relational database. This hour provides a broad overview of SQL, to cover some preliminary concepts that you need to know before you jump into hands-on exercises and coding. Be patient with this hour; the "boring" background material helps you build a solid starting foundation.

SQL Definition and History

Every modern business uses and stores data. Thus, every business requires some organized method or mechanism for maintaining and retrieving that data. When data is kept within a database, this mechanism is referred to as a *database management system (DBMS)*. Database management systems have been around for years; many of them started out as flat-file systems on a mainframe.

These days, information management is primarily achieved through a *relational database management system (RDBMS)*, derived from the traditional DBMS. Modern businesses typically use databases combined with client/server and web technologies to successfully manage their data and stay competitive in their appropriate markets. The trend for many businesses is to move from a client/server environment to the web, which sidesteps location as a restriction when users need access to important data.

The next few sections discuss SQL and the relational database, the most common DBMS implemented today. Having a good fundamental understanding of the relational database and how to use SQL to manage data in today's information technology world is important to your overall understanding of the SQL language.

The Importance of a Standard

Vendors of relational (SQL) database software adhere to the standard with various levels of compliance. If you work with a database implementation that does not fully comply with any given standard, workarounds normally are available, involving business logic that is incorporated into the database design. With any standard comes numerous obvious advantages as well as some disadvantages. Primarily, a standard steers vendors in the appropriate industry direction for development. For SQL, a standard provides the basic skeleton of necessary fundamentals, enabling consistency among various implementations and increasing portability (not only for database programs, but also for databases in general and individuals who manage databases).

Some people argue that a standard limits the flexibility and possible capabilities of a particular implementation. However, most vendors that comply with the standard add product-specific enhancements to standard SQL to fill in these gaps.

Considering the advantages and disadvantages, having a standard is desirable. Overall, a standard demands features that should be available in any complete SQL implementation and outlines basic concepts that not only force consistency among all competitive SQL implementations, but also increase the value of SQL programmers.

Vendor Implementations of the SQL Standard

A *SQL implementation* is a particular vendor's SQL product, or RDBMS. It is important to note, as this book states numerous times, that implementations of SQL vary widely. No single implementation follows the standard completely, although some implementations are mostly ANSI compliant. Also noteworthy is the fact that, in recent years, the ANSI standard has not dramatically changed the list of functionality that vendors must adhere to in order to be compliant. Thus, when new versions of RDBMS are released, they will most likely claim ANSI SQL compliance.

RDBMS market share leaders, as of publication, include the following:

- Oracle
- MySQL (owned by Oracle)
- Microsoft SQL
- PostgreSQL
- IBM Db2
- IBM Informix
- MariaDB
- SQLite
- Amazon RDS

NOTE

Free Relational Database Software

Many RDBMS vendors offer free use of their database software or trial downloads. Free versions of relational database software typically are allowed for development, personal, and educational purposes. Software vendors do this to gain exposure to their products and remain competitive in the RDBMS market. In addition, you can often find free relational databases that reside in the cloud.

SQL Implementation Used for This Book

The examples in this book primarily use the Oracle database. The code for creating the tables and data works seamlessly with Oracle. Nonetheless, all code is based on the SQL standard to the fullest extent possible. You can easily apply everything you learn in this book to any vendor implementation of SQL that you are using, with little or no changes to the code. The reason this book is based on the standard instead of any specific implementation of SQL is that SQL and relational databases are so widespread. Many organizations use multiple implementations of the relational database. Having a solid knowledge of standard SQL enables you to integrate various databases and data fairly easily, with few modifications.

The Right Implementation for You and Your Organization

Choosing the best implementation for you or your organization involves many factors, including the type of data, the size of the data, legacy information systems that are in place, and the cost of vendor implementations. You will find both for-profit leaders and open source products in the relational database world.

SQL Sessions

A *SQL session* occurs when a user interacts with a relational database through SQL commands. When a user initially connects to the database, a session is established. Within the scope of a SQL session, valid SQL commands can be entered to query the database, manipulate data in the database, and define database structures such as tables. A session is invoked either by direct connection to the database or through a front-end application. In both cases, a user normally establishes a session at a terminal or workstation that communicates through a network with the computer hosting the database.

CONNECT

When a user connects to a database, the SQL session is initialized. The `CONNECT` command establishes a database connection. With the `CONNECT` command, you either invoke a connection or change connections to the database. For example, if you connect as `USER1`, you can use the

The `SELECT` command is discussed in detail during Hour 12, "Introduction to Database Queries," through Hour 20, "Creating and Using Views and Synonyms."

Data Control Language

Data control commands in SQL enable you to control access to data within the database. These *Data Control Language (DCL)* commands are normally used to create objects related to user access and also control the distribution of privileges among users. Some data control commands follow:

- `ALTER PASSWORD`
- `GRANT`
- `REVOKE`
- `CREATE SYNONYM`

These commands often are grouped with other commands and appear in several lessons throughout this book.

Using Data Administration Commands

Data administration commands enable the user to perform audits and analyses on operations within the database. They can also help analyze system performance. Two general data administration commands follow:

- `START AUDIT`
- `STOP AUDIT`

Do not confuse data administration with database administration: *Database administration* is the overall administration of a database, which envelops the use of all levels of commands. *Data administration* is much more specific to each SQL implementation than the core commands of the SQL language.

Using Transactional Control Commands

In addition to the previously introduced categories of commands, these commands enable the user to manage database transactions:

- **`COMMIT`**—Saves database transactions
- **`ROLLBACK`**—Undoes database transactions
- **`SAVEPOINT`**—Creates points within groups of transactions for a `ROLLBACK`
- **`SET TRANSACTION`**—Places a name on a transaction

Transactional commands are discussed extensively during Hour 11, "Managing Database Transactions."

Summary

In this hour, you learned about the standard language of SQL and got a brief history of how the standard has evolved over the past several years. You took a look at database systems and current technologies, including the relational database, client/server systems, and web-based database systems, all of which are vital to your understanding of SQL. You also got an overview of the main SQL language components and learned that the relational database market has many players that produce various flavors of SQL. Despite ANSI SQL variations, most vendors comply to some extent with the current standard (SQL-2016), ensuring general consistency and forcing the development of portable SQL applications.

During this hour, you should have acquired overall background knowledge of the fundamentals of SQL and should understand the concept of a modern database. In Hour 3, "Getting to Know Your Data," you get an introduction to the database you use throughout this book. Soon you will be performing exercises to design, build, manage, and query a relational database using SQL.

Q&A

Q. Is SQL in one implementation of SQL portable to another implementation?

A. SQL code is typically portable from one implementation to another with minor changes to syntax. Also keep in mind that some implementations follow the SQL standard more closely than others, and implementations may offer features that might not exist in other implementations.

Q. If I learn SQL, can I use any implementation that uses SQL?

A. Yes, you can communicate with a database whose implementation is ANSI SQL compliant. If an implementation is not completely compliant, you most likely will pick it up quickly, with some adjustments.

Workshop

The following workshop consists of a series of quiz questions and practical exercises. The quiz questions are designed to test your overall understanding of the current material. The practical exercises give you the opportunity to apply the concepts discussed during the current hour, as well as build on the knowledge you acquired in previous hours of study. Be sure to complete the quiz questions and exercises before continuing to the next hour. Refer to Appendix C, "Answers to Quizzes and Exercises," for answers.

Quiz

1. What are the six main categories of SQL commands?
2. What is the difference between data administration commands and database administration?
3. What are some benefits to a SQL standard?

Exercises

1. Identify the categories for the following SQL commands:

```
CREATE TABLE
DELETE
SELECT
INSERT
ALTER TABLE
UPDATE
```

2. List the basic SQL statements to manipulate data.
3. List the SQL statement that is used to query a relational database.
4. Which transactional control command is used to save a transaction?
5. Which transactional control command is used to undo a transaction?

HOUR 3

Getting to Know Your Data

What You'll Learn in This Hour:

- An introduction to the database used in examples and exercises
- Diagrams that show data and relationships
- Lists of data by table

Welcome to Hour 3! Now you get to know the data you will use for all the exercises and examples in the rest of the book. In this hour, you look at the data itself, attributes of the data, the way data might be used, potential customers, and more. You also check out T relationship diagrams that focus on the tables used in this book and the columns in those tables; these diagrams illustrate the relationships between the tables. Finally, a list of data is provided from each table so that you can see what the data actually looks like. You get a copy of the scripts to create these tables and insert the data into the database. As you progress through the book, you will build upon this database. Remember that anytime you need to visually refer to the data used in his book or remember how the data is related, refer to this hour. Now let's get started.

The BIRD Database: Examples and Exercises in This Book

The database in this book focuses on birds. Virtually any database could have worked for the examples and exercises, but I wanted to use a different and interesting topic, to make the experience of learning SQL a little more fun. This first part of the hour accomplishes the following goals:

- Introduces you to the basic data
- Discusses organizations and users of this data
- Speculates how end users and customers might use the data
- Envisions opportunities for database expansion and growth down the road
- Envisions other data that might be integrated with this database

How to Talk About the Data

Before you continue your journey through SQL fundamentals, you need an introduction to the tables and data you will use throughout the book. The lessons all refer to an example database for a fictitious organization called Waterbird Photography.

Waterbird Photography data has been generated to create real-world scenarios for the examples and exercises in this book. The following sections provide an overview of the specific tables (the database) used, their relationship to one another, their structure, and examples of the data contained.

You can envision this database as one designed by a hobbyist/semipro wildlife photographer that, over time, evolves into something bigger. Within this database, you can look at any data you'd like and design anything you want. You can try to make sense of any information as usable data and convert it into a database for your organization that is not only usable, but makes your organization competitive in today's market, regardless of your industry.

Keep in mind that, in this hour, we are only *talking* about the data. Before you begin to design or create a database, you need to look at the potential information and determine how that information can become usable data in an organization. So here, we are simply talking about the data openly so that you can understand it, see how the data is related to other data, and think about how potential organizations might use that data down the road. This chapter is all about the data itself, not database structures or SQL. In future hours, you will use SQL to manipulate and query this data in great detail.

NOTE

Know Your Data

Every person and every organization has a goal to succeed in some manner. In a data-driven world, SQL and data management are critical contributors to those goals. Knowing your data is mandatory. If you don't know your data and maximize it, your competitors will.

Bird Information

Now let's talk about birds. Before looking at entity diagrams, tables, and data, it helps to simply discuss the data. A lot of information about birds exists, and it might or might not be stored in a database. This is a simple database—it does not include all birds or all information about birds. So consider the following basic information to get you started:

- Each bird category includes some standard information about the bird itself.
- Each bird may have photographs taken from different locations by different photographers.
- Information about each bird's diet will be stored.

- Information about each bird's migration habits will be stored.
- Information about the types of nests each bird builds will be stored.
- Each bird may have one or more nicknames.

Organizations and Users

A variety of organizations, users, and customers can benefit from the information in this bird database. Let's say that this database was created by a hobbyist wildlife photographer for personal use, but it evolved over time into something larger and multiple photographers now have access to it. With this in mind, you can speculate that the following types of organizations might use a database such as this:

- Photography and media
- Rescue organizations
- Parks
- Publications
- Online stores
- Government
- Birding groups

A few examples of some of the users within these organizations include the following:

- Individual photographers
- Volunteers
- Editors
- Park staff
- Retail customers

Opportunities for Expansion

As with any database, opportunities for expansion always exist. For example, if bird rescues start using the data within this database, you might create a set of tables about rescues that are integrated into the existing database. You also might end up storing more information about photographers and the equipment used in photographing various birds, such as cameras, lenses, and editing software. You can certainly think about other information that you could eventually integrate into a bird database, based on the previous information about organizations and users.

In addition to expansion, you need to consider the growth of data over time. Specific hardware is beyond the scope of this book, but the size and future growth of the database greatly influence hardware and software products that are used to manage the data. The size of the database also influences the database management system used.

Entity Relationship Diagrams

This section includes two *entity relationship diagrams (ERDs)*. Entity relationship diagrams illustrate entities within a database, as the attributes within each entity, and the relationships between entities. From a logical standpoint, the entities and attributes in a diagram will eventually become the tables and columns in a database when you move on to using SQL to create your tables. Diagrams such as these are important to consider during the design phase of a database and also provide a reference when using SQL to query a database and manage the data within.

Entities and Relationships

Figure 3.1 shows the first ERD, which illustrates all the basic entities in the bird database. Notice the line between each entity. This line represents some sort of relationship between entities or tables. For example, all the tables in this database will revolve around the birds table. A bird is related to food because a bird might eat many different types of food; conversely, each food item might be eaten by many different types of birds. Again, this is a simple diagram, to get you started.

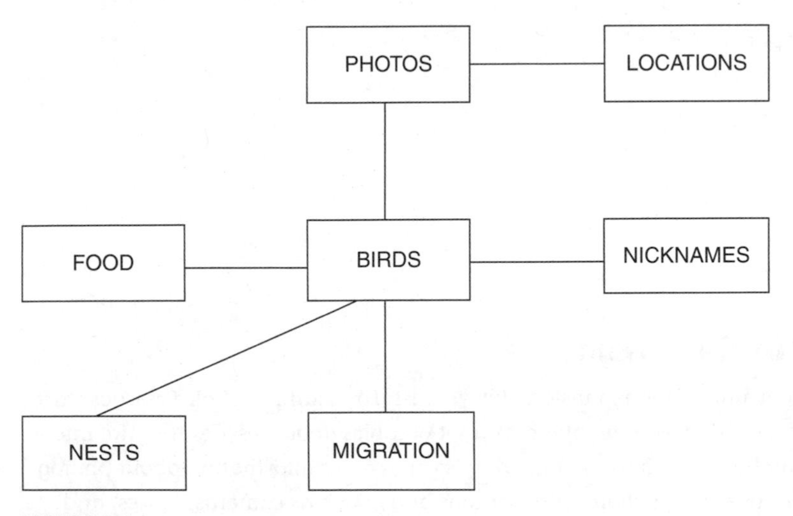

FIGURE 3.1
An ERD showing entities (tables) and basic relationships

Detailed Entities/Tables

In the ERD in Figure 3.2, you can see that attributes have been added to the entities. Attributes will become the columns when you build the tables using SQL. You can also see lines between the entities, illustrating that some sort of relationship exists. Later, you will look at the different types of relationships in a relational database and see how to illustrate those relationships more specifically in an ERD. You might also notice some extra entities in this figure that were not present in Figure 3.1. These entities are specifically used to facilitate a relationship between other entities, or tables, in the database. For example, a bird might eat many different types of foods, and each food item might be eaten by many different types of birds. The `BIRDS_FOOD` table simply facilitates a relationship between `BIRDS` and `FOOD`. We discuss relationships like this one in greater detail in Hour 6. You will also learn to use SQL to query the database and join tables.

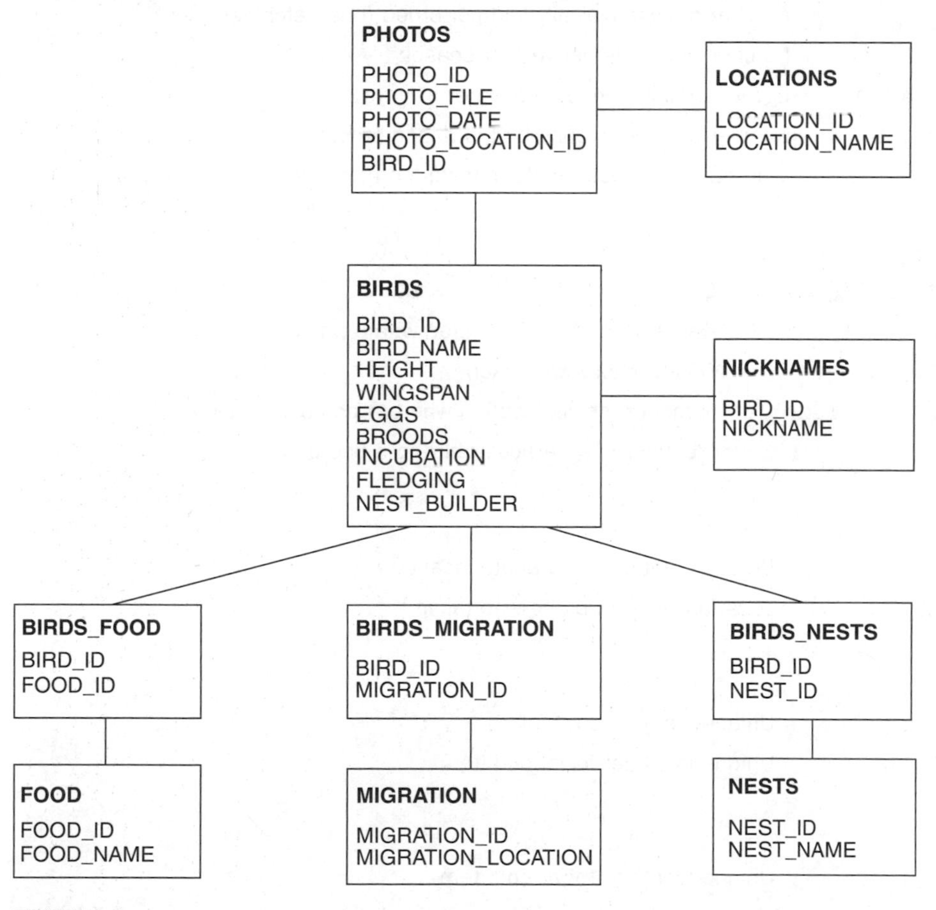

FIGURE 3.2
An ERD with attributes (columns)

Attribute (Column) Definition

Following is a list of all the entities and attributes that currently exist in the example database for this book. As previously stated, entities will become tables and attributes will become columns when you create the database. A description is provided for each attribute, although some are self-explanatory.

BIRDS

BIRD_ID	Unique identifier for each bird
BIRD_NAME	Name of the bird
HEIGHT	Height of the bird, in inches
WINGSPAN	Wingspan of the bird, in inches
EGGS	Number of eggs typically laid per brood (one hatching)
BROODS	Number of broods per year or season
INCUBATION	Egg incubation period, in number of days
FLEDGING	Number of days a young bird is raised before it can fly
NEST_BUILDER	Who builds the nest (male, female, both, neither)

PHOTOS

PHOTO_ID	Unique identifier for each photo
PHOTO_FILE	Name of the file associated with a photo
PHOTO_DATE	Date a photo was taken
PHOTO_LOCATION_ID	Identifier for the location where a photo was taken
BIRD_ID	Identifier of a particular bird in a photo

LOCATIONS

LOCATION_ID	Unique identifier for a photo location
LOCATION_NAME	Location where a photo was taken

BIRDS_FOOD

BIRD_ID	Unique identifier for a bird
FOOD_ID	Unique identifier for a food item

FOOD

FOOD_ID	Unique identifier for a food item
FOOD_NAME	Name of a food item

BIRDS_MIGRATION

BIRD_ID	Unique identifier for a bird
MIGRATION_ID	Unique identifier for a migration location

MIGRATION

MIGRATION_ID	Unique identifier for a migration location
MIGRATION_LOCATION	Name of a migration location

BIRDS_NESTS

BIRD_ID	Unique identifier for a bird
NEST_ID	Unique identifier for a nest type

NESTS

NEST_ID	Unique identifier for a nest type
NEST_NAME	Name or type of nest

NICKNAMES

BIRD_ID	Identifier for each bird
NICKNAME	Nickname for a bird

NOTE

Use This Hour As a Reference for Hands-on Exercises

Remember to refer back to this hour when performing hands-on exercises in this book.

Table Naming Standards

As with any standard within a business, table naming standards are critical to maintaining control. After studying the tables and data in the previous sections, you probably noticed consistency in the way entities (tables) and attributes (columns) are named. Naming standards, or naming conventions, exist almost exclusively for overall organization and are a big help in administering any relational database. Remember that, when naming objects in a relational database, you need to be consistent throughout and adhere to your organization's naming standards. Many approaches for naming standards exist; you just have to decide what works for you and your organization and then stick with it.

NOTE

Naming Standards

Not only should you adhere to the object naming syntax of any SQL implementation, but you also need to follow local business rules and create names that are both descriptive and related to the data groupings for the business. Consistent naming standards make it easier to manage databases with SQL.

Examples and Exercises

The exercises in this book primarily use the Oracle databases to generate the examples. The book concentrates on this database implementation for consistency and because Oracle is a dominant leader in the RDBMS market. Although Oracle offers a plethora of enhancements to the SQL standard, it also closely follows the SQL standard, making it easy for this book to show simplified examples with Oracle throughout the text. Microsoft SQL Server, MySQL, and other popular vendor implementations would have been adequate as well.

We also show examples of syntax from various implementations throughout, to illustrate how syntax might slightly vary from vendor to vendor. Many vendors provide freely distributed versions of their database for personal learning and development purposes. Whatever implementation you decide to use, you likely will find it easy to apply any examples in this book.

Finally, note that because most databases are not 100% compliant with the SQL standard, the exercises might vary slightly from the ANSI standard or other SQL implementations. However, learning the basics of the ANSI standard generally enables you to easily translate your skills among different database implementations.

Summary

In this hour, you took a look at the database that you will be using throughout this book for examples and hands-on exercises. You learned about the data itself and how it can be used. Then you looked at entity relationship diagrams (ERDs) and, after studying them, got a solid understanding of the data used in this book and the relationships between that data. Remember that entities and tables are basically the same: An entity is the name used during the design phase of a database. A table is the physical object that is created based on a concept or entity. Likewise, attributes become columns when the database is created. Use this hour as a reference for the hands-on exercises in the rest of the book, and feel free to come up with your own ideas to enhance this database as you progress.

Q&A

Q. How difficult is it to add entities to a database after it is well established?

A. If the database is well designed, adding entities to an existing database is simple: You define the data sets being added and define relationships with existing entities. Any data that you add to the new tables eventually must follow any constraints, or rules, that are already in place, such as primary and foreign keys.

Q. Can an entity be directly related to more than one other entity in a database?

A. Yes, an entity can be directly related to multiple entities. In the `Bird` database, each entity is directly related to only one other entity in the database. However, as you build upon this database, you will unveil more relationships.

Workshop

The following workshop consists of a series of quiz questions and practical exercises. The quiz questions are designed to test your overall understanding of the current material. The practical exercises give you the opportunity to apply the concepts discussed during the current hour, as well as build on the knowledge you acquired in previous hours of study. Be sure to complete the quiz questions and exercises before continuing to the next hour. Refer to Appendix C, "Answers to Quizzes and Exercises," for answers.

Quiz

1. What is the difference between entities and tables?
2. What is the purpose of the `BIRD_FOOD` entity?
3. How might photograph locations somehow be related to the food that birds eat?
4. What does the abbreviation ERD stand for?
5. How many direct relationships exist between entities in the `BIRDS` database?
6. What is another name for a naming standard?

Exercises

1. Give an example of an entity or attributes that might be added to this database.
2. Give some examples of candidates for primary keys, based on Figure 3.2.
3. Give some examples of candidates for foreign keys, based on Figure 3.2.

HOUR 4
Setting Up Your Database

What You'll Learn in This Hour:

- Locating the files you need for this book
- Downloading the database software used for examples in this book
- Understanding examples of other database software products available for download
- Creating the tables and data used in this book
- Getting to know the specific data in the `Birds` database
- Manually querying the bird database as a pathway into SQL code

In this hour, you look at the database software used for the examples in this book and check out the specific data in the bird database. You see how to download the software and also learn about other popular relational database software products available for download. After you install the appropriate database software, you can create your tables and data using the scripts provided with this book. Then you delve into the actual data and begin using that data to gather some basic information. Finally, you learn to manually query the data that is listed. Coding SQL is almost as simple as asking questions that anybody in your organization might ask about the data stored. Let's do this.

Locating the Files You Need

The file, or script, named `tables.sql` has the code to create the tables that will comprise your `Birds` database. The script `data.sql` has the code to insert the data into your tables. You can find these two files on the book's website, http:\\www.informit.com/9780137543120. When you download these files, make a note of the destination folder. The recommendation is to create a folder named c:\sqlbook\file_name for easy reference throughout the hands-on exercises in this book.

Getting Set Up for Hands-on Exercises

In this section, you learn how to download and install the database software used in this book. You also check out other options for database software and learn how to create a user with the required privileges in your database to create and manage objects. Additionally, you use the files created with this book to build the tables and then enter data into those tables that is used for all the examples and exercises in this book.

Downloading and Installing the Database Software

These are guidelines for installing a free version of the Oracle database that is used for the examples and hands-on exercises. Note that websites change, however; the destination of the free download could be different when you read this. Neither the author nor Pearson Education places any warranties on either the software or software support. For help with installation problems, or to inquire about software support, refer to the particular implementation's documentation or contact customer support for the specific implementation.

1. First, navigate to www.oracle.com in your web browser.

2. Click the Products link in the main menu (see Figure 4.1).

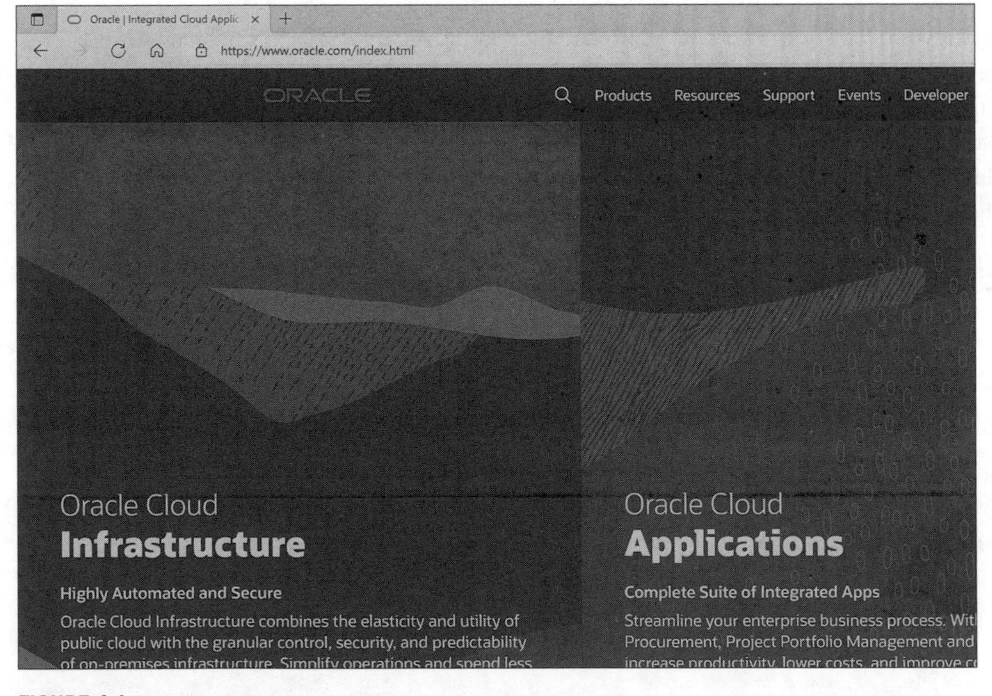

FIGURE 4.1
Oracle's website (image © 2021 Oracle)

3. Then click the Oracle Database link (see Figure 4.2).

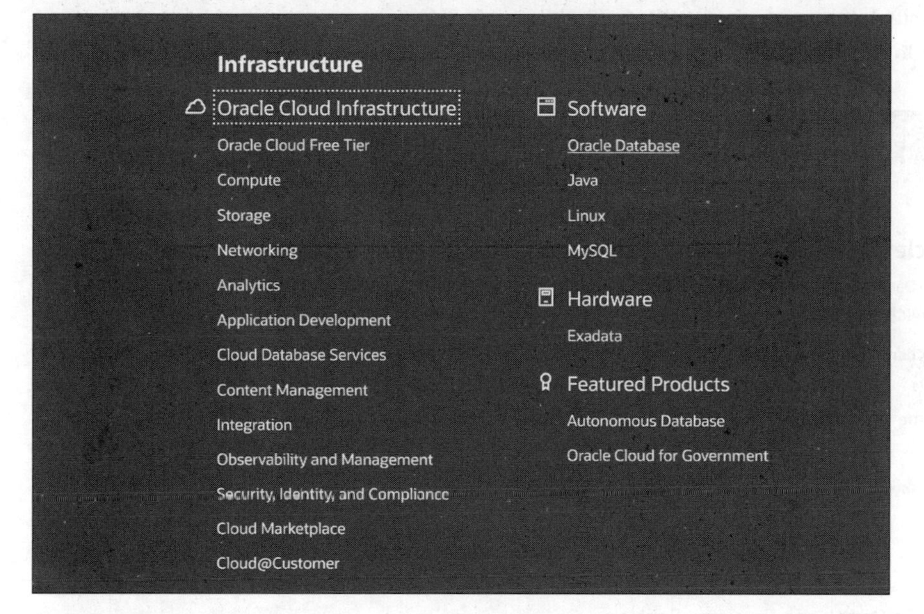

FIGURE 4.2
Download the Oracle Database product (image © 2021 Oracle)

4. Click Download Oracle Database 19c (see Figure 4.3).

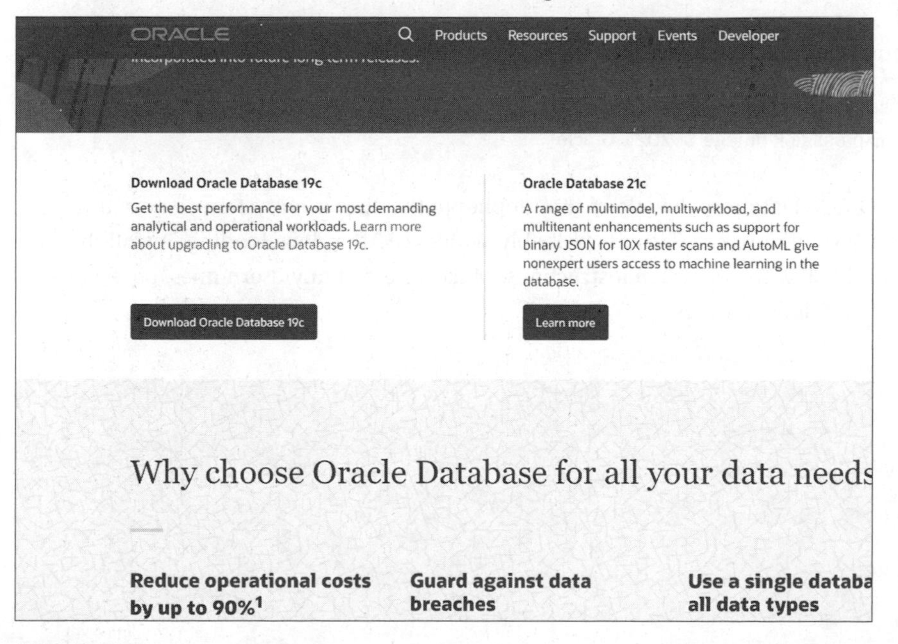

FIGURE 4.3
Oracle Database download (image © 2021 Oracle)

5. Scroll down and click Oracle Database 18c Express Edition (see Figure 4.4). Any version of the Oracle database works for the examples and hands-on exercises in this book. The recommendation is to select the latest version that has a license for free use.

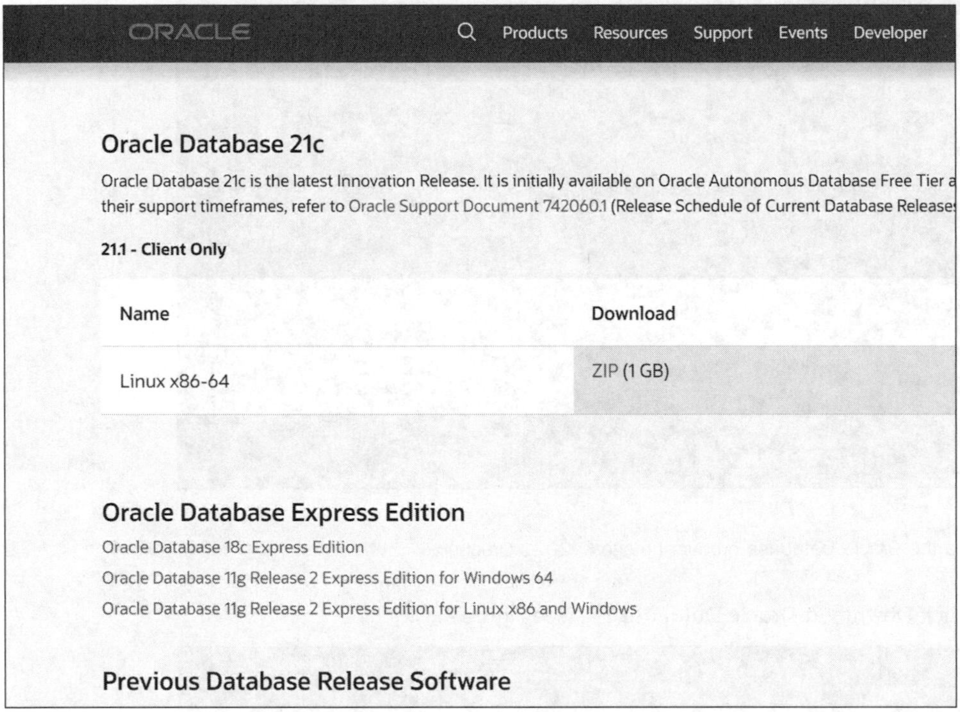

FIGURE 4.4
Oracle Database Express link (image © 2021 Oracle)

6. Select the Oracle Database download that applies to the operating system you are using (see Figure 4.5); in most cases, this is probably Windows. After downloading, install the software and follow the onscreen instructions. Make a note of any usernames, passwords, or destination folders for files.

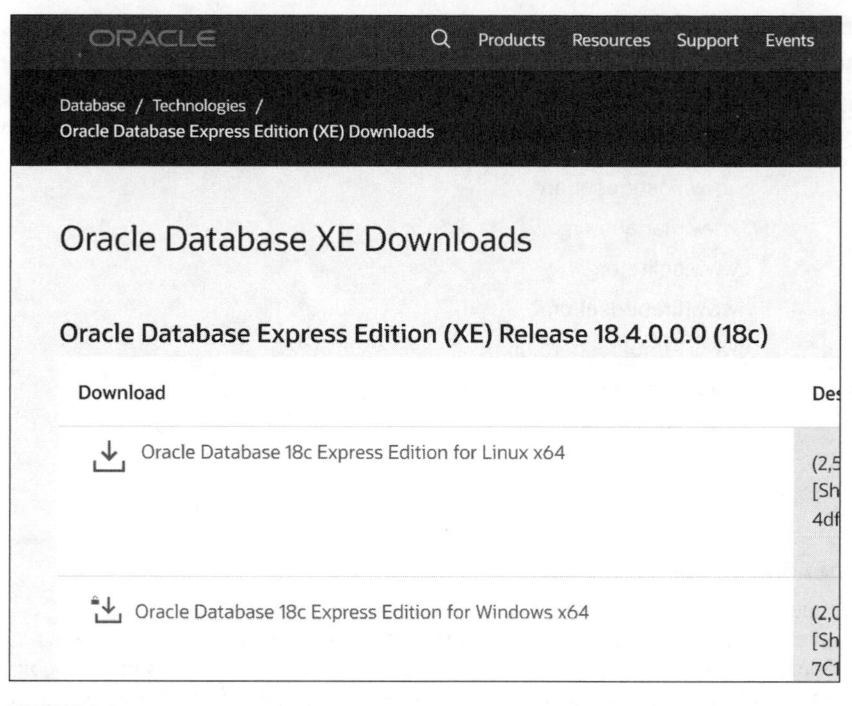

FIGURE 4.5
Oracle choices for the appropriate operating system (image © 2021 Oracle)

NOTE

Websites Change

As you know, websites change constantly. These instructions illustrate how to download the latest free version of Oracle Express as of the publication date of this book. Almost any version of the Oracle database is adequate for this book; the next section references other database implementation options.

Other Options for Database Software

So many vendors offer so many implementations of the relational database that this book cannot adequately show examples or syntax from even the top implementations. We have chosen Oracle for this book, but the examples stay as close to the SQL standard as possible so that they can easily be adapted to other database implementations. Following are some of the most popular implementations available as of the publication of this book, along with websites where you can access their database software. Many software products are available for free download or are freely distributed for personal, development, and educational purposes.

Oracle Database XE	www.oracle.com
Oracle Live SQL	livesql.oracle.com
Microsoft SQL Server	www.microsoft.com
MySQL	www.mysql.com
PostgreSQL	www.postgresql.org
MariaDB	www.mariadb.org
SQLite	www.sqlite.org
Firebirdsql	www.firebirdsql.org
InterBase	www.ermbarcadero.com
DB2 Express-C	www.ibm.com
CUBRID	www.cubrid.org

NOTE

RDBMS Recommendation for This Book

Oracle is the recommended database management system to use for this book—not because Oracle is necessarily the right database for you or your organization, but because you will have a seamless transition from examples to hands-on exercises. The examples and exercises in this book are simple and stay as close to the SQL standard as possible. Any code used in this book should thus be portable to most relational database management systems, with minor adjustments to vendor-specific SQL syntax.

Create a User with Required Privileges

Before you run the scripts to create the tables and data used in this book, you must create a database user within your database that has privileges to create and manage objects in the database. You then can run the scripts to build the tables and do everything else that you need to do within the scope of this book.

After you have installed the Oracle database software, do the following:

1. Click the Start button (if you are using Windows).
2. Type `sqlplus` in the search bar.
3. Click SQL Plus.

Figure 4.6 shows the SQL prompt after completing these steps.

```
SQL Plus

SQL*Plus: Release 18.0.0.0.0 - Production on Wed Jun 9 16:01:58 2021
Version 18.4.0.0.0

Copyright (c) 1982, 2018, Oracle.  All rights reserved.

Enter user-name: system
Enter password:
ERROR:
ORA-28002: the password will expire within 7 days

Last Successful login time: Wed Jun 09 2021 16:01:34 -07:00

Connected to:
Oracle Database 18c Express Edition Release 18.0.0.0.0 - Production
Version 18.4.0.0.0

SQL>
```

FIGURE 4.6
The SQL prompt (image © 2021 Oracle)

Log in at the `SQL>` prompt with the `SYSTEM`, `SYS`, or other administrative username and password that you set up when you installed the software.

NOTE

The SQL Command-Line Prompt

The examples in this class use the SQL command-line prompt, which is text based. This is because the code shown is as simple as possible, for learning purposes. You physically type the SQL code instead of using a product to generate the code because that is more effective for the initial learning. Many vendor-specific products provide a graphical interface for interacting with the database using SQL.

Now execute the following commands at the `SQL>` prompt to create a user for yourself to use for exercises throughout this book.

```
SQL> alter session set "_ORACLE_SCRIPT"=true;

Session altered.

SQL> create user your_username
  2  identified by your_passwd;

User created.
```

cannot delete data that does not exist. If you run this script again later with existing data in the tables, you will receive feedback that rows are deleted.

```
SQL> start c:\sqlbook\data.sql

0 rows deleted.


0 rows deleted.


0 rows deleted.


0 rows deleted.


0 rows deleted.


0 rows deleted.


0 rows deleted.
```

In the following second half of the output from the `data.sql` script, you can see feedback for every row that is created.

```
1 row created.


1 row created.


1 row created.


1 row created.


1 row created.


1 row created.

SQL>
```

List of Data by Table

Now it's time to look at the data that comprises the `Birds` database. This is a small database for learning purposes so it is not difficult to have a complete list of the data contained in it. Obviously, if this was a larger database with hundreds or thousands of tables and millions of rows of data, it would not be feasible to have a hard copy list of the data. However, even in a situation like that, you would ideally have diagrams and can always query the database to get a list of all the objects and columns within the database. You can also query the database at any time to get samples of data from various tables of your choosing within the database to see how the data looks.

The list of data follows for each table in our `Birds` database.

NOTE

Why There Are Two Sets of Output for the `Birds` Table

In the following list, you see a `Birds` table Part 1 of 2 and a `Birds` table Part 2 of 2. The output of the data in the `Birds` table was split only for readability purposes in this book. The bird and the bird name are included for your convenience in both data output sets.

BIRDS Table, Part 1 of 2

```
SQL> select bird_id, bird_name, height, wingspan, eggs, broods
  2  from birds;

BIRD_ID BIRD_NAME                  HEIGHT WINGSPAN EGGS BROODS
------- ------------------------- ------ -------- ---- ------
      1 Great Blue Heron              52       78    5      1
      2 Mallard                       28        3   10      1
      3 Common Loon                   36       54    2      1
      4 Bald Eagle                    37       84    2      1
      5 Golden Eagle                  40       90    3      1
      6 Red Tailed Hawk               25       48    3      1
      7 Osprey                        24       72    4      1
      8 Belted Kingfisher             13       23    7      1
      9 Canadian Goose                43       72   10      1
     10 Pied-billed Grebe             13        7    7      1
     11 American Coot                 16       29   12      1
     12 Common Sea Gull               18       18    3      1
     13 Ring-billed Gull              19       50    4      1
     14 Double-crested Cormorant      33       54    4      1
     15 Common Merganser              27       34   11      1
     16 Turkey Vulture                32       72    2      1
     17 American Crow                 18       40    6      1
     18 Green Heron                   22       27    4      2
     19 Mute Swan                     60       95    8      1
     20 Brown Pelican                 54       90    4      1
```

```
         5          2
         5         19
         5         25
         6          2
         6         12
         6         11
         6         19
         7          5
         8          5
         9          7
         9         19
         9          1
        10          8
        11          8
        11          7
        12          5
        12         23
        12         16
        13         19
        13          5
        13         16
        14          5
        14          8
        15          5
        15          8
        16         16
        17          3
        17          8
        17         13
        17          5
        17         16
        17          1
        18          5
        18         19
        18          7
        19          8
        19         20
        20          5
        20         23
        21          5
        21          8
        21          4
        21         22
        22          5
        22          8
        23          5
        23         23
        23          8

64 rows selected.
```

MIGRATION Table

```
SQL> select * from migration;

MIGRATION_ID MIGRATION_LOCATION
------------ ------------------------------
           1 Southern United States
           2 Mexico
           3 Central America
           4 South America
           5 No Significant Migration
           6 Partial, Open Water

6 rows selected.
```

BIRDS_MIGRATION Table

```
SQL> select * from birds_migration;

   BIRD_ID MIGRATION_ID
---------- ------------
         1            1
         1            2
         1            3
         1            4
         2            1
         3            1
         3            2
         3            3
         4            1
         5            5
         6            1
         7            1
         7            2
         7            3
         7            4
         8            1
         8            2
         8            3
         8            4
         9            1
         9            5
        10            1
        10            2
        10            3
        11            1
        11            2
        11            3
```

```
      12          1
      12          2
      12          3
      12          4
      13          1
      13          2
      14          1
      14          2
      14          3
      15          1
      15          2
      15          3
      16          1
      16          2
      16          3
      16          4
      17          5
      18          1
      18          2
      18          3
      18          4
      19          6
      20          5
      21          1
      21          2
      21          3
      22          1
      22          2
      23          5

56 rows selected.
```

NESTS Table

```
SQL> select * from nests;

   NEST_ID NEST_NAME
---------- --------------------
         1 Ground Nest
         2 Platform Nest
         3 Cup Nest
         4 Pendulous Nest
         5 Cavity Nest
         6 None/Minimal
         7 Floating Platform

7 rows selected.
```

BIRDS_NESTS Table

```
SQL> select * from birds_nests;

   BIRD_ID    NEST_ID
---------- ----------
         1          2
         2          1
         3          2
         4          2
         5          2
         6          2
         7          2
         8          5
         9          1
        10          7
        11          3
        12          1
        13          1
        14          2
        15          5
        16          6
        17          2
        18          2
        19          1
        20          1
        21          2
        22          2
        23          1

23 rows selected.
```

NICKNAMES Table

```
SQL> select * from nicknames;

   BIRD_ID NICKNAME
---------- ------------------------------
         1 Big Cranky
         1 Blue Crane
         2 Green Head
         2 Green Cap
         3 Great Northern Diver
         4 Sea Eagle
         4 Eagle
         5 War Eagle
         6 Chicken Hawk
         7 Sea Hawk
```

```
         8 Preacher Bird
         9 Honker
        10 Water Witch
        11 Soul Chicken
        11 Devil Duck
        12 Seagull
        13 Seagull
        14 Booby
        14 Sea Turkey
        15 Sawbill
        16 Turkey Buzzard
        16 Buzzard
        17 Crow
        18 Poke
        18 Chucklehead
        19 Tundra
        20 Pelican
        21 Common Egret
        21 White Egret
        22 Water Turkey
        22 Spanish Crossbird
        22 Snake Bird
        23 Sea Dog

33 rows selected.
```

LOCATIONS Table

```
SQL> select * from locations;

LOCATION_ID LOCATION_NAME
----------- ------------------------------
          1 Heron Lake
          2 Loon Creek
          3 Eagle Creek
          4 White River
          5 Sarasota Bridge
          6 Fort Lauderdale Beach

6 rows selected.
```

PHOTOS Table

```
SQL> select * from photos;

no rows selected
```

Summary

During this hour, you downloaded a relational database management system implementation to perform the hands-on exercises in this book. You saw how to install the software and create a user with the appropriate privileges in the database to create and manage database objects. You looked through the tables and data for the `Birds` database and, hopefully, ran the scripts to create the database. The last section gave you a hard copy of the data, which will come in handy as you progress with the exercises until you really get to know the data itself. Remember, you must know your data so that you can most effectively use it to benefit yourself and the organization.

Q&A

Q. Can I use an implementation other than Oracle for this book?

A. Oracle is the implementation used for the examples and exercises in this book. You can select virtually any relational database implementation, but you might need to make minor changes to the syntax that is specific to your implementation. The recommendation is to use the same software we are using in this book, for simplicity's sake, and then take your SQL knowledge with you to any other implementation that you choose. The examples and exercises given throughout this book are as compliant to the SQL standard as possible, for easy portability.

Q. If I make a mistake or just want to start over with a new database, can I do so?

A. Absolutely. If you make mistakes, delete data or tables accidentally, or simply want to reset or re-create the database, you can do so using the scripts provided. Simply log into SQL and rerun the script `tables.sql`. Then rerun the script `data.sql`. All the old tables will be dropped, new tables will be created, and data will be inserted as it was in the beginning.

Workshop

The following workshop consists of a series of quiz questions and practical exercises. The quiz questions are designed to test your overall understanding of the current material. The practical exercises give you the opportunity to apply the concepts discussed during the current hour, as well as build on the knowledge you acquired in previous hours of study. Be sure to complete the quiz questions and exercises before continuing to the next hour. Refer to Appendix C, "Answers to Quizzes and Exercises," for answers.

Quiz

Refer to the data for the `BIRDS` database that was listed during this hour.

1. Why is the `BIRDS` table split into two separate output sets?
2. Why do errors occur the first time you execute the file `tables.sql`?
3. Why are zero rows deleted the first time you execute the file `data.sql`?
4. What must an administrative user do after creating a user before that user can create and manage objects in the database?
5. How many tables are in the `BIRDS` database?

Exercises

Refer to the data for the BIRDS database that was listed during this hour.

1. Give some examples of parent tables in the BIRDS database.
2. Give some examples of child tables in the BIRDS database.
3. How many unique types of birds are in the database?
4. What foods does the Bald Eagle eat?
5. Who builds the most nests, male or female, or both?
6. How many birds migrate to Central America?
7. Which bird spends the most time raising its young?
8. Which birds have the term ***eagle*** in their nickname?
9. What is the most popular migration location for birds in the database?
10. Which bird(s) has/have the most diverse diet?
11. What is the average wingspan of birds that eat fish?

HOUR 5
Understanding the Basics of Relational (SQL) Database Design

What You'll Learn in This Hour:

- Database design's relation to SQL
- The general database design process
- Basic design techniques with the BIRDS database
- Database life cycle basics

In this hour, you learn the basics of designing a relational database. This is not by any means a database design book; however, you should understand not only the key elements of a relational database, but also what goes into design. This is because the design process is all about the data and the relationships with the data. The same is true when using SQL: The design process ties directly into how data is used. Here you learn the basics of design while reinforcing the foundation for your SQL journey.

Understanding What Database Design Has to Do with SQL

Database design has everything to do with SQL. SQL is about communicating with a database and accessing data so that an organization can use that data effectively. To access data and use it effectively, the database must be well designed. A solid database design provides a way to easily store, find, and use data for all sorts of purposes. In the business world, maximizing the use of your data for competitive advantage is critical. For individuals, having the right data at the right time makes us more efficient and better able to accomplish what we want to do. Understanding database design basics strengthens your knowledge of SQL and enables you to immediately apply what you learn.

The Database Design Process

Database design has numerous approaches, with many methodologies and industry best practices. Additionally, your organization might have its own standards and naming conventions. Database design can be a manual process or an automated one, with software products assisting you in the design process.

This book takes a simple manual approach, to focus on the basics of the relational database and SQL instead of a particular software product. When you learn the concepts covered in this book, however, you will be able to apply them to any software product that you or your organization choose.

Common approaches to just about any database design process involve the following:

- Choosing a database design methodology.
- Knowing your data. This involves understanding who uses the data, gathering information, and understanding how the data works within the organization.
- Establishing groups of data sets.
- Establishing lists of fields within these data sets.
- Identifying relationships between the data and how the data will be integrated with other components within an information system.
- Modeling your database.
- Planning ahead for database growth. This is where the database life cycle comes into play.

In the next few hours, you get a basic overview of this process by exploring the design of the `BIRDS` database and adding components to it. What you learn with basic relational (SQL) database design translates directly into your journey with SQL. The basic approach to examine and practice database design in this book follows:

- Requirements gathering
- Data modeling
- Design and normalization

This hour focuses mainly on gathering requirements and begins to scratch the surface of data modeling. As you progress through basic design and into hands-on use with SQL, the following hallmarks of a well-designed relational database also will become evident.

- Data storage needs have been met.
- Data is readily available to the end user.

- Data is protected through the use of built-in database constraints.
- Data is protected through the use of built-in database security options.
- Data is accurate and easy to manage, and database performance is acceptable.
- The database is scalable as the organization evolves and transforms over time.
- Redundant data is limited or minimized as much as possible.

NOTE

A Well-Designed Database Unlocks the Power of SQL

SQL is inherently a simple and powerful language, but this is even more true when you are using SQL with a well-designed database and you have a good knowledge of the data that is stored within your database. A well-designed database is scalable as data grows and enables you to unlock all the tools that SQL provides.

Choosing a Database Design Methodology

The database design methodology is the approach taken in designing a database. A sound plan is required from the beginning. For individuals who lack the proper knowledge and experience, designing a database probably involves a great deal of trial and error. Individuals who understand database fundamentals and design concepts, know the basic steps of the database design process, and have a structured plan have a better experience: Their design process generally produces a quality product for both the organization and the end users who will eventually access the database.

Some advantages of using a design methodology include the following:

- You can easily produce design plans, drawings that depict an organization's needs, and other deliverables that are specified during the design process.
- You can easily modify the database in the future because organization and planning ease the tasks of managing changes.

Choosing a design methodology or product does not involve any right or wrong answers. As stated earlier, many software products are available to assist you in the database design process, possibly including products made by the database vendor that you use. Finding the right choice for you and your organization involves looking at features and budgets and then choosing a methodology or product that supports the users of the design process and any standards or conventions that you choose along the way. Planning, documentation, and consistency are the keys.

NOTE

Our Simple Approach to Database Design

This book takes a simplistic yet systematic approach to designing a database so that you can better understand the relational database and how to use SQL to effectively access data. You can find more detailed information about specific database design methodologies that might work well for you, whether online or in physical bookstores. You'll see that countless approaches exist.

This book is intended to help you better understand the relational database and how you can use SQL to effectively access data. For that reason, the next few chapters take a simplistic yet systematic approach to designing a database and building on the example BIRDS database we have already seen:

- You first must ensure that you know your data. You have already begun to look at the data in the BIRDS database.
- You gather information that you can use to model a database.
- Then you model the data by establishing groups of data, lists of fields, and relationships between the data sets.
- Ultimately, you use this basic design and implement the database physically using SQL commands to create database objects, manage the data within the database, and effectively query the database to derive useful data that is critical to organizational success.

Using a Simple Process to Think Through the Design of the BIRDS Database

This section walks through some basic steps of the initial database design process for the sample BIRDS database. This process involves asking questions about the data and speculating about how the data might be used within various types of organizations that might need to access the database. As this section progresses, we will establish groups of data and a list of files that will eventually comprise a set of tables to be integrated with the BIRDS database. Hours 6 and 7 build on this exploration of the basic bird data and sample new data to be integrated by walking you through a hands-on example of how the database was designed.

As previously mentioned, this hour focuses on requirements gathering and the beginning phase of data modeling. The following subsections walk through the following process:

- Knowing your data
- Gathering information

- Modeling your data, or defining groups of data and lists of fields (Hours 6 and 7 discuss data modeling in more detail)

Knowing Your Data

To design a database, you must first know the data that must be modeled. Data consists of any information that a business is required to keep for any purpose. The objective of an information system is to maintain data for an organization. An organization might maintain internal or external information. For example, a company might keep track of health insurance claims submitted by many patients whose care was administered by various providers and doctors, at multiple times, and at different locations. In most cases, no single person can accurately and completely define all of this data. Therefore, you must also know who else knows about the data, who the end users of the data will be, and how the data will be used within the organization. Some basic questions can get you started, to better understand the information that will become critical data stored for your organization:

- What is the data about?
- From what sources will you get your data?
- Who within your organization knows about the data?
- Is the data internal to the organization or will it be used by users outside the organization?
- Who are the primary users of the data?
- How long must the data be kept?
- What are the current responsibilities of the end users?
- With whom do the end users interact?
- What service or product is provided to the customer?
- How are data sets related to other data sets?
- What information must be unique within the database? How will you grant access to the right users while restricting access from users that need less information?
- Does data within the database depend upon other data?
- Is data referenced by other data? Parent/child relationships?
- What reports might be generated from the data?
- How can the data be used as business intelligence?

NOTE

It's All About the Data

When designing and working with any database, it's all about the data. You have to know the data inside and out, including how it will be accessed by users and leveraged within your organization. As data changes and the way people utilize that data changes, the database will evolve accordingly. A good database design process facilitates this evolution. With SQL, you will always have relevant data at your fingertips.

Quick Review of the BIRDS Database

In previous chapters, you looked at the BIRDS database to find some basic and static information. In addition to the basic information about birds themselves, you saw that the database includes photographs taken of birds in different locations and information on birds eating different types of food, birds migrating to different locations, birds building nests, and birds with nicknames.

As a review, Figure 5.1 shows a very basic ERD of the BIRDS database which is also found in Hour 3, "Getting to Know Your Data." The entities diagramed here represent the basic groups of data about birds that were defined as entities at this point, and eventually will be converted into tables that store physical data in this database.

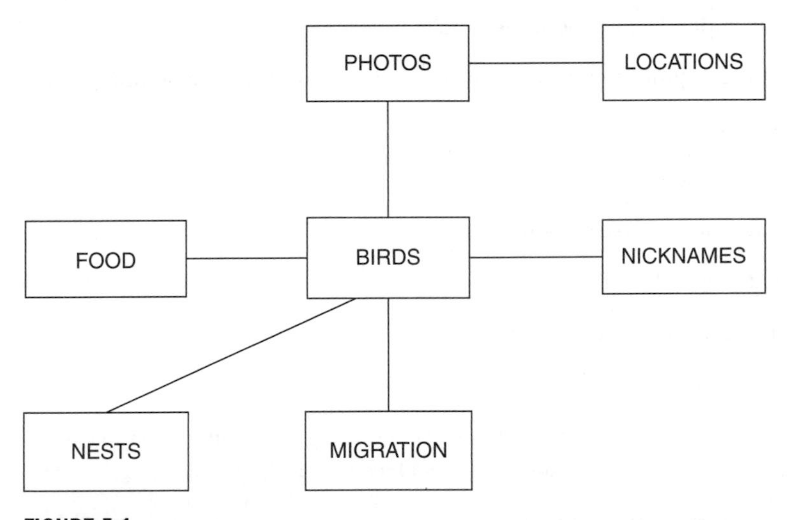

FIGURE 5.1
Basic entities in the BIRDS database

For your convenience, Figure 5.2 shows a more detailed ERD of the BIRDS database. This diagram contains not only the entities, or groups of data, but also a list of fields within each group of data. Each list of fields will comprise the attributes of each entity as you continue to model the database and eventually create a physical database using SQL commands. Refer back to Hour 3 whenever you need to refresh your memory on the details of the BIRDS database.

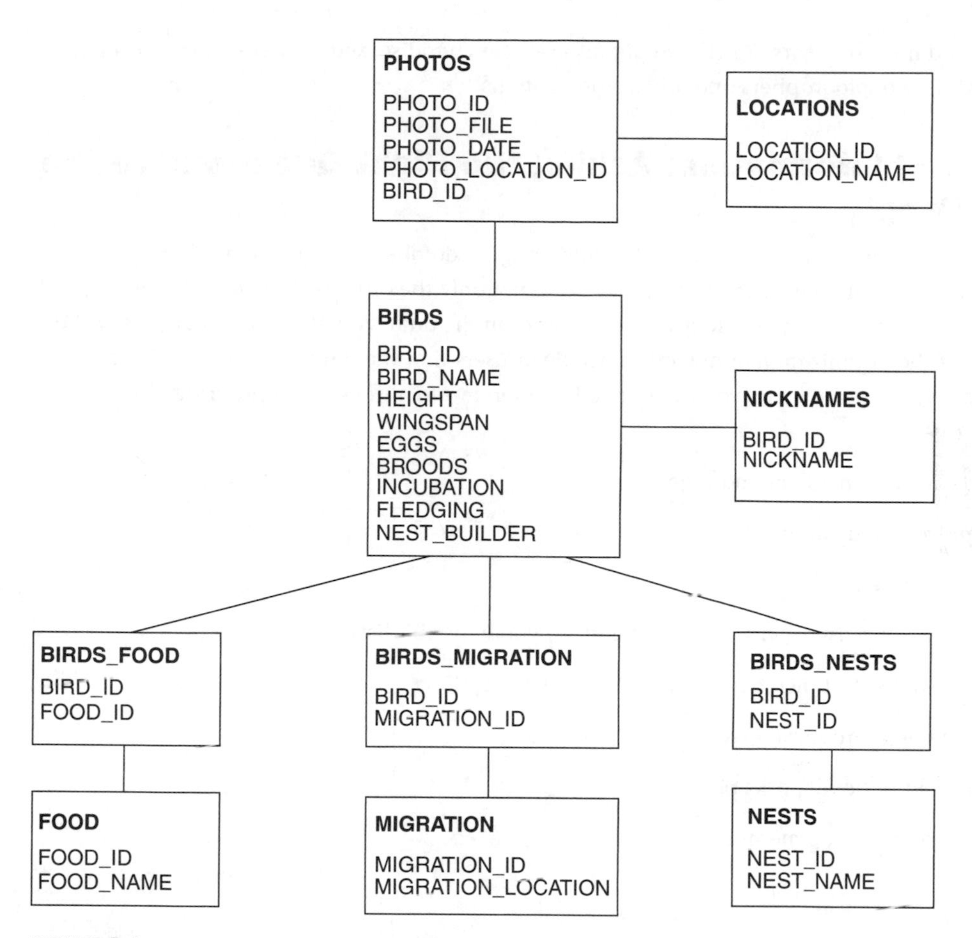

FIGURE 5.2
Entities, attributes, and relationships in the BIRDS database

Using Basic Database Design Principles to Add Data About Bird Rescues to the Existing BIRDS Database

This section begins to walk through the process of adding a related group of data to the BIRDS database. This data is about bird rescues, organizations that take in abandoned or injured birds and rehabilitate them, with the goal of releasing those birds back into the wild so that they can survive on their own. To get you started, here is some basic information about bird rescues that you can use to model data to add to the BIRDS database shown in the previous two figures.

Bird rescues have name, address, and contact information, as well as websites and social media sites. Various types of birds are taken in, and each rescue might have multiple facilities. Rescues are managed by full-time employees as well as volunteers, and they receive funding from various donors and fundraising events. A rescue might produce publications, distribute marketing material, and have sponsors. Rescues might also sell merchandise, share success stories, and interact with wildlife photographers and other organizations.

Gathering Information: Asking the Right Questions to the Right People

To gather the information necessary to plan and design a database, you need to ask the right questions to the right people. You must understand not only the organization, but all the people within the organization who interact with each other in the data. You also need to understand the customers of the organization or any other people or users that the data might affect. Consider, for example, a few groups that you might need to interview to gather the appropriate data to model:

- Bird rescue owners and management
- Employees and volunteers
- Photographers
- Database end users (which could include anybody on this list)
- Publications staff members, such as editorial staff
- Government organizations
- State and national parks personnel
- Bird interest group members

NOTE

Understanding Organization Processes and Business Rules

An important part of the overall design process of a database and the applications that surround the database is understanding organizational processes and business rules. This is part of the requirements gathering phase. This book focuses more on the data itself, so business processes and rules in application design itself lie outside its scope. Still, be sure to keep this in mind because requirements gathering ties closely into database design itself.

Modeling the Data

During this hour, you do not yet create entity relationship diagrams for the data on bird rescues that will be added to the database. You do, however, look at how to create a list of groups of data and a list of fields. You will build upon these lists in Hours 6 and 7 and also create the appropriate entity relationship diagrams. In the exercises at the end of this hour, you also have the opportunity to start modeling data.

Based on the previous information about bird rescues, you can begin to identify the initial groups of data and lists of fields.

Establishing Groups of Data

Following is a basic list of the groups of data that might be derived from the previous description of bird rescues that will not be integrated with the existing sample BIRDS database.

- Rescues
- Rescue_Facilities
- Staff
- Publications
- Events
- Online sites
- Sponsors

Keep in mind that these groups of data will become entities that will not only be related to one another either directly or indirectly, but to existing entities in the BIRDS database such as the BIRDS entity itself. Because the sample database is about birds, the most central entity which most entities will eventually refer back to is the BIRDS entity.

Establishing Lists of Fields

Based on the groups of data that you derived from the description for bird rescues, you might come up with lists of fields similar to the following:

RESCUES

    RESCUE_ID
    RESCUE_NAME
    PRIMARY_ADDRESS
    PRIMARY_CITY
    PRIMARY_STATE
    PRIMARY_ZIP
    PRIMARY_PHONE

```
RESCUE_FACILITIES
    RESCUE_FACILITY_ID
    RESCUE_FACILITY_NAME
    ADDRESS
    CITY
    STATE
    ZIP
    PHONE

STAFF
    STAFF_ID
    STAFF_NAME
    STAFF_TYPE
    STAFF_PAY
    STAFF_CONTACT_INFO

PUBLICATIONS
    PUBLICATION_ID
    PUBLICATION_NAME
    PUBLICATION_TYPE
    PUBLICATION_CONTACT_INFO

EVENTS
    EVENT_ID
    EVENT_NAME
    EVENT_LOCATION
    EVENT_DATE
    EVENT_DESCRIPTION

ONLINE SITES
    ONLINE_SITE_ID
    ONLINE_SITE_NAME
    ONLINE_SITE_TYPE
    ONLINE_SITE_ADDRESS
    ONLINE_SITE_DESCRIPTION
```

```
SPONSORS
    SPONSOR_ID
    SPONSOR_NAME
    SPONSOR_CONTACT_INFO
```

This is merely an example of a list of fields you might come up with for bird rescue information. There are no right or wrong solutions, especially at this point. The database will evolve as you think through the design, and even after the database is in production, it will continue to evolve overtime. Again, this is a simple example to help think through the process. Remember that this data and lists of fields will be modeled into entities that have relationships with one another, and then we will use SQL to create the physical database. At this point it is more important to focus on the basic concepts!

Logical Model vs. Physical Design

Although this is not a book about database design itself, it is important to understand the difference between logical data modeling and the physical design of a database. This is important because SQL is a standard language used to communicate with any relational database. Theoretically, a logical data model can be deployed to any relational database implementation. The tools used to logically model a database might or might not be vendor specific; the process could even be a manual one. However, the physical design and implementation of a database is very specific. It requires knowledge of a specific vendor's implementation of SQL. Fortunately, as already mentioned, most vendors do a pretty good job of adhering to the SQL standard. This means that most logical data mile models are portable to vendor implementations.

The logical data model lean process involves gathering the necessary information about the organization, users, processes, and information to model the data that will eventually comprise a database. From a database perspective, the information models that you produce represent the following:

- Entities
- Relationships between entities
- Attributes of entities

As stated, the physical design of a database involves starting with the logical model and then creating the database using SQL commands of the specific vendor implementation that your organization uses. The previous list is about entities and other elements that are created during the design process, which will eventually be used to create the physical database elements in the following list using SQL:

- Tables
- Keys and constraints
- Columns with data types
- Other physical database objects that are derived from the logical data model itself

NOTE

Logical vs. Physical Models

A logical model is simply a representation of the critical information, or data, that will comprise a database. The physical database consists of the actual physical objects, primarily tables, that contain data and are physically stored on a device using a particular technology—or, in the case of the database, a vendor-specific implementation of the relational database (SQL).

Database Life Cycle

The database life cycle starts with a requirement to have information available for the operation of a business. Requirements are gathered and the logical database design process commences. To effectively manage the life cycle of a database with minimal impact on the integrity of the data, the security of data, the performance of data, and so on, three minimal environments should be in place as a best practice (see Figure 5.3).

- Development
- Test
- Production

Development

The development environment represents the birth of a database—or an information system, for that matter. In the development environment, all database objects are initially created and relationships are established. No time limit governs development, other than the constraints of various milestones and deadlines specified in a design plan (or identified according to the organization's needs). The development environment should be kept active throughout the production life of the database. Any new objects or changes to existing objects should always begin in the development environment. All three database environments shown in Figure 5.3 must be kept in sync with one another, to most easily manage database changes. Having multiple environments keeps the production environment stable for end users until changes are properly developed and tested before production deployment. Making changes to a database in a production environment is too risky.

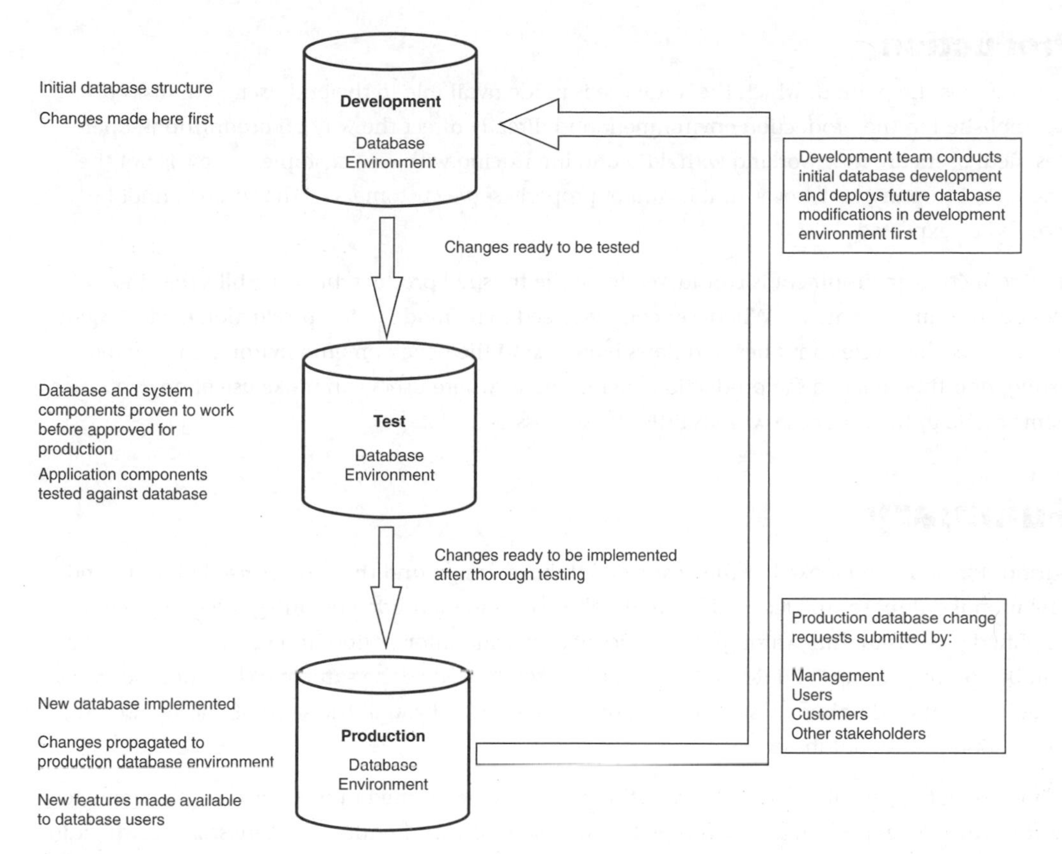

FIGURE 5.3
The database life cycle

Test

After the database has been fully designed and created in the development environment, it is time to migrate all development database structures into the test environment. During testing, the database is tested for overall functionality and accuracy. Any changes to the database are also tested with any applications that might access the database. Various users who have a good knowledge of the organization are typically involved in the testing phase of the database life cycle. Changes to an existing production database must be thoroughly tested before those changes are deployed into the production environment, to avoid potential data loss, degradation of performance, application functionality, and so on.

Production

Production is the point at which the database is made available to the end user. Real tasks are accomplished in the production environment and directly affect the way an organization operates. Real users are now working with data and interfacing with real customers. Now is not the time for a company to discover that it cannot properly serve customers or that data cannot be accessed as expected.

The production environment is considered to be the finished product, but it is still subject to changes and improvements. Whenever changes need to be made to the production environment, the database life cycle continues and flows back first to the development environment, then to testing, and then back to the production environment, where users can make use of any enhancements made to the database with as little risk as possible.

Summary

During this hour, you looked at the basics of database design and the process itself of designing a relational database. You learned about database design methodology and got a glimpse at a simplified process to think through the basics of gathering information and beginning to model data by creating groups of data and lists of fields. You looked at the sample `BIRDS` database and thought about its database design process, and you walked through the steps of adding data to the existing `BIRDS` database.

In future hours, you will build upon everything that you've learned in this hour as you complete a basic database design process. By completing the examples and hands-on exercises, you will gain a strong foundation that will lead you seamlessly into using SQL to define physical database components, manage data within the database, and effectively query the database. A well-designed database is crucial to the life cycle of a database and will help you maximize all the tools you have within the language of SQL.

Q&A

Q. Which approach works better, manually designing a database or using an automated tool?

A. For a small database, a manual design approach may be adequate. For larger and more complex databases, or even smaller databases with multiple people involved during the design process, using an automated design tool with an agreed upon design methodology is usually the best option. An automated tool will help keep everything straight and make documentation and diagrams much easier to produce. Many automated tools will generate the SQL code for you that's necessary to create the database that you have modeled.

Q. Can I deploy my database design to any relational database implementation?

A. When you design a relational database, you should be able to deploy that design to any relational database implementation without much trouble. The design process is more of a logical process whereas the actual use of a vendor's relational database system deals more with the physical database that is created after the design process. However, some vendors provide design tools that generate code specific to that implementation. In these situations, the logical design itself can be used, but you might have to modify the SQL code that is generated so that it follows a specific database implementation's exact syntax. For example, although the `create table` statement is a standard SQL command, it might vary slightly from vendor to vendor.

Workshop

The following workshop consists of a series of quiz questions and practical exercises. The quiz questions are designed to test your overall understanding of the current material. The practical exercises give you the opportunity to apply the concepts discussed during the current hour, as well as build on the knowledge you acquired in previous hours of study. Be sure to complete the quiz questions and exercises before continuing to the next hour. Refer to Appendix C, "Answers to Quizzes and Exercises," for answers.

Quiz

1. How is database design related to SQL?
2. What diagram is used to model data and relationships for a database? What are fields also called in a physical database?
3. During database design, groups of data (also referred to as entities) become what type of object in the physical database?
4. What is the difference between logical and physical design?
5. What are the three most common database environments that accommodate the database life cycle?

Exercises

1. During the next few hours, you will be designing a database about wildlife photographers who take pictures of birds. This database should be designed so that it can eventually be integrated with the existing `BIRDS` database. Take a minute and review the ERD for the `BIRDS` database. These exercises have no right or wrong solutions; what's important is the way you interpret the information and envision the data coming together into a database model. Also review the examples during this hour on adding entities to the `BIRDS` database about bird rescues.

2. Read and analyze the following information about photographer data that you will be adding to the `BIRDS` database. Consider what the database is about, the purpose of the database, the anticipated users, the potential customers, and so on.

   All photographers have names, addresses, and education information. They might have received awards and maintain various websites or social media sites. Each photographer also likely has a particular passion, an artistic approach, photographic style, preferred bird targets, and so on. Additionally, photographers use various cameras and lenses and might produce media in a variety of formats using editing software. They have different types of clients, often are published in certain products, and contribute images to publications. Photographers also might be mentors or volunteers for bird rescue groups or other nonprofit organizations. They definitely have varying skill levels—beginner, novice, hobbyist, competent photographer, skilled, artist, and world class. In addition, photographers might market and sell various products, whether they are self-employed or work for an organization.

   The equipment photographers use includes cameras, lenses, and editing software. Cameras have a make and model, sensor type (full frame or crop sensor), megapixels, frames per second, ISO range, and cost. Lenses have a make, lens type, aperture range, and cost.

3. Make a list of all of the basic entities, or groups of data, of wildlife photographers. This is then your basis for entities, and that eventually becomes your ERD.

4. Draw a basic data model based on the lists that you derived in the previous exercises. Draw lines between the entities in your diagram to depict relationships. This is the starting point for your ERD.

5. Make a list of all the basic attributes within each entity that you defined in the previous exercises, or fields, of wildlife photographers. This is the basis for your entities, and that eventually becomes your ERD.

HOUR 6
Defining Entities and Relationships

What You'll Learn in This Hour:

- Gain a deeper understanding of entities and relationships
- Understand how to model referential integrity
- Define parent and child relationships using primary and foreign keys
- Walk through defining entities and relationships with the BIRDS database
- Walk through the process of adding entities to the BIRDS database through hands-on exercises for modeling your own entities and relationships that will be integrated with the BIRDS database

During this hour, you learn about one of the most important phases of database design: defining entities and relationships. The entities and relationships that you define in this book are based on the groups of data and lists of fields that you defined in Hour 5, "Understanding the Basics of Relational (SQL) Database Design." In this hour, you walk through some of the design and modeling for the sample BIRDS database, think about how you might add components for bird rescues to the existing BIRDS database, and begin to model the data you defined in Hour 5. This is a crucial part of database design, and you must understand it so that you can fully take advantage of the SQL language. As you define entities and relationships in this hour, you'll gain a better understanding of the cornerstone of the relational database, referential integrity. As always, any hands-on exercises in this hour are immediately applicable to the real world.

Creating a Data Model Based on Your Data

Before you start modeling entities and relationships, let's dive a little deeper into data relationships and referential integrity. In the following sections, you look at the different types of relationships in a relational database and walk through examples based on the sample BIRDS database.

Data

As you know by now, data is at the heart of every organization and every individual. The sample database for this book is the BIRDS database. Output from the existing tables has been provided to show the actual data that currently exists in this database. Not only do you look deeper into the data itself and see how the different entities of the BIRDS database are related to one another, but you also get examples in this hour of how you might model data that can be added to the existing database. After looking at some examples of data about bird rescues that could be integrated into the BIRDS database, you move on to model data about photographers that can be integrated into the same database.

NOTE

Defining Data

In Hour 8, "Defining Data Structures," you learn how to define data structures using SQL data types. The most common data types are character, numeric, date, and time. These data types are initially defined using the SQL command `CREATE TABLE`.

Relationships

A relational database is all about relationships between data sets within a database. During the database design phase, you identify entities, or groups of data, and specify the relationships between those entities. For example, some entities are parent entities; some are child entities. These entities have relationships with one another and eventually define the database that will be created. Conceptually, you conceive the database and then use SQL to physically create the database and manage the data within that database. Different types of relationships are covered later in this hour.

Any relationship between entities is a two-way relationship and can be interpreted from either entity's side. Consider the following example between birds and the food items they eat (see Figure 6.1).

- Birds eat food.
- Food is eaten by birds.

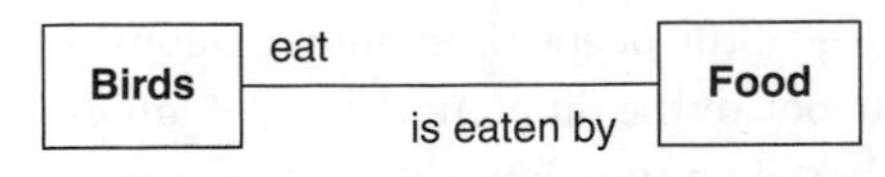

FIGURE 6.1
Reading a relationship between entities

Other examples from the `BIRDS` database include the following:

- Birds migrate to various locations, and each migration location has birds that migrate there.
- Birds have nicknames, and nicknames are given to birds.
- Birds have photographs taken of them, and photographs are taken of birds.
- Birds build nests, and nests are built by birds.

Referential Integrity

Referential integrity is a term used to describe parent and child relationships between entities within a database. Some entities that eventually become tables are parent entities; others are children. Children entities refer to parent entities: They depend on the data that already exists within parent entities. Of course, entities do not contain data; they are conceptual. But when you create the physical tables in the database, any data inserted into the database must comply with any rules that you have set forth within the database, according to the rules of the relational database implementation you are using and the constraints you have defined (such as primary key and foreign key constraints). The relational database is all about referential integrity.

Take a minute to study the parent and child relationship modeled in Figure 6.2.

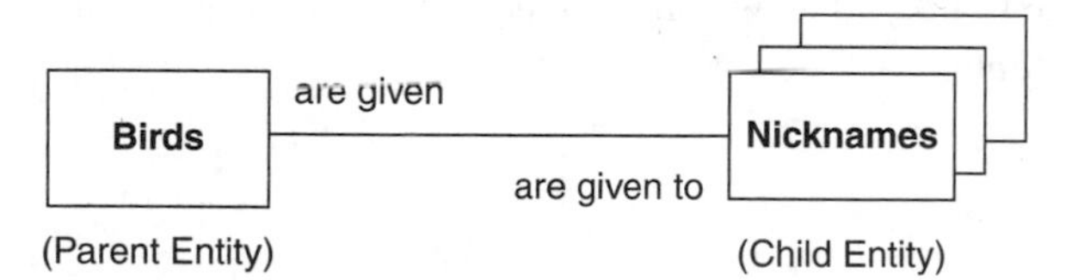

FIGURE 6.2
Parent and child relationship

All of the following information can be derived from the simple ERD shown in Figure 6.2.

- Birds are given one or more nicknames.
- A nickname may be given to a specific bird.
- The parent entity is about birds.
- The child entity is about nicknames.
- A bird may be given many nicknames.
- In this specific example, each nickname is associated with only a single bird.

- Because BIRDS is the parent entity, the NICKNAMES entity has dependencies on BIRDS.
- This means that you cannot have a nickname that is not associated with a specific bird.
- This also means that you cannot remove a bird if nicknames are associated with that specific bird.
- To add nicknames to the database that will eventually be created from this design, a corresponding entry for a bird must first exist.
- To remove a bird from the database that will eventually be created from this design, any corresponding nicknames that relate to that specific bird must first be deleted.

NOTE

Using SQL to Employ Referential Integrity

In Hour 9, "Creating and Managing Database Objects," you learn how to use referential integrity in a physical database by using SQL to create tables as well as constraints for primary and foreign keys. For example, the SQL commands CREATE TABLE and ALTER TABLE provide a simple mechanism for defining and managing database constraints to enforce referential integrity.

Figure 6.3 reveals more detail, showing sample data that might exist in the BIRDS table derived from this database design. The following section explains this in more detail, but you should easily see that BIRD_ID is a primary key in the BIRDS table, which uniquely identifies every row of data, or specific type of bird, in the BIRDS table.

Birds

Bird_Id	Bird_name
1	Great Blue Heron
2	Mallard
3	Common Loon
4	Bald Eagle

Primary
Key

FIGURE 6.3
Visual of data in the BIRDS table

Figure 6.4 expands on the previous example, showing more sample data that might exist in tables derived from this database design that are related to one another. The following sections also explain this in more detail, but you can see both a parent table and a child table. The child table contains the nicknames and relates back to the BIRDS table through a common column called BIRD_ID. Using a basic manual process, you can determine the nicknames of each bird in this example. Again, you are working with these basic concepts so that you can better understand how SQL works to get useful data from the database.

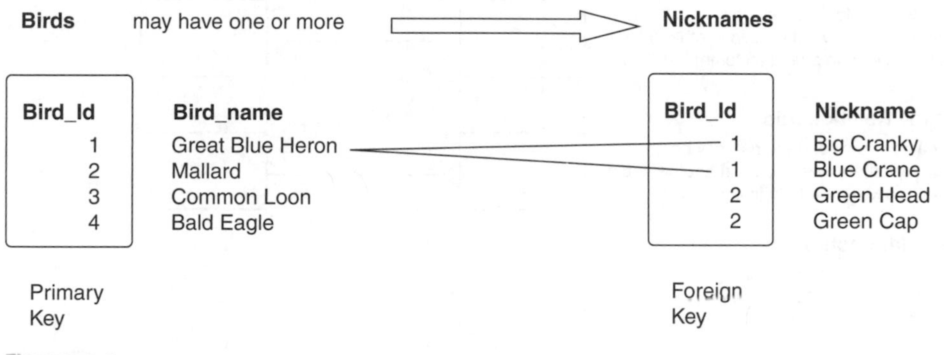

FIGURE 6.4
Data in parent and child relationships

Defining Relationships

In this section, you examine the basic relationships that can exist within a relational database. The four most common relationships in a relational database follow:

- One-to-one relationship
- One-to-many relationship
- Many-to-many relationship
- Recursive relationship

When drawing an ERD, the symbols in Figure 6.5 are commonly used to depict entities and their relationships.

Entity (Table)

One-to-one Relationship
A table has a row of data that is related
to only one other row of data in another table
through a common key on a field (column)

One-to-many Relationship
A table has a row of data that may be
related to one or more rows of data in another table
through a common key on a field (column)

Many-to-many Relationship
A table has multiple rows of data that may be
related to multiple other rows of data in another table
through a common key on a field (column)

Recursive Relationship
A table has a row of data that may be
related to another row of data in the same table
through a common key on a field (column)

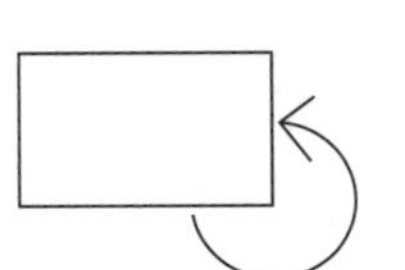

FIGURE 6.5
Common ERD symbols to depict entities and relationships

One-to-One

In a one-to-one relationship, one record in a table is related to only one record in another table. For example, each employee typically has only one pay record. In the bird example, each bird might have only one nickname.

Figure 6.6 shows a one-to-one relationship. In this example, every bird is assumed to have only one nickname; conversely, each nickname is associated with only one type of bird.

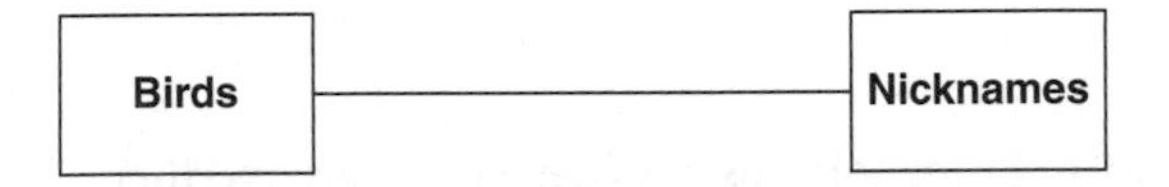

FIGURE 6.6
A one-to-one relationship in the BIRDS database

One-to-Many

In a one-to-many relationship, one record in a table can be related to one or more records in another table. For instance, each employee might have multiple dependents, or each bird might eat many different types of food.

Figure 6.7 shows two relationships that might exist in the BIRDS database. The first example shows a relationship between BIRDS and NICKNAMES. Unlike in the previous example, each bird can have multiple nicknames. However, each nickname can be related to only a specific type of bird. The second example shows a relationship between RESCUES and STAFF. Each bird rescue can have multiple staff members that work within that organization. This example also indicates that many staff members might work for a single bird rescue, but they work for only one bird rescue.

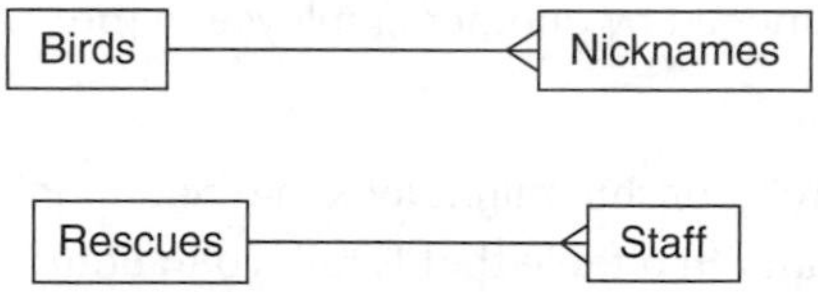

Birds
Nicknames
Rescues
Staff

FIGURE 6.7
A one-to-many relationship in the BIRDS database

Many-to-Many

In a many-to-many relationship, many records in a table can be related to many records in another table. For instance, in the case of birds and the food they eat, a bird might eat many different types of food and each type of food might be eaten by many different types of birds.

Figure 6.8 shows two many-to-many relationships that could exist in the BIRDS database. For the first example, suppose that staff members can work or volunteer at multiple bird rescues. Remember that staff members can be anybody—individuals, photographers, full time staff, part-time staff, and so on. Thus, that scenario is conceivable. This is an example of a many-to-many relationship within a database.

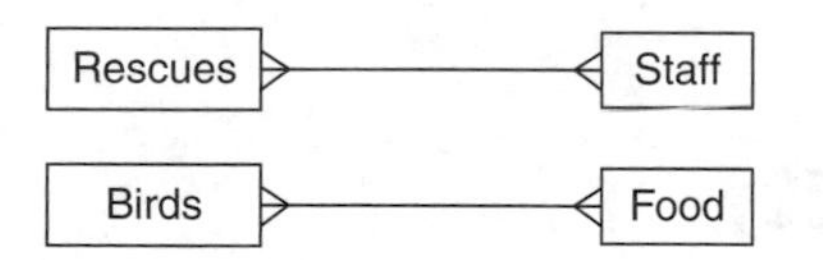

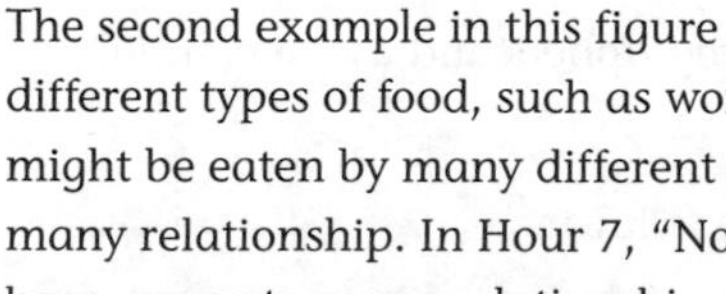

FIGURE 6.8
Examples of many-to-many relationships in the BIRDS database

The second example in this figure illustrates birds and the food they eat. A bird might eat many different types of food, such as worms, berries, and fish. Conversely, each specific type of food might be eaten by many different types of birds. These are two simple examples of a many-to-many relationship. In Hour 7, "Normalizing Your Database," you see that, in a relational database, many-to-many relationships are typically not a best practice for design. (However, they are a stepping stone to a strong relational database design; you learn later how many-to-many relationships can be resolved to eliminate redundant data in the database, thereby preserving the utmost integrity of data within the database.)

Recursive

In a recursive relationship, an attribute within one entity is related to an attribute within the same entity. Basically, an entity serves as both a parent entity and a child entity in a relationship. An attribute, or an eventual column in a table, depends on a column in the same table. You can place rules on attributes or columns within a table that other columns in a table must adhere to. (Later in this book, you use a self join to compare data to other data within the same table.) For example, each employee in an employees table might be managed by another employee in the same table.

Figure 6.9 shows two common examples of how a recursive relationship might look in a relational database. Remember that a recursive relationship involves data in a table that is related to data in the same table. In the first example in this figure, the recursive relationship involves staff members. For example, staff members might be managed by other staff members or, depending on which way you look at the relationship, staff members might manage other staff members. In the second example in this figure, photographers might be mentored by other photographers, or photographers might mentor other photographers that exist in the same entity.

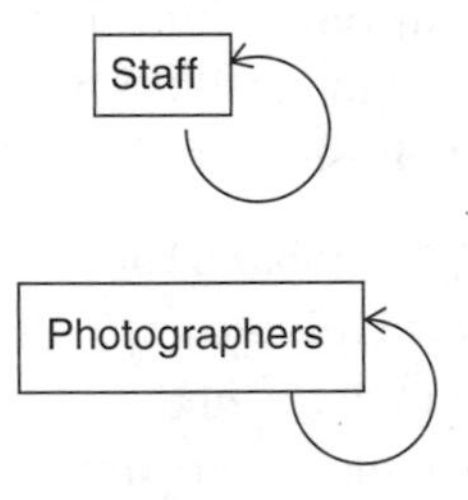

FIGURE 6.9
Examples of recursive relationships

Employing Referential Integrity

Next we look at an example of employee referential integrity. You have already seen referential integrity defined as it pertains to parent and child relationships in a relational database. Now you look at the BIRDS database and some objects that you might add for bird rescues. In the exercises at the end of this hour, you can add objects of your own for photographers and use referential integrity within those objects.

Referential integrity is defined in a relational database using the following:

- Primary keys
- Foreign keys

NOTE

Referential Integrity During Logical Database Design

At this point, the use of referential integrity concepts is still part of the logical process. Sometimes referential integrity is employed using primary key and foreign key constraints in the logical design process; other times, referential integrity is not fully employed until the physical database is created. These constraints are designated in a logical data model but are ultimately defined by constraints using SQL commands when you create the physical database.

Identifying Primary Keys

A primary key is simply a constraint placed on a column in a table that identifies each data value in that column, or field, as unique. A primary key designates a parent value in a parent/child relationship. A primary key is a required attribute within an entity.

Figure 6.4 shows the BIRD_ID entry in the BIRDS table as the primary key. This primary key ensures that every entry or row of data in the BIRDS table is a unique entry. A primary key not only identifies uniqueness, but also assumes that it is a parent record that can have child records in another table which are dependent.

In looking at the BIRDS database as a whole (at least, to this point), the primary keys are as follows:

- BIRD_ID in the BIRDS table
- FOOD_ID in the FOOD table
- MIGRATION_ID in the MIGRATION table
- NEST_ID in the NESTS table
- PHOTO_ID in the PHOTOS table
- LOCATION_ID in the LOCATIONS table

In the BIRDS database, the composite primary keys are as follows:

- BIRD_ID and FOOD_ID (combined) in the BIRDS_FOOD table
- BIRD_ID and MIGRATION_ID (combined) in the BIRDS_MIGRATION table
- BIRD_ID and NEST_ID (combined) in the BIRDS_NESTS tables
- BIRD_ID and NICKNAME (combined) in the NICKNAMES table

NOTE

Composite Primary Keys

A composite primary key is a primary key in a table that consists of more than one column. The combination of these columns must be unique for every row of data in the table. Future hours explain this concept in more detail.

Identifying Foreign Keys

A foreign key is a constraint placed on a column in a table—or, in this hour, an attribute within an entity—that depends on a data value in another entity. For example, a foreign key references a primary key in another entity. The foreign key designates the child record in a parent/child relationship. A foreign key can also be defined as a primary key and can be either a required attribute in an entity or optional.

Referring to Figure 6.4, you can see two tables there: the `BIRDS` table and the `NICKNAMES` table. `BIRD_ID` in the `BIRDS` table is a primary key, or a parent record. In the `NICKNAMES` table, `BIRD_ID` is a foreign key, or child record, that refers back to, or is dependent upon, the `BIRD_ID` in the `BIRDS` table.

In looking at the `BIRDS` database as a whole, the foreign keys are as follows:

- `BIRD_ID` in the `BIRDS_FOOD` table not only is a part of a composite primary key; it also is a foreign key representing a child record that references the `BIRD_ID` in the `BIRDS` table, which is a primary key that represents a parent record.
- `BIRD_ID` in the `BIRDS_MIGRATION` table is a foreign key representing a child record that references `BIRD_ID` in the `BIRDS` table, which is a primary key that represents a parent record.
- `BIRD_ID` in the `BIRDS_NESTS` table is a foreign key representing a child record that references `BIRD_ID` in the `BIRDS` table, which is a primary key that represents a parent record.
- `BIRD_ID` in the `NICKNAMES` table is a foreign key representing a child record that references `BIRD_ID` in the `BIRDS` table, which is a primary key that represents a parent record.
- `BIRD_ID` in the `PHOTOS` table is a foreign key representing a child record that references `BIRD_ID` in the `BIRDS` table, which is a primary key that represents a parent record.
- `FOOD_ID` in the `BIRDS_FOOD` table is a foreign key representing a child record that references `FOOD_ID` in the `FOOD` table, which is a primary key that represents a parent record.
- `MIGRATION_ID` in the `BIRDS_MIGRATION` table is a foreign key representing a child record that references `MIGRATION_ID` in the `MIGRATION` table, which is a primary key that represents a parent record.

- NEST_ID in the BIRDS_NESTS table is a foreign key representing a child record that references NEST_ID in the NESTS table, which is a primary key that represents a parent record.
- PHOTO_LOCATION_ID in the PHOTOS table is a foreign key representing a child record that references LOCATION_ID in the LOCATIONS table, which is a primary key that represents a parent record.

Creating an Entity Relationship

In this section, you create two basic entity relationship diagrams. Figure 6.10 shows the first one, an entity called RESCUES that represents the entire data set related to the bird rescues that will eventually be integrated into the BIRDS database. In this example, you can see that bird rescue information is primarily related to the BIRDS table in the BIRDS database. This does not mean that rescue information will not be related to any other information, such as locations and photographers. This figure is only a starting point to illustrate the basic relationship that might be visualized at this point.

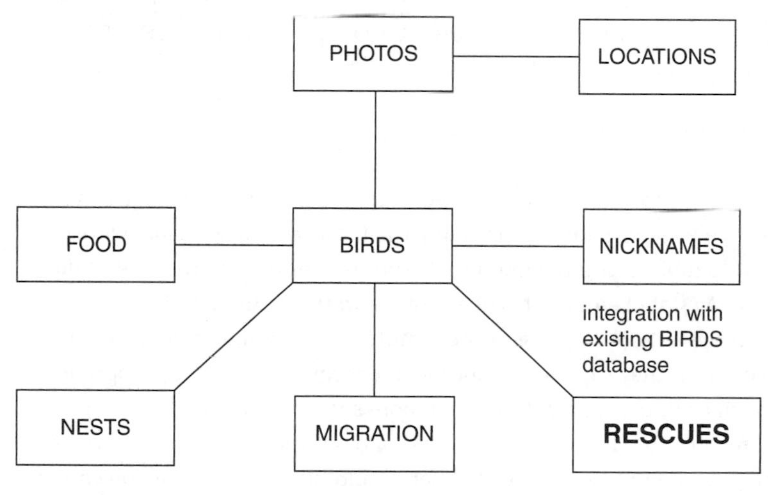

FIGURE 6.10
Basic ERD showing how bird rescues might be integrated into the BIRDS database

In Figure 6.11, you can see that the data set for bird rescues has been expanded upon. It is ultimately linked to the BIRDS database through the BIRDS table. Take a few minutes to study this figure and understand the relationships. Consider the data of the bird rescues and, beyond that, think about how the new data might be integrated and used with the existing BIRDS database.

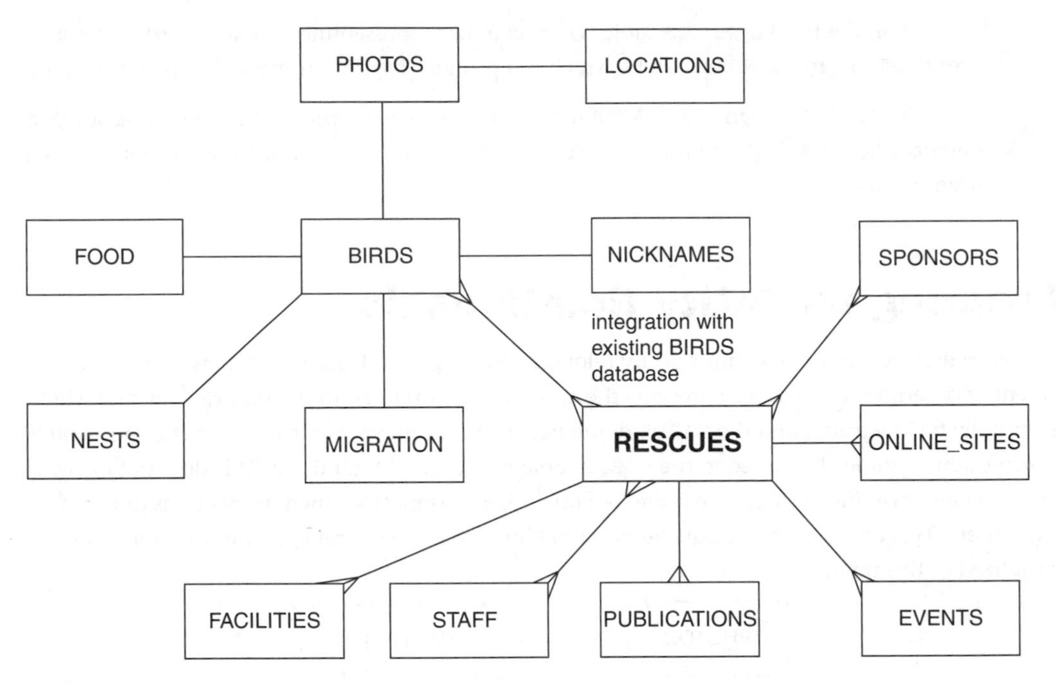

FIGURE 6.11
Basic ERD showing the high-level entities and relationship for bird rescue data

Let's look at the basic relationships that have been modeled in the ERD in Figure 6.11. The new data is about bird rescues, so the RESCUES table is probably the most centralized table within that new data set. The RESCUES table is also the main table that relates back to the BIRDS database through the BIRDS table. As stated earlier, this does not mean that other entities will not be related to other entities within the BIRDS database. For example, sponsors might have favorite birds that influence the rescues that they support. Various facilities might be most appropriate for different types of birds, such as larger raptors that need more space and eat different types of foods. Staff members within rescues could consist of sponsors, photographers, or paid personnel. Keep in mind, then, that the basic relationships modeled here could differ from what you came up with.

- The RESCUES entity is the parent entity.
- A rescue might house many different types of birds, and many different types of birds might be housed within each rescue.
- A rescue might have multiple facilities.
- Each rescue might have multiple staff members, and each staff member might also be a staff member at another rescue.

- A rescue might have multiple publications.
- Each rescue might host multiple events.
- Each rescue might have multiple sites, such as websites and various social media.
- Each rescue might have multiple sponsors or donors, and a sponsor might donate to many different rescues.

Summary

In this hour, you looked at entities and their relationships with one another. Data is initially modeled as entities. These entities eventually become tables using SQL commands as they are implemented into a physical database design. Attributes are implemented as columns in tables into a physical database design, and relationships are essentially defined as constraints using SQL in a physical database. Relationships are defined using SQL by constraints. The primary relationships in a relational database are based on referential integrity and are referred to as primary keys and foreign keys. Primary keys are parent values in a relational database. Foreign keys are child values in a relational database that are dependent upon primary keys, or parent values. The relationship between the primary key and the foreign key is the main concept behind a relational database.

You also walked through the thought process of modeling a basic database, and you analyzed some basic information so you could model your own entities that will eventually evolve into physical database objects that you can easily integrate into the sample BIRDS database. As you progress through the next few hours, you will see how SQL helps you both understand and implement these design concepts, ultimately leading to a well-designed database that unlocks the robustness of the standard SQL language. You can then use SQL to obtain critical information from a database that can help you and your organization succeed in today's competitive environment.

Q&A

Q. Can a primary key have multiple foreign keys associated with it?

A. Yes, a primary key can have multiple foreign keys that reference its data value.

Q. Do other constraints protect the integrity of data?

A. Yes, you can apply various other constraints with SQL to protect your data in addition to primary and foreign keys. Some of these constraints are covered in future hours, and other options might be available with your specific implementation of SQL.

Workshop

The following workshop consists of a series of quiz questions and practical exercises. The quiz questions are designed to test your overall understanding of the current material. The practical exercises give you the opportunity to apply the concepts discussed during the current hour, as well as build on the knowledge you acquired in previous hours of study. Be sure to complete the quiz questions and exercises before continuing to the next hour. Refer to Appendix C, "Answers to Quizzes and Exercises," for answers.

Quiz

1. What are the four basic types of relationships between entities in a relational database?
2. In which relationship does an attribute relate to another attribute in the same table?
3. What constraints, or keys, are used to enforce referential integrity in a relational database?
4. If a primary key represents a parent record, what represents a child record in a relational database?

Exercises

1. Suppose that you came up with a group of data and lists of fields similar to the following for the information on photographers that will be integrated into the `BIRDS` database. This baseline data is provided for your convenience so that you can build on it during the next few hours. However, feel free to use any list that you already have derived, or you can combine your list of data with this example. Keep in mind that the solutions that you come up with might vary from the example solutions provided. You will also find throughout this book that although many of your solutions might vary from the book solutions, they still yield the same results, similar results, or even better results, based on how you interpret the data. Also keep in mind that the following data is merely a subset of the data that can be derived from the description provided in Hour 5. Figure 6.12 hints at where you might find a recursive relationship. Complete the other relationships as you see fit.

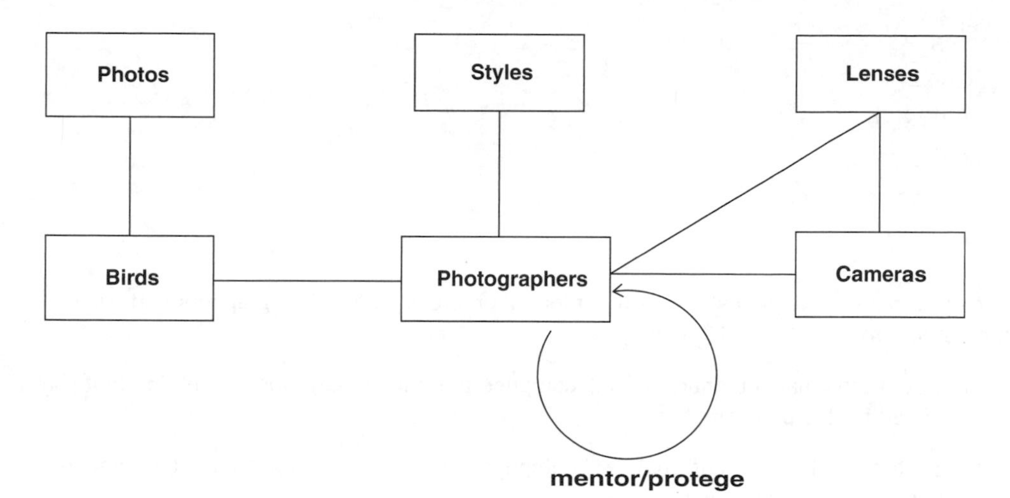

FIGURE 6.12
Example basic ERD for photographers

Sample limited lists of fields for photographer data might include the following:

```
PHOTOGRAPHERS
  Photographer_Id
  Photographer_Name
  Photographer_Contact_Info
  Education
  Website
  Mentor

STYLES
  Style_Id
  Style

CAMERAS
  Camera_Id
  Camera_Make
  Camera_Model
  Sensor_Type
  Megapixels
  Frames_Per_Second
  ISO_Range
  Cost
```

```
LENSES
  Lens_Id
  Lens_Make
  Lens_Type
  Aperature_Range
  Cost
```

2. List some possible relationships for the information provided for photographers that will be integrated into the BIRDS database.
3. List the attributes that you anticipate will comprise the primary keys for the entities that you have defined for the photographers.
4. List the attributes that you anticipate will comprise the foreign keys for the entities that you have defined for the photographers.
5. Draw a basic ERD depicting the entities and the relationships between those entities that you envision at this point for the photographer data.
6. Using words, describe the two-way relationships between your entities. The types of relationships should already be represented on your ERD from question 5 using the symbols introduced during this hour.
7. Refer to Figure 6.4 to answer the remaining questions in this exercise. Some of these questions might seem too simple, but these are the same types of questions you will be asking of the database using SQL commands. Remember that a major goal of this book is to get you to think the way that SQL does.
   - **A.** What are the nicknames of the Great Blue Heron?
   - **B.** What are the nicknames of the Mallard?
   - **C.** Which birds have the word ***green*** in their nickname?
   - **D.** Which birds have a nickname that starts with the letter ***B***?
   - **E.** Which birds do not have a nickname listed in the example?
   - **F.** How many unique birds are listed in this example?
   - **G.** What is the average number of nicknames per bird in this example?
   - **H.** Which birds do not have a nickname listed in the example?
   - **I.** Can any birds be deleted from the BIRDS table without first having to delete nicknames from the NICKNAMES table?
   - **J.** Which birds have child records in the NICKNAMES table?
   - **K.** Does any duplicate data exist in either table besides the BIRD_ID itself?

HOUR 7
Normalizing Your Database

What You'll Learn in This Hour:

- Definition of normalization
- Benefits of normalization
- Advantages of denormalization
- Normalization techniques using the most common normal forms
- How to expand upon your data model to the BIRDS database
- Normalization techniques used with the sample BIRDS database

In this hour, you learn how to expand upon the beginnings of the logical database design process that you've learned in previous hours. This hour focuses on normalization, which is a technique that eliminates redundant data in a database and optimizes relationships between data entities. As stated before, this is not a database design book and this hour does not exhaustively cover normalization; however you learn how to quickly apply the basic concepts of normalization to your database design. Using the auxiliary database that you have been modeling the past couple hours, you finalize an entity relationship diagram that is ready to be implemented as a physical database using SQL commands. Everything that you have learned up to this point serves as an extremely strong foundation so that you can immediately apply all the SQL concepts that you learn in this book.

As with nearly everything covered up to this point, the great part about the process of normalization is that it works the same regardless of which *relational database management system (RDBMS)* you use. The advantages and disadvantages of both normalization and denormalization of a database are also discussed in this hour, along with data integrity versus performance issues that pertain to normalization.

Defining Normalization

Normalization is the process of reducing redundancies of data in a database. It comes into play when you are designing and redesigning a database, to help you eliminate or reduce redundant data. The actual guidelines of normalization, called *normal forms*, are discussed later in this hour.

The decision to cover normalization in this book was difficult because of the complexity involved. Understanding the rules of the normal forms can be challenging this early in your SQL journey. However, normalization is an important process that, if understood, increases your understanding of SQL.

NOTE

Understanding Normalization

The material in this hour attempts to simplify the process of normalization as much as possible. At this point, don't be overly concerned with all the specifics of normalization; understanding the basic concepts is most important. Because this topic is not always easy to understand at first, several different types of examples are included, starting with standard employee-type data, then moving on to the `BIRDS` database, incorporating bird resource data into the `BIRDS` database, and finally finishing with your own opportunity to normalize photographer data that can also be integrated into the `BIRDS` database.

The Raw Database

A database that is not normalized might include data that is contained in one or more tables for no apparent reason. This is detrimental for security reasons, disk space usage, speed of queries, efficiency of database updates, and, maybe most important, data integrity. A database that has not been normalized has not been broken down logically into smaller, more manageable tables. Figure 7.1 illustrates an example of a simple database before normalization.

Determining the set of information that the raw database contains is one of the first and most important steps in logical database design, as previously discussed. You must know all the data elements that comprise your database to effectively apply the techniques discussed in this hour. Taking the time to gather the set of required data keeps you from having to backtrack your database design scheme because of missing data elements.

COMPANY_DATABASE	
emp_id	cust_id
last_name	cust_name
first_name	cust_address
middle_name	cust_city
address	cust_state
city	cust_zip
state	cust_phone
zip	cust_fax
phone	ord_num
pager	qty
position	ord_date
date_hire	prod_id
pay_rate	prod_desc
bonus	cost
date_last_raise	

FIGURE 7.1
The raw database

Logical Database Design

Any database should be designed with the end user in mind. As discussed in previous hours, logical database design, also referred to as the *logical model*, is the process of arranging data into logical, organized groups of objects that can easily be maintained. The logical design of a database should reduce data repetition or completely eliminate it. After all, why store the same data twice? In addition, the logical database design should strive to make the database easy to maintain and update. Naming conventions used in a database should also be standard and logical, to aid in this endeavor.

NOTE

The End User's Needs

The needs of the end user should be one of the top considerations when designing a database. Remember that the end user is the person who ultimately uses the database. The user's ***front-end tool*** (a client program that enables a user access to a database) should be easy to use, but this (along with optimal performance) cannot be achieved if the user's needs are not considered.

Data Redundancy

Data should not be redundant; duplicated data should be kept to a minimum. For example, storing an employee's home address in more than one table is unnecessary, as is storing a specific bird's name in more than one table. Duplicate data takes up unnecessary space. Confusion is also a threat when, for instance, an address for an employee in one table does not match the address for the same employee in another table. Which table is correct? Do you have documentation to verify the employee's current address? Data management is difficult enough; redundant data can be disastrous.

Reducing redundancy also ensures that updating the data within the database is a relatively simple process. If you have a single table for employees' addresses and you update that table with new addresses, you can rest assured that it is updated for everyone who is viewing the data.

NOTE

Eliminating Data Redundancy

One of the main objectives of database design and, specifically, normalization is to eliminate redundant data as much as possible. Even if you cannot completely eliminate redundant data, you should minimize redundant data, to avoid issues with data integrity, relationships, and general usability and scalability of the database in the future.

Exploring the Most Common Normal Forms of the Normalization Process

Normalizing a relational database is achieved by applying general guidelines that are organized progressively in two phases called normal forms. The next sections discuss normal forms, an integral concept in the process of database normalization.

A *normal form* is a way of measuring the levels, or depth, to which a database has been normalized. A database's level of normalization is determined by the normal form.

The following are the three most common normal forms in the normalization process:

- The first normal form
- The second normal form
- The third normal form

Additional normal forms exist beyond these, but they are used far less often than the three major ones noted here. Of the three major normal forms, each subsequent normal form depends on normalization steps taken in the previous normal form. For example, to normalize a database using the second normal form, the database must be in the first normal form.

First Normal Form (FNF): The Key

The objective of the first normal form is to divide the base data into logical entities and, ultimately, tables. When each entity has been designed, a primary key is assigned to most or all entities. Examine Figure 7.2, which illustrates how the raw database shown in Figure 7.1 has been redeveloped using the first normal form.

EMPLOYEE_TBL
emp_id
last_name
first_name
middle_name
address
city
state
zip
phone
pager
position
position_desc
date_hire
pay_rate
bonus
date_last_raise

COMPANY_DATABASE
emp_id
last_name
first_name
middle_name
address
city
state
zip
phone
pager
position
position_desc
date_hire
pay_rate
bonus
date_last_raise
cust_id
cust_name
cust_address
cust_city
cust_state
cust_zip
cust_phone
cust_fax
ord_num
qty
ord_date
prod_id
prod_desc
cost

CUSTOMER_TBL
cust_id
cust_name
cust_address
cust_city
cust_state
cust_zip
cust_phone
cust_fax
ord_num
qty
ord_date

PRODUCTS_TBL
prod_id
prod_desc
cost

FIGURE 7.2
The first normal form

You can see that, to achieve the first normal form, data had to be broken into logical units of related information, each with a primary key. No repeated groups appear in any of the tables. Instead of one large table, you have three smaller, more manageable tables: `EMPLOYEE_TBL`, `CUSTOMER_TBL`, and `PRODUCTS_TBL`. The primary keys are normally the first columns listed in a table—in this case, `EMP_ID`, `CUST_ID`, and `PROD_ID`. This is a normal convention to use when diagramming your database, to ensure that it is easily readable.

However, your primary key can also be made up of more than one column in the data set. Often these values are not simple database-generated numbers; they are logical points of data such as a product's name or a book's ISBN. These values are commonly referred to as natural keys because they uniquely define a specific object, regardless of whether it is in a database. The main point to remember in selecting your primary key for a table is that it must uniquely identify a single row. Without this, you introduce the possibility of adding duplication into your results of queries and prevent yourself from successfully performing even simple actions, such as removing a particular row of data based solely on the key.

Figure 7.3 shows another example of the first normal form being applied to the BIRDS database. This is only a subset of the data from the BIRDS database to have a simplified example. The figure also shows how the BIRDS database is related in some way to the bird rescue data as well as the photographer data that we were working with in examples and exercises in this book.

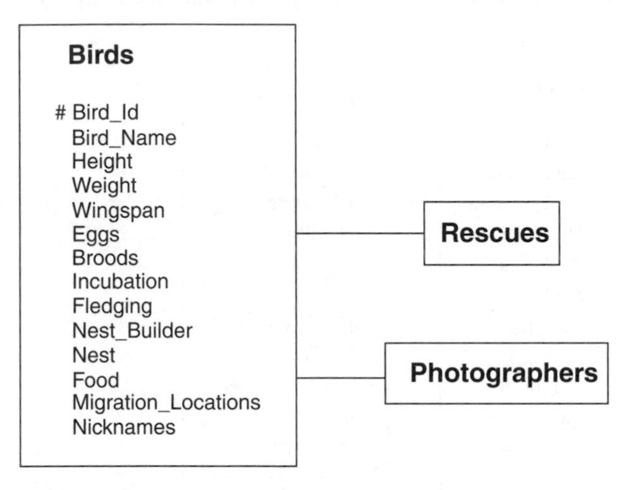

FIGURE 7.3
First normal form in the BIRDS database

After studying Figure 7.3, hopefully you can see that the basic bird information is grouped together into a single entity. The # represents a foreign key constraint that will eventually be placed on the BIRD_ID attribute of the BIRDS entity. When a table called BIRDS is later created based on this entity, a constraint will be placed on the BIRD_ID column. The BIRD_ID primary key is a unique identifier that ensures that every occurrence of a specific bird in the birds entity is unique. Maintaining duplicate records of the same bird is not necessary in this entity.

NOTE

First Normal Form

The objective of the first normal form is to divide the base data into logical units called entities. Each entity has attributes about the data contained within. These entities and attributes will become tables and columns eventually in the physical implementation based on the logical database design. When appropriate, a primary key should be assigned to each entity. To achieve first normal form, data is broken into logical units of related information. Assigning a primary key helps ensure that no duplicate records exist within a group of data.

Second Normal Form (SNF): The Whole Key

The objective of the second normal form is to enter data that is only partly dependent on the primary key into another table. Figure 7.4 illustrates the second normal form.

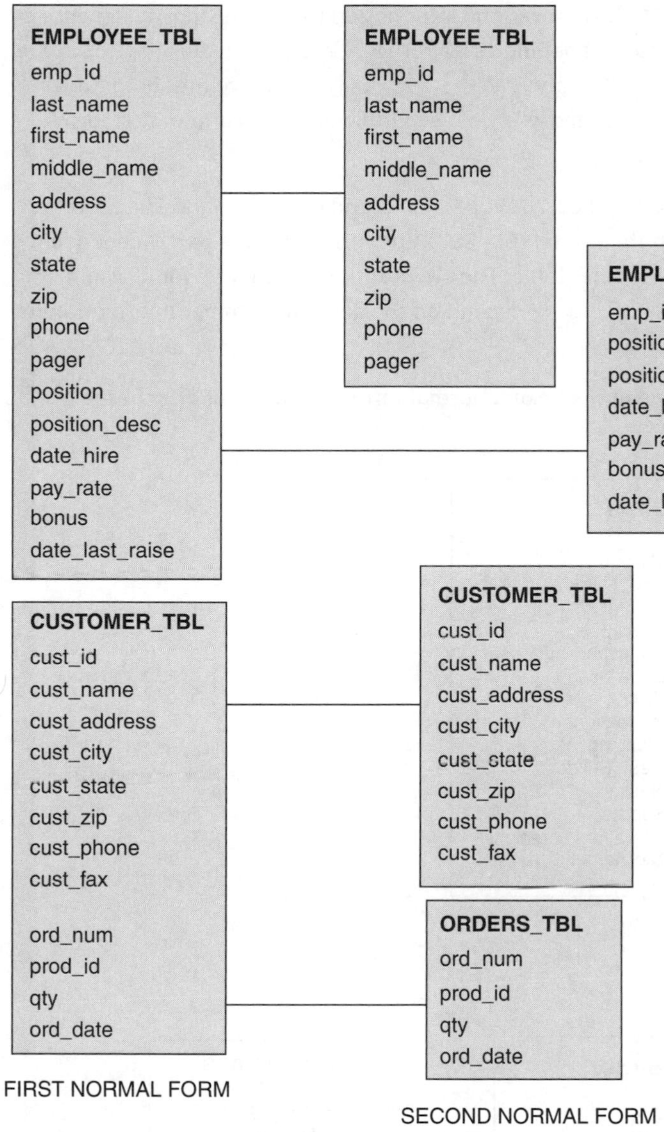

FIRST NORMAL FORM

EMPLOYEE_TBL
emp_id
last_name
first_name
middle_name
address
city
state
zip
phone
pager
position
position_desc
date_hire
pay_rate
bonus
date_last_raise

CUSTOMER_TBL
cust_id
cust_name
cust_address
cust_city
cust_state
cust_zip
cust_phone
cust_fax

ord_num
prod_id
qty
ord_date

SECOND NORMAL FORM

EMPLOYEE_TBL
emp_id
last_name
first_name
middle_name
address
city
state
zip
phone
pager

EMPLOYEE_PAY_TBL
emp_id
position
position_desc
date_hire
pay_rate
bonus
date_last_raise

CUSTOMER_TBL
cust_id
cust_name
cust_address
cust_city
cust_state
cust_zip
cust_phone
cust_fax

ORDERS_TBL
ord_num
prod_id
qty
ord_date

FIGURE 7.4
The second normal form

As you can see in the figure, the second normal form is derived from the first normal form by further breaking two tables into more specific units.

`EMPLOYEE_TBL` is split into two tables, called `EMPLOYEE_TBL` and `EMPLOYEE_PAY_TBL`. Personal employee information is dependent on the primary key (`EMP_ID`), so that information remains in the `EMPLOYEE_TBL` (`EMP_ID`, `LAST_NAME`, `FIRST_NAME`, `MIDDLE_NAME`, `ADDRESS`,

CITY, STATE, ZIP, PHONE, and PAGER). However, the information that is only partly dependent on the EMP_ID (each individual employee) populates EMPLOYEE_PAY_TBL (EMP_ID, POSITION, POSITION_DESC, DATE_HIRE, PAY_RATE, and DATE_LAST_RAISE). Notice that both tables contain the column EMP_ID. This is the primary key of each table and is used to match corresponding data between the two tables.

CUSTOMER_TBL is split into two tables, called CUSTOMER_TBL and ORDERS_TBL. The process here is similar to what occurred with the EMPLOYEE_TBL: Columns that were partly dependent on the primary key were directed to another table. The order of the information for a customer depends on each CUST_ID but does not directly depend on the general customer information in the original table.

Figure 7.5 illustrates another example of the second normal form in a subset of data in the BIRDS database (refer to Figure 7.3).

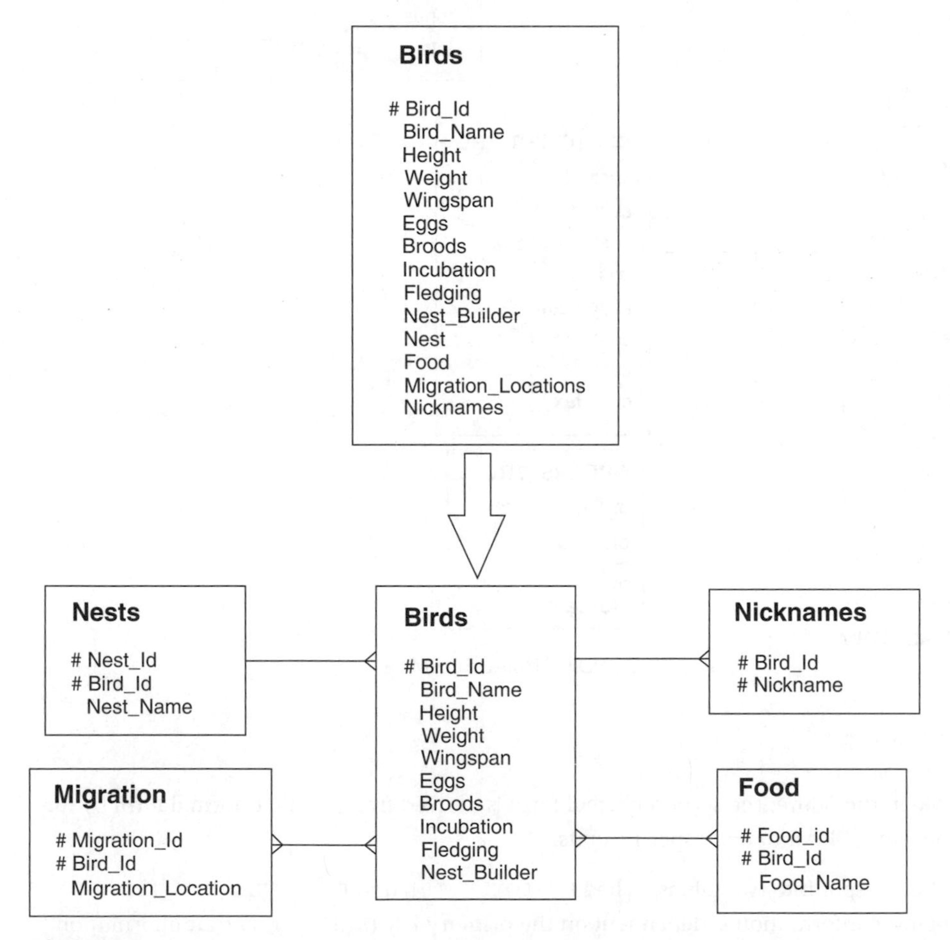

FIGURE 7.5
Second normal form in the BIRDS database

You can see here that, instead of having only one entity for birds, five entities have been derived from BIRDS. This is because the attributes that are only partly dependent on BIRDS, such as the food that a bird eats, have been separated into their own entities. The problem with the previous design shown in Figure 7.3 is that if food information is stored in the BIRDS entity, the only way for it to represent that a bird eats more than one type of food is to have multiple columns in the BIRDS entity for different foods (such as FOOD1, FOOD2, FOOD3, and so on). This is redundant information. Additionally, even though the food that a bird eats is partially dependent on a particular bird, a food is really an entity of its own and should become its own entity. This is the same case with nests, migration, and nicknames.

You can conclude the following relationships and information from Figure 7.5:

- BIRDS is the parent entity and the BIRD_ID in BIRDS is the primary key, which will be a parent key of entities that have foreign keys that reference birds. The BIRD_ID in BIRDS thus helps ensure that every record for a specific type of bird is unique within that entity.
- A bird builds only one type of nest. However, each specific type of nest can be built by many different types of birds. Therefore, the combination of NEST_ID and BIRD_ID comprises the primary key in NESTS. BIRD_ID is a foreign key that references the parent BIRD_ID in BIRDS.
- A bird might migrate to many different locations; conversely, each migration location might have many different types of birds that migrate there. Therefore, the primary key is the combination of MIGRATION_ID and BIRD_ID. MIGRATION_ID itself cannot represent uniqueness because multiple occurrences of migration location might still exist within that entity. BIRD_ID is a foreign key that references the BIRD_ID in BIRDS.
- A bird might have many nicknames; however, this figure indicates that each nickname is associated with only a single type of bird. Notice that, in this entity, the primary key is the combination of the BIRD_ID and NICKNAME itself.
- A bird might eat many different types of foods, and each different type of food might be eaten by many different types of birds. As with some of the other relationships in this figure, this is a many-to-many relationship. The FOOD_ID and BIRD_ID are two attributes that comprise the primary key in food because the combination of the two must be unique for every occurrence of data in this entity. The BIRD_ID is a foreign key that references the BIRD_ID in BIRDS.

NOTE

Second Normal Form

The objective of the second normal form is to move data that is only partly dependent on the primary key into another entity of its own. The second normal form is derived from the first normal form by further breaking down the original entity into two entities. Attributes that are only partly dependent on the primary key are moved to a new entity of their own.

Third Normal Form (TNF): Nothing but the Key

The third normal form's objective is to remove data from a table that is not dependent on the primary key. Figure 7.6 illustrates the third normal form.

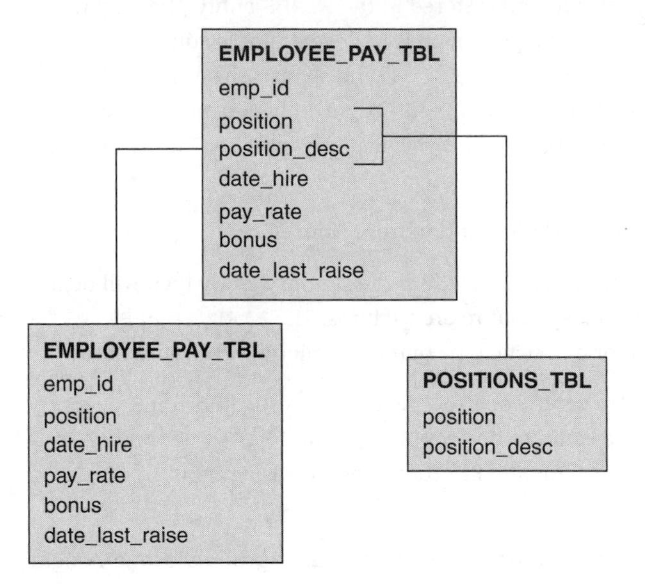

FIGURE 7.6
The third normal form

Another table was created to display the use of the third normal form. EMPLOYEE_PAY_TBL is split into two tables: One table contains the actual employee pay information; the other table contains the position descriptions, which do not need to reside in EMPLOYEE_PAY_TBL. The POSITION_DESC column is totally independent of the primary key, EMP_ID. As you can see, the normalization process is a series of steps that breaks down the data from the raw database into discrete tables of related data.

Figure 7.7 shows an example of taking data sets from the BIRDS database into the third normal form, based on what you started to model in Figure 7.5.

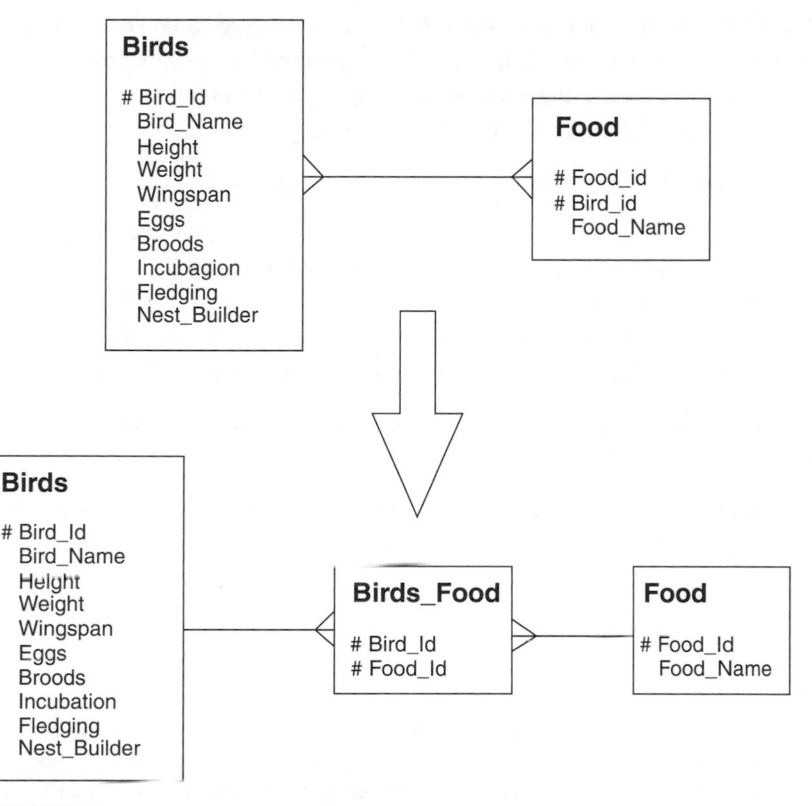

FIGURE 7.7
Third normal form in the BIRDS database

Figure 7.7 illustrates how the BIRDS and FOOD entities have been further broken down into three different entities, using the guidelines of the third normal form. The relationship between BIRDS and FOOD alone is a many-to-many relationship. Many-to-many relationships should generally be avoided in a relational database and should instead be resolved using the normalization process. The problem with many-to-many relationships is that redundant data will certainly exist. Figure 7.7 shows how these two tables, or entities, have been expanded into three entities, called BIRDS, BIRDS_FOOD, and FOOD. BIRDS has information only about birds. FOOD has information only about specific food items. BIRDS_FOOD is simply an intermediate entity whose sole purpose is to provide a relationship between birds and food. In BIRDS, the primary key is BIRD_ID. In FOOD, the primary key is FOOD_ID. In BIRDS_FOOD, the primary key is a combination of BIRD_ID and FOOD_ID. For example, the BIRDS_FOOD entity has only one occurrence of a bird and a food item because it is not necessary to store more than one record of a bird eating a specific type of food. This would be considered redundant data, and the purpose of normalization and this specific example is to remove the redundant data from the database. With third normal form, you can see that only a single record exists for every specific type of bird in the database and only a single record exists for each specific type of food in the database. Ideally, the name "Bald Eagle" should exist only once in the entire database. Likewise, the word "Fish" as a food item should exist only one time in the entire database. If the database is designed properly, other entities simply refer to those entities and then are linked to the appropriate related information.

You can conclude the following relationships and information from Figure 7.7:

- `BIRDS` and `FOOD` are both the parent entities in Figure 7.7. `BIRDS_FOOD` is a child entity that refers to both `BIRDS` and `FOOD`. Even though the primary key in `BIRDS_FOOD` is a composite primary key consisting of both `BIRD_ID` and `FOOD_ID`, the `BIRD_ID` attribute individually is also a foreign key that references `BIRD_ID` in `BIRDS`; likewise, the `FOOD_ID` attribute individually in `BIRDS_FOOD` is a foreign key that references `FOOD_ID` in `FOOD`.
- A bird can eat many different types of foods. This information is found using the `BIRDS_FOOD` entity to access the `FOOD` entity.
- A food item can be eaten by many different types of birds. This information is also found by accessing the `BIRDS_FOOD` entity to get information from `BIRDS`.

NOTE

Third Normal Form

The objective of the third normal form is to remove data that is not directly dependent on the primary key. Remember that attributes do not have attributes of their own. Any attribute that appears to have attributes of its own should be moved to another entity altogether; only attributes that are directly dependent on the key should remain in an entity.

Naming Conventions

Naming conventions are one of the foremost considerations when you normalize a database. Names are how you refer to objects in the database. You want to give your tables descriptive names that enable you to easily find the type of information they contain. Descriptive table names are especially important for users who had no part in the database design but who need to query the database.

Companies should have a company-wide naming convention to provide guidance for naming not only tables within the database, but also users, filenames, and other related objects. Naming conventions also help in database administration by enabling users to more easily discern the purpose of tables and locations of files within a database system. Designing and enforcing naming conventions is one of a company's first steps toward a successful database implementation.

Following are some examples of naming conventions you might use to name the BIRDS table. The best approach is to name objects in a way that describes the data contained or even the type of object; technically, though, the exact approach does not matter, as long as it is used consistently.

- Birds
- Bird
- BIRDS
- BIRD
- Bird_Table
- Birds_Table
- Birds_Tbl
- BIRDS_TABLE
- T_BIRDS
- t_Birds

One common debate among database designers is whether a table name should be singular or plural. For example, a table contains information about birds. However, another way of looking at the very same table is that the table contains information about *each specific type of bird*, in a singular sense. Again, the approach is based more on how you view the data; no real right or wrong solution exists, as long as you strive for consistency.

Benefits of Normalization

Normalization provides numerous benefits to a database. Some of the major benefits include the following:

- Greater overall database organization
- Reduction of redundant data
- Data consistency within the database
- A much more flexible database design
- A better handle on database security
- Reinforcement of referential integrity

The normalization process results in organization, which makes everyone's job easier, from the user who accesses tables, to the *database administrator (DBA)* who is responsible for the overall management of every object in the database. Data redundancy is reduced, which simplifies data structures and conserves disk space. Because duplicate data is minimized, the possibility of inconsistent data is greatly reduced. For example, in one table, an individual's name might read `STEVE SMITH`, whereas it might read `STEPHEN R. SMITH` in another table. Reducing duplicate data increases *data integrity*, or the assurance of consistent and accurate data within a database. Because the database has been normalized and broken into smaller tables, you have more flexibility in modifying existing structures. Modifying a small table with little data is much easier than modifying one big table that holds all the vital data in the database. Lastly, security is enhanced because the DBA can grant specific users access to a limited number of tables. Security is easier to control after normalization because data is grouped into neatly organized sets.

Drawbacks of Normalization

Most successful databases are normalized to some degree, but this process does incur one substantial drawback: reduced database performance. Query or transaction requests sent to the database then face limitations such as CPU usage, memory usage, and input/output (I/O) issues. To make a long story short, a normalized database requires much more CPU, memory, and I/O to process transactions and database queries than a denormalized database. A normalized database must locate the requested tables and then join the data from the tables to either get the requested information or process the wanted data. Hour 21, "Managing Database Users and Security," includes a more in-depth discussion of database performance.

Denormalizing a Database

Denormalization is the process of starting with a normalized database and modifying table structures to allow controlled redundancy for increased database performance. Attempting to improve performance is the only reason to denormalize a database. A denormalized database is not the same as a database that has not been normalized. Denormalizing a database is the process of taking the level of normalization within the database down a notch or two. Remember, normalization can actually slow performance with its frequent table join operations.

Denormalization might involve recombining separate tables or creating duplicate data within tables, to reduce the number of tables that need to be joined to retrieve the requested data. This would result in less I/O and CPU time. Denormalization is normally advantageous in larger data warehousing applications, where aggregate calculations are made across millions of rows of data within tables.

Denormalization comes at a cost. Data redundancy increases in a denormalized database, which can improve performance but requires more extraneous efforts to keep track of related data. Application coding is more complicated because the data has been spread across various tables and might be more difficult to locate. In addition, referential integrity is more of a chore because related data is divided among multiple tables.

You can achieve a happy medium in both normalization and denormalization, but both processes require a thorough knowledge of the actual data and the specific business requirements of the pertinent company. If you decide to denormalize parts of your database structure, carefully document the process so that you can see exactly how you are handling issues such as redundancy to maintain data integrity within your systems.

NOTE

The Most Effective Normal Form

The third normal form is usually the most common and effective normal form applied to the design of a relational database. In most cases, the third normal form also provides a good balance between optimal design with minimal data redundancy and overall performance.

Applying Normalization to Your Database

This section walks you through the basic process of normalizing a database, based on the guidelines of the first three normal forms with the bird rescue data that you have been modeling during the last few hours.

Applying First Normal Form to Bird Rescues Data

In the example in Figure 7.8, basic bird rescue information is modelled in the leftmost box. To adhere to the first normal form, entities are created for each group of data with primary key designations. This is only a subset of data that might exist within the bird rescue data; remember that any example shown can vary, depending on your interpretation of the data itself and the data relationships.

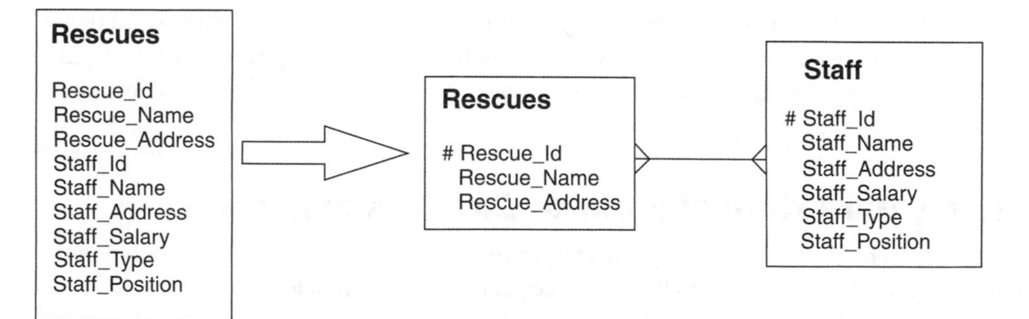

FIGURE 7.8
Integrating bird rescue data into the `BIRDS` data using first normal form

In this example in Figure 7.8, RESCUES is broken into two separate entities, called RESCUES and STAFF. This is because RESCUES is a group of data and a primary key of RESCUE_ID has been designated here. STAFF is another group of data and relates to RESCUES, but it has its own primary key of STAFF_ID that uniquely identifies every record within that entity. The relationship between RESCUES and STAFF in this example is a many-to-many relationship. Thus, each bird rescue might have many staff members, and each staff member might volunteer or work full time or part time at various different bird rescues. This is an example of first normal form.

Applying Second Normal Form to Bird Rescues Data

In the example in Figure 7.9, the bird rescue data that was shown in Figure 7.8 has been further expanded using the guidelines of the second normal form. Study this and try to understand both the relationships and why the data was further divided.

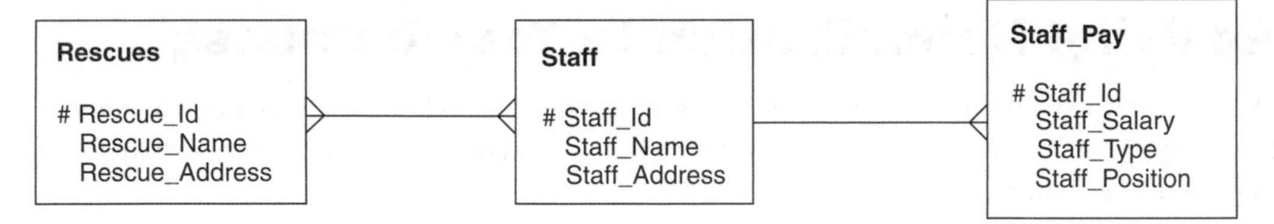

FIGURE 7.9
Integrating bird rescue data into the BIRDS data using second normal form

Looking at Figure 7.9, you can see that RESCUES and STAFF are further divided into three different entities. STAFF originally had pay information about each staff member. However, every staff member could conceivably have multiple pay records, and each different type of salary or position could be applicable to various different staff members. Therefore, STAFF was broken into STAFF and STAFF_PAY. STAFF_PAY has its own identifier as a primary key called STAFF_ID, which is a child record or foreign key that references the STAFF_ID in the STAFF entity. In the second normal form, you move attributes to their own entity that are only partly dependent on the parent entity. Pay information related to a staff member is related but only partly dependent, so it then becomes its own entity.

Applying Third Normal Form to Bird Rescues Data

Figure 7.10 shows how the data in Figure 7.9 for bird rescues has been expanded into additional entities and attributes when applying the guidelines of the third normal form. Study this figure and try to understand the relationships between the entities and all the primary and foreign keys that now exist.

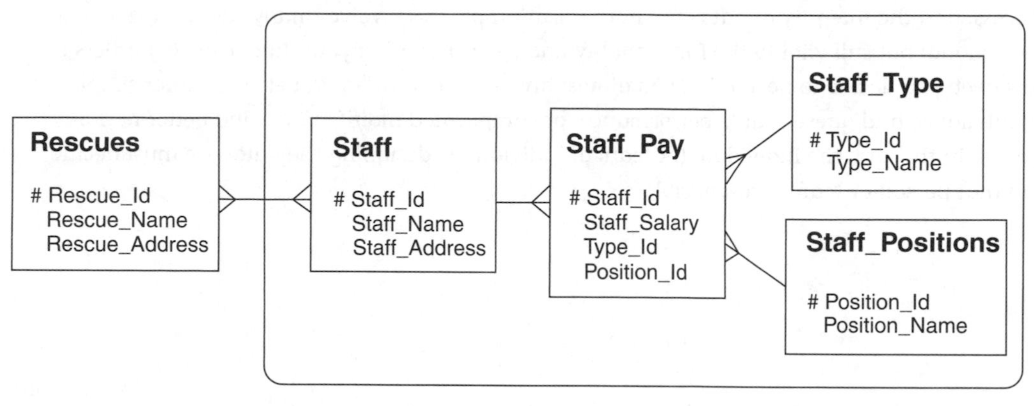

FIGURE 7.10
Integrating bird rescue data into the BIRDS data using third normal form

After reviewing Figure 7.10, you can see that STAFF, which originally was only one entity, is now a total of four entities. STAFF_PAY itself has been broken into three different entities: STAFF_PAY, STAFF_TYPE, and STAFF_POSITIONS. Remember that the goal of normalization is to eliminate or reduce redundant data. The STAFF_TYPE (which could be perhaps full time, part time, or volunteer) is a type that might apply to any staff member in any rescue. Therefore, the STAFF_TYPE name itself should really exist only one time in the database. There is no reason for a staff type to exist more than once by name, although it can be associated with any staff member or rescue in the database now through relationships. The staff position itself can be perhaps a manager, an owner, or a bird expert, but each position should exist only one time in the database. The POSITION_ID helps ensure that every position is unique in the database, just as TYPE_ID for the STAFF_TYPE ensures that each staff member exists only one time in the database. STAFF_POSITIONS is a child entity that references STAFF_PAY, just as STAFF_TYPE is a child entity that references STAFF_PAY. In Figure 7.10, all redundant data at this point that has been recognized has been isolated into its own entities. This is the third normal form.

Summary

The normalization process gives you a way to effectively design your relational database so that you eliminate or reduce redundant data as much as possible and also organize your data entities and attributes effectively. Sometimes you need to make a difficult decision: to normalize or not to normalize. You always want to normalize a database, to some degree. But how much do you normalize a database without destroying performance? The real decision relies on the application. How large is the database? What is its purpose? What types of users will access the data? This hour covered the three most common normal forms, the concepts behind the normalization process, and the integrity of data. The normalization process involves many steps, most of which are optional but still vital to the functionality and performance of your database. Regardless of how deep you decide to normalize, you almost always face a trade-off, between either simple maintenance and questionable performance, or complicated maintenance and better performance. In the end, the individual (or team of individuals) designing the database must decide, and that person or team is responsible.

Q&A

Q. Why should I be so concerned with the end users' needs when designing the database?

A. The end users might not have the technical knowledge, but they are some of the most knowledgeable data experts who use the database. Therefore, they should be at the center of any database design effort. The database designer only helps organize the data.

Q. Is normalization more advantageous than denormalization?

A. Normalization can be more advantageous. However, denormalization also can be more advantageous in some situations. Remember, many factors help determine which way to go. You will probably normalize your database to reduce repetition in the database, but you might denormalize it to a certain extent, to improve performance.

Q. Are there more than three levels of normalization?

A. More levels of normalization can be achieved in a relational database. However, keep in mind that this is not a database design book. The third normal form is the most common normal form that is used to model most relational databases. This book simply provides a general overview of the relational database and database design. The third normal form is really all you need to know to fully understand and unleash the power of SQL in most situations.

Workshop

The following workshop consists of a series of quiz questions and practical exercises. The quiz questions are designed to test your overall understanding of the current material. The practical exercises give you the opportunity to apply the concepts discussed during the current hour, as well as build on the knowledge you acquired in previous hours of study. Be sure to complete the quiz questions and exercises before continuing to the next hour. Refer to Appendix C, "Answers to Quizzes and Exercises," for answers.

Quiz

1. True or false: Normalization is the process of grouping data into logical related groups.
2. True or false: Having no duplicate data or redundant data in a database, and having everything in the database normalized, is always the best way to go.
3. True or false: If data is in the third normal form, it is automatically in the first and second normal forms.
4. What is a major advantage of a denormalized database versus a normalized database?
5. What are some major disadvantages of denormalization?
6. How do you determine whether data needs to be moved to a separate table when normalizing your database?

7. What are the disadvantages of overnormalizing your database design?
8. Why is it important to eliminate redundant data?
9. What is the most common level of normalization?

Exercises

1. Assuming that you came up with a similar configuration to the entities shown in Figure 7.11 for the photographer data set that is to be incorporated into the `BIRDS` database, take a minute to compare this example to yours. Feel free to use this example as a baseline for these exercises, use your own, or combine the two as you see fit. Also review Figure 6.12 in Hour 6, "Defining Entities and Relationships," to envision how this data might be integrated into the original `BIRDS` database.

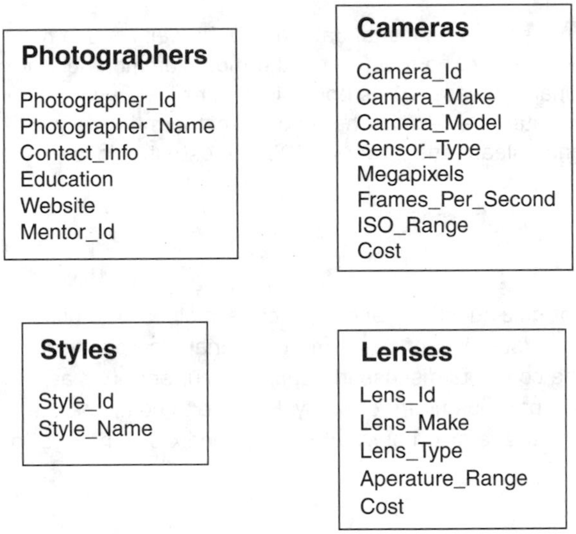

Photographers
Photographer_Id
Photographer_Name
Contact_Info
Education
Website
Mentor_Id

Cameras
Camera_Id
Camera_Make
Camera_Model
Sensor_Type
Megapixels
Frames_Per_Second
ISO_Range
Cost

Styles
Style_Id
Style_Name

Lenses
Lens_Id
Lens_Make
Lens_Type
Aperature_Range
Cost

FIGURE 7.11
Example entities and attributes for photographer data

2. List some of the redundant data that you see in this example and the ERD you modeled.
3. Use the guidelines of the first normal form to model your database appropriately.
4. Use the guidelines in this hour to take your data model to the second normal form.
5. Finally, use the guidelines in this hour to take your data model to the third normal form.
6. Verbally describe all relationships in your third normal form model.
7. List all primary and foreign keys from your third normal form model.
8. Can you envision any other data that could be added to your ERD?

HOUR 8
Defining Data Structures

What You'll Learn in This Hour:

- A look at the underlying data of a table
- An introduction to the basic data types
- Instruction on using the various data types
- Examples depicting differences between data types
- Data types applied to the `BIRDS` database
- Hands-on exercises to apply data types to your database design

In this hour, you learn about the characteristics of data and how such data is stored in a relational database. After a brief discussion of data itself, you learn the basic data types that exist within the standard language of SQL. You see examples of different types of data and then apply those to the `BIRDS` database. You will walk through how to assign data types to the bird rescue data and, finally, assign data types to the photographer database that you have been designing to this point. Up to now, this book has focused on the concepts and logical design for building a foundation for a strong SQL database and applying SQL to everything you have learned. Now, we move on to the application of data types in SQL to begin defining the data that you have modeled.

NOTE

Moving from Logical to Physical Databases

So far, this book has mostly dealt with the logical design of a database. During the planning and design of a database, you typically refer to groups of data, or entities. You also refer to attributes, or fields within those entities. This hour uses more physical database terminology, which involves entities seen as tables that actually store physical data, and what we see now as columns within tables that were previously represented logically as attributes. A table is a group of data and columns or attributes that physically store the data.

Defining Data

Data is a collection of information stored in a database as one of several different data types. Data includes names, numbers, dollar amounts, text, graphics, decimals, figures, calculations, summarization, and just about anything else you can possibly imagine. Data can be stored in upper case, lower case, or mixed case. Data can be manipulated or changed; most data does not remain static for its lifetime.

Data types provide rules for data for particular columns. A data type deals with the way values are stored in a column for the length allocated for a column and whether certain values (such as alphanumeric, numeric, and date and time data) are allowed. A data type exists for every possible bit or combination of data that can be stored in a particular database. These data types store data such as characters, numbers, date and time, images, and other binary data. More specifically, the data might consist of names, descriptions, numbers, calculations, images, image descriptions, documents, and so forth.

Understanding Basic Data Types

The following sections discuss the basic data types that ANSI SQL supports. Data types are characteristics of the data itself whose attributes are placed in fields within a table. For example, you can specify that a field must contain numeric values, disallowing alphanumeric strings to be entered. After all, you would not want to enter alphabetic characters in a field for a dollar amount. Defining each field in the database with a data type eliminates much of the incorrect data found in a database from data entry errors. *Field definition* (data type definition) is a form of data validation that controls the type of data that may be entered into each given field.

Depending on your implementation of the *relational database management system (RDBMS)*, certain data types can be converted automatically to other data types. This type of conversion is known as an *implicit conversion*, which means that the database handles the conversion for you. An example of this is taking a numeric value of 1000.92 from a numeric field and inputting it into a string field. Other data types cannot be converted implicitly by the host RDBMS and, therefore, must undergo an explicit conversion. This usually involves using a SQL function, such as `CAST` or `CONVERT`. In the following Oracle example, the current system date is retrieved from the database in the default date format, which is a date data type:

```
SELECT CAST('12/27/1974' AS DATETIME) AS MYDATE

SQL> SELECT SYSDATE FROM DUAL;

SYSDATE
---------
08-SEP-15
```

NOTE

The `SELECT` Statement

The SELECT statement is one of the most important SQL commands. SELECT enables you to query data from within the database. The following examples are simple SELECT statements that show simple data within a database. Hour 12, "Introduction to Database Queries," covers the SELECT statement in detail; subsequent chapters deal with how to effectively manage and get data from the database.

If you want to change or display the date in a format other than the default data type, you can apply the Oracle TO_CHAR function to display the date as a character string. In the next example, this function retrieves only the current month:

```
SQL> SELECT TO_CHAR(SYSDATE, 'Month') MONTH
  2  FROM DUAL;

MONTH
------------------------------------
September
```

As with most other languages, the basic data types in SQL are as follows:

- String types
- Numeric types
- Date and time types

TIP

SQL Data Types

Every implementation of SQL has its own specific set of data types. Using implementation-specific data types is necessary to support each implementation's approach to storing data. However, the basics are the same among all implementations.

Fixed-Length Strings

Constant characters, or strings that always have the same length, are stored using a fixed-length data type. The following is the standard for a SQL fixed-length character:

```
CHARACTER(n)
```

Here, n represents a number identifying the allocated or maximum length of the particular field with this definition.

Some implementations of SQL use the CHAR data type to store fixed-length data. You can store alphanumeric data in this data type. An example of a constant-length data type is a state abbreviation; all state abbreviations are two characters.

Spaces normally fill any extra spots when using a fixed-length data type. If a field's length is set to 10 and the data entered fills only 5 places, the remaining 5 spaces are recorded as spaces. This padding of spaces ensures that each value in a field is a fixed length.

CAUTION

Fixed-Length Data Types

Be careful not to use a fixed-length data type for fields that might contain varying-length values, such as an individual's name. If you use the fixed-length data type inappropriately, you will eventually encounter problems, such as wasted available space and the inability to make accurate comparisons between data.

Always use the varying-length data type for nonconstant character strings, to save database space.

Varying-Length Strings

SQL supports the use of *varying-length strings*, or strings whose length is not constant for all data. The following is the standard for a SQL varying-length character:

```
CHARACTER VARYING(n)
```

Here, n represents a number identifying the allocated or maximum length of the particular field with this definition.

Common data types for variable-length character values are the VARCHAR, VARBINARY, and VARCHAR2 data types. VARCHAR is the ANSI standard, which Microsoft SQL Server and MySQL use; Oracle uses both VARCHAR and VARCHAR2. The data stored in a character-defined column can be alphanumeric, which means that the data value may contain numeric characters. VARBINARY is similar to VARCHAR and VARCHAR2, except that it contains a variable length of bytes. Normally, you use a type such as this to store some kind of digital data such as an image file.

Remember that fixed-length data types typically pad spaces to fill in allocated places that the field is not using. The varying-length data type does not work this way. For instance, if the allocated length of a varying-length field is 10 and a string of 5 characters is entered, the total length of that particular value is only 5. Spaces are not used to fill unused places in a column.

Large Object Types

Some variable-length data types need to hold longer lengths of data than what is traditionally reserved for a `VARCHAR` field. The `BLOB` and `TEXT` data types are two examples of such data types in modern database implementations. These data types are specifically made to hold large sets of data. The `BLOB` is a binary large object, so its data is treated as a large binary string (a byte string). A `BLOB` is especially useful in an implementation that needs to store binary media files in the database, such as images or MP3s.

The `TEXT` data type is a large character string data type that can be treated as a large `VARCHAR` field. It is often used when an implementation needs to store large sets of character data in the database. An example of this is storing HTML input from the entries of a blog site. Storing this type of data in the database enables the site to be dynamically updated.

Numeric Types

Numeric values are stored in fields that are defined as some type of number, typically referred to as `NUMBER`, `INTEGER`, `REAL`, `DECIMAL`, and so on.

The following are the standards for SQL numeric values:

- `BIT(n)`
- `BIT VARYING(n)`
- `DECIMAL(p,s)`
- `INTEGER`
- `SMALLINT`
- `BIGINT`
- `FLOAT(p,s)`
- `DOUBLE PRECISION(p,s)`
- `REAL(s)`

Here, `p` represents a number that identifies the allocated or maximum length of the particular field for each appropriate definition.

Additionally, `s` is a number to the right of the decimal point, as in `34.ss`.

A common numeric data type in SQL implementations is `NUMERIC`, which accommodates the direction for numeric values provided by ANSI. Numeric values can be stored as zero, positive, negative, fixed, and floating-point numbers. The following is an example using `NUMERIC`:

```
NUMERIC(5)
```

This example restricts the maximum value entered in a particular field to `99999`. Note that all the database implementations used for the examples support the `NUMERIC` type but implement it as a `DECIMAL`.

Decimal Types

Decimal values are numeric values that include the use of a decimal point. The standard for a decimal in SQL follows, where `p` is the precision and `s` is the decimal's scale:

```
DECIMAL(p,s)
```

The *precision* is the total length of the numeric value. In a numeric defined `DECIMAL(4,2)`, the precision is 4, which is the total length allocated for a numeric value. The scale is the number of digits to the right of the decimal point. The scale is 2 in the previous `DECIMAL(4,2)` example. If a value has more places to the right side of the decimal point than the scale allows, the value is rounded; for instance, `34.33` inserted into a `DECIMAL(3,1)` is typically rounded to `34.3`.

If a numeric value is defined as the following data type, the maximum value allowed is `99.99`:

```
DECIMAL(4,2)
```

The precision is 4, which represents the total length allocated for an associated value. The scale is 2, which represents the number of *places*, or *bytes*, reserved to the right side of the decimal point. The decimal point does not count as a character.

Allowed values for a column defined as `DECIMAL(4,2)` include the following:

- `12`
- `12.4`
- `12.44`
- `12.449`

The last numeric value, `12.449`, is rounded off to `12.45` upon input into the column. In this case, any numbers between `12.445` and `12.449` are rounded to `12.45`.

Integers

An *integer* is a numeric value that does not contain a decimal; it contains only whole numbers (both positive and negative).

Valid integers include the following:

- `1`
- `0`
- `-1`

- `99`
- `-99`
- `199`

Floating-Point Decimals

Floating-point decimals are decimal values whose precision and scale are variable lengths and virtually without limit. Any precision and scale is acceptable. The `REAL` data type designates a column with single-precision floating-point numbers. The `DOUBLE PRECISION` data type designates a column that contains double-precision floating-point numbers. To be considered a single-precision floating point, the precision must be between 1 and 21, inclusive. To be considered a double-precision floating point, the precision must be between 22 and 53, inclusive. The following are examples of the `FLOAT` data type:

- `FLOAT`
- `FLOAT(15)`
- `FLOAT(50)`

Date and Time Types

Date and time data types are used to keep track of information concerning dates and time. Standard SQL supports `DATETIME` data types, which include the following specific data types:

- `DATE`
- `TIME`
- `DATETIME`
- `TIMESTAMP`

The elements of a `DATETIME` data type consist of the following:

- `YEAR`
- `MONTH`
- `DAY`
- `HOUR`
- `MINUTE`
- `SECOND`

NOTE

Fractions and Leap Seconds

The `SECOND` element can also be broken down to fractions of a second. The range is from `00.000` to `61.999`, although some implementations of SQL do not support this range. The extra 1.999 seconds is used for leap seconds.

Be aware that each implementation of SQL might have its own customized data type for dates and times. The previous data types and elements are standards to which each SQL vendor should adhere, but most implementations have their own data type for date values. Those variations can affect both appearance and the way date information is actually stored internally. A length is not normally specified for a date data type.

Literal Strings

A *literal string* is a series of characters, such as a name or a phone number, that is explicitly specified by a user or program. Literal strings consist of data with the same attributes as the previously discussed data types, but the value of the string is known. The value of a column is usually unknown because a column typically has a different value associated with each row of data in a table.

You do not actually specify data types with literal strings; you simply specify the string. Some examples of literal strings follow:

- `'Hello'`
- `45000`
- `"45000"`
- `3.14`
- `'November 1, 1997'`

The alphanumeric strings are enclosed by single quotation marks, whereas the number value `45000` is not. Also notice that the second numeric value of `45000` is enclosed in quotation marks. Generally, character strings require quotation marks, whereas numeric strings do not.

The process that converts a number to a numeric type is known as an *implicit conversion*. In this process, the database attempts to figure out what type it needs to create for the object. Thus, if you do not have a number enclosed within single quotation marks, the SQL compiler assumes that you want a numeric type. When working with data, make sure that the data is being represented as you want it to be. Otherwise, it might skew your results or result in an unexpected error. You will see later how literal strings are used with database queries.

NULL Data Types

As you should know from Hour 1, "Understanding the Relational Database and SQL," a NULL value is a missing value or a column in a row of data that has not been assigned a value. NULL values are used in nearly all parts of SQL, including the creation of tables, search conditions for queries, and even literal strings.

A NULL value is designated using the keyword NULL.

Because the following is in quotations, it represents not a NULL value, but a literal string containing the characters N-U-L-L:

```
'NULL'
```

When using the NULL data type, it is important to realize that data is not required in a particular field. If data is always required for a given field, always use NOT NULL with a data type. If there is a chance that a field might not always contain data, using NULL is a better practice.

Boolean Values

A Boolean value is a value of TRUE, FALSE, or NULL. Boolean values are used to make data comparisons. For example, when criteria specified for a query return the Boolean value of TRUE, then data is returned. If a Boolean value of FALSE or NULL is returned, data might not be returned.

Consider the following example:

```
WHERE NAME = 'SMITH'
```

This line might be a condition found in a query. The condition is evaluated for every row of data in the table that is queried. If the value of NAME is SMITH for a row of data in the table, the condition returns the value TRUE, thereby returning the data associated with that record.

Most database implementations do not implement a strict Boolean type and instead opt to use their own methodology. MySQL contains the Boolean type, but it is merely a synonym for its existing TINYINT type. Oracle prefers to direct its users to use a CHAR(1) value to denote a Boolean, and Microsoft SQL Server uses a value known as BIT.

NOTE

Differences in Data Type Implementations

Some of the data types mentioned during this hour are not available by name in some implementations of SQL. Data types are often named differently among implementations of SQL, but the concept behind each data type remains. Most, if not all, data types are supported by relational databases.

User-Defined Types

A *user-defined type* is a data type that the user defines. User-defined types allow users to customize their own data types to meet data storage needs and are based on existing data types. User-defined data types can assist the developer by providing greater flexibility during database application development because they maximize the number of possibilities for data storage. The `CREATE TYPE` statement is used to create a user-defined type.

For example, you can create a type as follows in Oracle:

```
CREATE TYPE PERSON AS OBJECT
(NAME         VARCHAR (30),
 SSN          VARCHAR (9));
```

You can reference your user-defined type as follows:

```
CREATE TABLE EMP_PAY
(EMPLOYEE    PERSON,
 SALARY      DECIMAL(10,2),
 HIRE_DATE   DATE);
```

Notice that the data type referenced for the first column, `EMPLOYEE`, is `PERSON`. `PERSON` is the user-defined type you created in the first example.

Domains

A *domain* is a set of valid data types that can be used. A domain is associated with a data type, so only certain data is accepted. After you create a domain, you can add constraints to the domain. Constraints work with data types, allowing you to further specify acceptable data for a field. The domain is used like the user-defined type.

User-defined domains are not nearly as common as user-defined types; for example, they are not supported by Oracle. The following syntax does not work with the implementations downloaded for this book, but it is an example of a basic syntax to create a domain:

```
CREATE DOMAIN MONEY_D AS NUMBER(8,2);
```

You add constraints to your domain as follows:

```
ALTER DOMAIN MONEY_D
ADD CONSTRAINT MONEY_CON1
CHECK (VALUE > 5);
```

You reference the domain as follows:

```
CREATE TABLE EMP_PAY
(EMP_ID         NUMBER(9),
 EMP_NAME       VARCHAR2(30),
 PAY_RATE       MONEY_D);
```

Using Data Types in the BIRDS Database

At this point, you have seen a detailed ERD for the BIRDS database with entities, attributes, and relationships. Primary and foreign keys have also been discussed. Additionally, you have also been provided a list of the actual data contained within the BIRDS database so that you understand what the data looks like. Following is a list of the columns in each table in the BIRDS database, along with their assigned data types and whether each column is mandatory (meaning NULL or NOT NULL, by definition). Primary and foreign keys are also identified here for your convenience.

```
BIRDS
bird_id        number(3)     not null    PK
bird_name      varchar(30)   not null
height         number(4,2)   not null
weight         number(4,2)   not null
wingspan       number(4,2)   null
eggs           number(2)     not null
broods         number(1)     null
incubation     number(2)     not null
fledging       number(3)     not null
nest_builder   char(1)       not null
```

```
NICKNAMES
bird_id     number(3)     not null    PK, FK
nickname    varchar(30)   not null    PK, FK
```

```
LOCATIONS
location_id     number(2)     not null    PK
location_name   varchar(30)   not null
```

```
PHOTOS
photo_id             number(5)     not null  PK
photo_file           varchar(30)   not null
photo_date           date          not null
photo_location_id    number(2)     not null
bird_id              number(3)     not null  FK
```

```
FOOD
food_id     number(3)      not null   PK
food_name   varchar(30)    not null
```

```
BIRDS_FOOD
bird_id     number(3)     not null    PK, FK
food_id     number(3)     not null    PK, FK


NESTS
nest_id      number(1)      not null     PK
nest_name    varchar(20)    not null


BIRDS_NESTS
bird_id     number(3)      not null    PK, FK
nest_id     number(1)      not null    PK, FK


MIGRATION
migration_id          number(2)    not null    PK
migration_location    varchar(30)  not null


BIRDS_MIGRATION
bird_id          number(3)  not null    PK, FK
migration_id     number(2)  not null    PK, FK
```

Summary

Countless data types are available with SQL. If you have programmed in other languages, you probably recognize many of the data types mentioned. Data types allow different types of data to be stored in the database, ranging from simple characters, to decimal points, to date and time. Data types also place rules on data that can be inserted into columns in a table. This helps maintain the integrity of data, along with constraints such as primary and foreign keys. The concept of data types is the same in all languages, whether programming in a third-generation language such as C and passing variables, or using a relational database implementation and coding in SQL. Of course, each implementation has its own names for standard data types, but they basically work the same. Also remember that an RDBMS does not have to implement all the data types in the ANSI standard to be considered ANSI compliant. Therefore, it is prudent to check with the documentation of your specific RDBMS implementation to see what options you have available.

Take care in planning for both the near future and the distant future when deciding on data types, lengths, scales, and precisions in which to store your data. Business rules and how you want the end user to access the data are other factors in deciding on specific data types. To assign proper data types, you should know the nature of the data and how the data in the database is related. Everything you have learned in this hour is immediately applicable to your database design and the relational data you encounter in the real world.

Q&A

Q. Why can I enter numbers such as a person's Social Security number in fields defined as character fields?

A. Numeric values are still alphanumeric, which are allowed in string data types. The process is called an implicit conversion because the database system handles it automatically. Typically, the only data stored as numeric values are values used in computations. However, it might be helpful to define all numeric fields with a numeric data type, to control the data entered in that field.

Q. I still do not understand the difference between constant-length and varying-length data types. Can you explain?

A. Say you have an individual's last name defined as a constant-length data type with a length of 20 bytes. Suppose that the individual's name is Smith. When the data is inserted into the table, 20 bytes are taken: 5 for the name and 15 for the extra spaces. (Remember that this is a constant-length data type.) If you use a varying-length data type with a length of 20 and insert `Smith`, only 5 bytes of space are taken. If you then imagine that you are inserting 100,000 rows of data into this system, you could possibly save 1.5 million bytes of data.

Q. Are there limits on the lengths of data types?

A. Yes, there are limits on the lengths of data types. These vary among the various implementations.

Workshop

The following workshop consists of a series of quiz questions and practical exercises. The quiz questions are designed to test your overall understanding of the current material. The practical exercises give you the opportunity to apply the concepts discussed during the current hour, as well as build on the knowledge you acquired in previous hours of study. Be sure to complete the quiz questions and exercises before continuing to the next hour. Refer to Appendix C, "Answers to Quizzes and Exercises," for answers.

Quiz

1. What are the three most basic categories of data types?
2. True or false: An individual's Social Security number, entered in the format `'111111111'`, can be any of the following data types: constant-length character, varying-length character, or numeric.
3. True or false: The scale of a numeric value is the total length allowed for values.
4. Do all implementations use the same data types?

5. What are the precision and scale of the following?

```
DECIMAL(4,2)
DECIMAL(10,2)
DECIMAL(14,1)
```

6. Which numbers can be inserted into a column whose data type is `DECIMAL(4,1)`?

   A. `16.2`

   B. `116.2`

   C. `16.21`

   D. `1116.2`

   E. `1116.21`

Exercises

1. Assign the following column titles to a data type, decide on the proper length, and give an example of the data you would enter into that column:

   A. `ssn`

   B. `state`

   C. `city`

   D. `phone_number`

   E. `zip`

   F. `last_name`

   G. `first_name`

   H. `middle_name`

   I. `salary`

   J. `hourly_pay_rate`

   K. `date_hired`

2. Using the same column titles, decide whether they should be `NULL` or `NOT NULL`. Be sure to realize that, for some columns that would normally be `NOT NULL`, the column could be `NULL`, or vice versa, depending on the application:

   A. `ssn`

   B. `state`

   C. `city`

   D. `phone_number`

E. `zip`

F. `last_name`

G. `first_name`

H. `middle_name`

I. `salary`

J. `hourly_pay_rate`

K. `date_hired`

3. Based on the birds rescue data from previous hours, assign data types and nullability as you see fit.

4. Based on the photographer data you have modeled, assign data types and nullability as you see fit.

HOUR 9
Creating and Managing Database Objects

What You'll Learn in This Hour:

- An introduction to database objects
- An introduction to schemas
- An introduction to tables
- The nature and attributes of tables
- Examples of creating and manipulating tables
- Table storage options
- Referential integrity and data consistency

In this hour, you learn about database objects: what they are, how they act, how they are stored, and how they relate to one another. Database objects are the logical units that compose the building blocks of the database. Most of the instruction during this hour revolves around tables, but keep in mind other database objects exist, many of which are discussed in later hours of study.

Database Objects and Schemas

A *database object* is any defined object in a database that is used to store or reference data. Some examples of database objects include tables, views, clusters, sequences, indexes, and synonyms. The table is this hour's focus because it is the primary and simplest form of data storage in a relational database.

A *schema* is a collection of database objects normally associated with one particular database username. This username is called the *schema owner*, or the owner of the related group of objects. You might have one schema or multiple schemas in a database. The user is associated with only the schema of the same name, and often the terms are used interchangeably. Basically, any user who creates an object has just created it in his or her own schema unless that user specifically instructs it to be created in another one. Based on a user's privileges within the database, then, the user has control over objects that are created, manipulated, and deleted. A schema can consist of a single table and has no limits to the number of objects that it may contain, unless restricted by a specific database implementation.

Say that the database administrator issues you a database username and password. Your username is USER1. Suppose that you log on to the database and create a table called EMPLOYEE_TBL. According to the database, your table's actual name is USER1.EMPLOYEE_TBL. The schema name for that table is USER1, which is also the owner of that table. You have just created the first table of a schema.

The good part about schemas is that when you access a table that you own (in your own schema), you do not have to refer to the schema name. For instance, you can refer to your table as either one of the following:

```
EMPLOYEE_TBL
USER1.EMPLOYEE_TBL
```

The first option is preferred because it requires fewer keystrokes. If another user queries one of your tables, the user must specify the schema as follows:

```
USER1.EMPLOYEE_TBL
```

As you progress through your SQL journey in this book, you learn how to grant users privileges to your schema so that they may access your objects. You also learn about synonyms, which enable you to give a table another name so that you do not have to specify the schema name when accessing a table. Figure 9.1 illustrates two schemas in a relational database.

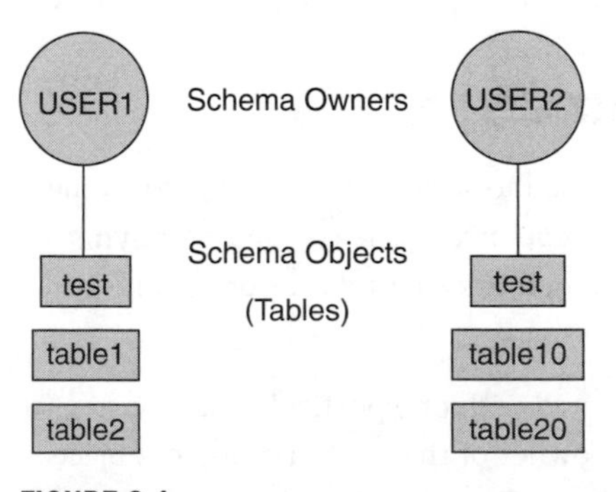

FIGURE 9.1
Schemas in a database

In Figure 9.1, two user accounts in the database own tables: USER1 and USER2. Each user account has its own schema. Take a look at some examples of how the two users can access their own tables and the tables owned by the other user:

```
USER1 accesses own TABLE1:          TABLE1

USER1 accesses own TEST:            TEST

USER1 accesses USER2's TABLE10      USER2.TABLE10

USER1 accesses USER2's TEST         USER2.TEST
```

In this example, both users have a table called TEST. Tables can have the same names in a database, as long as they belong to different schemas. If you look at it this way, table names are always unique in a database because the schema owner is actually part of the table name. For instance, USER1.TEST is a different table than USER2.TEST. If you do not specify a schema with the table name when accessing tables in a database, the database server looks for a table that you own, by default. That is, if USER1 tries to access TEST, the database server looks for a USER1-owned table named TEST before it looks for other objects owned by USER1, such as synonyms to tables in another schema. Hour 24, "Working with the System Catalog," helps you fully understand how synonyms work.

Be sure to understand the distinction between objects in your own schema and objects in another schema. If you do not provide a schema when performing operations that alter the table, such as a DROP command, the database assumes that you mean a table in your own schema. Always pay careful attention as to which user you are currently logged into the database with, to avoid unintentionally dropping the wrong object.

CAUTION

Object Naming Rules Differ Between Systems

Every database server has rules concerning how you can name objects and elements of objects, such as field names. Check your particular implementation for the exact naming conventions or rules.

Tables: The Primary Storage for Data

The table is the primary storage object for data in a relational database. In its simplest form, a table consists of row(s) and column(s), both of which hold the data. A table takes up physical space in a database and can be permanent or temporary.

Columns

A *field*, also called a *column* in a relational database, is part of a table that is assigned a specific data type. The data type determines what kind of data the column is allowed to hold. This enables the designer of the table to help maintain the integrity of the data.

Every database table must consist of at least one column. Columns are elements within a table that hold specific types of data, such as a person's name or address. For example, a valid column in a customer table might be the customer's name. The following data illustrates a column in a table:

```
BIRD_NAME                        WINGSPAN
------------------------------ ----------
Eastern Kingbird                       15
Great Blue Heron                       78
Mallard                               3.2
Common Loon                            54
Bald Eagle                             84
Golden Eagle                           90
Red Tailed Hawk                        48
Osprey                                 72
Belted Kingfisher                      23
Canadian Goose                         72
Pied-billed Grebe                     6.5
American Coot                          29
Common Sea Gull                        18
Ring-billed Gull                       50
Double-crested Cormorant               54
Common Merganser                       34
Turkey Vulture                         72
American Crow                        39.6
Green Heron                          26.8
Mute Swan                            94.8
Brown Pelican                          90
Great Egret                          67.2
Anhinga                                42
Black Skimmer                          15
```

Generally, a column name must be one continuous string and can be limited to the number of characters used according to each implementation of SQL. Underscores typically are used with names to provide separation between characters. For example, a column for the bird's name can be named `BIRD_NAME` instead of `BIRDNAME`. This is normally done to increase the readability of database objects. You can use other naming conventions as well, such as CamelCase, to fit your specific preferences. As such, it is important for a database development team to agree upon a standard naming convention, to maintain order within the development process.

The most common form of data stored within a column is string data. This data can be stored as either upper case or lower case for character-defined fields. The case that you use for data is simply a matter of preference and should be based on how the data will be used. In many cases, data is stored in upper case for simplicity and consistency. However, if data is stored in different case types throughout the database (upper case, lower case, and mixed case), functions can be applied to convert the data to either upper case or lower case, if needed. Hour 15, "Restructuring the Appearance of Data," covers these functions.

Columns also can be specified as `NULL` or `NOT NULL`. If a column is `NOT NULL`, something must be entered. If a column is specified as `NULL`, nothing has to be entered. `NULL` is different from an empty set, such as an empty string, and holds a special place in database design. As such, you can relate a `NULL` value to a lack of any data in the field.

Rows

A *row* is a record of data in a database table. For example, a row of data in a customer table might consist of a particular customer's identification number, name, address, phone number, and fax number. A row consists of fields that contain data from one record in a table. A table can contain as little as one row of data and as many as several million rows of data or records. The following data from a table called FOOD provides an example of the distinct food items that birds eat from our database.

```
   FOOD_ID FOOD_NAME
---------- ------------------------------
         1 Seeds
         2 Birds
         3 Fruit
         4 Frogs
         5 Fish
         6 Berries
         7 Aquatic Plants
         8 Aquatic Insects
         9 Worms
        10 Nuts
        11 Rodents
        12 Snakes
        13 Small Mammals
        14 Nectar
        15 Pollen
        16 Carrion
        17 Moths
        18 Ducks
        19 Insects
        20 Plants
        21 Corn
        22 Crayfish
        23 Crustaceans
        24 Reptiles
        25 Deer
```

In the previous example, the table has 25 rows of data. The first row of data in the table appears as follows, consisting of the FOOD_ID and the FOOD_NAME:

```
1 Seeds
```

The CREATE TABLE Statement

The CREATE TABLE statement in SQL creates a table. Although the act of creating a table is quite simple, much time and effort should be put into planning the table structures before actually executing the CREATE TABLE statement. Carefully planning your table structure before implementation saves you from having to reconfigure in production.

NOTE

Types Used in This Hour

This hour's examples use the popular data types CHAR (constant-length character), VARCHAR (variable-length character), NUMBER (numeric values, decimal, and nondecimal), and DATE (date and time values).

Some elementary questions need to be answered when creating a table:

- What type of data will be entered into the table?
- What will be the table's name?
- What column(s) will comprise the primary key?
- What names will be given to the columns (fields)?
- What data type will be assigned to each column?
- What will be the allocated length for each column?
- Which columns in a table can be left as a null, or missing, value?

NOTE

Existing Systems Often Have Existing Naming Rules

Be sure to check your implementation for rules when naming objects and other database elements. Often database administrators adopt a ***naming convention*** that explains how to name the objects within the database so that you can easily discern how they are used.

After you answer these questions, using the actual CREATE TABLE statement is simple. The basic syntax for creating a table follows:

```
CREATE TABLE table_name
( field1  data_type  [ not null ],
  field2  data_type  [ not null ],
  field3  data_type  [ not null ],
  field4  data_type  [ not null ],
  field5  data_type  [ not null ] );
```

Note that a semicolon is the last character in the previous statement. Also, brackets indicate portions that are optional. Most SQL implementations have some character that terminates a statement or submits a statement to the database server. Oracle, Microsoft SQL Server, and MySQL use the semicolon. Although Transact-SQL, Microsoft SQL Server's ANSI SQL version, has no such requirement, it is considered best practice to use it. This book uses the semicolon.

Notice that the syntax to create a table looks very similar to the list of tables, columns, and data types at the end of the previous hour, as shown again:

```
BIRDS
bird_id        number(3)      not null
bird_name      varchar(30)    not null
height         number(4,2)    not null
weight         number(4,2)    not null
wingspan       number(4,2)    null
eggs           number(2)      not null
broods         number(1)      null
incubation     number(2)      not null
fledging       number(3)      not null
nest_builder   char(1)        not null
```

When you define a table using SQL, you simply provide the name of the table and a list of the columns in that table, along with their data types and whether the columns can contain null values. The default is null if it is not specified, which means that data is optional for that particular column.

To create a table called BIRDS, you simply substitute the table and column names that you previously defined during database design and substitute that information into the CREATE TABLE statement as follows:

```
create table birds
(bird_id        number(3)        not null,
bird_name       varchar(30)      not null,
height          number(4,2)      not null,
weight          number(4,2)      not null,
wingspan        number(4,2)      null,
```

```
eggs           number(2)          not null,
broods         number(1)          null,
incubation     number(2)          not null,
fledging       number(3)          not null,
nest_builder   char(1)            not null);
```

NOTE

Case Sensitivity of SQL Commands

Note that, with most implementations, the SQL command itself is not case sensitive. However, if you choose to store data a certain way, case sensitivity does matter when searching for that data. If you're not sure of the case, SQL has functions that enable you to convert the case of data, as covered beginning in Hour 15 of this book.

In this example, each record, or row of data, in the table consists of the following columns:

```
BIRD_ID, BIRD_NAME, HEIGHT, WEIGHT, WINGSPAN, EGGS, BROODS, INCUBATION, FLEDGIN,
NEST_BUILDER
```

In this table, each field is a column. The column `BIRD_ID` can consist of one bird's identification number or many birds' identification numbers, depending on the requirements of a database query or transaction.

Eight different columns comprise this table. Notice the use of the underscore character to break up the column names into what appears to be separate words. (The bird identification is stored as the `BIRD_ID`.) This technique makes the table or column name more readable. Each column has been assigned a specific data type and length. By using the `NULL/NOT NULL` constraint, you specify which columns require values for every row of data in the table. The `EMP_PHONE` is defined as `NULL`, meaning that null values are allowed in this column because some individuals might not have a telephone number. A comma separates the information for each column, with parentheses surrounding all columns (a left parenthesis before the first column and a right parenthesis following the information on the last column).

CAUTION

Limitations on Data Types Vary

Check your particular implementation for the allowed name length limits and characters; they differ among implementations.

Naming Conventions

When selecting names for objects, specifically tables and columns, make sure the name reflects the data that is to be stored. For example, the name for a table pertaining to employee information might be named EMPLOYEE_TBL. Names for columns should follow the same logic. When storing an employee's phone number, an obvious name for that column might be PHONE_NUMBER.

Using the ALTER TABLE Command

You can modify a table after the table has been created by using the ALTER TABLE command. You can add column(s), drop column(s), change column definitions, add and drop constraints, and, in some implementations, modify table STORAGE values. The standard syntax for the ALTER TABLE command follows:

```
alter table table_name [modify] [column column_name][datatype | null not null]
[restrict|cascade]
[drop]    [constraint constraint_name]
[add]     [column] column definition
```

For example, let's say that you want to remove the WINGSPAN column from the BIRDS table. Keep in mind that if you drop a column, the data is removed. On a related note, you cannot drop a column that has data that other child records in the database depend upon.

```
SQL> alter table birds
  2  drop column wingspan;

Table altered.

SQL> desc birds
 Name                                      Null?    Type
 ----------------------------------------- -------- ----------------------------
 BIRD_ID                                   NOT NULL NUMBER(3)
 BIRD_NAME                                 NOT NULL VARCHAR2(30)
 HEIGHT                                    NOT NULL NUMBER(4,2)
 WEIGHT                                    NOT NULL NUMBER(4,2)
 EGGS                                      NOT NULL NUMBER(2)
 BROODS                                             NUMBER(1)
 INCUBATION                                NOT NULL NUMBER(2)
 FLEDGING                                  NOT NULL NUMBER(3)
 NEST_BUILDER                              NOT NULL CHAR(1)
```

In the following example, you attempt to remove the BIRD_ID from the BIRDS table. An error is received from the database because the BIRD_ID is defined as a primary key that has dependent child records in other tables. You cannot drop a column or remove data if that modification to the database violates any constraints or definitions that have previously been defined.

```
SQL> alter table birds
  2  drop column bird_id;
drop column bird_id
            *
ERROR at line 2:
ORA-12992: cannot drop parent key column
```

NOTE

Object Modifications Cannot Violate Existing Constraints

Remember that you cannot violate any rules that are previously set up for a database object when modifying a table or when inserting or modifying any data within a table.

In the following example, you add a column called BEAK_LENGTH to the BIRDS table.

```
SQL> alter table birds
  2  add beak_length number(5,2);

Table altered.

SQL> desc birds
 Name                          Null?    Type
 ----------------------------- -------- -----------------
 BIRD_ID                       NOT NULL NUMBER(3)
 BIRD_NAME                     NOT NULL VARCHAR2(30)
 HEIGHT                        NOT NULL NUMBER(4,2)
 WEIGHT                        NOT NULL NUMBER(4,2)
 WINGSPAN                      NUMBER(4,2)
 EGGS                          NOT NULL NUMBER(2)
 BROODS                                 NUMBER(1)
 INCUBATION                    NOT NULL NUMBER(2)
 FLEDGING                      NOT NULL NUMBER(3)
 NEST_BUILDER                  NOT NULL CHAR(1)
 BEAK_LENGTH                            NUMBER(5,2)
```

CAUTION

Altering or Dropping Tables Can Be Dangerous

Take heed when altering and dropping tables. If you make logical or typing mistakes when issuing these statements, you can lose important data.

Modifying Elements of a Table

The *attributes* of a column refer to the rules and behavior of data in a column. You can modify the attributes of a column by using the ALTER TABLE command. The word *attributes* here refers to the following:

- The data type of a column
- The length, precision, or scale of a column
- Whether the column can contain NULL values

The following example uses the ALTER TABLE command on the BIRDS table to modify the attributes of the column BROODS:

```
SQL> alter table birds
  2  modify broods not null;

Table altered.

SQL> desc birds
 Name                Null?    Type
 ------------------ -------- --------------------------
 BIRD_ID             NOT NULL NUMBER(3)
 BIRD_NAME           NOT NULL VARCHAR2(30)
 HEIGHT              NOT NULL NUMBER(4,2)
 WEIGHT              NOT NULL NUMBER(4,2)
 WINGSPAN                     NUMBER(4,2)
 EGGS                NOT NULL NUMBER(2)
 BROODS              NOT NULL NUMBER(1)
 INCUBATION          NOT NULL NUMBER(2)
 FLEDGING            NOT NULL NUMBER(3)
 NEST_BUILDER        NOT NULL CHAR(1)
 BEAK_LENGTH                  NUMBER(5,2)
```

Adding Mandatory Columns to a Table

One of the basic rules for adding columns to an existing table is that the column you are adding cannot be defined as NOT NULL if data currently exists in the table. NOT NULL means that a column must contain some value for every row of data in the table. If you are adding a column defined as NOT NULL, you are contradicting the NOT NULL constraint from the beginning if the preexisting rows of data in the table do not have values for the new column.

The following example attempts to modify the BEAK_LENGTH column in the birds table as Not Null, or as a mandatory column. You see in this example that an error is returned; you cannot identify an existing column as Not Null if rows of data already exist in that table and null values are found in that particular column.

```
SQL> alter table birds
  2  modify beak_length not null;
alter table birds
*
ERROR at line 1:
ORA-02296: cannot enable (RYAN.) - null values found
```

However, you do have a way to add a mandatory column to a table:

1. Add the column and define it as NULL. (The column does not have to contain a value.)
2. Insert a value into the new column for every row of data in the table.
3. Alter the table to change the column's attribute to NOT NULL.

For example:

```
SQL> update birds
  2  set beak_length = 0;

23 rows updated.

SQL> commit;

Commit complete.

SQL> alter table birds
  2  modify beak_length not null;

Table altered.
```

Adding Autoincrementing Columns to a Table

Sometimes it is necessary to create a column that autoincrements itself, to give a unique sequence number for a particular row. You might do this for many reasons, such as if you do not have a natural key for the data or if you want to use a unique sequence number to sort the data. Creating an autoincrementing column is generally easy. In MySQL, the implementation provides the SERIAL method, to produce a truly unique value for the table. Following is an example:

```
CREATE TABLE TEST_INCREMENT(
        ID            SERIAL,
        TEST_NAME    VARCHAR(20));
```

NOTE

Using NULL for Table Creation

NULL is a default attribute for a column; therefore, it does not have to be entered in the CREATE TABLE statement. NOT NULL must always be specified.

In Microsoft SQL Server, you have an IDENTITY column type. The following is an example for the SQL Server implementation:

```
CREATE TABLE TEST_INCREMENT(
        ID            INT IDENTITY(1,1) NOT NULL,
        TEST_NAME    VARCHAR(20));
```

Oracle does not provide a direct method for an autoincrementing column. However, one method, using an object called a SEQUENCE and a TRIGGER, simulates the effect in Oracle.

Now you can insert values into the newly created table without specifying a value for the autoincrementing column:

```
INSERT INTO TEST_INCREMENT(TEST_NAME)
VALUES ('FRED'),('JOE'),('MIKE'),('TED');
SELECT * FROM TEST_INCREMENT;
| ID |      TEST_NAME |
|  1 |      FRED      |
|  2 |      JOE       |
|  3 |      MIKE      |
|  4 |      TED       |
```

Modifying Columns

You need to consider many factors when modifying the existing columns of a table. Following are some common rules for modifying columns:

- The length of a column can be increased to the maximum length of the given data type.
- The length of a column can be decreased only if the largest value for that column in the table is less than or equal to the new length of the column.
- The number of digits for a number data type can always be increased.
- The number of digits for a number data type can be decreased only if the value with the most number of digits for that column is less than or equal to the new number of digits specified for the column.
- The number of decimal places for a number data type can be either increased or decreased.
- The data type of a column can normally be changed.

Some implementations restrict you from using certain ALTER TABLE options. For example, you might not be allowed to drop columns from a table. To do this, you have to drop the table itself and then rebuild the table with the desired columns. You might run into problems by dropping a column in one table that is dependent on a column in another table, or dropping a column that is referenced by a column in another table. Be sure to refer to your specific implementation documentation.

How to Create a Table from an Existing Table

You can create a copy of an existing table using a combination of the CREATE TABLE statement and the SELECT statement. The new table has the same column definitions. You can select any or all columns. New columns that you create using functions or a combination of columns automatically assume the size necessary to hold the data. The basic syntax for creating a table from another table follows:

```
create table new_table_name as
select [ *|column1, column2 ]
from table_name
[ where ]
```

Take a look at some data in the BIRDS table. In this example, you're looking at only the BIRD_NAME itself and the WINGSPAN. Notice that this table has 23 rows of data, in no particular order.

```
SQL> select bird_name, wingspan
  2  from birds;

BIRD_NAME                        WINGSPAN
------------------------------ ----------
Great Blue Heron                       78
Mallard                               3.2
Common Loon                            54
Bald Eagle                             84
Golden Eagle                           90
Red Tailed Hawk                        48
Osprey                                 72
Belted Kingfisher                      23
Canadian Goose                         72
Pied-billed Grebe                     6.5
American Coot                          29
Common Sea Gull                        18
Ring-billed Gull                       50
Double-crested Cormorant               54
Common Merganser                       34
Turkey Vulture                         72
American Crow                        39.6
Green Heron                          26.8
Mute Swan                            94.8
Brown Pelican                          90
Great Egret                          67.2
Anhinga                                42
Black Skimmer                          15

23 rows selected.
```

You can create a copy of the BIRDS table with the CREATE TABLE AS statement, as follows. In this example, you're creating a table called BIG_BIRDS that will contain only birds that have a wingspan of more than 48 inches.

```
SQL> create table big_birds as
  2  select * from birds
  3  where wingspan > 48;

Table created.
```

Now if you query data from the BIG_BIRDS table, you get an idea of the capabilities of creating a table based on another table. In this example, the new table has only 12 rows; these are the big birds.

```
SQL> select bird_name, wingspan
  2  from big_birds;

BIRD_NAME                        WINGSPAN
------------------------------ ----------
Great Blue Heron                       78
Common Loon                            54
Bald Eagle                             84
Golden Eagle                           90
Osprey                                 72
Canadian Goose                         72
Ring-billed Gull                       50
Double-crested Cormorant               54
Turkey Vulture                         72
Mute Swan                            94.8
Brown Pelican                          90
Great Egret                          67.2

12 rows selected.
```

Notice the new keywords in the syntax, particularly the SELECT keyword. SELECT is a database query and is discussed in more detail in Hour 12, "Introduction to Database Queries." However, it is important to know that you can create a table based on the results from a query.

Both MySQL and Oracle support the CREATE TABLE AS SELECT method of creating a table based on another table. Microsoft SQL Server uses a different statement. For that database implementation, you use a SELECT ... INTO statement, like this:

```
select [ *|column1, column2]
into new_table_name
from table_name
[ where ]
```

You can take a look at some examples of using this method next. First, you do a simple query to view the data in the MIGRATION table:

```
select * from migration;
SQL> select * from migration;

MIGRATION_ID MIGRATION_LOCATION
------------ ------------------------------
           1 Southern United States
           2 Mexico
           3 Central America
           4 South America
           5 No Significant Migration
           6 Partial, Open Water
```

Next, you create a table called MIGRATION_NEW that is based on the previous query:

```
create table migration_new as
select * from migration;
Table created.
```

In SQL Server, the same statement is written like this:

```
select *
into migration_new
from migration;
Table created.
```

Now if you run a query on the MIGRATION_NEW table, your results appear the same as if you selected data from the original table:

```
MIGRATION_ID MIGRATION_LOCATION
------------ ------------------------------
           1 Southern United States
           2 Mexico
           3 Central America
           4 South America
           5 No Significant Migration
           6 Partial, Open Water
```

TIP

What the * Means

SELECT * selects data from all fields in the given table. The * represents a complete row of data, or record, in the table. In other words, the query to the database is asking to show all columns for each row of data the query returns.

The Process of Dropping Tables

Dropping a table is one of the easiest actions to complete. When the RESTRICT option is used and the table is referenced by a view or a constraint, the DROP statement returns an error. When the CASCADE option is used, the drop succeeds and all referencing views and constraints are dropped. The syntax to drop a table follows:

```
drop table table_name [ restrict | cascade ]
```

SQL Server does not allow the use of the CASCADE option. For that particular implementation, you must ensure that you drop all objects that reference the table you are removing, to make sure you are not leaving an invalid object in your system.

In the first example that follows, you attempt to drop the BIRDS table:

```
SQL> drop table birds;
drop table birds
           *
ERROR at line 1:
ORA-02449: unique/primary keys in table referenced by foreign keys
```

You can see that an error is returned because you cannot drop a table (or remove any data from the database, for that matter) that other data in the database depends on. BIRDS is one of the main tables in the database and is a parent table with primary keys that foreign keys in other tables reference.

In the next example, you drop the NICKNAMES table. The NICKNAMES table does have data, but it does not have any parent primary keys that other foreign keys in the database reference. Therefore, the table is dropped, along with all the data within it. The SELECT statement after the DROP TABLE statement shows that the table does not exist; an error is returned if you try to query a table that does not exist.

```
SQL> drop table nicknames;

Table dropped.

SQL> select * from nicknames;
select * from nicknames
              *
ERROR at line 1:
ORA-00942: table or view does not exist
drop table products_tmp;
Table dropped.
```

CAUTION

Be Specific When Dropping a Table

Whenever you drop a table, be sure to specify the schema name or owner of the table before you submit your command, to avoid dropping the incorrect table. If you have access to multiple user accounts, make sure that you are connected to the database through the correct user account before you drop a table. For example, a safer way to drop the NICKNAMES table in the previous example is to fully qualify the table name with the table owner, as with DROP TABLE RYAN.NICKNAMES.

Integrity Constraints

Integrity constraints ensure the accuracy and consistency of data in a relational database. Data integrity is handled in a relational database through the concept of referential integrity. Many types of integrity constraints play a role in *referential integrity (RI)*. Referential integrity consists of rules that are in place in the database to ensure that the data in tables remains consistent.

Primary Key Constraints

The *primary key* identifies one or more columns in a table that make a row of data unique. Although the primary key typically consists of one column in a table, more than one column can comprise the primary key. For example, either the employee's Social Security number or an assigned employee identification number is the logical primary key for an employee table. The objective is for every record to have a unique primary key or value for the employee's identification number. Because there is probably no need to have more than one record for each employee in an employee table, the employee identification number makes a logical primary key. The primary key is assigned upon table creation.

The following example identifies the BIRD_ID column as the PRIMARY KEY for the BIRDS table:

```
create table birds
(bird_id         number(3)       not null        primary key,
bird_name        varchar(30)     not null,
height           number(4,2)     not null,
weight           number(4,2)     not null,
wingspan         number(4,2)     null,
eggs             number(2)       not null,
broods           number(1)       null,
incubation       number(2)       not null,
fledging         number(3)       not null,
nest_builder     char(1)         not null);
```

This method of defining a primary key is accomplished during table creation. In this case, the primary key is an implied constraint. You can also specify a primary key explicitly as a constraint when setting up a table, as follows:

```
create table birds
(bird_id          number(3)       not null,
bird_name         varchar(30)     not null,
height            number(4,2)     not null,
weight            number(4,2)     not null,
wingspan          number(4,2)     null,
eggs              number(2)       not null,
broods            number(1)       null,
incubation        number(2)       not null,
fledging          number(3)       not null,
nest_builder      char(1)         not null);
PRIMARY KEY (BIRD_ID));
```

The primary key constraint in this example is defined after the column comma list in the CREATE TABLE statement.

You can define a primary key that consists of more than one column in either of the following methods, which demonstrate creating a primary key in an Oracle table:

```
create table nicknames
(bird_id        number(3)       not null,
nickname        varchar(30)     not null,
constraint nicknames_pk primary key (bird_id, nickname));
```

In this example, let's say that you did not specify the primary key when you created the NICKNAMES table. The following example shows how you can use the ALTER TABLE statement to add a constraint to an existing table.

```
ALTER TABLE NICKNAMES
ADD CONSTRAINT NICKNAMES_PK PRIMARY KEY (BIRD_ID, NICKNAME) ;
```

Unique Constraints

A *unique column constraint* in a table is similar to a primary key: Each value in a column must be a unique value. Although a primary key constraint is placed on one column, you can place a unique constraint on another column even though it is not actually for use as the primary key.

Study the following example:

```
create table birds
(bird_id         number(3)       not null        primary key,
bird_name        varchar(30)     not null        unique,
height           number(4,2)     not null,
weight           number(4,2)     not null,
```

```
wingspan        number(4,2)     null,
eggs            number(2)       not null,
broods          number(1)       null,
incubation      number(2)       not null,
fledging        number(3)       not null,
nest_builder    char(1)         not null);
```

The primary key in this example is BIRD_ID, meaning that the bird identification number is the column that ensures that every record in the table is unique. The primary key is a column that is normally referenced in queries, particularly queries to join tables. The column BIRD_NAME has been designated as a UNIQUE value, meaning that no two birds can have the same name. Not a lot of difference exists between the two, except that the primary key provides an order to data in a table and, in the same respect, joins related tables.

Foreign Key Constraints

A *foreign key* is a column in a child table that references a primary key in the parent table. A *foreign key constraint* is the main mechanism that enforces referential integrity between tables in a relational database. A column defined as a foreign key references a column defined as a primary key in another table.

Study the creation of the foreign key in the following example:

```
create table nicknames
(bird_id        number(3)         not null,
nickname        varchar(30)       not null,
constraint nicknames_pk primary key (bird_id, nickname),
constraint nicknames_bird_id_fk foreign key (bird_id) references birds (bird_id));
```

The BIRD_ID column in this example has been designated as the foreign key for the NICKNAMES table. As you can see, this foreign key references the BIRD_ID column in the BIRDS table. This foreign key ensures that, for every BIRD_ID in the NICKNAMES table, there is a corresponding BIRD_ID in the BIRDS table. You might recall that this is called a *parent/child relationship*. The parent table is the BIRDS table, and the child table is the NICKNAMES table.

For every data value to be inserted for BIRD_ID in the child table of NICKNAMES, a value for BIRD_ID must first exist in the parent table of BIRDS. Likewise, for a value to be removed for BIRD_ID in the parent table, all corresponding first values for BIRD_ID must be removed from the child table. This is how referential integrity works—and how you use SQL to protect your data.

You can add a foreign key to a table using the ALTER TABLE command, as shown in the following example:

```
alter table nicknames
add constraint nicknames_bird_id_fk foreign key (bird_id)
references birds (bird_id);
```

NOTE

ALTER TABLE Variations

The options available with the ALTER TABLE command differ among implementations of SQL, particularly when dealing with constraints. In addition, the actual use and definitions of constraints vary. However, the concept of referential integrity works the same for all relational databases.

NOT NULL Constraints

Previous examples use the keywords NULL and NOT NULL listed on the same line as each column and after the data type. NOT NULL is a constraint that you can place on a table's column. This constraint disallows the entrance of NULL values into a column; in other words, data is required in a NOT NULL column for each row of data in the table. NULL is generally the default for a column if NOT NULL is not specified, allowing NULL values in a column.

Using Check Constraints

You can use check (CHK) constraints to test the validity of data entered into particular table columns. Check constraints provide back-end database edits, although edits are commonly found in the front-end application as well. General edits restrict values that can be entered into columns or objects, whether within the database or on a front-end application. The check constraint is a way of providing another protective layer for the data.

The following example illustrates the use of a check constraint in Oracle:

```
create table birds
(bird_id          number(3)        not null         primary key,
bird_name         varchar(30)      not null         unique,
height            number(4,2)      not null,
weight            number(4,2)      not null,
wingspan          number(4,2)      null,
eggs              number(2)        not null,
broods            number(1)        null,
incubation        number(2)        not null,
fledging          number(3)        not null,
nest_builder      char(1)          not null,
constraint chk_wingspan check (wingspan between 1 and 100));
```

In this example, the check constraint has been placed on the WINGSPAN column in the BIRDS table. For every row of data inserted into the BIRDS table, you place a rule or constraint here that the database checks to ensure that any value entered is between 1 and 100 inches. (We don't imagine a bird having a wingspan greater than 100 inches. However, if that situation occurs in the future as the database grows, you can simply modify the table to accept a greater range of WINGSPAN.)

The Process of Dropping Constraints

Using the ALTER TABLE command with the DROP CONSTRAINT option, you can drop any constraint that you have defined. For example, to drop the primary key constraint in the EMPLOYEES table, you use the following command:

```
ALTER TABLE BIRDS DROP CONSTRAINT CHK_WINGSPAN;
Table altered.
```

Some implementations provide shortcuts for dropping certain constraints. For example, to drop the primary key constraint for a table in MySQL, you use the following command:

```
ALTER TABLE BIRDS DROP PRIMARY KEY;
Table altered.
```

TIP

Other Ways of Dealing with Constraints

Instead of permanently dropping a constraint from the database, some implementations allow you to temporarily disable constraints and then enable them later. The problem with this approach is that you cannot enable a constraint if data in a table violates the rules of the constraint.

Summary

During this hour, you learned a little about database objects in general, specifically about tables. The table is the simplest form of data storage in a relational database. Tables contain groups of logical information, such as employee, customer, or product information. A table consists of various columns, each with attributes; those attributes mainly consist of data types and constraints, such as NOT NULL values, primary keys, foreign keys, and unique values.

You learned about the CREATE TABLE command and options, such as storage parameters, that might be available with this command. You also learned how to modify the structure of existing tables using the ALTER TABLE command. Although the process of managing database tables might not be the most basic process in SQL, learning the structure and nature of tables helps you more easily grasp the concept of accessing the tables, whether through data manipulation operations or database queries. In later hours, you learn about managing other objects in SQL, such as indexes on tables and views.

Q&A

Q. When I name a table that I am creating, do I have to use a suffix such as _TBL?

A. Absolutely not. For example, a table that holds employee information can literally be named anything, but most likely similar to the following, so that the table is descriptive of the data it contains:

```
EMPLOYEES
EMP_TBL
EMPLOYEE_TBL
EMPLOYEE_TABLE
WORKER
```

Q. Why is using the schema name so important when dropping a table?

A. Consider this true story about a new DBA who dropped a table: A programmer had created a table under his schema with the same name as a production table. That particular programmer left the company. His database account was being deleted from the database, but the `DROP USER` statement returned an error because he owned outstanding objects. After some investigation, it was determined that his table was not needed, so a `DROP TABLE` statement was issued.

It worked like a charm, but the problem was that the DBA was logged in as the production schema when the `DROP TABLE` statement was issued. The DBA should have specified a schema name, or owner, for the table to be dropped. You guessed it: The wrong table in the wrong schema was dropped. Restoring the production database took approximately 8 hours.

Workshop

The following workshop consists of a series of quiz questions and practical exercises. The quiz questions are designed to test your overall understanding of the current material. The practical exercises give you the opportunity to apply the concepts discussed during the current hour, as well as build on the knowledge you acquired in previous hours of study. Be sure to complete the quiz questions and exercises before continuing to the next hour. Refer to Appendix C, "Answers to Quizzes and Exercises," for answers.

Quiz

1. What is the most common object created in a database to store data?
2. Can you drop a column from a table?
3. What statement do you issue to create a primary key constraint on the preceding `BIRDS` table?
4. What statement do you issue on the preceding `BIRDS` table to allow the `WINGSPAN` column to accept `NULL` values?

5. What statement do you use to restrict the birds added into the preceding MIGRATION table to migrate only to certain migration locations?

6. What statement do you use to add an autoincrementing column called BIRD_ID to the preceding BIRDS table using both the MySQL and SQL Server syntax?

7. What SQL statement can be used to create a copy of an existing table?

8. Can you drop a column from a table?

Exercises

In this exercise, refer to the examples in the previous hours for the BIRDS database, as well as the information provided for rescues and photographers that are integrated into the BIRDS database. At this point, you have been designing entities for photographer data that will be integrated into the BIRDS database. Review what you have come up with so far and use that information for the following exercises.

1. Using the SQL commands that you've learned during this hour, create a physical database based on the photographer data that you previously modeled that will be integrated with the BIRDS database.

2. Think about any columns in your tables that can be altered in any way. Use the ALTER TABLE command as an example to change the way one of your tables is defined.

3. Have you used SQL and the CREATE TABLE statements to define all primary key and foreign key constraints? If not, use the ALTER TABLE statement to define at least one.

4. Can you think of any check constraints that you can add to the photographer data? If so, use the ALTER TABLE statement to add the appropriate constraints.

HOUR 10
Manipulating Data

What You'll Learn in This Hour:

- Getting an overview of DML
- Manipulating data in tables
- Understanding table population of data
- Deleting data from tables
- Changing or modifying data in tables
- Applying DML to the BIRDS database

In this hour, you learn how to use the piece of SQL known as *Data Manipulation Language (DML)* to change data and tables in a relational database.

Getting an Overview of Data Manipulation

DML is the part of SQL that enables a database user to actually propagate changes among data in a relational database. With DML, the user can populate tables with new data, update existing data in tables, and delete data from tables. Simple database queries can also be performed within a DML command.

SQL uses three basic DML commands:

- `INSERT`
- `UPDATE`
- `DELETE`

The `SELECT` command, which can be used with DML commands, is discussed in more detail in Hour 12, "Introduction to Database Queries." The `SELECT` command is the basic query command that you can use after you enter data into the database with the `INSERT` command. In this hour, you concentrate on getting the data into your tables so that you have something interesting to use the SELECT command on.

Populating Tables with New Data

Populating a table with data is simply the process of entering new data into a table, whether manually using individual commands or through batch processes using programs or other related software. *Manual population of data* refers to data entry using a keyboard. *Automated population* normally deals with obtaining data from an external data source (such as another database or possibly a flat file) and loading the obtained data into the database.

Many factors can affect what data and how much data can be put into a table when populating tables with data. Major factors include existing table constraints, the physical table size, column data types, the length of columns, and other integrity constraints, such as primary and foreign keys. The following sections help you learn the basics of inserting new data into a table.

Inserting Data into a Table

You use the INSERT statement to insert new data into a table. This statement has a few options; look at the basic syntax to begin:

```
INSERT INTO TABLE_NAME
VALUES ('value1', 'value2', [ NULL ] );
```

CAUTION

Data Is Case Sensitive

SQL statements can be in upper or lower case. However, data is sometimes case sensitive. For example, if you enter data into the database as upper case, depending on your database, you might have to reference that data in upper case. These examples use both lower- and upper-case statements, just to show that case does not affect the outcome.

Using this INSERT statement syntax, you must include every column in the specified table in the VALUES list. Notice that each value in this list is separated by a comma. Enclose the values inserted into the table in single quotation marks for character and date/time data types. Single quotation marks are not required for numeric data types or NULL values that use the NULL keyword. A value should be present for each column in the table, and those values must be in the same order as the columns are listed in the table. In later sections, you learn how to specify the column ordering; for now just know that the SQL engine you are working with assumes that you want to enter the data in the same order in which the columns were created.

In the following example, you insert a new record into the BIRDS table.

This is the table structure:

```
 Name                     Null?    Type
 ------------------------ -------- ---------------------------
 BIRD_ID                  NOT NULL NUMBER(3)
 BIRD_NAME                NOT NULL VARCHAR2(30)
 HEIGHT                   NOT NULL NUMBER(4,2)
 WEIGHT                   NOT NULL NUMBER(4,2)
 WINGSPAN                          NUMBER(4,2)
 EGGS                     NOT NULL NUMBER(2)
 BROODS                   NOT NULL NUMBER(1)
 INCUBATION               NOT NULL NUMBER(2)
 FLEDGING                 NOT NULL NUMBER(3)
 NEST_BUILDER             NOT NULL CHAR(1)
```

This is the sample `INSERT` statement:

```
insert into birds (bird_id, bird_name, height, weight, wingspan, eggs, broods,
incubation, fledging, nest_builder)
values (1, 'Great Blue Heron', 52, 5.5, 78, 5, 1, 28, 60, 'B');

1 row created.
```

In this example, 10 values were inserted into a table with 10 columns. The inserted values are in the same order as the columns listed in the table. Character values are inserted using single quotation marks, and numeric values are inserted without single quotation marks, although this is optional with numeric values.

The following example is the exact same `insert` statement, but notice that the list of column names is not included. If you do not include a list of columns into which the data is being inserted, the assumption is that you are inserting into all columns in the same order they are listed in the table.

```
insert into birds
values (1, 'Great Blue Heron', 52, 5.5, 78, 5, 1, 28, 60, 'B');

1 row created.
```

NOTE

When to Use Quotation Marks

Although single quotation marks are not required around numeric data that is inserted, they can be used with any data type. In other words, single quotation marks are optional when referring to numeric data values in the database, but they are required for all other data values (data types). Including them is usually a matter of preference, but most SQL users choose not to use quotation marks with numeric values because their queries are more readable without them.

Inserting Data into Limited Columns of a Table

You can insert data into specified columns as well. For instance, suppose that you want to insert data into the BIRDS table for every column except the WINGSPAN column. Remember that if a column is defined as mandatory or not null, data must be inserted into that particular column for every row of data in the table. The WINGSPAN column in the BIRDS table is optional or defined as null, so leaving that column empty is acceptable when inserting a row of data into the BIRDS table.

The syntax for inserting values into a limited number of columns in a table follows:

```
INSERT INTO TABLE_NAME ('COLUMN1', 'COLUMN2')
VALUES ('VALUE1', 'VALUE2');
```

This is the sample INSERT statement:

```
insert into birds (bird_id, bird_name, height, weight, eggs, broods, incubation,
fledging, nest_builder)
values (1, 'Great Blue Heron', 52, 5.5, 5, 1, 28, 60, 'B');

1 row created.
```

You have specified a column list enclosed by parentheses after the table name in the INSERT statement. You have listed all columns into which you want to insert data. WINGSPAN is the only excluded column. If you look at the table definition, you can see that WINGSPAN does not require data for every record in the table. You know that WINGSPAN does not require data because NULL is specified in the table definition. NULL tells us that NULL values are allowed in the column. Furthermore, the list of values must appear in the same order as the column list.

TIP

Column List Ordering Can Differ

The column list in the INSERT statement does not have to reflect the same order of columns as in the definition of the associated table. However, the list of values must be in the order of the associated columns in the column list. In addition, you can leave off the NULL syntax for a column because the defaults for most RDBMSs specify that columns allow NULL values.

Inserting Data from Another Table

You can insert data into a table based on the results of a query from another table using a combination of the INSERT statement and the SELECT statement. Briefly, a *query* is an inquiry to the database that either expects or does not expect data to be returned. (See Hour 12, "Introduction to Database Queries," for more information on queries.) A query is a question that the user asks the database, and the data returned is the answer. When combining the INSERT statement with the SELECT statement, you can insert the data retrieved from a query into a table.

The syntax for inserting data from another table follows:

```
insert into table_name [('column1', 'column2')]
select [*|('column1', 'column2')]
from table_name
[where condition(s)];
```

You see three new keywords in this syntax: SELECT, FROM, and WHERE. SELECT is the main command used to initiate a query in SQL. FROM is a clause in the query that specifies the names of tables where the target data should be found. The WHERE clause, also part of the query, places conditions on the query. A *condition* is a way of placing criteria on data affected by a SQL statement. A sample condition might state this: WHERE LASTNAME = 'SMITH'.

In the following example, let's say that you want to create a table called SHORT_BIRDS. This table will have some of the information from the original BIRDS table but will store only information about birds that are short, or less than a certain height. Here you see a simple CREATE TABLE statement with three columns that will have data that is to be pulled from the BIRDS table.

```
SQL> create table short_birds
  2  (bird_id             number(3)           not null,
  3   bird_name           varchar2(30)        not null,
  4   height              number(3));

Table created.
```

Next, you use the INSERT statement to insert data into the SHORT_BIRDS table based on the output of a SELECT statement, from the BIRDS table itself. Only three columns are being pulled from the BIRDS table: BIRD_ID, BIRD_NAME, and HEIGHT. Notice the WHERE clause on line 4 of this INSERT statement. You are placing a condition on the query within the INSERT statement to consider only birds that have a height less than 20 inches. All rows of data from the BIRDS table will be inserted into the SHORT_BIRDS table if they meet this height criteria. This is a SELECT statement that is embedded within an INSERT statement. All the main components of the SELECT statement are discussed starting in Hour 12.

```
SQL> insert into short_birds
  2  select bird_id, bird_name, height
  3  from birds
  4  where height < 20;

6 rows created.
```

Finally, study the results of the following query. You now have a table with information about birds that are shorter than 20 inches in height.

```
SQL> select * from short_birds;

   BIRD_ID BIRD_NAME                          HEIGHT
---------- ------------------------------ ----------
         8 Belted Kingfisher                      13
        10 Pied-billed Grebe                      13
        11 American Coot                          16
        12 Common Sea Gull                        18
        13 Ring-billed Gull                       19
        17 American Crow                          18

6 rows selected.
```

Inserting NULL Values

Inserting a NULL value into a column of a table is simple. You might want to insert a NULL value into a column if the value of the column in question is unknown. For instance, not every bird in the database has a logged wingspan. You can insert a NULL value into a column of a table using the keyword NULL.

The syntax for inserting a NULL value follows:

```
insert into schema.table_name values
('column1', NULL, 'column3');
```

Use the NULL keyword in the proper sequence of the associated column that exists in the table. That column will not have data in it for that row if you enter NULL. In the syntax, a NULL value is entered in the place of COLUMN2.

Updating Existing Data

You can modify existing data in a table using the UPDATE command. This command does not add new records to a table, nor does it remove records—UPDATE simply updates the existing data. The update is generally used to update one table at a time in a database, but you also can use it to update multiple columns of a table at the same time. Depending on your needs, you can use a single statement to update an individual row of data in a table or numerous rows.

Updating the Value of a Single Column

The simplest use of the UPDATE statement is to update a single column in a table. Either a single row of data or numerous records can be updated when updating a single column in a table.

The syntax for updating a single column follows:

```
update table_name
set column_name = 'value'
[where condition];
```

Take a look at the MIGRATION table. This table has six rows of data that indicate different locations to which the birds in the database migrate.

```
SQL> select * from migration;
MIGRATION_ID MIGRATION_LOCATION
------------ ------------------------------
           1 Southern United States
           2 Mexico
           3 Central America
           4 South America
           5 No Significant Migration
           6 Partial, Open Water

6 rows selected.
```

Now let's update the MIGRATION table for MIGRATION_ID of 5, which has a MIGRATION_LOCATION value of No significant migration. The following UPDATE statement updates the value of the MIGRATION_LOCATION to None for that specific MIGRATION_ID.

```
SQL> update migration
  2  set migration_location = 'None'
  3  where migration_id = 5;

1 row updated.
```

After the update, you can query the MIGRATION table with the SELECT statement to verify that the MIGRATION_LOCATION value was successfully changed as intended.

```
SQL> select * from migration;

MIGRATION_ID MIGRATION_LOCATION
------------ ------------------------------
           3 Central America
           2 Mexico
           5 None
           6 Partial, Open Water
           4 South America
           1 Southern United States

6 rows selected.
```

Now let's look at an example of performing an UPDATE on a table without using the where clause. First, take a look at the table you previously created, called SHORT_BIRDS.

```
SQL> select * from short_birds;

   BIRD_ID BIRD_NAME                          HEIGHT
---------- ------------------------------ ----------
         8 Belted Kingfisher                      13
        10 Pied-billed Grebe                      13
        11 American Coot                          16
        12 Common Sea Gull                        18
        13 Ring-billed Gull                       19
        17 American Crow                          18

6 rows selected.
```

The following update statement is performed on the SHORT_BIRDS table, setting the BIRD_NAME to Some Sort of Bird for every row of data in the table. As you can see, six rows were updated. The SELECT statement that follows verifies this. All the rows were updated because criteria was not placed on the update using the where clause.

```
SQL> update short_birds
  2  set bird_name = 'Some Sort of Bird';

6 rows updated.

SQL> select * from short_birds;

   BIRD_ID BIRD_NAME                          HEIGHT
---------- ------------------------------ ----------
         8 Some Sort of Bird                      13
        10 Some Sort of Bird                      13
        11 Some Sort of Bird                      16
        12 Some Sort of Bird                      18
        13 Some Sort of Bird                      19
        17 Some Sort of Bird                      18

6 rows selected.
```

In this example, all six rows of data were updated. We set the value for BIRD_NAME to Some Sort of Bird for every row of data in the table. Was this actually the intention of the table update? Perhaps in some cases, but rarely do you issue an UPDATE statement without a WHERE clause. An easy way to check to see whether you will be updating the correct data set is to write a SELECT statement for the same table with your WHERE clause that you are using in the INSERT statement. Then you can physically verify that these are the rows you want to update.

CAUTION

Test Your UPDATE and DELETE Statements

Use extreme caution when using the UPDATE statement without a WHERE clause. The target column is updated for all rows of data in the table if conditions are not designated using the WHERE clause. In most situations, using of the WHERE clause with a DML command is appropriate.

Updating Multiple Columns in One or More Records

Next, you see how to update multiple columns with a single UPDATE statement. Study the following syntax:

```
update table_name
set column1 = 'value',
   [column2 = 'value',]
   [column3 = 'value']
[where condition];
```

Notice the use of SET in this syntax—there is only one SET, but multiple columns. Each column is separated by a comma. You should start to see a trend in SQL: The comma usually separates different types of arguments in SQL statements. In the following code, a comma separates the two columns being updated. Again, the WHERE clause is optional, but it is usually necessary.

As you take another look at the SHORT_BIRDS table, you will update the table and set the value of multiple columns to a new value using the UPDATE statement. You start by looking at BIRD_ID number 8.

```
SQL> select * from short_birds;

   BIRD_ID BIRD_NAME                          HEIGHT
---------- ------------------------------ ----------
         8 Belted Kingfisher                      13
        10 Pied-billed Grebe                      13
        11 American Coot                          16
        12 Common Sea Gull                        18
        13 Ring-billed Gull                       19
        17 American Crow                          18

6 rows selected.
```

Here, an update is performed on SHORT_BIRDS, setting the value for BIRD_NAME to Kingfisher and the height to 12 instead of 13 for BIRD_ID number 8, or the Belted Kingfisher.

```
SQL> update short_birds
  2  set bird_name = 'Kingfisher',
  3      height = 12
  4  where bird_id = 8;

1 row updated.
```

The following query verifies that this update was successful.

```
SQL> select * from short_birds;

   BIRD_ID BIRD_NAME                          HEIGHT
---------- ------------------------------ ----------
         8 Kingfisher                             12
        10 Pied-billed Grebe                      13
        11 American Coot                          16
        12 Common Sea Gull                        18
        13 Ring-billed Gull                       19
        17 American Crow                          18

6 rows selected.
```

NOTE

When to Use the SET Keyword

The SET keyword is used only once for each UPDATE statement. If you want to update more than one column, use a comma to separate the columns to be updated.

In Hour 14, "Joining Tables in Queries," you learn how to write more complex statements through a construct known as a JOIN. This construct enables you to update values in one table using values from one or more outside tables.

Deleting Data from Tables

The DELETE command removes entire rows of data from a table. It does not remove values from specific columns; a full record, including all columns, is removed. Use the DELETE statement with caution.

To delete a single record or selected records from a table, use the DELETE statement with the following syntax:

```
delete from table_name
[where condition];
```

In the following example, suppose that you want to delete the row of data for the Belted Kingfisher altogether. The BIRD_ID for the Belted Kingfisher is number 8. Study the following DELETE statement.

```
SQL> delete from short_birds
  2  where bird_id = 8;

1 row deleted.
```

The following query verifies that one row of data was successfully deleted from the SHORT_BIRDS table. BIRD_ID number 8, Belted Kingfisher, no longer exists in that table.

```
SQL> select * from short_birds;

   BIRD_ID BIRD_NAME                          HEIGHT
---------- ------------------------------ ----------
        10 Pied-billed Grebe                      13
        11 American Coot                          16
        12 Common Sea Gull                        18
        13 Ring-billed Gull                       19
        17 American Crow                          18

5 rows selected.
```

So what happens if you perform a DELETE statement with no WHERE clause? The situation is similar to that of using an UPDATE without the WHERE clause. All rows of data are affected within the table. The following DELETE statement from the SHORT_BIRDS table lacks a WHERE clause; you can see that the remaining five rows in the SHORT_BIRDS table were deleted.

```
SQL> delete from short_birds;

5 rows deleted.

SQL> select * from short_birds;

no rows selected
```

CAUTION

Don't Omit the WHERE Clause

If the WHERE clause is omitted from the DELETE statement, all rows of data are deleted from the table. As a general rule, always use a WHERE clause with the DELETE statement. In addition, first test your WHERE clause with a SELECT statement.

Also remember that the DELETE command might have a permanent effect on the database. Ideally, recovering erroneously deleted data should be possible using a backup, but in some cases, recovering data is difficult or even impossible. If you cannot recover data, you must re-enter it into the database—this is trivial if you are dealing with only one row of data, but not so trivial if you have thousands of rows of data. You can see the importance of the WHERE clause.

The temporary table that was populated from the original table earlier in this hour can be useful for testing the DELETE and UPDATE commands before issuing them against the original table. Also remember the technique discussed earlier when you looked at the UPDATE command: Write a SELECT statement using the same WHERE clause that you want to use for the DELETE statement. That way, you can verify that the data being deleted is actually the data you want.

Summary

During this hour, you learned about the three basic commands in DML: the `INSERT`, `UPDATE`, and `DELETE` statements. As you have seen, data manipulation is a powerful part of SQL that allows the database user to populate tables with new data, update existing data, and delete data.

An important lesson when updating or deleting data from tables in a database is sometimes learned when neglecting the use of the `WHERE` clause. Remember that the `WHERE` clause places conditions on a SQL statement—particularly in the case of `UDPATE` and `DELETE` operations, when you specify rows of data that are affected during a transaction. All target table data rows are affected if the `WHERE` clause is not used, which could be disastrous to the database. Protect your data and be cautious during data manipulation operations.

Q&A

Q. With all the warnings about `DELETE` and `UPDATE`, I'm apprehensive about using them. If I accidentally update all the records in a table because I didn't use the `WHERE` clause, can I reverse the changes?

A. You have no reason to be afraid: You can correct almost anything you do to the database, although it might involve considerable time and work. Hour 11, "Managing Database Transactions," discusses the concept of transactional control, which allows you to finalize or undo data manipulation operations.

Q. Is the `INSERT` statement the only way to enter data into a table?

A. No, but remember that the `INSERT` statement is an ANSI standard. Various implementations have their own tools for entering data into tables. For example, Oracle has a SQL*Loader utility, whereas SQL Server has a SQL Server Integration Services (SSIS) utility. Many other implementations have `IMPORT` utilities that can insert data.

Workshop

The following workshop consists of a series of quiz questions and practical exercises. The quiz questions are designed to test your overall understanding of the current material. The practical exercises give you the opportunity to apply the concepts discussed during the current hour, as well as build on the knowledge you acquired in previous hours of study. Be sure to complete the quiz questions and exercises before continuing to the next hour. Refer to Appendix C, "Answers to Quizzes and Exercises," for answers.

Quiz

1. Do you always need to supply a column list for the table that you use an `INSERT` statement on?
2. What can you do if you do not want to enter a value for one particular column?
3. Why is it important to use a `WHERE` clause with `UPDATE` and `DELETE`?
4. What is an easy way to check that an `UPDATE` or `DELETE` will affect the rows that you want?

Exercises

1. Review the table structures in the `BIRDS` database, particularly the data in the `BIRDS` table itself. You will use this data to perform the exercises.
2. Use the `SELECT` statement to display all the data currently in the `BIRDS` table.

3. Create a new table called TALL_BIRDS that is based on the BIRDS table itself, with the following columns: BIRD_ID, BIRD_NAME, and WINGSPAN.

4. Insert data from the BIRDS table into the TALL_BIRDS table for birds taller than 30 inches.

5. Use the SELECT statement to display all the new data in the TALL_BIRDS table.

6. Insert the following data into the TALL_BIRDS table:

```
BIRD_NAME = Great Egret
HEIGHT = 40
WINGSPAN = 66
```

7. Update every data value in the BIRDS table for the bird name column to read Bird. Was this command successful? Why or why not?

8. Update the wingspan of every bird in the TALL_BIRDS table to a NULL value.

9. Delete the record for Great Egret from the TALL_BIRDS table.

10. Delete every remaining row of data from the TALL_BIRDS table.

11. Drop the TALL_BIRDS table.

HOUR 11

Managing Database Transactions

What You'll Learn in This Hour:

- The definition of a transaction
- The commands used to control transactions
- The syntax and examples of transaction commands
- When to use transactional commands
- The consequences of poor transactional control

So far, this book has discussed all-or-nothing scenarios for manipulating data inside a database. However, in more complicated processes, you need the capability to isolate changes so that they can be applied or rolled back to an original state at will. This is where transactions come in. Transactions give you the additional flexibility to isolate database changes into discrete batches and undo those changes if something goes wrong. In this hour, you learn the concepts behind managing database transactions, how to implement them, and how to properly control transactions.

Defining Transactions

A *transaction* is a unit of work that is performed against a database. Transactions are units or sequences of work accomplished in a logical order, whether manually by a user or automatically by some sort of a database program. In a relational database that uses SQL, transactions are accomplished using the *Data Manipulation Language (DML)* commands that were discussed during Hour 10, "Manipulating Data" (`INSERT`, `UPDATE`, and `DELETE`). A transaction is the propagation of one or more changes to the database. For instance, you are performing a transaction if you perform an `UPDATE` statement on a table to change an individual's name.

A transaction can be either one DML statement or a group of statements. When managing transactions, each designated transaction (group of DML statements) must be successful as one entity, or none of them will be successful.

The following list describes the nature of transactions:

- All transactions have a beginning and an end.
- A transaction can be saved or undone.
- If a transaction fails in the middle, no part of the transaction can be saved to the database.

Controlling Transactions

Transactional control is the capability to manage various transactions that might occur within a *relational database management system (RDBMS)*. When you speak of transactions, you are referring to the `INSERT`, `UPDATE`, and `DELETE` commands, which you looked at during the previous hour.

NOTE

Transactions Are Implementation Specific

Starting or executing transactions is implementation specific. Check your particular implementation for how to begin transactions.

When a transaction is executed and completes successfully, the target table is not immediately changed (even though this might appear to be the case, according to the output). When a transaction successfully completes, transactional control commands are used to finalize the transaction, either saving the changes made by the transaction to the database or reversing the changes made by the transaction. During the transaction execution, the information is stored either in an allocated area or in a temporary rollback area in the database. All changes are held in this temporary rollback area until a transactional control command is issued. When a transactional control command is issued, changes are either made to the database or discarded; then the temporary rollback area is emptied. Figure 11.1 illustrates how changes are applied to a relational database.

Three commands are used to control transactions:

- `COMMIT`
- `ROLLBACK`
- `SAVEPOINT`

Each of these is discussed in detail in the following sections.

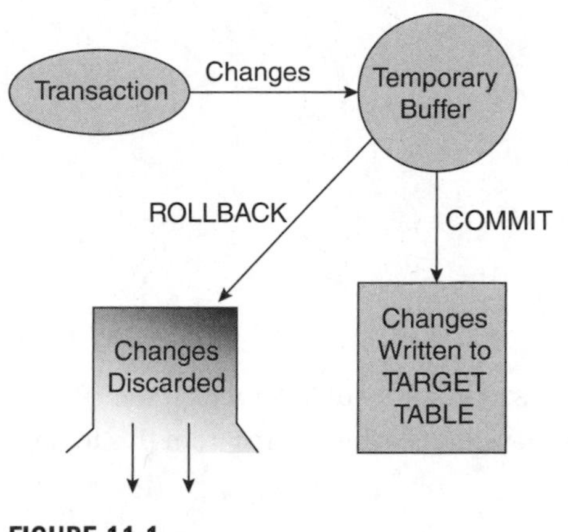

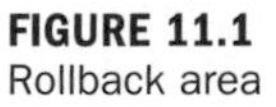

FIGURE 11.1
Rollback area

The COMMIT Command

The COMMIT command is the transactional command used to save changes invoked by a transaction to the database. The COMMIT command saves all transactions to the database since the last COMMIT or ROLLBACK command.

The syntax for this command follows:

```
commit [ work ];
```

The keyword COMMIT is the only mandatory part of the syntax, along with the character or command that terminates a statement, according to each implementation. WORK is a keyword that is completely optional; its only purpose is to make the command user friendly.

In the following example, you begin by creating a copy of the MIGRATION table, called the MIGRATION_TEST_DELETE table, and querying the table for all records, to familiarize yourself with the data.

```
SQL> create table migration_test_delete as
  2  select * from migration;

Table created.

SQL> select * from migration_test_delete;

MIGRATION_ID MIGRATION_LOCATION
```

```
------------ ------------------------------
           3 Central America
           2 Mexico
           5 No Significant Migration
           6 Partial, Open Water
           4 South America
           1 Southern United States

6 rows selected.
```

Next, you delete all rows of data from the MIGRATION_TEST_DELETE table for which the MIGRATION_ID is greater than 3. In other words, you remove half of the records from this table, for example purposes.

```
SQL> delete from migration_test_delete
  2  where migration_id > 3;

3 rows deleted.
```

A COMMIT statement is issued to save the changes to the database, completing the transaction:

```
SQL> commit;

Commit complete.
```

Finally, you query all records within the MIGRATION_TEST_DELETE table to verify the results of the transaction.

```
SQL> select * from migration_test_delete;

MIGRATION_ID MIGRATION_LOCATION
------------ ------------------------------
           3 Central America
           2 Mexico
           1 Southern United States

3 rows selected.
```

As a reminder, throughout the book, some implementations have minor variations. Oracle is used for examples in this book, for consistency, but an example of a variation occurs with Microsoft SQL Server. For example, if you issue a COMMIT statement and use SQL Server, you get the following error:

```
The COMMIT TRANSACTION request has no corresponding BEGIN TRANSACTION.
```

This is because SQL Server uses an autocommit. This simply means that it treats any statement as a transaction—SQL Server automatically issues a commit if the statement is successful and issues a rollback if it is not. To change this, you need to issue a SET IMPLICIT_TRANSACTIONS command and set the mode to ON:

```
SET IMPLICIT_TRANSACTIONS ON;
Command(s) completed successfully.
```

If you want your current connection to go back to autocommit mode, you simply issue the same statement and set the mode to OFF:

```
SET IMPLICIT_TRANSACTIONS OFF;
Command(s) completed successfully.
```

Frequent COMMIT statements in large loads or unloads of the database are highly recommended; however, too many COMMIT statements cause the job to take a lot of extra time to complete. Remember that all changes are first sent to the temporary rollback area. If this temporary rollback area runs out of space and cannot store information about changes made to the database, the database will probably halt, disallowing further transactional activity.

When an UPDATE, INSERT, or DELETE is issued, most RDBMSs use a form of transaction in the background so that if the query is canceled or runs into an error, changes are not committed. Therefore, issuing a transaction is more of an action to ensure that a set of transactions is run. This set is commonly referred to as a *unit of work*. In a real-world example, you might process a bank transaction at an ATM with a client that wants to withdraw money. In such a situation, you need to both insert a transaction for the money being withdrawn and update the client's balance to reflect the new total. Obviously, you want either both of these statements to succeed or both of them to fail. Otherwise, the system's data integrity is compromised. In this instance, you wrap your unit of work in a transaction to ensure that you can control the outcome of both statements.

CAUTION

Some Implementations Treat COMMIT Differently

In some implementations, transactions are committed without issuing the COMMIT command; merely signing out of the database causes a commit to occur. However, in some implementations, such as MySQL, after you perform a SET TRANSACTION command, the autocommit functionality does not resume until it has received a COMMIT or ROLLBACK statement. In addition, in other implementations, such as Microsoft SQL Server, statements are autocommitted unless a transaction is specifically used. Check the documentation of your particular RDBMS to understand exactly how transactions and statement commits are handled.

The ROLLBACK Command

The ROLLBACK command is the transactional control command that undoes transactions that have not already been saved to the database. You can use the ROLLBACK command to undo transactions only since the last COMMIT or ROLLBACK command was issued.

The syntax for the ROLLBACK command follows:

```
rollback [ work ];
```

Again, as in the COMMIT statement, the WORK keyword is an optional part of the ROLLBACK syntax.

For the rest of the exercise, if you use SQL Server, you need to turn on IMPLICIT_TRANSACTIONS to make the examples easier to follow:

```
SET IMPLICIT_TRANSACTIONS ON;
Command(s) completed successfully.
```

The following examples demonstrate the behavior of the ROLLBACK command using a table called BIG_BIRDS that is derived from the BIRDS table.

```
SQL> create table big_birds as
  2  select bird_id, bird_name, height, weight, wingspan, eggs
  3  from birds
  4  where wingspan > 48;

Table created.

SQL> select * from big_birds;

   BIRD_ID BIRD_NAME                          HEIGHT     WEIGHT   WINGSPAN     EGGS
---------- ------------------------------ ---------- ---------- ---------- --------
         1 Great Blue Heron                       52        5.5         78        5
         3 Common Loon                            36         18         54        2
         4 Bald Eagle                             37         14         84        2
         5 Golden Eagle                           40         15         90        3
         7 Osprey                                 24          3         72        4
         9 Canadian Goose                         43         14         72       10
        13 Ring-billed Gull                       19        1.1         50        4
        14 Double-crested Cormorant               33        5.5         54        4
        16 Turkey Vulture                         32        3.3         72        2
        19 Mute Swan                              60         26       94.8        8
        20 Brown Pelican                          54        7.6         90        4
        21 Great Egret                            38        3.3       67.2        3

12 rows selected.
```

In the previous output from the BIG_BIRDS table, you can see that the number of records from the BIRDS table was reduced to 12. The BIG_BIRDS table also consists of fewer columns than the BIRDS table. Less data makes it easier to see the results as you make changes to this table and study the behavior of the ROLLBACK command.

Next, let's create a table called LOCATIONS2 that is based on the original locations table. This table has six records.

```
SQL> create table locations2 as
  2  select * from locations;

Table created.

SQL> select * from locations2;

LOCATION_ID LOCATION_NAME
----------- ------------------------------
          3 Eagle Creek
          6 Fort Lauderdale Beach
          1 Heron Lake
          2 Loon Creek
          5 Sarasota Bridge
          4 White River

6 rows selected.
```

After you create the two tables, you issue a ROLLBACK command. However, you can see that all records still exist in the LOCATIONS2 table that was created prior to the rollback. The ROLLBACK did not undo that transaction because the command issued before the ROLLBACK was a data definition command. COMMIT and ROLLBACK commands apply to Data Manipulation Language, not Data Definition Language.

```
SQL> rollback;

Rollback complete.

SQL> select * from locations2;

LOCATION_ID LOCATION_NAME
----------- ------------------------------
          3 Eagle Creek
          6 Fort Lauderdale Beach
          1 Heron Lake
          2 Loon Creek
          5 Sarasota Bridge
          4 White River

6 rows selected.
```

Next, you insert a new row of data into the LOCATIONS2 table for Lake Michigan. The following query verifies that a new row of data was successfully inserted into the table:

```
SQL> insert into locations2
  2  values (7, 'Lake Michigan');

1 row created.

SQL> select * from locations2;

LOCATION_ID LOCATION_NAME
----------- ------------------------------
          3 Eagle Creek
          6 Fort Lauderdale Beach
          1 Heron Lake
          7 Lake Michigan
          2 Loon Creek
          5 Sarasota Bridge
          4 White River

7 rows selected.
```

Next, you issue the COMMIT command to save the previous transaction to the database:

```
SQL> commit;

Commit complete.
```

Now you can insert another row of data into the LOCATIONS2 table for the Gulf of Mexico. The query that follows shows that the Gulf of Mexico was successfully added and the previous entry for Lake Michigan is there as well:

```
SQL> insert into locations2
  2  values (8, 'Gulf of Mexico');

1 row created.
```

```
SQL> select * from locations2;
```

```
LOCATION_ID LOCATION_NAME
----------- ------------------------------
          3 Eagle Creek
          6 Fort Lauderdale Beach
          8 Gulf of Mexico
          1 Heron Lake
          7 Lake Michigan
          2 Loon Creek
          5 Sarasota Bridge
          4 White River

8 rows selected.
```

Now let's issue the ROLLBACK command and see what happens:

```
SQL> rollback;

Rollback complete.
```

In the results, the entry for Lake Michigan still exists in the LOCATIONS2 table, but the most recent record for the Gulf of Mexico is no longer there. The previous ROLLBACK command negated any transactions since the last COMMIT. Because a COMMIT command was issued after Lake Michigan was added to the table, the only transaction that was rolled back involved the entry of the Gulf of Mexico.

```
SQL> select * from locations;

LOCATION_ID LOCATION_NAME
----------- ------------------------------
          3 Eagle Creek
          6 Fort Lauderdale Beach
          1 Heron Lake
          7 Lake Michigan
          2 Loon Creek
          5 Sarasota Bridge
          4 White River

7 rows selected.
```

In the next example, let's delete Lake Michigan from the LOCATIONS2 table. The LOCATION_ID for Lake Michigan is 7, so you can simply refer to the LOCATION_ID of 7 in the DELETE statement that follows:

```
SQL> delete from locations
  2  where location_id = 7;

1 row deleted.
```

```
SQL> delete from locations;

6 rows deleted.
```

After deleting the record for Lake Michigan, you issue another DELETE statement to delete the remaining rows of data from the LOCATIONS2 table. The following query shows that no rows exist any longer in the LOCATIONS2 table:

```
SQL> select * from locations;

no rows selected
```

Finally, let's issue another ROLLBACK command and perform a query from the LOCATIONS2 table. Take a minute to study the results:

```
SQL> rollback;

Rollback complete.

SQL> select * from locations;

LOCATION_ID LOCATION_NAME
----------- ------------------------------
          3 Eagle Creek
          6 Fort Lauderdale Beach
          1 Heron Lake
          7 Lake Michigan
          2 Loon Creek
          5 Sarasota Bridge
          4 White River

7 rows selected.
```

The previous ROLLBACK command rolled back, or undid, all transactions since the last COMMIT. This includes both previous DELETE statements. Because no COMMIT commands were issued, all rows that were deleted remain in the LOCATIONS2 table.

The SAVEPOINT Command

A *savepoint* is a point in a transaction where you can roll back the transaction without rolling back the entire transaction.

The syntax for the SAVEPOINT command follows:

```
savepoint savepoint_name
```

This command serves only to create a savepoint among transactional statements. The ROLLBACK command undoes a group of transactions. The savepoint is a way of managing transactions by breaking large numbers of transactions into smaller, more manageable groups.

Microsoft SQL Server uses a slightly different syntax. In SQL Server, you use the statement SAVE TRANSACTION instead of SAVEPOINT, as shown in the following statement:

```
save transaction savepoint_name
```

Otherwise, the procedure works exactly the same as in the other implementations.

The ROLLBACK TO SAVEPOINT Command

The syntax for rolling back to a savepoint follows:

```
ROLLBACK TO SAVEPOINT_NAME;
```

In this example, you are working with the BIG_BIRDS table again. Review the table data:

```
SQL> select * from big_birds;

   BIRD_ID BIRD_NAME                          HEIGHT     WEIGHT   WINGSPAN       EGGS
---------- ------------------------------ ---------- ---------- ---------- ----------
         1 Great Blue Heron                       52        5.5         78          5
         3 Common Loon                            36         18         54          2
         4 Bald Eagle                             37         14         84          2
         5 Golden Eagle                           40         15         90          3
         7 Osprey                                 24          3         72          4
         9 Canadian Goose                         43         14         72         10
        13 Ring-billed Gull                       19        1.1         50          4
        14 Double-crested Cormorant               33        5.5         54          4
        16 Turkey Vulture                         32        3.3         72          2
        19 Mute Swan                              60         26       94.8          8
        20 Brown Pelican                          54        7.6         90          4
        21 Great Egret                            38        3.3       67.2          3

12 rows selected.
```

This table has 12 records. Next, the DELETE statement is issued to delete the row of data from BIG_BIRDS corresponding to Great Blue Heron. The following result provides feedback that one row of data was deleted from the table:

```
SQL> delete from big_birds
  2  where bird_name = 'Great Blue Heron';

1 row deleted.
```

Next, you create a SAVEPOINT to create a reference point within this transaction as a whole. The following feedback indicates that the SAVEPOINT was successfully created:

```
SQL> savepoint sp1;

Savepoint created.
```

Now you delete the record from the BIG_BIRDS table that corresponds to the BIRD_NAME of Bald Eagle and create a SAVEPOINT called SP2 after that DELETE statement. After that DELETE, you also update the BIG_BIRDS table and set the value for the EGGS column to 20 for every row of data in that table. As you can see, this affects 10 rows. A SAVEPOINT was also created after that update, called SP3.

```
SQL> delete from big_birds
  2  where bird_name = 'Bald Eagle';

1 row deleted.

SQL> savepoint sp2;

Savepoint created.

SQL> update big_birds
  2  set eggs = 0;

10 rows updated.

SQL> savepoint sp3
  2  ;

Savepoint created.
```

NOTE

SAVEPOINT Names Must Be Unique

A savepoint's name must be unique to the associated group of transactions. However, it can have the same name as a table or other object. Refer to your specific implementation documentation for more details on naming conventions. Otherwise, savepoint names are a matter of personal preference and are used by the database application developer to manage groups of transactions.

Now that the three deletions have taken place, let's say that you change your mind and decide to issue a ROLLBACK command to the savepoint that you identify as SP2. Because SP2 was created after the first deletion, the last two deletions are undone. In Oracle, you use the following syntax:

```
ROLLBACK TO sp2;
Rollback complete.
```

In SQL Server, you use the following syntax:

```
ROLLBACK TRANSACTION sp2;
Command(s) completed successfully.
```

Now you can apply the syntax of the ROLLBACK to a SAVEPOINT to the previous examples in which you created three different SAVEPOINTS after deleting and updating rows of data in the BIG_BIRDS table. First, you query the BIG_BIRDS table to review the data that was affected. You can see that the records for Great Blue Heron and Bald Eagle are no longer in the BIG_BIRDS table. Also notice that every value in the EGGS column has been updated to zero.

```
SQL> select * from big_birds;

  BIRD_ID BIRD_NAME                          HEIGHT     WEIGHT   WINGSPAN     EGGS
---------- ------------------------------ ---------- ---------- ---------- --------
         3 Common Loon                           36         18         54        0
         5 Golden Eagle                          40         15         90        0
         7 Osprey                                24          3         72        0
         9 Canadian Goose                        43         14         72        0
        13 Ring-billed Gull                      19        1.1         50        0
        14 Double-crested Cormorant              33        5.5         54        0
        16 Turkey Vulture                        32        3.3         72        0
        19 Mute Swan                             60         26       94.8        0
        20 Brown Pelican                         54        7.6         90        0
        21 Great Egret                           38        3.3       67.2        0

10 rows selected.
```

Let's issue the ROLLBACK command back to SAVEPOINT SP2. SP2 was a SAVEPOINT created after both the Great Blue Heron and Bald Eagle records were removed, but before the value of every row of data in the EGGS column was set to zero. Therefore, the only transaction rolled back is the update to the EGGS column. You can still see in the output of the following SELECT statement that the Great Blue Heron and Bald Eagle records still no longer exist in that table:

```
SQL> rollback to sp2;

Rollback complete.

SQL> select * from big_birds;

  BIRD_ID BIRD_NAME                          HEIGHT     WEIGHT   WINGSPAN     EGGS
---------- ------------------------------ ---------- ---------- ---------- --------
         3 Common Loon                           36         18         54        2
         5 Golden Eagle                          40         15         90        3
         7 Osprey                                24          3         72        4
         9 Canadian Goose                        43         14         72       10
        13 Ring-billed Gull                      19        1.1         50        4
        14 Double-crested Cormorant              33        5.5         54        4
```

```
        16 Turkey Vulture                         32         3.3         72          2
        19 Mute Swan                              60          26       94.8          8
        20 Brown Pelican                          54         7.6         90          4
        21 Great Egret                            38         3.3       67.2          3

10 rows selected.
```

Let's issue a basic ROLLBACK command to see what happens. Take a minute to examine the following output from the query of the BIG_BIRDS table:

```
SQL> rollback;

Rollback complete.

SQL> select * from big_birds;

   BIRD_ID BIRD_NAME                          HEIGHT     WEIGHT   WINGSPAN     EGGS
---------- ------------------------------ ---------- ---------- ---------- --------
         1 Great Blue Heron                       52        5.5         78        5
         3 Common Loon                            36         18         54        2
         4 Bald Eagle                             37         14         84        2
         5 Golden Eagle                           40         15         90        3
         7 Osprey                                 24          3         72        4
         9 Canadian Goose                         43         14         72       10
        13 Ring-billed Gull                       19        1.1         50        4
        14 Double-crested Cormorant               33        5.5         54        4
        16 Turkey Vulture                         32        3.3         72        2
        19 Mute Swan                              60         26       94.8        8
        20 Brown Pelican                          54        7.6         90        4
        21 Great Egret                            38        3.3       67.2        3

12 rows selected.
```

After reviewing the output, you can see that the Great Blue Heron and Bald Eagle entries are both back in the BIG_BIRDS table. The ROLLBACK worked in this situation because a COMMIT was never performed after those records were deleted; the ROLLBACK thus negated any transactions that occurred since the last COMMIT.

Remember, the ROLLBACK command by itself rolls back to the last COMMIT or ROLLBACK statement.

The RELEASE SAVEPOINT Command

The RELEASE SAVEPOINT command removes a savepoint that you have created. After a savepoint has been released, you can no longer use the ROLLBACK command to undo transactions performed since the savepoint. You might want to issue a RELEASE SAVEPOINT command to avoid an accidental rollback to a savepoint that is no longer needed:

```
RELEASE SAVEPOINT savepoint_name;
```

Microsoft SQL Server does not support the RELEASE SAVEPOINT syntax; instead, all SAVEPOINTs are released when the transaction is completed, either by the COMMIT or the ROLLBACK of the transaction. Remember this point when you structure your transactions within your environment.

The SET TRANSACTION Command

You can use the SET TRANSACTION command to initiate a database transaction. This command specifies characteristics for the transaction that follows. For example, you can specify a transaction to be read-only or read/write:

```
SET TRANSACTION READ WRITE;
SET TRANSACTION READ ONLY;
```

READ WRITE is used for transactions that are allowed to query and manipulate data in the database. READ ONLY is used for transactions that require query-only access. READ ONLY is useful for generating reports and increasing the speed at which transactions are accomplished. If a transaction is READ WRITE, the database must create locks on database objects to maintain data integrity if multiple transactions are happening concurrently. If a transaction is READ ONLY, no locks are established by the database, thereby improving transaction performance.

Dealing with Poor Transactional Control

Poor transactional control can hurt database performance and even bring the database to a halt. Repeated poor database performance might result from a lack of transactional control during large inserts, updates, or deletes. Large batch processes also cause temporary storage for rollback information to grow until either a COMMIT or a ROLLBACK command is issued.

When a COMMIT is issued, rollback transactional information is written to the target table and the rollback information in temporary storage is cleared. When a ROLLBACK is issued, no changes are made to the database and the rollback information in the temporary storage is cleared. If neither a COMMIT nor ROLLBACK is issued, the temporary storage for rollback information continues to grow until no more space is left, thus forcing the database to stop all processes until space is freed. Although the database administrator (DBA) ultimately controls space usage, a lack of transactional control can still cause database processing to stop, sometimes forcing the DBA to take action that involves killing running user processes.

Summary

During this hour, you learned the preliminary concepts of transactional management through the use of three transactional control commands: COMMIT, ROLLBACK, and SAVEPOINT. You use COMMIT to save a transaction to the database. You use ROLLBACK to undo a transaction you performed. You use SAVEPOINT to break a transaction or transactions into groups, which enables you to roll back to specific logical points in transaction processing.

Remember that you should frequently use the COMMIT and ROLLBACK commands when running large transactional jobs, to keep space free in the database. Also keep in mind that these transactional commands are used only with the three DML commands (INSERT, UPDATE, and DELETE).

Q&A

Q. Is it necessary to issue a commit after every `INSERT` statement?

A. No, absolutely not. Some systems, such as SQL Server, automatically issue a commit after your `INSERT` statement. However, if you have large inserts or updates, you might consider doing them in batches; large updates to tables can negatively affect performance.

Q. How does the `ROLLBACK` command undo a transaction?

A. The ROLLBACK command clears all changes from the rollback area.

Q. If I issue a transaction and 99% of the transaction completes but the other 1% errs, can I redo only the error part?

A. No, the entire transaction must succeed; otherwise, data integrity is compromised. Therefore, you should always perform a `ROLLBACK` on an error unless there is a compelling reason not to.

Q. A transaction is permanent after I issue a `COMMIT`, but can I change data with an `UPDATE` command?

A. The word ***permanent*** in this case means that it is now a part of the database. You can always use the `UPDATE` statement to make modifications or corrections to the data.

Workshop

The following workshop consists of a series of quiz questions and practical exercises. The quiz questions are designed to test your overall understanding of the current material. The practical exercises give you the opportunity to apply the concepts discussed during the current hour, as well as build on the knowledge you acquired in previous hours of study. Be sure to complete the quiz questions and exercises before continuing to the next hour. Refer to Appendix C, "Answers to Quizzes and Exercises," for answers.

Quiz

1. True or false: If you have committed several transactions, you have several more transactions that have not been committed, and you issue a `ROLLBACK` command, all your transactions for the same session are undone.
2. True or false: A `SAVEPOINT` or `SAVE TRANSACTION` command saves transactions after a specified number of transactions have executed.
3. Briefly describe the purpose of each one of the following commands: `COMMIT`, `ROLLBACK`, and `SAVEPOINT`.
4. What are some differences in the implementation of transactions in Microsoft SQL Server?

5. What are some performance implications when using transactions?
6. When using several SAVEPOINT or SAVE TRANSACTION commands, can you roll back more than one?

Exercises

1. For the following exercises, create the following tables based on the BIRDS database:
   A. Use the SQL statement CREATE TABLE *table_name* AS SELECT... to create a table called BIG_BIRDS that is based on the original BIRDS table. Include only the following columns in the BIG_BIRDS table: BIRD_ID, BIRD_NAME, HEIGHT, WEIGHT, and WINGSPAN. Use the WHERE clause to include only records for birds that have a wingspan greater than 48 inches.
   B. Create a table called LOCATIONS2 that is based on the original LOCATIONS table.
2. Write a simple query to display all records in the BIG_BIRDS table, to familiarize yourself with the data.
3. Write a simple query to display all records in the LOCATIONS2 table, to familiarize yourself with the data.
4. Modify the BIG_BIRDS table to change the name of the column WINGSPAN to AVG_WINGSPAN.
5. Manually compute the average wingspan of birds in the BIG_BIRDS table, and use the UPDATE statement to update the value of all birds' wingspans to the average wingspan value that you calculated.
6. Issue the ROLLBACK command.
7. Query all data in the BIG_BIRDS table using the SELECT statement. You should see in the output from the query that all the values for WINGSPAN have been restored to their original values; however, the name of the column is still the updated value of AVG_WINGSPAN.
8. Why did the ROLLBACK negate the update to data values in the AVG_WINGSPAN column, but not the UPDATE TABLE statement to rename the WINGSPAN column?
9. Insert a new row of data into the LOCATIONS2 table for a location called Lake Tahoe.
10. Issue the COMMIT command.
11. Query the LOCATIONS2 table to verify the changes you made.
12. Insert another new row of data into the LOCATIONS2 table for a location of Atlantic Ocean.
13. Create a SAVEPOINT called SP1.
14. Update the value of Atlantic Ocean to Pacific Ocean.
15. Create a SAVEPOINT called SP2.

16. Update the value of Lake Tahoe that you previously added to Lake Erie.
17. Create a SAVEPOINT called SP3.
18. Issue the ROLLBACK command back to SAVEPOINT SP2.
19. Query the LOCATIONS2 table and study the behavior of the ROLLBACK command to SAVEPOINT.
20. Get creative with some transactions of your own on these two tables. Remember that these tables are copies of the original tables, so anything you do should not affect the original data. Also remember that, at any point during your progression through this book, you can rerun the scripts provided called tables.sql and, subsequently, data.sql to restore your tables and the data for the BIRDS database back to its original state.

HOUR 12

Introduction to Database Queries

What You'll Learn in This Hour:

- Defining a database query
- Using the SELECT statement
- Adding conditions to queries using the WHERE clause
- Using column aliases
- Selecting data from another user's table

In this hour, you learn about database queries, which involve using the SELECT statement. The SELECT statement is the most frequently used of all SQL commands after a database is created. The SELECT statement enables you to view data that is stored in the database.

Using the SELECT Statement

The SELECT statement, which is known as the Data Query Language (DQL) command, is the basic statement used to construct database queries. A *query* is an inquiry into the database to extract data from the database in a readable format according to the user's request. For instance, in the sample database, you have the BIRDS table. You might issue a SQL statement that returns the smallest bird in the database based on columns such as WINGSPAN, HEIGHT, and WEIGHT. This request to the database for usable bird information is a typical query that can be performed in a relational database.

The SELECT statement is by far one of the most powerful statements in SQL. The SELECT statement is not a standalone statement; one or more additional clauses (elements) are required for a syntactically correct query. In addition, optional clauses increase the overall functionality of the SELECT statement. The FROM clause is a mandatory clause and must always be used with the SELECT statement.

Four keywords, or *clauses*, are valuable parts of a `SELECT` statement:

- `SELECT`
- `FROM`
- `WHERE`
- `ORDER BY`

Each of these clauses is covered in detail in the following sections.

The capability to effectively and simply retrieve useful data is what SQL and the relational database are all about. Writing SQL queries is simple. Queries allow for fast retrieval of data, they are powerful, and they enable you to easily view deeper perspectives of the data within your database. Writing queries in SQL is very English-like, or language-like. For example, consider these examples of questions a user might ask to get useful information from the `BIRDS` database:

- How many types of birds are in the database?
- Which bird has the most diverse diet?
- Which is the largest bird?
- Which birds have a wingspan that is greater than average?
- In which species of birds do both males and females contribute to building the nest?
- List all birds in order of their size.
- Which bird spends the most total time with its young?
- What percentage of birds eat fish?
- Which birds are "big" (very subjective)?

SQL makes it easy to communicate with a relational database to ask questions such as these and get useful information back.

Understanding the SELECT Clause

The `SELECT` statement is used with the `FROM` clause to extract data from the database in an organized, readable format. The `SELECT` clause of the query is used to select the data you want to see, according to the columns in which they are stored in a table.

The syntax for a simple SELECT statement follows:

```
SELECT [ * | ALL | DISTINCT COLUMN1, COLUMN2 ]
FROM TABLE1 [ , TABLE2 ];
```

The SELECT clause in a query is followed by a comma-delimited list of column names that you want displayed as part of the query output. The asterisk (*) denotes that all columns in a table should display as part of the output. Check your particular implementation for its usage. The ALL option displays all values for a column, including duplicates. The DISTINCT option suppresses duplicate rows from displaying in the output. The ALL option is an inferred option; think of it as the default—therefore, it does not necessarily need to be used in the SELECT statement. The FROM keyword is followed by a list of one or more tables from which you want to select data. Notice that the columns following the SELECT clause are separated by commas, as is the table list following the FROM clause.

NOTE

Constructing Lists

Commas separate arguments in a list in SQL statements. ***Arguments*** are values that are either required or optional to the syntax of a SQL statement or command. Some common lists include lists of columns in a query, lists of tables to be selected from in a query, values to be inserted into a table, and values grouped as a condition in a query's WHERE clause.

First, you create two tables here based on the BIRDS table. This is the same syntax that was introduced previously in this book. The first table, called BIG_BIRDS, lists all data about birds whose WINGSPAN is greater than 48 inches. The second table, SMALL_BIRDS, is also based on the BIRDS table and includes any bird that has a WINGSPAN less than or equal to 48 inches. These two tables are used for two reasons. One reason is simply for readability; the BIRDS table has a lot of columns that would wrap on the page in this book. The second reason is to show you how to separate data and categorize it, or look at it differently, as you begin to query a database.

```
SQL> create table big_birds as
  2  select * from birds
  3  where wingspan > 48;

Table created.

SQL> create table small_birds as
  2  select * from birds
  3  where wingspan <= 48;

Table created.
```

Now let's perform a simple query from the BIG_BIRDS table to show all records, or rows of data, in that new table. Following that output are the data results from a query showing all records from the SMALL_BIRDS table.

```
SQL> select * from big_birds;

   BIRD_ID BIRD_NAME                          HEIGHT     WEIGHT   WINGSPAN
---------- ------------------------------ ---------- ---------- ----------
         1 Great Blue Heron                       52        5.5         78
         3 Common Loon                            36         18         54
         4 Bald Eagle                             37         14         84
         5 Golden Eagle                           40         15         90
         7 Osprey                                 24          3         72
         9 Canadian Goose                         43         14         72
        13 Ring-billed Gull                       19        1.1         50
        14 Double-crested Cormorant               33        5.5         54
        16 Turkey Vulture                         32        3.3         72
        19 Mute Swan                              60         26       94.8
        20 Brown Pelican                          54        7.6         90
        21 Great Egret                            38        3.3       67.2

12 rows selected.

SQL> select * from small_birds;

   BIRD_ID BIRD_NAME                          HEIGHT     WEIGHT   WINGSPAN
---------- ------------------------------ ---------- ---------- ----------
         2 Mallard                                28        3.5        3.2
         6 Red Tailed Hawk                        25        2.4         48
         8 Belted Kingfisher                      13        .33         23
        10 Pied-billed Grebe                      13          1        6.5
        11 American Coot                          16          1         29
        12 Common Sea Gull                        18          1         18
        15 Common Merganser                       27        3.2         34
        17 American Crow                          18        1.4       39.6
        18 Green Heron                            22         .4       26.8
        22 Anhinga                                35        2.4         42
        23 Black Skimmer                          20          1         15

11 rows selected.
```

Notice that, between the two queries, 23 rows of data are returned. The BIRDS table itself has 23 rows of data, or 23 distinct birds, in the database. Therefore, based on the criteria of these two CREATE TABLE statements, all 23 rows of data should be returned from the BIRDS table itself. The first query in the CREATE TABLE statement looks for any birds that have a wingspan greater than 48 inches. The second CREATE TABLE statement looks for birds that have a wingspan of less than or equal to 48 inches in length.

The asterisk represents all columns in the table. Each column in the output displays in the order that it appears in the table. This table has 23 records, identified by the feedback (12 rows selected and 11 rows selected). This feedback message differs among implementations; for example, another feedback for the same query might be 14 rows affected. Although the asterisk is a helpful piece of shorthand when writing SQL queries, some people consider it best practice to explicitly name the columns that you are returning.

Selecting DISTINCT Values from a Table

A table can have thousands or millions of rows of data. Sometimes you need to see only distinct or unique values. SQL provides a DISTINCT keyword, or function, that can be used in a query to show only the distinct or unique values within a column of a table. The following example shows a query that returns only the distinct values of the NEST_BUILDER column from the BIRDS table. The NEST_BUILDER column in the BIRDS table is a one-character code that represents male and female birds: F for female, M for male, or N for neither.

```
SQL> select distinct nest_builder
  2  from birds;

N
-
B
F
N

3 rows selected.
```

You can also use DISTINCT with parentheses enclosing the associated column, as follows. Parentheses are often used in SQL—as well as many other languages—to improve readability. In the following examples, you select the distinct number of broods from the BIRDS table for a bird. The number of broods represents the number of times birds lay eggs within a season or a year. The first query shows the same results as the first query. The only difference is that the column name is enclosed by parentheses, which is optional in most cases and assists in readability.

```
SQL> select distinct broods
  2  from birds;

    BROODS
----------
         1
         2
```

```
2 rows selected.


SQL> select distinct(broods)
  2  from birds;

    BROODS
----------
         1
         2

2 rows selected.
```

Understanding the FROM Clause

The FROM clause must be used with the SELECT statement. It is a required element for any query. The purpose of the FROM clause is to tell the database what table(s) to access to retrieve the wanted data for the query. The FROM clause may contain one or more tables. The FROM clause must always list at least one table.

The syntax for the FROM clause follows:

```
from table1 [ , table2 ]
```

Understanding the WHERE Clause

A *condition* is part of a query that displays selective information as specified by the user. The value of a condition is either TRUE or FALSE, thereby limiting the data received from the query. The WHERE clause places conditions on a query by eliminating rows that would normally be returned by a query without conditions.

You can have more than one condition in the WHERE clause. If more than one condition exists, the conditions connect by the AND and OR operators, which are discussed during Hour 13, "Using Operators to Categorize Data." As you also learn during the next hour, several conditional operators enable you to specify conditions in a query. This hour deals with only a single condition for each query.

An *operator* is a character or keyword in SQL that combines elements in a SQL statement.

The syntax for the WHERE clause follows:

```
select [ all | * | distinct column1, column2 ]
from table1 [ , table2 ]
where [ condition1 | expression1 ]
[ and|OR condition2 | expression2 ]
```

The following example queries the BIRDS table to show only the BIRD_ID and the BIRD_NAME, but only for birds whose BIRD_NAME is equal to Great Blue Heron.

```
SQL> select bird_id, bird_name
  2  from birds
  3  where bird_name = 'Great Blue Heron';

   BIRD_ID BIRD_NAME
---------- ------------------------------
         1 Great Blue Heron

1 row selected.
```

The following example uses the BIRD_ID that was obtained from the previous query to select all the nicknames associated with the Great Blue Heron, or any bird that has a BIRD_ID of 1. This is a manual way of selecting data from two tables. Getting information from two tables (joining tables) is discussed in great deal in Hour 14, "Joining Tables in Queries." In this example, the Great Blue Heron has two nicknames stored in the database, Big Cranky and Blue Crane.

```
SQL> select nickname
  2  from nicknames
  3  where bird_id = 1;

NICKNAME
------------------------------
Big Cranky
Blue Crane

2 rows selected.
```

Sometimes when querying the database, you are searching not for equality but for potential multiple records. The following example produces a list of birds that have wingspan of greater than 48 inches. Again, this is a similar query used to create a table called BIG_BIRDS that has a subset of data from the main BIRDS table.

```
SQL> select bird_name, height, weight, wingspan
  2  from birds
  3  where wingspan > 48;

BIRD_NAME                          HEIGHT     WEIGHT   WINGSPAN
------------------------------ ---------- ---------- ----------
Great Blue Heron                       52        5.5         78
Common Loon                            36         18         54
Bald Eagle                             37         14         84
Golden Eagle                           40         15         90
Osprey                                 24          3         72
Canadian Goose                         43         14         72
Ring-billed Gull                       19        1.1         50
```

```
Double-crested Cormorant                 33       5.5        54
Turkey Vulture                           32       3.3        72
Mute Swan                                60        26      94.8
Brown Pelican                            54       7.6        90
Great Egret                              38       3.3      67.2

12 rows selected.
```

NOTE

Conditions in a Query

Conditions do not always have to be exact matches of exact terms. Sometimes you want a range of values, as you see in the previous query. There you want to see only birds that have wingspan greater than 48 inches. This is actually the same query used previously to create a table called `BIG_BIRDS`, based on the `BIRDS` table.

The following example shows two queries. The first query returns a list of birds that lay exactly five eggs. The second query returns a list of birds that lay more than five eggs.

```
SQL> select bird_name, eggs
  2  from birds
  3  where eggs = 5;

BIRD_NAME                            EGGS
------------------------------ ----------
Great Blue Heron                        5
Black Skimmer                           5

2 rows selected.

SQL> select bird_name, eggs
  2  from birds
  3  where eggs > 5;

BIRD_NAME                            EGGS
------------------------------ ----------
Mallard                                10
Belted Kingfisher                       7
Canadian Goose                         10
Pied-billed Grebe                       7
American Coot                          12
Common Merganser                       11
American Crow                           6
Mute Swan                               8

8 rows selected.
```

Understanding the ORDER BY Clause

You usually want your output to have some kind of order. Data can be sorted using the ORDER BY clause, which arranges the results of a query in a listing format that you specify. The default ordering of the ORDER BY clause is *ascending order*; the sort displays in the order A–Z if it is sorting output names alphabetically. *Descending order* for alphabetical output is displayed in the order Z–A. Ascending order for output for numeric values between 1 and 9 is displayed as 1–9; descending order is displayed as 9–1.

The syntax for the ORDER BY clause follows:

```
select [ all | * | distinct column1, column2 ]
from table1 [ , table2 ]
where [ condition1 | expression1 ]
[ and|OR condition2 | expression2 ]
ORDER BY column1|integer [ ASC|DESC ]
```

You begin your exploration of the ORDER BY clause here with an extension of one of the previous statements. Suppose that you want to see a list of birds and their associated wingspans from the BIRDS table for birds whose wingspan is greater than 40 inches, but we want to order it by the WINGSPAN column. By default, the ORDER BY clause orders from least to greatest—in other words, from 0 to 10 or from A to Z. In this example, then, birds with the smallest wingspan are listed first, up to the birds with the greatest wingspan.

```
SQL> select bird_name, wingspan
  2  from birds
  3  where wingspan > 48
  4  order by wingspan;

BIRD_NAME                        WINGSPAN
------------------------------ ----------
Ring-billed Gull                       50
Double-crested Cormorant               54
Common Loon                            54
Great Egret                          67.2
Osprey                                 72
Canadian Goose                         72
Turkey Vulture                         72
Great Blue Heron                       78
Bald Eagle                             84
Brown Pelican                          90
Golden Eagle                           90
Mute Swan                            94.8

12 rows selected.
```

NOTE

Rules for Sorting

SQL sorts are ASCII, character-based sorts. The numeric values 0–9 are sorted as character values and are sorted before the characters A–Z. Because numeric values are treated like characters during a sort, an example list of numeric values is sorted in the following order: 1, 12, 2, 255, 3.

You can use DESC, as in the following statement, if you want the same output to be sorted in reverse alphabetical order, or descending order. This example works exactly the same as the previous one, except that you sort the results from the query to show the birds with the greatest wingspan first, all the way down to the birds with the smallest wingspan. Thus, here you show the bigger birds first in the result set.

```
SQL> select bird_name, wingspan
  2  from birds
  3  where wingspan > 48
  4  order by wingspan desc;

BIRD_NAME                       WINGSPAN
------------------------------ ----------
Mute Swan                           94.8
Brown Pelican                         90
Golden Eagle                          90
Bald Eagle                            84
Great Blue Heron                      78
Osprey                                72
Canadian Goose                        72
Turkey Vulture                        72
Great Egret                         67.2
Common Loon                           54
Double-crested Cormorant              54
Ring-billed Gull                      50

12 rows selected.
```

TIP

There Is a Default for Ordering

Because ascending order for output is the default, you do not have to specify ASC.

Shortcuts do exist in SQL. A column listed in the ORDER BY clause can be abbreviated with an integer. An *integer* is a substitution for the actual column name (an alias, for the purpose of the sort operation), identifying the position of the column after the SELECT keyword.

An example of using an integer as an identifier in the ORDER BY clause follows:

```
SQL> select bird_name, wingspan
  2  from birds
  3  where wingspan > 48
  4  order by 1;

BIRD_NAME                        WINGSPAN
------------------------------ ----------
Bald Eagle                             84
Brown Pelican                          90
Canadian Goose                         72
Common Loon                            54
Double-crested Cormorant               54
Golden Eagle                           90
Great Blue Heron                       78
Great Egret                          67.2
Mute Swan                            94.8
Osprey                                 72
Ring-billed Gull                       50
Turkey Vulture                         72

12 rows selected.
```

In this query, the integer 1 represents the column BIRD_NAME, and 2 theoretically represents the WINGSPAN column.

You can order by multiple columns in a query, using either the column name or the associated number of the column in the SELECT:

```
ORDER BY 1,2,3
```

Columns in an ORDER BY clause are not required to appear in the same order as the associated columns following the SELECT, as the following example shows:

```
ORDER BY 1,3,2
```

The order in which the columns are specified within the ORDER BY clause is the manner in which the ordering process is done. The following statement orders first by the LASTNAME column and then by the FIRSTNAME column:

```
ORDER BY BIRD_NAME,NICKNAME
```

Case Sensitivity

Case sensitivity is an important concept to understand when coding with SQL. Typically, SQL commands and keywords are not case sensitive, which enables you to enter your commands and keywords in either upper or lower case, as you prefer. The case may also be mixed (both upper and lower case for a single word or statement), which is often referred to as *CamelCase*. See Hour 10, "Manipulating Data," for more on case sensitivity.

Collation is the mechanism that determines how the relational database management system (RDBMS) interprets data. This includes methods of ordering the data, as well as case sensitivity. Case sensitivity in your data is important because it determines how your `WHERE` clauses, among other components, interpret matches. Check with your specific RDBMS implementation to determine the default collation on your system. Some systems, such as MySQL and Microsoft SQL Server, have a default collation that is not case sensitive; this means that it matches strings without considering their case. Other systems, such as Oracle, have a default collation that is case sensitive; this means that strings are matched with case taken into account. Because case sensitivity is a factor at the database level, its importance as a factor in your queries varies.

CAUTION

Use a Standard Case in Your Queries

It is a good practice to use the same case in your query as the data that is stored in your database. Moreover, good corporate policy ensures that data entry is handled in the same manner across an enterprise.

Case sensitivity is a factor in maintaining data consistency within your RDBMS. For instance, your data is not consistent if you arbitrarily enter your data using random case:

- `BALD EAGLE`
- `Bald Eagle`
- `bald eagle`

In the `BIRDS` database, data is stored in mixed case. This is a matter of preference and can vary between different databases—for that matter, your own preference can vary. In the `BIRDS` database, the value for `Bald Eagle` is stored as `Bald Eagle`. With that in mind, review the following queries and the output of the queries; make sure you understand why rows are returned in some instances and no rows are returned in other instances because of the specific data (including case) being searched for within the query.

```
SQL> select bird_name
  2  from birds
  3  where bird_name = 'BALD EAGLE';

no rows selected

SQL> select bird_name
  2  from birds
  3  where bird_name = 'bald eagle';
```

```
no rows selected

SQL> select bird_name
  2  from birds
  3  where bird_name = 'Bald Eagle';

BIRD_NAME
------------------------------
Bald Eagle

1 row selected.

SQL> SELECT BIRD_NAME
  2  FROM BIRDS
  3  WHERE BIRD_NAME = 'Bald Eagle';

BIRD_NAME
------------------------------
Bald Eagle

1 row selected.
```

Fundamentals of Query Writing

This section provides several examples of queries based on the concepts that have already been discussed. It begins with the simplest query you can issue and progressively builds upon the initial query. All queries use the `BIRDS` table.

Select all records from the `FOOD` table and display all columns:

```
SQL> select * from food;

   FOOD_ID FOOD_NAME
---------- ------------------------------
         1 Seeds
         2 Birds
         3 Fruit
         4 Frogs
         5 Fish
         6 Berries
         7 Aquatic Plants
         8 Aquatic Insects
         9 Worms
        10 Nuts
        11 Rodents
        12 Snakes
        13 Small Mammals
```

```
        14 Nectar
        15 Pollen
        16 Carrion
        17 Moths
        18 Ducks
        19 Insects
        20 Plants
        21 Corn
        22 Crayfish
        23 Crustaceans
        24 Reptiles
        25 Deer

25 rows selected.
```

Select the BIRD_ID, BIRD_NAME, and HEIGHT from the BIRDS table for only birds that have a height greater than 50 inches. Sort the results by HEIGHT in ascending order, which is the default.

```
SQL> select bird_id, bird_name, height
  2  from birds
  3  where height > 50
  4  order by height;

   BIRD_ID BIRD_NAME                          HEIGHT
---------- ------------------------------ ----------
         1 Great Blue Heron                       52
        20 Brown Pelican                          54
        19 Mute Swan                              60

3 rows selected.
```

Create a report that shows the identification of the bird, the bird's name, the bird's wingspan, the height, and the weight of only birds that have a wingspan greater than 48 inches. Sort the results by the bird's wingspan first, then height and weight progressively.

```
SQL> select bird_id, bird_name, wingspan, height, weight
  2  from birds
  3  where wingspan > 48
  4  order by wingspan, height, weight;

   BIRD_ID BIRD_NAME                        WINGSPAN     HEIGHT     WEIGHT
---------- ------------------------------ ---------- ---------- ----------
        13 Ring-billed Gull                       50         19        1.1
        14 Double-crested Cormorant               54         33        5.5
         3 Common Loon                            54         36         18
        21 Great Egret                          67.2         38        3.3
         7 Osprey                                 72         24          3
        16 Turkey Vulture                         72         32        3.3
```

```
         9 Canadian Goose                              72         43         14
         1 Great Blue Heron                            78         52        5.5
         4 Bald Eagle                                  84         37         14
         5 Golden Eagle                                90         40         15
        20 Brown Pelican                               90         54        7.6
        19 Mute Swan                                 94.8         60         26

12 rows selected.
```

Perform the same query as the previous one, but sort the results by wingspan, height, and weight in descending order.

```
SQL> select bird_id, bird_name, wingspan, height, weight
  2  from birds
  3  where wingspan > 48
  4  order by wingspan desc, height desc, weight desc;

   BIRD_ID BIRD_NAME                        WINGSPAN     HEIGHT     WEIGHT
---------- ------------------------------ ---------- ---------- ----------
        19 Mute Swan                            94.8         60         26
        20 Brown Pelican                          90         54        7.6
         5 Golden Eagle                           90         40         15
         4 Bald Eagle                             84         37         14
         1 Great Blue Heron                       78         52        5.5
         9 Canadian Goose                         72         43         14
        16 Turkey Vulture                         72         32        3.3
         7 Osprey                                 72         24          3
        21 Great Egret                          67.2         38        3.3
         3 Common Loon                            54         36         18
        14 Double-crested Cormorant               54         33        5.5
        13 Ring-billed Gull                       50         19        1.1

12 rows selected.
```

Write a query that displays the bird identification, the bird name, the wingspan, the height, and the weight of all birds that have a wingspan greater than 40 inches, but sort the results according to the values in the columns of `WINGSPAN`, `HEIGHT`, and `WEIGHT` in progressive order using integers instead of the column name itself.

```
SQL> select bird_id, bird_name, wingspan, height, weight
  2  from birds
  3  where wingspan > 48
  4  order by 3, 4, 5;

   BIRD_ID BIRD_NAME                        WINGSPAN     HEIGHT     WEIGHT
---------- ------------------------------ ---------- ---------- ----------
        13 Ring-billed Gull                       50         19        1.1
        14 Double-crested Cormorant               54         33        5.5
```

```
  3 Common Loon                          54         36         18
 21 Great Egret                        67.2         38        3.3
  7 Osprey                               72         24          3
 16 Turkey Vulture                       72         32        3.3
  9 Canadian Goose                       72         43         14
  1 Great Blue Heron                     78         52        5.5
  4 Bald Eagle                           84         37         14
  5 Golden Eagle                         90         40         15
 20 Brown Pelican                        90         54        7.6
 19 Mute Swan                          94.8         60         26

12 rows selected.
```

CAUTION

Ensure That Your Queries Are Constrained

When you select all rows of data from a large table, the results might return a substantial amount of data. In highly transactional databases, this can slow performance not only for the query that is executed but also for the system. Use WHERE clauses whenever possible to work on the smallest subset of your data as possible, to limit the effect your query has on precious database resources.

Counting the Records in a Table

You can issue a simple query on a table to get a quick count of the number of records in the table or the number of values for a column in the table. A count is accomplished by the function COUNT. Although functions are not discussed until Hours 15 through 17, this function is introduced here because it is often part of one of the simplest queries you can create.

The syntax of the COUNT function follows:

```
SELECT COUNT(*)
FROM TABLE_NAME;
```

The COUNT function is used with parentheses, which enclose the target column or the asterisk to count all rows of data in the table.

TIP

Counting Basics

Counting the number of values for a column is the same as counting the number of records in a table if the column being counted is NOT NULL (a required column). However, COUNT(*) is typically used to count the number of rows for a table.

The following example is a query that provides a count of the number of birds stored in the BIRDS table.

```
SQL> select count(*) from birds;

  COUNT(*)
----------
        23

1 row selected.
```

The next query provides a count of the birds that have an entry for the WINGSPAN column, which is an optional column, in the BIRDS table. In this situation, every bird in the database has an entry for WINGSPAN, even though it is optional.

```
SQL> select count(wingspan) from birds;

COUNT(WINGSPAN)
---------------
             23

1 row selected.
```

The following example is the same as the first example; it provides a count of the birds in the BIRDS table. The only characteristic that makes this example different is that it specifies the column name of BIRD_ID (which happens to be a primary key and thus is a required column) instead of using the asterisk (*), which represents every row of data in the table. Again, the same output is derived in this situation.

```
SQL> select count(bird_id) from birds;

COUNT(BIRD_ID)
--------------
            23

1 row selected.
```

The next query provides a count of the birds that have an entry for the WINGSPAN column, which is an optional column in the BIRDS table. In this situation, every bird in the database has an entry for WINGSPAN, even though it is optional.

This final example shows how to find out how many nicknames a specific bird has. In Hour 14, you learn how to easily join tables to get this information in a single query. This example demonstrates a manual, common-sense process for getting the same information and lays a foundation for better understanding table joins as you progress through your SQL journey.

Let's say that you want to find out how many nicknames are in the database for the Great Blue Heron. First, you perform the following query from the BIRDS table to get the BIRD_ID for the Great Blue Heron from the database. You do this because only the BIRD_ID itself is stored in the NICKNAMES table, not the BIRD_NAME itself.

```
SQL> select bird_id
  2  from birds
  3  where bird_name = 'Great Blue Heron';

   BIRD_ID
----------
         1
```

Finally, you write a simple query to select a count of the birds associated with the Great Blue Heron from the NICKNAMES table. This query produces a simple numeric value of 2, which represents the number of nicknames in the NICKNAMES table that are stored at this point for the Great Blue Heron. If you manually look at the data set in the BIRDS table, you can easily verify that the Great Blue Heron has two nicknames associated with it.

```
SQL> select count(bird_id)
  2  from nicknames
  3  where bird_id = 1;

COUNT(BIRD_ID)
--------------
             2

1 row selected.
```

Selecting Data from Another User's Table

Permission must be granted to a user to access another user's table. If no permission has been granted, access is not allowed. You can select data from another user's table after access has been granted. (Hour 20, "Creating and Using Views and Synonyms," discusses the GRANT command.) To access another user's table in a SELECT statement, precede the table name with the schema name or the username that owns (that is, created) the table, as in the following example:

```
SELECT BIRD_NAME
FROM another_user.BIRDS;
```

Using Column Aliases

Column aliases temporarily rename a table's columns for the purpose of a particular query. The following syntax illustrates the use of column aliases:

```
SELECT COLUMN_NAME ALIAS_NAME
FROM TABLE_NAME;
```

The following example is a simple query that shows the BIRD_NAME column. The literal string bird is used as a column alias, which you can see in the result set from the query. Notice that, by default (at least, within Oracle), the literal string of bird is converted to all upper case. Keep in mind that minor variations can occur between relational database implementations, but the concept is the same.

```
SQL> select bird_name bird
  2  from birds
  3  where wingspan > 48;

BIRD
------------------------------
Great Blue Heron
Common Loon
Bald Eagle
Golden Eagle
Osprey
Canadian Goose
Ring-billed Gull
Double-crested Cormorant
Turkey Vulture
Mute Swan
Brown Pelican
Great Egret

12 rows selected.
```

In Oracle, for example, if you want to create an alias that is more than one word, you simply use double quotation marks to identify the alias, as in the following example.

```
SQL> select bird_name "BIG BIRD"
  2  from birds
  3  where wingspan > 48;

BIG BIRD
------------------------------
Great Blue Heron
Common Loon
Bald Eagle
Golden Eagle
Osprey
Canadian Goose
Ring-billed Gull
Double-crested Cormorant
Turkey Vulture
Mute Swan
Brown Pelican
Great Egret

12 rows selected.
```

You can use column aliases to customize names for column headers and reference a column with a shorter name in some SQL implementations.

NOTE

Aliasing a Column in a Query

When a column is renamed in a `SELECT` statement, the name is not a permanent change. The change is only for that particular `SELECT` statement.

Summary

This hour introduced you to the database query, a means of obtaining useful information from a relational database. The `SELECT` statement creates queries in SQL. You must include the `FROM` clause with every `SELECT` statement. You learned how to place a condition on a query using the `WHERE` clause and how to sort data using the `ORDER BY` clause. You also learned the fundamentals of writing queries. After a few exercises, you should be prepared to learn more about queries during the next hour.

Q&A

Q. Why doesn't the SELECT clause work without the FROM clause?

A. The SELECT clause merely tells the database what data you want to see. The FROM clause tells the database where to get the data.

Q. What is the purpose of using the DISTINCT option?

A. The DISTINCT option causes the query to suppress duplicate rows of columns from appearing in the result set.

Q. When I use the ORDER BY clause and choose the descending option, what does that actually do to the data?

A. Say that you use the ORDER BY clause and select BIRD_NAME from the BIRDS table. If you use the descending option, the order starts with the letter Z and finishes with the letter A. Now say that you use the ORDER BY clause and select the WINGSPAN from BIRDS. If you use the descending option, the order starts with the greatest value for WINGSPAN and goes down to the least.

Q. If I have a DISTINCT option, a WHERE clause, and an ORDER BY clause, in which order are they performed?

A. The WHERE clause is applied first, to constrain the results. Then the DISTINCT is applied and, lastly, the ORDER BY clause is used to order the finalized result set.

Q. What advantage is there to renaming columns?

A. The new column name can fit the description of the returned data more closely for a particular report.

Q. What is the proper ordering of the following statement?

```
SELECT BIRD_NAME,WINGSPAN,EGGS FROM BIRDS
ORDER BY 3,1
```

A. The query is properly ordered by the EGGS column and then by the BIRD_NAME column. Because no ordering preference is specified, they are properly ordered in ascending order, and the birds that lay the least number of eggs are shown first.

Workshop

The following workshop consists of a series of quiz questions and practical exercises. The quiz questions are designed to test your overall understanding of the current material. The practical exercises give you the opportunity to apply the concepts discussed during the current hour, as well as build on the knowledge you acquired in previous hours of study. Be sure to complete the quiz questions and exercises before continuing to the next hour. Refer to Appendix C, "Answers to Quizzes and Exercises," for answers.

Quiz

1. Name the required parts for any `SELECT` statement.
2. In the `WHERE` clause, are single quotation marks required for all the data?
3. Can multiple conditions be used in the `WHERE` clause?
4. Is the `DISTINCT` option applied before or after the `WHERE` clause?
5. Is the `ALL` option required?
6. How are numeric characters treated when ordering based on a character field?
7. How does Oracle handle its default case sensitivity differently from Microsoft SQL Server?
8. How is the ordering of the fields in the `ORDER BY` clause important?
9. How is the ordering determined in the `ORDER BY` clause when you use numbers instead of column names?

Exercises

1. Write a query that tells you how many birds are stored in the database.
2. How many types of nest builders exist in the database?
3. Which birds lay more than seven eggs?
4. Which birds have more than one brood per year?
5. Write a query from the `BIRDS` table showing only the bird's name, the number of eggs the bird typically lays, and the incubation period.
6. Modify the previous query in exercise 5 to show only the birds that have a wingspan greater than 48 inches.
7. Sort the previous query by `WINGSPAN` in ascending order.
8. Sort the previous query by `WINGSPAN` in descending order, to show the biggest birds first.
9. How many nicknames are stored in the database?
10. How many different food items are stored in the database?
11. Using the manual process described in this hour, determine which food items the Bald Eagle consumes.
12. Bonus exercise: Using a manual process and simple SQL queries, provide a list of birds that eat fish.

HOUR 13

Using Operators to Categorize Data

What You'll Learn in This Hour:

- Defining operators
- Understanding operators in SQL
- Using operators singularly
- Using operators in combinations

Operators are used with the SELECT command's WHERE clause to place extended constraints on data that a query returns. Various operators are available to SQL users that support all data querying needs. This hour shows you what operators are available for you to use and how to utilize them properly within the WHERE clause.

Defining an Operator in SQL

An operator is a reserved word or character used primarily in a SQL statement's WHERE clause to perform operation(s) such as comparisons and arithmetic operations. *Operators* specify conditions in a SQL statement and serve as conjunctions for multiple conditions in a statement.

The operators discussed during this hour are listed here:

- Comparison operators
- Logical operators
- Operators used to negate conditions
- Arithmetic operators

Using Comparison Operators

Comparison operators test single values in a SQL statement. The comparison operators discussed consist of =, <>, <, and >.

These operators are used to test the following conditions:

- Equality
- Non-equality
- Less than
- Greater than

These comparison operators, including examples, are covered in the following sections.

Equality

The *equal operator* compares single values in a SQL statement. The equals sign (=) symbolizes equality. When testing for equality, the compared values must match exactly, or no data is returned. If two values are equal during a comparison for equality, the returned value for the comparison is `TRUE`; the returned value is `FALSE` if equality is not found. This Boolean value (`TRUE/FALSE`) determines whether data is returned according to the condition.

You can use the = operator by itself or combine it with other operators. Remember from the previous hour that character data comparisons can either be case sensitive or not case sensitive, depending on how your relational database management system (RDBMS) is set up. Make sure you understand exactly how the query engine compares your values.

The following example shows that `WINGSPAN` is equal to `48`:

```
WHERE WINGSPAN = 48
```

The following query returns the bird's name and wingspan of any birds that have a wingspan of exactly 48 inches.

```
SQL> select bird_name, wingspan
  2  from birds
  3  where wingspan = 48;

BIRD_NAME                        WINGSPAN
------------------------------ ----------
Red Tailed Hawk                        48

1 row selected.
```

Non-Equality

For every equality, multiple non-equalities exist. In SQL, the operator used to measure non-equality is <> (the less than sign combined with the greater than sign). The condition returns `TRUE` if the condition finds non-equality; `FALSE` is returned if equality is found.

The following example shows that `WINGSPAN` is not equal to `48`:

```
WHERE WINGSPAN<>400
```

TIP

Options for Non-Equality

Another option for non-equality is `!=`. Many of the major implementations have adopted `!=` to represent not equal. Microsoft SQL Server, MySQL, and Oracle support both versions of the operator. Oracle actually supports a third, `^=`, as another version, but it is rarely used because most people are accustomed to using the earlier two versions.

The following query is similar to the previous one, but it is looking at non-equality: The output returns any birds that do not have a wingspan of exactly 48 inches.

```
SQL> select bird_name, wingspan
  2  from birds
  3  where wingspan <> 48;

BIRD_NAME                        WINGSPAN
------------------------------ ----------
Great Blue Heron                       78
Mallard                               3.2
Common Loon                            54
Bald Eagle                             84
Golden Eagle                           90
Osprey                                 72
Belted Kingfisher                      23
Canadian Goose                         72
Pied-billed Grebe                     6.5
American Coot                          29
Common Sea Gull                        18
Ring-billed Gull                       50
Double-crested Cormorant               54
Common Merganser                       34
Turkey Vulture                         72
American Crow                        39.6
Green Heron                          26.8
Mute Swan                            94.8
Brown Pelican                          90
```

```
Great Egret                           67.2
Anhinga                                 42
Black Skimmer                           15

22 rows selected.
```

Again, remember that your collation and whether your specific system is set up as case sensitive play a critical role in these comparisons. If your system is case sensitive, then `OSPREY`, `Osprey`, and `osprey` are considered different values, which might not be your intention.

Less Than and Greater Than

Two of the most widely used comparison operators are greater than and less than. Greater than works the opposite of less than. You can use the symbols < (less than) and > (greater than) by themselves or in combination with each other or other operators to perform a comparison of non-null values. The results of both are a Boolean value that shows whether the comparison is accurate.

The following examples show that `WINGSPAN` is less than or greater than `48`:

```
WHERE WINGSPAN < 400
WHERE WINGSPAN > 400
```

The following query returns any birds that have a wingspan that is greater than 72 inches.

```
SQL> select bird_name, wingspan
  2  from birds
  3  where wingspan > 72;

BIRD_NAME                        WINGSPAN
------------------------------ ----------
Great Blue Heron                       78
Bald Eagle                             84
Golden Eagle                           90
Mute Swan                            94.8
Brown Pelican                          90

5 rows selected.
```

In the next example, the result set returns any birds that have a wingspan less than 72 inches. Notice that some bird records are not included between the two queries. This is because the less than operator is not inclusive of the value it is compared against.

```
SQL> select bird_name, wingspan
  2  from birds
  3  where wingspan < 72;
```

```
BIRD_NAME                      WINGSPAN
------------------------------ ----------
Mallard                               3.2
Common Loon                            54
Red Tailed Hawk                        48
Belted Kingfisher                      23
Pied-billed Grebe                     6.5
American Coot                          29
Common Sea Gull                        18
Ring-billed Gull                       50
Double-crested Cormorant               54
Common Merganser                       34
American Crow                        39.6
Green Heron                          26.8
Great Egret                          67.2
Anhinga                                42
Black Skimmer                          15

15 rows selected.
```

Combinations of Comparison Operators

The equal operator can be combined with the less than and greater than operators to have them include the value they are compared against.

The following example shows that WINGSPAN is less than or equal to 400:

```
WHERE WINGSPAN <= 400
```

The next example shows that WINGSPAN is greater than or equal to 400:

```
WHERE WINGSPAN >= 400
```

"Less than or equal to 48" includes 48 and all values less than 48. Any value in that range returns TRUE; any value greater than 48 returns FALSE. "Greater than or equal to" also includes the value 48 in this case and works the same as the <= operator. The following example demonstrates how to use the combined operator to find all birds that have a wingspan of 72 or more. Notice the three records in the result set that were not included previously.

```
SQL> select bird_name, wingspan
  2  from birds
  3  where wingspan >= 72;

BIRD_NAME                      WINGSPAN
------------------------------ ----------
Great Blue Heron                       78
Bald Eagle                             84
Golden Eagle                           90
```

```
Osprey                                    72
Canadian Goose                            72
Turkey Vulture                            72
Mute Swan                               94.8
Brown Pelican                             90

8 rows selected.
```

Using Logical Operators

Logical operators are operators that use SQL keywords instead of symbols to make comparisons. Following are the logical operators in SQL, which are covered in the following subsections:

- IS NULL
- BETWEEN
- IN
- LIKE
- EXISTS
- UNIQUE
- ALL, SOME, and ANY

IS NULL

The IS NULL operator compares a value with a NULL value. For example, you might look for birds that do not have a wingspan entered by searching for NULL values in the WINGSPAN column of the BIRDS table.

The following example compares a value to a NULL value; here, WINGSPAN has no value:

```
WHERE WINGSPAN IS NULL
```

The following example demonstrates finding all the birds from the BIRDS table that do not have a wingspan listed in the table. First, the overall result set from the BIRDS table is shown. You can see here that some of the values for WINGSPAN have been temporarily removed from this table, to better illustrate the IS NULL operator.

```
SQL> select bird_name, wingspan
  2  from birds;
```

```
BIRD_NAME                        WINGSPAN
------------------------------ ----------
Great Blue Heron                       78
Mallard
Common Loon                            54
Bald Eagle                             84
Golden Eagle                           90
Red Tailed Hawk                        48
Osprey                                 72
Belted Kingfisher
Canadian Goose                         72
Pied-billed Grebe
American Coot
Common Sea Gull
Ring-billed Gull                       50
Double-crested Cormorant               54
Common Merganser
Turkey Vulture                         72
American Crow
Green Heron
Mute Swan                            94.8
Brown Pelican                          90
Great Egret                          67.2
Anhinga
Black Skimmer

23 rows selected.

SQL> select bird_name, wingspan
  2  from birds
  3  where wingspan is null;

BIRD_NAME                        WINGSPAN
------------------------------ ----------
Mallard
Belted Kingfisher
Pied-billed Grebe
American Coot
Common Sea Gull
Common Merganser
American Crow
Green Heron
Anhinga
Black Skimmer

10 rows selected.
```

The literal word *null* is different from a NULL value. Examine the following example and observe that you cannot interchange the string value 'NULL' because it does not mean the same as a NULL value:

```
SQL> update birds
  2  set wingspan = ''
  3  where bird_name = 'American Coot';

1 row updated.

SQL>
SQL> select bird_name
  2  from birds
  3  where wingspan is null;

BIRD_NAME
------------------------------
American Coot

1 row selected.

SQL> select bird_name
  2  from birds
  3  where wingspan = 'null';
where wingspan = 'null'
                 *
ERROR at line 3:
ORA-01722: invalid number
```

BETWEEN

The BETWEEN operator searches for values that are within a set of values, given the minimum value and the maximum value. The minimum and maximum values are included as part of the conditional set.

The following example shows that wingspans must fall between 48 and 90, including the values 48 and 90:

```
WHERE WINGSPAN BETWEEN 48 AND 90
```

TIP

Proper Use of BETWEEN

BETWEEN is inclusive and, therefore, includes the minimum and maximum values in the query results.

The following example shows birds that have a wingspan between 48 and 90 inches:

```
SQL> select bird_name, wingspan
  2  from birds
  3  where wingspan between 48 and 90;

BIRD_NAME                        WINGSPAN
------------------------------ ----------
Great Blue Heron                       78
Common Loon                            54
Bald Eagle                             84
Golden Eagle                           90
Red Tailed Hawk                        48
Osprey                                 72
Canadian Goose                         72
Ring-billed Gull                       50
Double-crested Cormorant               54
Turkey Vulture                         72
Brown Pelican                          90
Great Egret                          67.2

12 rows selected.
```

Notice that the value `90` is included in the output.

IN

The `IN` operator compares a value to a list of literal values that have been specified. For `TRUE` to be returned, the compared value must match at least one of the values in the list.

The following example shows that the migration location must match one of the values `Mexico` or `South America`:

```
WHERE MIGRATION_LOCATION IN ('Mexico', 'South America')
```

The following example uses the `IN` operator to match all the migration locations that have a location name within a certain range of values (the first query shows all values in the `MIGRATION` table, for comparison purposes):

```
SQL> select * from migration;

MIGRATION_ID MIGRATION_LOCATION
------------ ------------------------------
           1 Southern United States
           2 Mexico
           3 Central America
           4 South America
           5 No Significant Migration
           6 Partial, Open Water
```

```
6 rows selected.

SQL> select migration_location
  2  from migration
  3  where migration_location in ('Mexico', 'South America');

MIGRATION_LOCATION
------------------------------
Mexico
South America

2 rows selected.
```

Using the IN operator achieves the same results as using the OR operator, but it returns the results more quickly because it is optimized in the database.

LIKE

The LIKE operator compares a value to similar values using wildcard operators. Two wildcards are used with the LIKE operator:

- The percent sign (%)
- The underscore (_)

The following example shows that two locations have the word *America* in the migration location name:

```
SQL> select migration_location
  2  from migration
  3  where migration_location like '%America%';

MIGRATION_LOCATION
------------------------------
Central America
South America

2 rows selected.
```

The following example shows that only one bird has a nickname that starts with the word *eagle*:

```
SQL> select nickname
  2  from nicknames
  3  where nickname like 'Eagle%';

NICKNAME
------------------------------
Eagle

1 row selected.
```

The following example shows that three nicknames have the word *eagle* anywhere in the nickname:

```
SQL> select nickname
  2  from nicknames
  3  where nickname like '%Eagle%';

NICKNAME
------------------------------
Eagle
Sea Eagle
War Eagle

3 rows selected.
```

The final example shows three nicknames that end with the word *eagle*:

```
SQL> select nickname
  2  from nicknames
  3  where nickname like '%Eagle';

NICKNAME
------------------------------
Eagle
Sea Eagle
War Eagle

3 rows selected.
```

EXISTS

The `EXISTS` operator searches for the presence of a row in a specified table that meets certain criteria.

The following query returns the birds that have a nickname with the word *eagle* somewhere in it:

```
SQL> select bird_id, bird_name
  2  from birds
  3  where exists (select bird_id
  4                from nicknames
  5                where birds.bird_id = nicknames.bird_id
  6                  and nicknames.nickname like '%Eagle%');

   BIRD_ID BIRD_NAME
---------- ------------------------------
         4 Bald Eagle
         5 Golden Eagle

2 rows selected.
```

ALL, SOME, and ANY

The ALL operator compares a value to all values in another value set.

The following example tests WINGSPAN to see whether it is greater than the seating wingspan of the Bald Eagle:

```
where wingspan > ALL (select wingspan
            from birds
            where bird_name = 'Bald Eagle')
```

The following example shows how the ALL operator is used with a subquery:

```
SQL> select bird_name, wingspan
  2  from birds
  3  where wingspan > ALL (select wingspan
  4                        from birds
  5                        where bird_name = 'Bald Eagle');

BIRD_NAME                        WINGSPAN
------------------------------ ----------
Brown Pelican                          90
Golden Eagle                           90
Mute Swan                            94.8

3 rows selected.
```

In this output, three birds have a wingspan that is greater than that of the bald eagle.

The ANY operator compares a value to any applicable value in the list, according to the condition. SOME is an alias for ANY, so you can use them interchangeably.

The following example tests WINGSPAN to see whether it is greater than any of the wingspans of birds greater than 48 inches:

```
where wingspan > ANY (select wingspan
                      from birds
                      where wingspan > 48);
```

The following example shows the ANY operator used with a subquery:

```
SQL> select bird_name, wingspan
  2  from birds
  3  where wingspan > ANY (select wingspan
  4                        from birds
  5                        where wingspan > 48);

BIRD_NAME                        WINGSPAN
------------------------------ ----------
Mute Swan                            94.8
Brown Pelican                          90
```

```
Golden Eagle                           90
Bald Eagle                             84
Great Blue Heron                       78
Osprey                                 72
Canadian Goose                         72
Turkey Vulture                         72
Great Egret                          67.2
Common Loon                            54
Double-crested Cormorant               54

11 rows selected.
```

Using Conjunctive Operators

Suppose you want to use multiple conditions to narrow data in a SQL statement. You must be able to combine the conditions. You can do this with the following conjunctive operators:

- AND
- OR

Conjunctive operators provide a means to make multiple comparisons with different operators in the same SQL statement. The following sections describe each operator's behavior.

AND

The AND operator allows the existence of multiple conditions in a SQL statement's WHERE clause. For an action to be taken by the SQL statement, whether it be a transaction or a query, all conditions separated by the AND must be TRUE.

The following example shows that the WINGSPAN must be between the values of 48 and 90:

```
WHERE WINGSPAN > 48 AND WINGSPAN < 90
```

The following example shows the use of the AND operator to find the birds with a wingspan between two limiting values:

```
SQL> select bird_name, height, weight, wingspan
  2  from birds
  3  where wingspan > 48
  4    and wingspan < 90;

BIRD_NAME                          HEIGHT     WEIGHT   WINGSPAN
------------------------------ ---------- ---------- ----------
Great Blue Heron                       52        5.5         78
Common Loon                            36         18         54
Bald Eagle                             37         14         84
```

```
Osprey                                 24          3         72
Canadian Goose                         43         14         72
Ring-billed Gull                       19        1.1         50
Double-crested Cormorant               33        5.5         54
Turkey Vulture                         32        3.3         72
Great Egret                            38        3.3       67.2

9 rows selected.
```

In this output, the value for WINGSPAN must be both greater than 48 and less than 90 for data to be retrieved.

This statement retrieves no data because with the AND operator, both conditions must be true for data to be returned; here, it is impossible for a bird to have a wingspan that is both less than 48 inches and greater than 90 inches.

```
SQL> select bird_name, height, weight, wingspan
  2  from birds
  3  where wingspan < 48
  4    and wingspan > 90;

no rows selected
```

OR

The OR operator combines multiple conditions in a SQL statement's WHERE clause. For an action to be taken by the SQL statement, whether it is a transaction or a query, at least one of the conditions that are separated by OR must be TRUE.

The following example shows that WINGSPAN must match either greater than 48 inches or less than 90 inches.

```
WHERE WINGSPAN > 48 AND WINGSPAN < 90
```

The following example shows the use of the OR operator to limit a query on the BIRDS table:

```
SQL> select bird_name, height, weight, wingspan
  2  from birds
  3  where wingspan > 48
  4     or wingspan < 90;

BIRD_NAME                          HEIGHT     WEIGHT   WINGSPAN
------------------------------ ---------- ---------- ----------
Great Blue Heron                       52        5.5         78
Common Loon                            36         18         54
Bald Eagle                             37         14         84
Golden Eagle                           40         15         90
Red Tailed Hawk                        25        2.4         48
```

```
Osprey                                 24          3         72
Canadian Goose                         43         14         72
Ring-billed Gull                       19        1.1         50
Double-crested Cormorant               33        5.5         54
Turkey Vulture                         32        3.3         72
Mute Swan                              60         26       94.8
Brown Pelican                          54        7.6         90
Great Egret                            38        3.3       67.2

13 rows selected.
```

In this output, either one of the conditions must be TRUE for data to be retrieved.

```
SQL> select bird_name, height, weight, wingspan
  2  from birds
  3  where wingspan > 70
  4    and height < 60
  5    and weight < 18;

BIRD_NAME                          HEIGHT     WEIGHT   WINGSPAN
------------------------------ ---------- ---------- ----------
Great Blue Heron                       52        5.5         78
Bald Eagle                             37         14         84
Golden Eagle                           40         15         90
Osprey                                 24          3         72
Canadian Goose                         43         14         72
Turkey Vulture                         32        3.3         72
Brown Pelican                          54        7.6         90

7 rows selected.
```

NOTE

Comparison Operators Can Be Stacked

Each of the comparison and logical operators can be used singularly or in combination with each other. This can be important in modeling complex statements, where you test for several different criteria. Utilizing AND and OR statements to stack both comparison and logical operators becomes an important tool in getting correct query results.

In the next example, notice the use of the AND and two OR operators. In addition, notice the logical placement of the parentheses to make the statement more readable.

```
SQL> select bird_name, height, weight, wingspan
  2  from birds
  3  where bird_name like '%Eagle%'
  4    and (wingspan > 85
  5      or height > 36);
```

```
BIRD_NAME                          HEIGHT     WEIGHT   WINGSPAN
------------------------------ ---------- ---------- ----------
Bald Eagle                             37         14         84
Golden Eagle                           40         15         90

2 rows selected.
```

TIP

Group Your Queries to Make Them Easily Understandable

When using multiple conditions and operators in a SQL statement, you might find that using parentheses to separate statements into logical groups improves overall readability. However, be aware misusing parentheses can adversely affect your output results.

If you remove the parentheses, the result is much different, as you can see in the following example:

```
SQL> select bird_name, height, weight, wingspan
  2  from birds
  3  where bird_name like '%Eagle%'
  4    and wingspan > 85
  5     or height > 36;

BIRD_NAME                          HEIGHT     WEIGHT   WINGSPAN
------------------------------ ---------- ---------- ----------
Great Blue Heron                       52        5.5         78
Bald Eagle                             37         14         84
Golden Eagle                           40         15         90
Canadian Goose                         43         14         72
Mute Swan                              60         26       94.8
Brown Pelican                          54        7.6         90
Great Egret                            38        3.3       67.2

7 rows selected.
```

More rows of data are returned in the results of this query than in the previous query. This is because, without proper placement of parentheses, the `OR` operator allows for data to be returned if *any*, not *all*, of the conditions are met. Anything within the parentheses is treated as one condition, and conditions within the innermost parentheses are resolved first. Use parentheses properly within your `WHERE` clause to ensure that you are returning the correct logical result set. Otherwise, remember that your operators are evaluated in a certain order, which is normally from left to right.

Using Negative Operators

Each logical operator can be negated, to change the tested condition's viewpoint.

The NOT operator reverses the meaning of the logical operator with which it is used. NOT can be used with other operators to form the following methods:

- <>, != (NOT EQUAL)
- NOT BETWEEN
- NOT IN
- NOT LIKE
- IS NOT NULL
- NOT EXISTS
- NOT UNIQUE

Each method is discussed in the following sections.

NOT EQUAL

Earlier this hour, you learned how to test for inequality using the <> operator. To test for inequality, you negate the equality operator. Here you can see a second method for testing inequality that is available in some SQL implementations.

The following examples show that WINGSPAN is not equal to 48:

```
WHERE WINGSPAN <> 48
WHERE WINGSPAN != 48
```

In the second example, you can see that the exclamation mark negates the equality comparison. Some implementations allow the use of the exclamation mark in addition to the standard operator for inequality <>.

NOTE

Check Your Implementation

Check your particular implementation for the validity of using the exclamation mark to negate the inequality operator. The other operators mentioned are almost always the same when compared among different SQL implementations.

NOT BETWEEN

The BETWEEN operator is negated with the NOT operator as follows:

```
WHERE WINGSPAN NOT BETWEEN 30 AND 60
```

The value for WINGSPAN cannot fall between 30 and 60 or include the values 30 and 60. Now let's see how this works on the BIRDS table:

```
SQL> select bird_name, wingspan
  2  from birds
  3  where wingspan not between 30 and 60;

BIRD_NAME                        WINGSPAN
------------------------------ ----------
Great Blue Heron                       78
Bald Eagle                             84
Golden Eagle                           90
Osprey                                 72
Canadian Goose                         72
Turkey Vulture                         72
Mute Swan                            94.8
Brown Pelican                          90
Great Egret                          67.2

9 rows selected.
```

NOT IN

The IN operator is negated as NOT IN. All migration locations in the following example that are not in the listed values, if any, are returned:

```
where migration_location not in ('Mexico', 'South America')
```

The following example demonstrates using the negation of the IN operator:

```
SQL> select *
  2  from migration
  3  where migration_location not in ('Mexico', 'South America');

MIGRATION_ID MIGRATION_LOCATION
------------ ------------------------------
           3 Central America
           5 No Significant Migration
           6 Partial, Open Water
           1 Southern United States

4 rows selected.
```

In this output, records are not displayed for the listed identifications after the NOT IN operator.

NOT LIKE

The LIKE, or wildcard, operator is negated as NOT LIKE. When NOT LIKE is used, only values that are not similar are returned.

The following example demonstrates using the NOT LIKE operator to display a list of values:

```
SQL> select bird_name
  2  from big_birds
  3  where bird_name not like '%Eagle%';

BIRD_NAME
------------------------------
Great Blue Heron
Common Loon
Osprey
Canadian Goose
Ring-billed Gull
Double-crested Cormorant
Turkey Vulture
Mute Swan
Brown Pelican
Great Egret

10 rows selected.
```

In this output, birds that have the word *eagle* anywhere in their name are not displayed.

IS NOT NULL

The IS NULL operator is negated as IS NOT NULL to test for values that are not NULL. The following example returns only NOT NULL rows:

```
WHERE WINGSPAN IS NOT NULL
```

The following example demonstrates using the IS NOT NULL operator to retrieve a list of birds whose WINGSPAN is NOT NULL:

```
SQL> select bird_name, wingspan
  2  from big_birds
  3  where wingspan is not null;

BIRD_NAME                        WINGSPAN
------------------------------ ----------
Great Blue Heron                       78
Common Loon                            54
Bald Eagle                             84
Golden Eagle                           90
Osprey                                 72
```

```
Canadian Goose                          72
Ring-billed Gull                        50
Double-crested Cormorant                54
Turkey Vulture                          72
Mute Swan                             94.8
Brown Pelican                           90
Great Egret                           67.2

12 rows selected.
```

NOT EXISTS

EXISTS is negated as NOT EXISTS.

The following example demonstrates the use of the NOT EXISTS operator with a subquery by returning only birds in the BIG_BIRDS table that do not have a nickname that has the word *eagle* in it:

```
SQL> select bird_id, bird_name
  2  from big_birds
  3  where not exists (select bird_id
  4                    from nicknames
  5                    where big_birds.bird_id = nicknames.bird_id
  6                      and nicknames.nickname like '%Eagle%');

   BIRD_ID BIRD_NAME
---------- ------------------------------
        14 Double-crested Cormorant
         1 Great Blue Heron
         7 Osprey
        21 Great Egret
         3 Common Loon
         9 Canadian Goose
        20 Brown Pelican
        13 Ring-billed Gull
        19 Mute Swan
        16 Turkey Vulture

10 rows selected.
```

Using Arithmetic Operators

Arithmetic operators perform mathematical functions in SQL—the same as in most other languages. The four conventional operators for mathematical functions are listed here:

- + (addition)
- – (subtraction)

- * (multiplication)
- / (division)

Addition

Addition is performed by using the plus (+) symbol.

The following example begins by selecting the BIRD_NAME, EGGS, INCUBATION, and FLEDGING columns from the SMALL_BIRDS table, which was previously created based on the BIRDS table.

```
SQL> select bird_name, eggs, incubation, fledging
  2  from small_birds;

BIRD_NAME                            EGGS INCUBATION   FLEDGING
------------------------------ ---------- ---------- ----------
Mallard                                10         30         52
Red Tailed Hawk                         3         35         46
Belted Kingfisher                       7         24         24
Pied-billed Grebe                       7         24         24
American Coot                          12         25         52
Common Sea Gull                         3         28         36
Common Merganser                       11         33         80
American Crow                           6         18         35
Green Heron                             4         25         36
Anhinga                                 4         30         42
Black Skimmer                           5         25         30

11 rows selected.
```

The following query from the SMALL_BIRDS table returns only birds that have a combined incubation and fledging period greater than 60 days combined.

```
SQL> select bird_name, eggs, incubation, fledging
  2  from small_birds
  3  where incubation + fledging > 60;

BIRD_NAME                            EGGS INCUBATION   FLEDGING
------------------------------ ---------- ---------- ----------
Mallard                                10         30         52
Red Tailed Hawk                         3         35         46
American Coot                          12         25         52
Common Sea Gull                         3         28         36
Common Merganser                       11         33         80
Green Heron                             4         25         36
Anhinga                                 4         30         42

7 rows selected.
```

Subtraction

Subtraction is performed using the minus (-) symbol.

This example returns any birds for which the difference between the fledging and incubation periods is less than 30 days:

```
SQL> select bird_name, eggs, incubation, fledging
  2  from small_birds
  3  where fledging - incubation > 30;

BIRD_NAME                            EGGS INCUBATION   FLEDGING
------------------------------ ---------- ---------- ----------
Common Merganser                       11         33         80

1 row selected.
```

Multiplication

Multiplication is performed using the asterisk (*) symbol.

The next example returns any birds from the SMALL_BIRDS table that have a total number of eggs per year greater than or equal to 10. The total number of eggs per year is derived by multiplying the number of broods per year by the number of eggs per brood.

```
SQL> select bird_name, eggs, broods
  2  from small_birds
  3  where eggs * broods >= 10;

BIRD_NAME                            EGGS     BROODS
------------------------------ ---------- ----------
Mallard                                10          1
American Coot                          12          1
Common Merganser                       11          1

3 rows selected.
```

The example that follows shows the arithmetic in the SELECT clause, not the WHERE clause. This query returns any small birds and shows the number of eggs they lay, the number of broods per year, and the estimated eggs per year, based on a calculation.

```
SQL> select bird_name "SMALL BIRD", eggs, broods, eggs * broods "EGGS PER YEAR"
  2  from small_birds;

SMALL BIRD             EGGS      BROODS EGGS PER YEAR
-------------------------- ---------- ---------- -------------
Mallard                10        1             10
Red Tailed Hawk        3         1              3
```

```
Belted Kingfisher   7       1           7
Pied-billed Grebe   7       1           7
American Coot       12      1          12
Common Sea Gull     3       1           3
Common Merganser    11      1          11
American Crow       6       1           6
Green Heron         4       2           8
Anhinga             4       1           4
Black Skimmer       5       1           5

11 rows selected.
```

Division

Division is performed by using the slash (/) symbol.

This example starts by showing a query that lists the birds and the number of days spent with their young, which is derived by a calculation in the SELECT clause.

```
SQL> select bird_name, incubation + fledging "DAYS SPENT WITH YOUNG"
  2  from small_birds;

BIRD_NAME                      DAYS SPENT WITH YOUNG
------------------------------ ---------------------
Mallard                                           82
Red Tailed Hawk                                   81
Belted Kingfisher                                 48
Pied-billed Grebe                                 48
American Coot                                     77
Common Sea Gull                                   64
Common Merganser                                 113
American Crow                                     53
Green Heron                                       61
Anhinga                                           72
Black Skimmer                                     55

11 rows selected.
```

Finally, the following query uses a calculation to estimate the average days spent with each young individually, based on the previous query.

```
SQL> select bird_name,
  2         (incubation + fledging) / (eggs * broods) "AVG DAYS SPENT WITH EACH
YOUNG"
  3  from small_birds;
```

```
BIRD_NAME                      AVG DAYS SPENT WITH EACH YOUNG
------------------------------ ------------------------------
Mallard                                                   8.2
Red Tailed Hawk                                            27
Belted Kingfisher                                  6.85714286
Pied-billed Grebe                                  6.85714286
American Coot                                      6.41666667
Common Sea Gull                                    21.3333333
Common Merganser                                   10.2727273
American Crow                                      8.83333333
Green Heron                                             7.625
Anhinga                                                    18
Black Skimmer                                              11

11 rows selected.
```

Arithmetic Operator Combinations

You can use the arithmetic operators in combination with one another. Remember the rules of precedence in basic mathematics. Multiplication and division operations are performed first, then addition and subtraction operations. The only way the user has control over the order of the mathematical operations is to use parentheses. Parentheses surrounding an expression cause that expression to be evaluated as a block.

Precedence is the order in which expressions are resolved in a mathematical expression or with embedded functions in SQL. The following table shows some simple examples of how operator precedence can affect the outcome of a calculation:

Expression	Result
1 + 1 * 5	6
(1 + 1) * 5	10
10 – 4 / 2 +1	9
(10 – 4) / (2 + 1)	2

In the following examples, notice that the placement of parentheses in an expression does not affect the outcome if only multiplication and division are involved.

CAUTION

Make Sure Your Math Is Correct

When combining arithmetic operators, remember to consider the rules of precedence. The absence of parentheses in a statement can render inaccurate results. Although the syntax of a SQL statement is correct, a logical error might result.

Summary

This hour introduced you to various operators available in SQL. You learned the hows and whys of operators, and you saw examples of operators used both by themselves and in various combinations with one another, using the conjunctive-type operators `AND` and `OR`. You learned the basic arithmetic functions: addition, subtraction, multiplication, and division. Comparison operators test equality, inequality, less than values, and greater than values. Logical operators include `BETWEEN`, `IN`, `LIKE`, `EXISTS`, `ANY`, and `ALL`. You can now see how elements are added to SQL statements to further specify conditions and better control the processing and retrieving capabilities provided with SQL. You saw numerous examples of applying these operators to the `BIRDS` database and now have the opportunity to apply what you have learned to the example `BIRDS` database—and to any other data you have created to this point. Remember to have fun with these exercises; the same questions often have multiple solutions. Take some time to experiment with your data because the last couple hours are extremely important as you build upon your knowledge of the `SELECT` statement.

Q&A

Q. Can I have more than one AND in the WHERE clause?

A. Yes, you can use all the operators multiple times.

Q. What happens if I use single quotation marks around a NUMBER data type in a WHERE clause?

A. Your query still processes, but quotation marks are not necessary for NUMBER fields.

Workshop

The following workshop consists of a series of quiz questions and practical exercises. The quiz questions are designed to test your overall understanding of the current material. The practical exercises give you the opportunity to apply the concepts discussed during the current hour, as well as build on the knowledge you acquired in previous hours of study. Be sure to complete the quiz questions and exercises before continuing to the next hour. Refer to Appendix C, "Answers to Quizzes and Exercises," for answers.

Quiz

1. True or false: When using the OR operator, both conditions must be TRUE for data to be returned.
2. True or false: All specified values must match when using the IN operator for data to be returned.
3. True or false: The AND operator can be used in the SELECT and the WHERE clauses.
4. True or false: The ANY operator can accept an expression list.
5. What is the logical negation of the IN operator?
6. What is the logical negation of the ANY and ALL operators?

Exercises

1. Use the original BIRDS database for these exercises. Write a SELECT statement from the BIRDS table to return all rows of data, to familiarize yourself with the data. Then write the appropriate SELECT statements using the operators you learned in this chapter for the remaining exercises.
2. Which birds have more than two broods per year?
3. Show all records in the MIGRATIONS table in which the MIGRATION_LOCATION is not Mexico.

4. List all birds that have a wingspan less than 48 inches.
5. List all birds that have a wingspan greater than or equal to 72 inches.
6. Write a query to return the `BIRD_NAME` and `WINGSPAN` of birds that have a wingspan between 30 and 70 inches.
7. Select all migration locations that are in Central America and South America.
8. List all birds by name that have the word ***green*** in their name.
9. List all birds that begin with the word ***bald***.
10. Do any birds have a wingspan less than 20 inches or a height shorter than 12 inches?
11. Do any birds have a weight more than 5 pounds and a height shorter than 36 inches?
12. List all bird names that do not have the word ***green*** in their name.
13. List all bird names that have one of the three primary colors in their name.
14. How many birds spend more than 75 days total with their young?
15. Experiment with some of your own queries using the operators you learned in this chapter.

HOUR 14
Joining Tables in Queries

What You'll Learn in This Hour:

- Defining table joins
- Identifying the different types of joins
- Understanding how and when joins are used
- Taking a look at practical examples of table joins
- Understanding the effects of improperly joined tables
- Renaming tables in a query using an alias

To this point, all database queries you have executed in this book have extracted data from a single table. However, examples of manual joins have been shown in exercises. In a manual join, you separately select data for multiple tables to get the final result set that you want. During this hour, you learn how to join tables in a query so that you can efficiently and automatically retrieve data from multiple tables.

Selecting Data from Multiple Tables

One of the most powerful features of SQL is the capability to select data from multiple tables. Without this capability, the entire relational database concept would not be feasible. Single-table queries are sometimes quite informative, but in the real world, the most practical queries are the ones whose data is acquired from multiple tables within the database.

As you witnessed throughout this book, especially during the database design hours, a relational database is broken into smaller, more manageable tables for simplicity and the ease of overall management. As tables are divided into smaller tables, the related tables are created with common columns: *primary keys* and *foreign keys*. These keys are used to join related tables to one another.

Why should you normalize tables if, in the end, you are going to rejoin the tables to retrieve the data you want? You rarely select all data from all tables, so picking and choosing according to the needs of each query is more beneficial. Performance might suffer slightly from a normalized database, but overall coding and maintenance are much simpler. Remember that you generally normalize the database to reduce redundancy and increase data integrity. Your overreaching task as a database administrator is to safeguard data.

Understanding Joins

A *join* combines two or more tables to retrieve data from multiple tables. Different implementations have many ways of joining tables, so you concentrate on the most common joins in this lesson. This hour covers the following types of joins:

- Equijoins, or inner joins
- Non-equijoins
- Outer joins
- Self joins

As you have learned in previous hours, both the SELECT and FROM clauses are required SQL statement elements; the WHERE clause is a required element of a SQL statement when joining tables. The tables joined are listed in the FROM clause. The join is performed in the WHERE clause. Several operators can be used to join tables, including =, <, >, <>, <=, >=, !=, BETWEEN, LIKE, and NOT. However, the most common operator is the equals symbol.

Figure 14.1 shows two tables in a database, EMPLOYEES and DEPENDENTS, that have a relationship through the ID column. Each employee can have multiple dependents or none. Each dependent must have an associated employee record. (This is an example shown in Hour 1, "Understanding the Relational Database and SQL.") This concept encapsulates the primary concepts of a relational database. In this case, two tables are shown with a parent/child relationship. A parent record can have zero to many children. Each child record must have a parent (at least, if primary key and foreign key relationships are properly defined). Study the data in Figure 14.1.

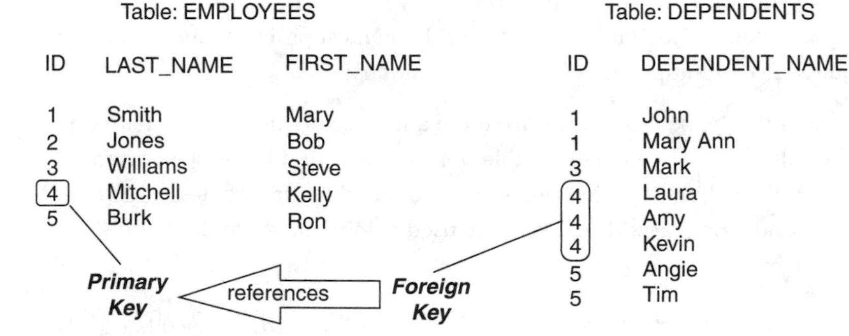

FIGURE 14.1
Joining tables

Let's query data from the two tables in Figure 14.1. Who are the dependents of Kelly Mitchell? This is easy to resolve because you can see all the data. Kelly Mitchell's `ID` is `4`. If you look to the `DEPENDENTS` table and search for Kelly Mitchell's `ID` of `4`, you can easily see that Kelly Mitchell has three records, or rows of data, associated with her `ID`: `Laura`, `Amy`, and `Kevin`. This is a simple yet effective example of a table join. The rest of the hour elaborates on this concept.

Joins of Equality

Perhaps the most used and most important of the joins is the equijoin, also referred to as an *inner join*. The equijoin joins two tables with a common column, in which each is usually the primary key.

The syntax for an equijoin follows:

```
SELECT TABLE1.COLUMN1, TABLE2.COLUMN2...
FROM TABLE1, TABLE2 [, TABLE3 ]
WHERE TABLE1.COLUMN_NAME = TABLE2.COLUMN_NAME
[ AND TABLE1.COLUMN_NAME = TABLE3.COLUMN_NAME ]
```

Look at the following example:

```
SQL> select birds.bird_id, birds.bird_name,
  2  nicknames.bird_id, nicknames.nickname
  3  from birds, nicknames
  4  where birds.bird_id = nicknames.bird_id
  5  order by 1;

   BIRD_ID BIRD_NAME                         BIRD_ID NICKNAME
---------- ------------------------------ ---------- ------------------------------
         1 Great Blue Heron                        1 Big Cranky
         1 Great Blue Heron                        1 Blue Crane
         2 Mallard                                 2 Green Cap
         2 Mallard                                 2 Green Head
         3 Common Loon                             3 Great Northern Diver
         4 Bald Eagle                              4 Eagle
         4 Bald Eagle                              4 Sea Eagle
         5 Golden Eagle                            5 War Eagle
         6 Red Tailed Hawk                         6 Chicken Hawk
         7 Osprey                                  7 Sea Hawk
         8 Belted Kingfisher                       8 Preacher Bird
        19 Mute Swan                              19 Tundra
        20 Brown Pelican                          20 Pelican
        21 Great Egret                            21 Common Egret
        21 Great Egret                            21 White Egret
        22 Anhinga                                22 Snake Bird
        22 Anhinga                                22 Spanish Crossbird
        22 Anhinga                                22 Water Turkey
        23 Black Skimmer                          23 Sea Dog

19 rows selected.
```

This SQL statement is a query against the BIRDS and NICKNAMES tables. It displays the BIRD_NAME and the associated NICKNAME for each bird. The BIRD_ID is selected twice, to prove that the two tables have been properly joined. For this example, numerous records were deleted from the NICKNAMES table so that the result set displays easily on one page in the book. You need to tell the query how the tables are related, which is the purpose of the WHERE clause. Here you specify that the two tables are linked through the BIRD_ID column. Because the BIRD_ID exists in both tables, you must justify both columns with the table name in your column listing. By justifying the columns with the table names, you tell the database server where to get the data.

Data in the following example is selected from BIRDS and NICKNAMES because the desired data resides in each of the two tables. An equijoin is used.

```
SQL> select birds.bird_id, birds.bird_name,
  2         nicknames.bird_id, nicknames.nickname
  3  from birds, nicknames
  4  where birds.bird_id = nicknames.bird_id
  5    and birds.bird_name like '%Eagle%'
  6  order by 1;

   BIRD_ID BIRD_NAME                         BIRD_ID NICKNAME
---------- ------------------------------ ---------- ------------------------------
         4 Bald Eagle                              4 Eagle
         4 Bald Eagle                              4 Sea Eagle
         5 Golden Eagle                            5 War Eagle

3 rows selected.
```

Notice that each column in the SELECT clause is preceded by the associated table name to identify each column. This is called *qualifying columns* in a query. Qualifying columns is necessary only for columns that exist in more than one table referenced by a query. You usually qualify all columns, for consistency and to avoid questions when debugging or modifying SQL code.

In addition, the SQL syntax provides a version by introducing the JOIN syntax. The JOIN syntax follows; it is essentially the same as performing the join in the WHERE clause if you study the syntax:

```
SELECT TABLE1.COLUMN1, TABLE2.COLUMN2...
FROM TABLE1
INNER JOIN TABLE2 ON TABLE1.COLUMN_NAME = TABLE2.COLUMN_NAME
```

As you can see, the JOIN operator is removed from the WHERE clause and instead is replaced with the JOIN syntax. The table joined is added after the JOIN syntax; then the JOIN operators are placed after the ON qualifier.

Table Aliases

You use *table aliases* to rename a table in a particular SQL statement. Renaming is temporary; the actual table name does not change in the database. As you learn later in the "Self Joins" section, giving the tables aliases is a necessity for the self join. Aliases are most often used to save keystrokes, which results in a shorter and easier-to-read SQL statement. In addition, fewer keystrokes means fewer keystroke errors. Programming errors also are typically less frequent if you can refer to an alias, which is often shorter and more descriptive of the data you are working with. Using table aliases also means that the columns selected must be qualified with the table alias.

Following is the same query as the previous one, but aliases have been assigned to table names. After you assign an alias to a table name, you can use that alias within the query for shorthand and better readability.

```
SQL> select B.bird_id, B.bird_name,
  2  N.bird_id, N.nickname
  3  from birds B,
  4  nicknames N
  5  where B.bird_id = N.bird_id
  6    and B.bird_name like '%Eagle%'
  7  order by 1;

   BIRD_ID BIRD_NAME                                 BIRD_ID NICKNAME
---------- ------------------------------ ---------- ------------------------------
         4 Bald Eagle                                      4 Eagle
         4 Bald Eagle                                      4 Sea Eagle
         5 Golden Eagle                                    5 War Eagle

3 rows selected.
```

In the preceding SQL statement, `BIRDS` has been renamed `B` and `NICKNAMES` has been renamed `N`. The choice of what to rename the tables is arbitrary; these letters were chosen here because `BIRDS` starts with `B` and `NICKNAMES` starts with `N`. The selected columns were justified with the corresponding table alias. Note that `BIRD_NAME` was used in the `WHERE` clause and was justified with the table alias as well.

Joins of Non-Equality

A *non-equijoin* joins two or more tables based on a specified column value not equaling a specified column value in another table. The syntax for the non-equijoin follows:

```
FROM TABLE1, TABLE2 [, TABLE3 ]
WHERE TABLE1.COLUMN_NAME != TABLE2.COLUMN_NAME
[ AND TABLE1.COLUMN_NAME != TABLE2.COLUMN_NAME ]
```

The example that follows issues the same query as before, but it replaces the join of equality on line 5 with a test for non-equality. Every row of data in the BIRDS table is paired with every unrelated row of data in the NICKNAMES table, so this query basically tells you which nicknames each bird does not have. Again, this is a subset of data from the NICKNAMES table.

```
SQL> select B.bird_id, B.bird_name,
  2       N.bird_id, N.nickname
  3  from birds B,
  4    nicknames N
  5  where B.bird_id != N.bird_id
  6    and B.bird_name like '%Eagle%'
  7  order by 1;

   BIRD_ID BIRD_NAME                        BIRD_ID NICKNAME
---------- ------------------------------ ---------- ------------------------------
         4 Bald Eagle                             1 Big Cranky
         4 Bald Eagle                             1 Blue Crane
         4 Bald Eagle                             2 Green Cap
         4 Bald Eagle                             2 Green Head
         4 Bald Eagle                             3 Great Northern Diver
         4 Bald Eagle                             5 War Eagle
         4 Bald Eagle                             6 Chicken Hawk
         4 Bald Eagle                             7 Sea Hawk
         4 Bald Eagle                             8 Preacher Bird
         4 Bald Eagle                            19 Tundra
         4 Bald Eagle                            20 Pelican
         4 Bald Eagle                            21 Common Egret
         4 Bald Eagle                            21 White Egret
         4 Bald Eagle                            22 Snake Bird
         4 Bald Eagle                            22 Spanish Crossbird
         4 Bald Eagle                            22 Water Turkey
         4 Bald Eagle                            23 Sea Dog
         5 Golden Eagle                           1 Big Cranky
         5 Golden Eagle                           1 Blue Crane
         5 Golden Eagle                           2 Green Cap
         5 Golden Eagle                           2 Green Head
         5 Golden Eagle                           3 Great Northern Diver
         5 Golden Eagle                           4 Eagle
         5 Golden Eagle                           4 Sea Eagle
         5 Golden Eagle                           6 Chicken Hawk
         5 Golden Eagle                           7 Sea Hawk
         5 Golden Eagle                           8 Preacher Bird
         5 Golden Eagle                          19 Tundra
         5 Golden Eagle                          20 Pelican
         5 Golden Eagle                          21 Common Egret
         5 Golden Eagle                          21 White Egret
         5 Golden Eagle                          22 Snake Bird
```

```
        5 Golden Eagle             22 Spanish Crossbird
        5 Golden Eagle             22 Water Turkey
        5 Golden Eagle             23 Sea Dog

35 rows selected.
```

CAUTION

Non-Equijoins Can Add Data

When using non-equijoins, you might receive several rows of data that are of no use to you. Check your results carefully.

In the earlier section's example test for equality, each row in the first table was paired with only one row in the second table (each row's corresponding row).

Outer Joins

An *outer join* returns all rows that exist in one table, even though corresponding rows do not exist in the joined table. The `(+)` symbol denotes an outer join in a query and is placed at the end of the table name in the `WHERE` clause. The table with the `(+)` should be the table that does not have matching rows. In many implementations, the outer join is broken into joins called *left outer join*, *right outer join*, and *full outer join*. The outer join in these implementations is normally optional.

CAUTION

Join Syntax Varies Widely

Check your particular implementation for the exact use and syntax of the outer join. The `(+)` symbol is used in some major implementations, but it is nonstandard. This varies somewhat among versions of implementations. For example, Microsoft SQL Server 2000 supports this type of join syntax, but SQL Server 2005 and newer versions do not. Be sure to carefully consider using this syntax before implementing it.

The general syntax for an outer join follows:

```
FROM TABLE1
{RIGHT | LEFT | FULL} [OUTER] JOIN
ON TABLE2
```

The Oracle syntax is

```
FROM TABLE1, TABLE2 [, TABLE3 ]
WHERE TABLE1.COLUMN_NAME[(+)] = TABLE2.COLUMN_NAME[(+)]
[ AND TABLE1.COLUMN_NAME[(+)] = TABLE3.COLUMN_NAME[(+)]]
```

To understand how the outer join works, first write a query as before to acquire the bird name and associated nicknames from the database. You can see in the following example that 19 rows of data are returned. Now, even though you previously temporarily deleted some records from the NICKNAMES table to create a subset of data, some birds still are not listed here. Also prior to this particular example, the NICKNAME column was updated in the NICKNAMES table to a NULL value for many of the birds, to illustrate the example. The following 19 rows thus represent only the birds in the database that currently have nicknames.

```
SQL> select B.bird_id, B.bird_name,
  2  N.bird_id, N.nickname
  3  from birds B,
  4  nicknames N
  5  where B.bird_id = N.bird_id
  6  order by 1;

   BIRD_ID BIRD_NAME                     BIRD_ID NICKNAME
---------- -------------------- ---------- ------------------------------
         1 Great Blue Heron                    1 Big Cranky
         1 Great Blue Heron                    1 Blue Crane
         2 Mallard                             2 Green Cap
         2 Mallard                             2 Green Head
         3 Common Loon                         3 Great Northern Diver
         4 Bald Eagle                          4 Eagle
         4 Bald Eagle                          4 Sea Eagle
         5 Golden Eagle                        5 War Eagle
         6 Red Tailed Hawk                     6 Chicken Hawk
         7 Osprey                              7 Sea Hawk
         8 Belted Kingfisher                   8 Preacher Bird
        19 Mute Swan                          19 Tundra
        20 Brown Pelican                      20 Pelican
        21 Great Egret                        21 Common Egret
        21 Great Egret                        21 White Egret
        22 Anhinga                            22 Snake Bird
        22 Anhinga                            22 Spanish Crossbird
        22 Anhinga                            22 Water Turkey
        23 Black Skimmer                      23 Sea Dog

19 rows selected.
```

If you wanted to show all birds in the result set, regardless of whether they have an associated nickname, you would use an outer join. The BIRDS table has a list of all birds in the database. However, some birds do not have related rows of data in the NICKNAMES table in this situation. To show a list of all birds, the outer join operator (+) was used next to the BIRD_ID in the join associated with the NICKNAMES table (see line 5 in the query), which is where missing entries of birds are found. When you look at the result set, now you can see that all birds from the database are listed, whether they have a nickname or not.

```
SQL> select B.bird_id, B.bird_name,
  2  N.bird_id, N.nickname
  3  from birds B,
  4  nicknames N
  5  where B.bird_id = N.bird_id(+)
  6  order by 1;

   BIRD_ID BIRD_NAME                    BIRD_ID NICKNAME
---------- ---------------------- ---------- ------------------------------
         1 Great Blue Heron                 1 Big Cranky
         1 Great Blue Heron                 1 Blue Crane
         2 Mallard                          2 Green Cap
         2 Mallard                          2 Green Head
         3 Common Loon                      3 Great Northern Diver
         4 Bald Eagle                       4 Eagle
         4 Bald Eagle                       4 Sea Eagle
         5 Golden Eagle                     5 War Eagle
         6 Red Tailed Hawk                  6 Chicken Hawk
         7 Osprey                           7 Sea Hawk
         8 Belted Kingfisher                8 Preacher Bird
         9 Canadian Goose
        10 Pied-billed Grebe
        11 American Coot
        12 Common Sea Gull
        13 Ring-billed Gull
        14 Double-crested Cormorant
        15 Common Merganser
        16 Turkey Vulture
        17 American Crow
        18 Green Heron
        19 Mute Swan                       19 Tundra
        20 Brown Pelican                   20 Pelican
        21 Great Egret                     21 White Egret
        21 Great Egret                     21 Common Egret
        22 Anhinga                         22 Snake Bird
        22 Anhinga                         22 Spanish Crossbird
        22 Anhinga                         22 Water Turkey
        23 Black Skimmer                   23 Sea Dog

29 rows selected.
```

TIP

Use of Outer Joins

You can use the outer join on only one side of a JOIN condition; however, you can use an outer join on more than one column of the same table in the JOIN condition.

Self Joins

A *self join* joins a table to itself, as if the table were two tables. Then it temporarily renames at least one table in the SQL statement using a table alias. The syntax follows:

```
SELECT A.COLUMN_NAME, B.COLUMN_NAME, [ C.COLUMN_NAME ]
FROM TABLE1 A, TABLE2 B [, TABLE3 C ]
WHERE A.COLUMN_NAME = B.COLUMN_NAME
[ AND A.COLUMN_NAME = C.COLUMN_NAME ]
```

Following is an example with a table called PHOTOGRAPHERS. First, take a look at the CREATE TABLE statement. This is a very simple table of photographers that contains the identification number, the photographer's name, and the identification number of a photographer's mentor, which is another photographer in the PHOTOGRAPHERS table. So in this example, the PHOTOGRAPHER_ID is the primary key, which ensures that every row of data in the table contains a unique value for the identification. A foreign key constraint was also created on the MENTOR_PHOTOGRAPHER_ID column, which references the PHOTOGRAPHER_ID column in the same table.

```
SQL> create table photographers
  2  (photographer_id      number(3)       not null    primary key,
  3   photographer         varchar(30)     not null,
  4   mentor_photographer_id number(3)     null,
  5   constraint p_fk1 foreign key (mentor_photographer_id) references
photographers (photographer_id));

Table created.
```

Next, sample records were inserted into the PHOTOGRAPHERS table, as follows.

```
SQL> insert into photographers values ( 7, 'Ryan Notstephens' , null);

1 row created.

SQL> insert into photographers values ( 8, 'Susan Willamson' , null);

1 row created.

SQL> insert into photographers values ( 9, 'Mark Fife' , null);

1 row created.

SQL> insert into photographers values ( 1, 'Shooter McGavin' , null);

1 row created.

SQL> insert into photographers values ( 2, 'Jenny Forest' , 8);

1 row created.
```

```
SQL> insert into photographers values ( 3, 'Steve Hamm' , null);

1 row created.

SQL> insert into photographers values ( 4, 'Harry Henderson' , 9);

1 row created.

SQL> insert into photographers values ( 5, 'Kelly Hairtrigger' , 8);

1 row created.

SQL> insert into photographers values ( 6, 'Gordon Flash' , null);

1 row created.

SQL> insert into photographers values ( 10, 'Kate Kapteur' , 7);

1 row created.
```

Now you can query the PHOTOGRAPHERS table to show all the data. In the result set that follows, you can see 10 photographers in the table. Four of the photographers have mentors who are other photographers in the same table. This also means that some photographers mentor other photographers, if you look at the relationship from the other side. Some photographers are neither mentored nor mentor anyone. Familiarize yourself with the data. Look at the following returned data set and determine who Kate Kapteur's mentor is.

```
SQL> select * from photographers;

PHOTOGRAPHER_ID PHOTOGRAPHER         MENTOR_PHOTOGRAPHER_ID
--------------- -------------------- ----------------------
              7 Ryan Notstephens
              8 Susan Willamson
              9 Mark Fife
              1 Shooter McGavin
              2 Jenny Forest                  8
              3 Steve Hamm
              4 Harry Henderson               9
              5 Kelly Hairtrigger             8
              6 Gordon Flash
             10 Kate Kapteur                  7

10 rows selected.
```

Kate Kapteur's mentor is Ryan Notstephens. You can see this because the MENTOR_PHOTOGRAPHER_ID associated with Kate Kapteur is 7, which corresponds to Ryan Notstephens'

PHOTOGRAPHER_ID. Remember that in this table, MENTOR_PHOTOGRAPHER_ID is a foreign key that references the primary key of PHOTOGRAPHER_ID in the very same table.

In the next example, you apply the concept of a self join to the PHOTOGRAPHERS table. Suppose that you want to produce a list of mentors and their protégé. Looking at the SELECT statement, you can see that you are selecting from the PHOTOGRAPHERS table twice. The first occurrence of the PHOTOGRAPHERS table in the FROM clause has an alias of "mentors"; the second occurrence of the PHOTOGRAPHERS table in the FROM clause has an alias of "proteges". Essentially, you are seeing the PHOTOGRAPHERS table as two separate tables, for the purpose of this query. The PHOTOGRAPHER_ID in the "mentors" version of the PHOTOGRAPHERS table is being joined to the MENTOR_PHOTOGRAPHER_ID column of the "proteges" version of the same table. Study the results and compare to them the complete output in the previous example. Notice that this output lists only photographers who have protégé.

```
SQL> select mentors.photographer mentor,
  2  proteges.photographer protege
  3  from photographers mentors,
  4  photographers proteges
  5  where mentors.photographer_id = proteges.mentor_photographer_id
  6  order by 1;

MENTOR                         PROTEGE
------------------------------ ------------------------------
Mark Fife                      Harry Henderson
Ryan Notstephens               Kate Kapteur
Susan Willamson                Kelly Hairtrigger
Susan Willamson                Jenny Forest

4 rows selected.
```

This final example uses the exact same query as before but applies the concept of an outer join along with the self join. If you want to see all photographers, regardless of whether there is an associated record as a mentor or protégé, the outer join allows for this. Study the results and review the previous discussion of the outer join, if necessary. The PROTEGES.PHOTOGRAPHER column was left as "photographer" because some of the photographers in this output are not necessarily protégés.

```
SQL> select mentors.photographer mentor,
  2  proteges.photographer "PHOTOGRAPHER"
  3  from photographers mentors,
  4  photographers proteges
  5  where mentors.photographer_id(+) = proteges.mentor_photographer_id
  6  order by 1;
```

```
MENTOR                         PHOTOGRAPHER
------------------------------ ------------------------------
Mark Fife                      Harry Henderson
Ryan Notstephens               Kate Kapteur
Susan Willamson                Kelly Hairtrigger
Susan Willamson                Jenny Forest
                               Steve Hamm
                               Shooter McGavin
                               Mark Fife
                               Susan Willamson
                               Gordon Flash
                               Ryan Notstephens

10 rows selected.
```

Self joins are useful when all the data that you want to retrieve resides in one table, but you must somehow compare records in the table to other records in the table.

Joins on Multiple Keys

Most join operations involve merging data based on a key in one table and a key in another table. Depending on how your database has been designed, you might have to join on more than one key field to accurately depict that data in your database. You might have a table with a primary key that consists of more than one column. You might also have a foreign key in a table that consists of more than one column, which references the multiple-column primary key.

The `BIRDS` database has not been designed in this way, but consider the following example tables:

```
SQL> desc products

Name                                  Null?    Type
------------------------------------- -------- ------------------------------
SERIAL_NUMBER                         NOT NULL NUMBER(10)
VENDOR_NUMBER                         NOT NULL NUMBER(10)
PRODUCT_NAME                          NOT NULL VARCHAR2(30)
COST                                  NOT NULL NUMBER(8,2)

SQL> desc orders

Name                                  Null?    Type
------------------------------------- -------- ------------------------------
ORD_NO                                NOT NULL NUMBER(10)
PROD_NUMBER                           NOT NULL NUMBER(10)
VENDOR_NUMBER                         NOT NULL NUMBER(10)
QUANTITY                              NOT NULL NUMBER(5)
ORD_DATE                              NOT NULL DATE
```

The primary key in PROD is the combination of the columns SERIAL_NUMBER and VENDOR_NUMBER. Perhaps two products can have the same serial number within the distribution company, but each serial number is unique per vendor.

The foreign key in ORD is also the combination of the columns SERIAL_NUMBER and VENDOR_NUMBER.

When selecting data from both tables (PROD and ORD), the join operation might appear as follows:

```
SELECT P.PRODUCT_NAME, O.ORD_DATE, O.QUANTITY
FROM PRODUCTS P, ORDERS O
WHERE P.SERIAL_NUMBER = O.SERIAL_NUMBER
  AND P.VENDOR_NUMBER = O.VENDOR_NUMBER;
```

Join Considerations

Consider several points before using joins: what columns(s) to join on, whether there is a common column to join on, and any performance issues. More joins in a query means the database server has to do more work, which means that more time is taken to retrieve data. You cannot avoid joins when retrieving data from a normalized database, but it is imperative to ensure that joins are performed correctly from a logical standpoint. Incorrect joins can result in serious performance degradation and inaccurate query results. Hour 23, "Improving Database Performance," discusses performance issues in more detail.

Base Tables

In a normalized database, a common need involves selecting data from multiple tables that do not have a direct relationship. What should you join on? If you need to retrieve data from two tables that do not have a common column to join, you must join on another table that has a common column or columns to both tables. That table becomes the *base table*. A base table joins one or more tables that have common columns, or joins tables that do not have common columns.

Thinking back to the previous database design, Hours 5 through 7 (particularly Hour 7 on normalization), you should recall that several intermediate, or base tables, have been created. For instance, Figure 14.1 shows how the original BIRDS and FOOD entities are related via a many-to-many relationship. Many-to-many relationships have redundant data; as you continue to normalize the database and remove that redundant data, you end up with tables in between. Figure 14.2 shows how the two tables are normalized into three tables. The middle table is used as a base table to provide a relationship between the BIRDS and FOOD tables. Take a minute to refresh your memory on this concept.

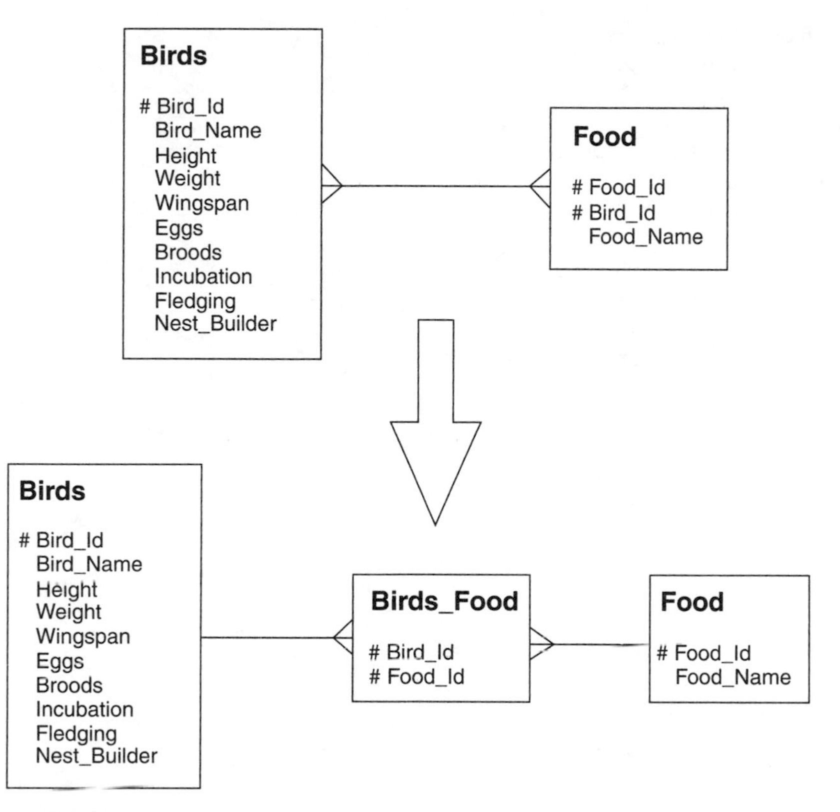

FIGURE 14.2
Joining tables through a base table

In the following query, you need to get information about the food items that specific birds eat. To get this information, you need to use the three tables in Figure 14.2. You can see in the FROM clause that all three tables are listed and given an alias, to simplify and for better readability. You want to see only the BIRD_NAME and the FOOD columns. Notice that because table aliases are used, every column in the query is qualified using the alias, which indicates the table in which that column resides. The join operation consists of lines 3 and 4 in the WHERE clause. The BIRDS table is joined to the BIRDS_FOOD table using the BIRD_ID column, and the FOOD table is joined to the BIRDS_FOOD table using the FOOD_ID column. The BIRDS table has only one row of data for each bird in the database. The FOOD table has only one row of data for each food item in the database. The BIRDS_FOOD table consists of the BIRD_ID and FOOD_ID, which together comprise the primary key in that table. Thus, you can have only one combination in that table of a specific bird and a specific food item. You can also see in the following query that you want to see only birds that eat fish, insects, or plants and have a valid entry in the WINGSPAN column. Finally, you are sorting the results by the bird's name here. Take some time to study the query and results.

```
SQL> select B.bird_name, F.food_name
  2  from birds B, food F, birds_food BF
  3  where B.bird_id = BF.bird_id
  4    and F.food_id = BF.food_id
  5    and F.food_name in ('Fish', 'Insects', 'Plants')
  6    and B.wingspan is not null
  7  order by 1;

BIRD_NAME                      FOOD_NAME
------------------------------ ------------------------------
Bald Eagle                     Fish
Brown Pelican                  Fish
Canadian Goose                 Insects
Common Loon                    Fish
Double-crested Cormorant       Fish
Golden Eagle                   Insects
Golden Eagle                   Fish
Great Blue Heron               Insects
Great Blue Heron               Fish
Great Egret                    Fish
Mute Swan                      Plants
Osprey                         Fish
Red Tailed Hawk                Insects
Ring-billed Gull               Fish
Ring-billed Gull               Insects

15 rows selected.
```

The Cartesian Product

The *Cartesian product* is a result of a Cartesian join or "no join." If you select from two or more tables and do not join the tables, your output is all possible rows from all the tables selected. If your tables are large, the result could be hundreds of thousands, or even millions, of rows of data. A WHERE clause is highly recommended for SQL statements that retrieve data from two or more tables. The Cartesian product is also known as a *cross join*.

The syntax follows:

```
FROM TABLE1, TABLE2 [, TABLE3 ]
WHERE TABLE1, TABLE2 [, TABLE3 ]
```

Following is an example of a cross join, or the dreaded Cartesian product:

```
SQL> select bird_name, food_name
  2  from birds, food;
```

```
BIRD_NAME                      FOOD_NAME
------------------------------ ---------------
American Coot                  Aquatic Insects
American Coot                  Aquatic Plants
American Coot                  Berries
American Coot                  Birds
American Coot                  Carrion
American Coot                  Corn
American Coot                  Crayfish
American Coot                  Crustaceans
American Coot                  Deer
American Coot                  Ducks
American Coot                  Fish
American Coot                  Frogs
American Coot                  Fruit
American Coot                  Insects
American Coot                  Moths
American Coot                  Nectar
American Coot                  Nuts
American Coot                  Plants
American Coot                  Pollen
American Coot                  Reptiles
American Coot                  Rodents
American Coot                  Seeds
American Coot                  Small Mammals
American Coot                  Snakes
American Coot                  Worms
American Crow                  Aquatic Insects
American Crow                  Aquatic Plants
American Crow                  Berries
.........
Turkey Vulture                 Crustaceans
Turkey Vulture                 Deer
Turkey Vulture                 Ducks
Turkey Vulture                 Fish
Turkey Vulture                 Frogs
Turkey Vulture                 Fruit
Turkey Vulture                 Insects
Turkey Vulture                 Moths
Turkey Vulture                 Nectar
Turkey Vulture                 Nuts
Turkey Vulture                 Plants
Turkey Vulture                 Pollen
Turkey Vulture                 Reptiles
Turkey Vulture                 Rodents
Turkey Vulture                 Seeds
```

```
Turkey Vulture                Small Mammals
Turkey Vulture                Snakes
Turkey Vulture                Worms

575 rows selected.
```

Data is selected from two separate tables, yet no `JOIN` operation is performed. Because you have not specified how to join rows in the first table with rows in the second table, the database server pairs every row in the first table with every row in the second table. Because each table has numerous rows of data each, the product of 575 rows selected is achieved from 23 rows multiplied by 25 rows. The `BIRDS` database is a small sample database with limited data, but you can imagine the results of a Cartesian product in a real-world database that has thousands or even millions of rows of data in various tables.

To fully understand exactly how the Cartesian product is derived, study the following example:

```
SQL> SELECT X FROM TABLE1;

X
-
A
B
C
D

4 rows selected.

SQL> SELECT V FROM TABLE2;

X
-
A
B
C
D

4 rows selected.

SQL> SELECT TABLE1.X, TABLE2.X
  2* FROM TABLE1, TABLE2;

X X
- -
A A
B A
C A
D A
```

```
A B
B B
C B
D B
A C
B C
C C
D C
A D
B D
C D
D D

16 rows selected.
```

CAUTION

Ensure That All Tables Are Joined

Be careful to join all tables in a query. If two tables in a query have not been joined and each table contains 1,000 rows of data, the Cartesian product then consists of 1,000 rows multiplied by 1,000 rows, which results in a total of 1,000,000 rows of data returned. Cartesian products dealing with large amounts of data can cause the host computer to stall or crash, in some cases, based on resource usage on the host computer. Therefore, it is important for the database administrator (DBA) and the system administrator to closely monitor for long-running queries.

Summary

This hour introduced you to one of the most robust features of SQL: the table join. Imagine the limits and intense manual effort needed if you could not extract data from more than one table in a single query. You saw several types of joins in this hour, each serving its own purpose based on the conditions placed on the query. Joins are used to link data from tables based on equality and non-equality. Outer joins are powerful, allowing data to be retrieved from one table even though associated data is not found in a joined table. Self joins are used to join a table to itself. Beware of the cross join, more commonly known as the Cartesian product. The Cartesian product is the result set of a multiple-table query without a join, often yielding a large amount of unwanted output. When selecting data from more than one table, be sure to properly join the tables according to the related columns (normally, primary keys). Failing to properly join tables can result in incomplete or inaccurate output.

Q&A

Q. When joining tables, must they be joined in the same order that they appear in the FROM clause?

A. No, they do not have to appear in the same order; however, performance might be impacted, depending on the order of tables in the FROM clause and the order in which tables are joined.

Q. When using a base table to join unrelated tables, must I select any columns from the base table?

A. No, using a base table to join unrelated tables does not mandate selecting columns from the base table.

Q. Can I join on more than one column between tables?

A. Yes, some queries might require you to join on more than one column per table, to provide a complete relationship between rows of data in the joined tables.

Workshop

The following workshop consists of a series of quiz questions and practical exercises. The quiz questions are designed to test your overall understanding of the current material. The practical exercises give you the opportunity to apply the concepts discussed during the current hour, as well as build on the knowledge you acquired in previous hours of study. Be sure to complete the quiz questions and exercises before continuing to the next hour. Refer to Appendix C, "Answers to Quizzes and Exercises," for answers.

Quiz

1. What type of join do you use to return records from one table, regardless of the existence of associated records in the related table?
2. The JOIN conditions are located in which parts of the SQL statement?
3. What type of JOIN do you use to evaluate equality among rows of related tables?
4. What happens if you select from two different tables but fail to join the tables?

Exercises

1. Type the following code into the database and study the result set (Cartesian product):

```
select bird_name, migration_location
from birds, migration;
```

2. Now modify the previous query with a proper table join to return useful data and avoid the Cartesian product. You might have to review the ERD for the BIRDS database in Hour 3, "Getting to Know Your Data," to refresh your memory on how these two tables are related to one another.

3. Generate a list of the food items eaten by the Great Blue Heron.

4. Which birds in the database eat fish?

5. Create a report showing the BIRD_NAME and MIGRATION_LOCATION for birds that migrate to South America.

6. Do any birds have a wingspan less than 30 inches and also eat fish?

7. Write a query to display the following results: the BIRD_NAME, FOOD_NAME, and NEST_TYPE for any birds that eat fish or build a platform nest.

8. Ask some questions you would anticipate database users, photographers, bird rescues, and so forth might inquire about the BIRDS database. Experiment with some of your own queries using table joins.

HOUR 15
Restructuring the Appearance of Data

What You'll Learn in This Hour:

- Introduction to character functions
- How and when to use character functions
- Examples of ANSI SQL functions
- Examples of common implementation-specific functions
- Overview of conversion functions
- How and when to use conversion functions

In this hour, you learn how to restructure the appearance of output results using some American National Standards Institute (ANSI) standard functions, other functions based on the standard, and several variations used by the major SQL implementations.

NOTE

The ANSI Standard Is Not Rigid

The ANSI concepts discussed in this book are just that—concepts. Standards provided by ANSI are simply guidelines for how to use SQL in a relational database. Keep in mind, therefore, that the specific functions discussed in this hour are not necessarily the exact functions that you might use in your particular implementation. Yes, the concepts are the same and the functions generally work the same, but function names and actual syntax might differ.

ANSI Character Functions

Character functions are functions that transform strings in SQL into different formats than the way they are stored in the table. The first part of this hour discusses the concepts for character functions as covered by ANSI. The second part of this hour shows real-world examples using functions that are specific to various SQL implementations. Some of the most common forms of ANSI character functions deal with operations for concatenation, substrings, and translation.

Concatenation is the process of combining two strings into one. For example, you might want to concatenate an individual's first and last names into a single string for the complete name. For example, `JOHN` concatenated with `SMITH` produces `JOHN SMITH`.

The concept of substrings is the capability to extract part of a string, or a "sub" of the string. For example, the following values are substrings of `Bald Eagle`:

- `B`
- `Bald`
- `Ba`
- `E`
- `Eagle`
- `d E`

The following example illustrates how a literal string might appear in a query. The literal string `Somewhere in the world` is selected here from the `MIGRATION_LOCATIONS` table. The literal string itself is irrelevant to the data in this case; it could have been anything. This is merely an example to show that if you select a literal string from a table, the literal string is shown in the results for every row of data in the table—or at least every row of data returned by the results according to the conditions of the query. This simple example is important to remember as you progress through this hour with SQL functions.

```
SQL> select 'Somewhere in the world.' "MIGRATION LOCATION"
  2  from migration locations;

MIGRATION LOCATION
-----------------------
Somewhere in the world.
Somewhere in the world.
Somewhere in the world.
Somewhere in the world.
Somewhere in the world.
Somewhere in the world.

6 rows selected.
```

Common Character Functions

You use character functions mainly to compare, join, search, and extract a segment of a string or a value in a column. Several character functions are available to SQL programmers.

The following sections illustrate the application of ANSI concepts in some of the leading implementations of SQL. Although this book uses Oracle for the examples, they apply to most other implementations as well, although you might find slight variations of syntax.

The CONCAT Function

The `CONCAT` function, along with most other functions, is represented slightly differently among various implementations. The following examples show the use of concatenation in Oracle and SQL Server.

Say you want to concatenate `Bald` and `Eagle` to produce `Bald Eagle`. In Oracle, your code looks like this:

```
SELECT 'Bald' || ' Eagle'
```

In SQL Server, your code appears as follows:

```
SELECT 'Bald' + ' Eagle'
```

In SQL Server or Oracle, your code using `CONCAT` looks like this:

```
SELECT CONCAT('Bald' , ' Eagle')
```

Now for an overview of the syntaxes. The syntax for Oracle follows:

```
COLUMN_NAME || [ '' || ] COLUMN_NAME [ COLUMN_NAME ]
```

The syntax for SQL Server is this:

```
COLUMN_NAME + [ '' + ] COLUMN_NAME [ COLUMN_NAME ]
```

The syntax for the `CONCAT` function appears as follows:

```
CONCAT(COLUMN_NAME , [ '' , ] COLUMN_NAME [ COLUMN_NAME ])
```

Both SQL Server and Oracle employ the `CONCAT` function. You can use it to get the concatenation of pairs of strings, just like the shortened syntax of + for SQL Server and the double pipe (||) for Oracle. In addition, remember that because this operation is for string values, any numeric values must be converted to strings before concatenation. Some examples of utilizing concatenation in its various formats are shown next.

This SQL Server statement concatenates the values for city and state into one value:

```
SELECT CITY + STATE FROM BIRD_RESCUES;
```

This Oracle statement concatenates the values for city and state into one value, placing a comma between the values for city and state:

```
SELECT CITY ||', '|| STATE FROM BIRD_RESCUES;
```

Alternatively, for Oracle, if you want to use the CONCAT statement to achieve the preceding result, you cannot do so because you are concatenating more than two values.

NOTE

Use of Quotation Marks for Special Characters

Notice the use of single quotation marks and a comma in the preceding SQL statement. Most characters and symbols are allowed if they are enclosed by single quotation marks. Some implementations use double quotation marks for literal string values.

This SQL Server statement concatenates the values for city and state into one value, placing a space between the two original values:

```
SELECT CITY + '' + STATE FROM BIRD_RESCUES;
```

The following example consists of two queries. The first query selects the literal string Great Blue Heron from the NICKNAMES table, where the BIRD_ID is equal to 1. The BIRD_ID of 1 is associated with the Great Blue Heron, which you know at this point. This is simply an example to reiterate the previous example showing the selection of a literal string from a table as opposed to an actual data value in a table. It just so happens in this case that the BIRD_ID with the value of 1 is associated with the Great Blue Heron.

```
SQL> select 'Great Blue Heron'
  2  from nicknames
  3  where bird_id = 1;

'GREATBLUEHERON'
----------------
Great Blue Heron
Great Blue Heron

2 rows selected.
```

In this query, the concept of concatenation is used to essentially create a sentence from the database that states, "We combine the literal string 'Another name for' with the value for BIRD_NAME, which is collectively concatenated with ' is: ' and the value for NICKNAME associated with each specific value for BIRD_NAME." The result set here shows nicknames only for the Great Blue Heron because the WHERE clause has a condition that limits the data returned to the Great Blue Heron on line 4 of the query.

```
SQL> select 'Another name for ' || birds.bird_name || ' is: ' || nicknames.nickname
"NICKNAMES"
  2  from birds, nicknames
  3  where birds.bird_id = nicknames.bird_id
  4    and birds.bird_name = 'Great Blue Heron';
```

```
NICKNAMES
-------------------------------------------------------
Another name for Great Blue Heron is: Big Cranky
Another name for Great Blue Heron is: Blue Crane

2 rows selected.
```

The UPPER Function

Most implementations have a way to control the case of data by using functions. The UPPER function converts lowercase letters to uppercase letters for a specific string.

The syntax follows:

```
UPPER(character string)
```

The following query simply converts the output of the migration location to all upper case. Remember that we have chosen to store data in mixed case in this database, which is simply a matter of preference.

```
SQL> select upper(migration_location)
  2  from migration;

UPPER(MIGRATION_LOCATION)
------------------------------
CENTRAL AMERICA
MEXICO
NO SIGNIFICANT MIGRATION
PARTIAL, OPEN WATER
SOUTH AMERICA
SOUTHERN UNITED STATES

6 rows selected.
```

Microsoft SQL Server, MySQL, and Oracle all support this syntax. In addition, MySQL supports an alternative to the UPPER function called UCASE. Because both functions accomplish the same task, you are better off following the ANSI syntax.

The LOWER Function

The converse of the UPPER function, the LOWER function, converts uppercase letters to lowercase letters for a specific string.

The syntax follows:

```
LOWER(character string)
```

The following query is the same as the previous query, except that you are converting the migration location names to all lower case from mixed case, as they are stored in the database.

```
SQL> select lower(migration_location)
  2  from migration;

LOWER(MIGRATION_LOCATION)
------------------------------
central america
mexico
no significant migration
partial, open water
south america
southern united states

6 rows selected.
```

The LOWER function is supported in Microsoft SQL Server, Oracle, and MySQL. As with the UPPER function, MySQL supports an alternative, LCASE. However, as discussed with the UPPER function, following the ANSI standard is generally preferred.

The DECODE Function

DECODE is more specific to Oracle. Even though most implementations do a good job of using the SQL standard as a guide, some implementations have functions that provide additional functionality. The DECODE function supplies an IF/THEM option in a query. The DECODE function is performed on values in a column and searches for a value within the list of values that you provide in the query. If value1 is found, then new_value1 is shown in the query results. If value2 is found in the column, then new_value2 is shown the results, and so forth through any number of values that you choose. Finally, if none of the values listed is found, the default value that you specified is the output for the column. Study the syntax here:

```
DECODE (column, value1, new1, value2, new2, default_value)
```

The following query selects the DISTINCT value of data in the NEST_BUILDER column of the BIRDS table. The NEST_BUILDER column has the following potential values: M for a male bird, F for a female bird, B if both parents build the nest, and N for neither (which means that the birds do not build a nest—they take over another nest).

```
SQL> select distinct(nest_builder) from birds;

N
-
B
F
N

3 rows selected.
```

In the following query, the DECODE function is applied to the NEST_BUILDER column. The DECODE function tells the database engine to return the literal string Neither if a value of N is found in the column, return the literal string Female if F is found, and return the literal string Male if M is found. No default is included in this case, nor is a value for B. This is because, in the WHERE clause, you are looking for only nest builders that do not have a value of B. As you can see in the results, you have successfully changed the way the data appears using the DECODE function.

```
SQL>
SQL> select distinct(decode(nest_builder, 'N', 'Neither', 'F', 'Female', 'M',
'Male')) "NESTER"
  2  from birds
  3  where nest_builder != 'B';

NESTER
-------
Neither
Female

2 rows selected.
```

The SUBSTR Function

Taking an expression's substring is common in most implementations of SQL, but the function name might differ, as shown in the following Oracle and SQL Server examples.

The syntax for Oracle follows:

```
SUBSTR(COLUMN NAME, STARTING POSITION, LENGTH)
```

The syntax for SQL Server is shown here:

```
SUBSTRING(COLUMN NAME, STARTING POSITION, LENGTH)
```

The following query uses the SUBSTR function to display only the first three characters of a location's name from our database where birds might be photographed.

```
SQL> select location_name, substr(location_name,1, 3)
  2  from locations;

LOCATION_NAME                  SUBSTR(LOCAT
------------------------------ ------------
Eagle Creek                    Eag
Fort Lauderdale Beach          For
Heron Lake                     Her
Loon Creek                     Loo
Sarasota Bridge                Sar
White River                    Whi

6 rows selected.
```

The TRANSLATE Function

The TRANSLATE function searches a string of characters and checks for a specific character, makes note of the position found, searches the replacement string at the same position, and then replaces that character with the new value. The syntax follows:

```
TRANSLATE(CHARACTER SET, VALUE1, VALUE2)
```

The next SQL statement substitutes every occurrence of I in the string with A, every occurrence of N with B, and all occurrences of D with C:

```
SELECT TRANSLATE (CITY,'IND','ABC' FROM EMPLOYEES) CITY_TRANSLATION
```

The following example illustrates the use of TRANSLATE with data in the BIG_BIRDS table:

```
SQL> select bird_name,
  2  translate(bird_name, 'BGH', 'ZZZ') "TRANSLATED NAME"
  3  from big_birds;

BIRD_NAME                      TRANSLATED NAME
------------------------------ ----------------------------
Great Blue Heron               Zreat Zlue Zeron
Common Loon                    Common Loon
Bald Eagle                     Zald Eagle
Golden Eagle                   Zolden Eagle
Osprey                         Osprey
Canadian Goose                 Canadian Zoose
Ring-billed Gull               Ring-billed Zull
Double-crested Cormorant       Double-crested Cormorant
Turkey Vulture                 Turkey Vulture
Mute Swan                      Mute Swan
Brown Pelican                  Zrown Pelican
Great Egret                    Zreat Egret

12 rows selected.
```

Notice that all occurrences of B were replaced with Z, G with Z, and H with Z.

Both MySQL and Oracle support the use of the TRANSLATE function. Microsoft SQL Server does not currently support the use of TRANSLATE.

The REPLACE Function

The REPLACE function replaces every occurrence of a character or string with another specified character or string. The use of this function is similar to the TRANSLATE function, except that only one specific character or string is replaced within another string. The syntax follows:

```
REPLACE('VALUE', 'VALUE', [ NULL ] 'VALUE')
```

The following statement returns the MIGRATION_LOCATION and a new version of the MIGRATION_LOCATION using the REPLACE function, which basically does a search and replace. In this example, it replaces every occurrence of a space with a dash. Study the results:

```
SQL> select migration_location, replace(migration_location, ' ', '-')
"NEW LOCATION"
  2  from migration;

MIGRATION_LOCATION             NEW LOCATION
------------------------------ ----------------------------
Central America                Central-America
Mexico                         Mexico
No Significant Migration       No-Significant-Migration
Partial, Open Water            Partial,-Open-Water
South America                  South-America
Southern United States         Southern-United-States

6 rows selected.
```

Microsoft SQL Server, MySQL, and Oracle all support the ANSI version of the syntax.

The LTRIM Function

The LTRIM function provides another way of clipping part of a string. This function and SUBSTRING are in the same family. LTRIM trims characters from the left of a string. The syntax follows:

```
LTRIM(CHARACTER STRING [ ,'set' ])
```

The following SQL statement trims all characters to the left that have a value of 'Bald ' in the BIRD_NAME column. Note that a single space is included in the application of the LTRIM function.

```
SQL> select bird_name, ltrim(bird_name, 'Bald ') "TRIMMED NAME"
  2  from birds
  3  where bird_name like '%Eagle%';

BIRD_NAME                      TRIMMED NAME
------------------------------ ---------------------
Bald Eagle                     Eagle
Golden Eagle                   Golden Eagle

2 rows selected.
```

The LTRIM function is supported in Microsoft SQL Server, MySQL, and Oracle.

The RTRIM Function

Similar to LTRIM, the RTRIM function trims characters, but this time from the right of a string. The syntax follows

```
RTRIM(CHARACTER STRING [ ,'set' ])
```

Remember that the SQL Server version removes only the blank spaces from the right side of the string; therefore, it does not require the [,'set'] portion of the syntax.

```
RTRIM(CHARACTER STRING)
```

This SQL statement trims everything to the right of the literal string ' Eagle'. Thus, the result set shows a second column that indicates a type of eagle.

```
SQL> select bird_name, rtrim(bird_name, ' Eagle') "TYPE OF EAGLE"
  2  from birds
  3  where bird_name like '%Eagle%';

BIRD_NAME                      TYPE OF EAGLE
------------------------------ ----------------------
Bald Eagle                     Bald
Golden Eagle                   Golden

2 rows selected.
```

The RTRIM function is supported in Microsoft SQL Server, MySQL, and Oracle.

Miscellaneous Character Functions

The following sections show a few other character functions worth mentioning. Again, these are functions that are fairly common among major implementations. Remember that each implementation of SQL has different syntax and different options to communicate with a relational database. When it comes to character functions, a wide variety of options are available among implementations. For any implementation that you choose to use to store your data, you must work within the limits of the functions and other options that are available. Still, you can capitalize on those options to maximize the use of the data that is stored within your database.

The LENGTH Function

The LENGTH function is a common function that finds the length of a string, number, date, or expression in bytes. The syntax follows:

```
LENGTH(CHARACTER STRING)
```

The following query returns the length and characters of a bird's name.

```
SQL> select bird_name, length(bird_name) "LENGTH OF NAME"
  2  from big_birds;

BIRD_NAME                      LENGTH OF NAME
------------------------------ --------------
Great Blue Heron                           16
Common Loon                                11
Bald Eagle                                 10
Golden Eagle                               12
Osprey                                      6
Canadian Goose                             14
Ring-billed Gull                           16
Double-crested Cormorant                   24
Turkey Vulture                             14
Mute Swan                                   9
Brown Pelican                              13
Great Egret                                11

12 rows selected.
```

The LENGTH function is supported in both MySQL and Oracle. Microsoft SQL Server uses the shortened version LEN instead, but the functionality is the same.

The COALESCE Function

The COALESCE function replaces NULL values within the result set.

The following example demonstrates the COALESCE function by replacing every NULL value of WINGSPAN with a 0. This gives you the first non-NULL value of WINGSPAN, or the string value of 0:

```
SQL> select bird_name, coalesce(wingspan, 0) wingspan
  2  from birds;

BIRD_NAME                        WINGSPAN
------------------------------ ----------
Great Blue Heron                       78
Mallard                                 0
Common Loon                            54
Bald Eagle                             84
Golden Eagle                           90
Red Tailed Hawk                        48
Osprey                                 72
Belted Kingfisher                       0
Canadian Goose                         72
Pied-billed Grebe                       0
American Coot                           0
```

```
Common Sea Gull                            0
Ring-billed Gull                          50
Double-crested Cormorant                  54
Common Merganser                           0
Turkey Vulture                            72
American Crow                              0
Green Heron                                0
Mute Swan                               94.8
Brown Pelican                             90
Great Egret                             67.2
Anhinga                                    0
Black Skimmer                              0

23 rows selected.
```

The COALESCE function is supported in Microsoft SQL Server, Oracle, and MySQL.

The LPAD Function

LPAD (left pad) adds characters or spaces to the left of a string. The syntax follows:

```
LPAD(CHARACTER SET)
```

The following example pads periods to the left of MIGRATION_LOCATION in the second column to fill a total of 25 characters. This is also a way to right-justify a value if you pad it with spaces.

```
SQL> select migration_location,
  2  lpad(migration_location, 25, '.') "LEFT PADDED LOCATION"
  3  from migration;

MIGRATION_LOCATION             LEFT PADDED LOCATION
------------------------------ ----------------------------------------------------------
------------------------------------
Central America                ..........Central America
Mexico                         ...................Mexico
No Significant Migration       .No Significant Migration
Partial, Open Water            ......Partial, Open Water
South America                  ............South America
Southern United States         ...Southern United States

6 rows selected.
```

The LPAD function is supported in both MySQL and Oracle. Unfortunately, no alternative is available for Microsoft SQL Server.

The RPAD Function

The RPAD (right pad) function adds characters or spaces to the right of a string. The syntax follows:

```
RPAD(CHARACTER SET)
```

As with LPAD, the following query pads periods to the right of MIGRATION_LOCATION in the second column to fill a total of 25 characters.

```
SQL> select migration_location,
  2  rpad(migration_location, 25, '.') "RIGHT PADDED LOCATION"
  3  from migration;

MIGRATION_LOCATION             RIGHT PADDED LOCATION
------------------------------ -------------------------------------------------------
-------------------------------------------
Central America                Central America..........
Mexico                         Mexico...................
No Significant Migration       No Significant Migration.
Partial, Open Water            Partial, Open Water......
South America                  South America............
Southern United States         Southern United States...

6 rows selected.
```

The RPAD function is available in both MySQL and Oracle. Unfortunately, no substitute is available for Microsoft SQL Server.

The ASCII Function

The ASCII function returns the ASCII representation of the leftmost character of a string. The syntax follows:

```
ASCII(CHARACTER SET)
```

Following are some examples:

- ASCII('A') returns 65.
- ASCII('B') returns 66.
- ASCII('C') returns 67.
- ASCII('a') returns 97.

For more information, refer to the ASCII chart located at www.asciitable.com.

The ASCII function is supported in Microsoft SQL Server, MySQL, and Oracle.

Mathematical Functions

Mathematical functions are standard across implementations. These functions enable you to manipulate numeric values in a database according to mathematical rules.

The most common functions include the following:

- Absolute value (`ABS`)
- Rounding (`ROUND`)
- Square root (`SQRT`)
- Sign values (`SIGN`)
- Power (`POWER`)
- Ceiling and floor values (`CEIL(ING)`, `FLOOR`)
- Exponential values (`EXP`)
- `SIN`, `COS`, `TAN`

The general syntax of most mathematical functions follows:

```
FUNCTION(EXPRESSION)
```

All the mathematical functions are supported in Microsoft SQL Server, MySQL, and Oracle, as well as most other implementations.

Conversion Functions

Conversion functions convert a data type into another data type. For example, you might have data that is normally stored in character format, but occasionally you want to convert the character format to numeric so that you can make calculations. Mathematical functions and computations are not allowed on data that is represented in character format.

The following are general types of data conversions:

- Numeric to character
- Character to numeric
- Character to date
- Date to character

The first two types of conversions are discussed in this hour. The remaining conversion types are discussed in Hour 16, "Understanding Dates and Times."

Converting Numbers to Character Strings

Converting numeric values to character strings is precisely the opposite of converting characters to numbers.

Following is an example of converting the height, which is stored as a numeric value, into a character value. Notice that the height column was selected twice, and the third column is left-justified because the height is now seen as a character value for the purpose of this query. You're not changing the data type of the column; you're simply changing the way it is displayed in the output.

```
SQL> select bird_name, height, to_char(height) "HEIGHT AS A CHARACTER"
  2  from big_birds;

BIRD_NAME                  HEIGHT HEIGHT AS A CHARACTER ------------------ ----------
------------------------ ------ --------------------

Great Blue Heron               52 52
Common Loon                    36 36
Bald Eagle                     37 37
Golden Eagle                   40 40
Osprey                         24 24
Canadian Goose                 43 43
Ring-billed Gull               19 19
Double-crested Cormorant       33 33
Turkey Vulture                 32 32
Mute Swan                      60 60
Brown Pelican                  54 54
Great Egret                    38 38

12 rows selected.
```

TIP

Different Data Is Output in Different Ways

The data's justification is the simplest way to identify a column's data type. Character data is most often left-justified, whereas numeric data is often right-justified. You can quickly determine what kind of data is returned from a given query.

Converting Character Strings to Numbers

You should notice two differences between numeric data types and character string data types:

- You can use arithmetic expressions and functions on numeric values.
- Numeric values are right-justified in the output results, whereas character string data types are left-justified.

NOTE

Converting to Numeric Values

For a character string to be converted to a number, the characters must typically be 0 through 9. The addition symbol (+), minus symbol (−), and period (.) can also be used to represent positive numbers, negative numbers, and decimals. For example, the string STEVE cannot be converted to a number, whereas an individual's Social Security number can be stored as a character string but can easily be converted to a numeric value using a conversion function.

When a character string is converted to a numeric value, the value takes on the two attributes just mentioned.

Some implementations might not have functions to convert character strings to numbers; others offer such conversion functions. In either case, consult your implementation documentation for the specific syntax and rules for conversions.

NOTE

Some Systems Do the Conversions for You

Some implementations implicitly convert data types when necessary. In these cases, the system makes the conversion for you when changing between data types and the use of conversion functions is unnecessary. Check your implementation's documentation to see which types of implicit conversions are supported.

In this example, you use the TO_NUMBER function within the exact same query as before, to convert HEIGHT back to a numeric value. In the result set, this value in the third column is right-justified as a number. This is also an example of embedding functions within other functions.

```
SQL> select bird_name, height, to_number(to_char(height)) "HEIGHT BACK TO A NUMBER"
  2  from big_birds;

BIRD_NAME                HEIGHT HEIGHT BACK TO A NUMBER
------------------------ ------ -----------------------


Common Loon              36     36
Bald Eagle               37     37
Golden Eagle             40     40
Osprey                   24     24
Canadian Goose           43     43
Ring-billed Gull         19     19
Double-crested Cormorant 33     33
Turkey Vulture           32     32
Mute Swan                60     60
```

```
Brown Pelican                54      54
Great Egret                  38      38

12 rows selected.
```

The employee identification is right-justified following the conversion.

Combined Character Functions

You can combine most functions in a SQL statement. After all, SQL would be far too limited if function combinations were not allowed. When combining functions in an SQL statement, all functions are resolved separately. When you embed a function within another function, the innermost function is resolved first. Virtually no limit governs what you can do with a `SELECT` statement to look at data and control how the data appears when it is returned as output.

NOTE

How Embedded Functions Are Resolved

When embedding functions within functions in a SQL statement, remember that the innermost function is resolved first; and then each function is resolved from the inside out.

Summary

This hour introduced you to various functions used in a SQL statement—usually a query—to modify or enhance the way output is represented. Those functions include character, mathematical, and conversion functions. It is important to realize that the ANSI standard is a guideline for how vendors should implement SQL, but it does not dictate the exact syntax or necessarily place limits on vendor innovations. Most vendors have standard functions and conform to the ANSI concepts, but each vendor has its own specific list of available functions. The function name and exact syntax might differ, but the concepts among the functions are the same.

Q&A

Q. Are all functions in the ANSI standard?

A. No, not all functions are exactly ANSI SQL. As with data types, functions are often implementation dependent. Most implementations contain supersets of the ANSI functions; many have a wide range of functions with extended capability, whereas other implementations seem to be somewhat limited. This hour included several examples of functions from various implementations. However, because so many implementations use similar functions (with perhaps slight differences), check your particular implementation for the available functions and their usage.

Q. Is the data actually changed in the database when using functions?

A. No, data is not changed in the database when using functions. Functions are typically used in queries to manipulate the output's appearance.

Workshop

The following workshop consists of a series of quiz questions and practical exercises. The quiz questions are designed to test your overall understanding of the current material. The practical exercises give you the opportunity to apply the concepts discussed during the current hour, as well as build on the knowledge you acquired in previous hours of study. Be sure to complete the quiz questions and exercises before continuing to the next hour. Refer to Appendix C, "Answers to Quizzes and Exercises," for answers.

Quiz

1. Match the descriptions with the possible functions:

Descriptions	Functions
a. Selects a portion of a character string	`||`
	`RPAD`
b. Trims characters from either the right or the left of a string	`LPAD`
	`UPPER`
c. Changes all letters to lower case	`RTRIM`
d. Finds the length of a string	`LTRIM`
	`LENGTH`
e. Combines strings	`LOWER`
	`SUBSTR`
	`LEN`

2. True or false: Using functions in a SELECT statement to restructure the appearance of data in output also affects the way the data is stored in the database.

3. True or false: The outermost function is always resolved first when functions are embedded within other functions in a query.

Exercises

1. Write a query to select (display) the word Somewhere for every MIGRATION_LOCATION in the MIGRATION_LOCATIONS table.

2. Write a query to produce results for every bird in the BIRDS table that looks like the following:

```
The Bald Eagle eats Fish.
The Bald Eagle eats Mammals.
Etc.
```

3. Write a query to convert all nicknames to upper case.

4. Use the REPLACE function to replace the occurrence of every MIGRATION_LOCATION that has the word United States in it with US.

5. Write a query using the RPAD function to produce output to display every numeric column in the BIRDS table as a character, or left-justify.

6. Write a query to produce the following results for types of herons in the BIRDS table.

```
BIRD_NAME                      TYPE OF HERON
------------------------------ ------------------
Great Blue Heron               Great Blue
Green Heron                    Green

2 rows selected.
```

7. Experiment with the functions in this hour on your own. Trial and error is a good way to learn with queries because you do not affect any data that is actually stored in the database.

HOUR 16

Understanding Dates and Times

What You'll Learn in This Hour:

- Understanding how date and time are stored
- Understanding typical date and time formats
- Using date functions
- Using date conversions

In this hour, you learn about the nature of dates and times in SQL. Not only does this hour discuss the DATETIME data type in more detail, but you also see how some implementations use dates, learn how to extract the date and time in your desired format, and familiarize yourself with some of the common rules.

NOTE

Variations in the SQL Syntax

As you know by now, many different SQL implementations exist. This book follows the American National Standards Institute (ANSI) standard and illustrates the most common nonstandard functions, commands, and operators. Oracle is used for the examples. Even in Oracle, however, the date can be stored in different formats, so check your particular implementation for details. No matter how it is stored, your implementation should have functions that convert date formats.

Understanding How a Date Is Stored

Each implementation has a default storage format for the date and time. This default storage often varies among different implementations, as do other data types for each implementation. The following sections begin by reviewing the standard format of the DATETIME data type and its elements. Then you see the data types for date and time in some popular implementations of SQL, including Oracle, MySQL, and Microsoft SQL Server.

Standard Data Types for the Date and Time

Three standard SQL data types are used for date and time (`DATETIME`) storage. In a relational database, the date can be stored and retrieved as a basic date format, or can include a time of day, or can include a time stamp based on certain intervals (according to the options available in each SQL implementation):

- **`DATE`**—Stores date literals. `DATE` is formatted as `YYYY-MM-DD` and ranges from `0001-01-01` to `9999-12-31`.
- **`TIME`**—Stores time literals. `TIME` is formatted as `HH:MI:SS.nn`... and ranges from `00:00:00`... to `23:59:61.999`....
- **`TIMESTAMP`**—Stores date and time literals. `TIMESTAMP` is formatted as `YYYY-MM-DD HH:MI:SS.nn`... and ranges from `0001-01-01 00:00:00`... to `9999-12-31 23:59:61.999`....

`DATETIME` Elements

`DATETIME` elements pertain to the date and time and are included as part of a `DATETIME` definition. The following is a list of the constrained `DATETIME` elements and a valid range of values for each element.

DATETIME Element	Valid Ranges
`YEAR`	`0001 to 9999`
`MONTH`	`01 to 12`
`DAY`	`01 to 31`
`HOUR`	`00 to 23`
`MINUTE`	`00 to 59`
`SECOND`	`00.000... to 61.999...`

Each of these is an element of time that you deal with on a daily basis. Seconds can be represented as a decimal, enabling you to express tenths of a second, hundredths of a second, milliseconds, and so on. According to the ANSI standard, a minute is defined as 61.999 seconds, due to the possible insertion or omission of a leap second in a minute, which is a rare occurrence. Refer to your implementation on the allowed values; date and time storage can vary widely.

TIP

Databases Handle Leap Years

Date variances, such as leap seconds and leap years, are handled internally by the database if the data is stored in a `DATETIME` data type.

Implementation-Specific Data Types

As with other data types, each implementation provides its own representation and syntax. Table 16.1 shows how three products (Microsoft SQL Server, MySQL, and Oracle) have been implemented with a date and time.

TABLE 16.1 `DATETIME` **Types Across Platforms**

Product	Data Type	Use
Oracle	`DATE`	Stores both date and time information
SQL Server	`DATETIME`	Stores both date and time information
	`SMALLDATETIME`	Same as `DATETIME`, except that it has a small range
	`DATE`	Stores a date value
	`TIME`	Stores a time value
MySQL	`DATETIME`	Stores both date and time information
	`TIMESTAMP`	Stores both date and time information
	`DATE`	Stores a date value
	`TIME`	Stores a time value
	`YEAR`	1-byte type that represents the year

TIP

Even Date and Time Types Can Differ

Each implementation has its own specific data type(s) for date and time information. However, most implementations comply with the ANSI standard; all elements of the date and time are included in their associated data types. The way the date is internally stored is implementation dependent.

Using Date Functions

Date functions are available in SQL, depending on the options with each specific implementation. *Date functions*, similar to character string functions, manipulate the representation of date and time data. Available date functions are often used to format the output of dates and time in an appealing format, compare date values with one another, compute intervals between dates, and so on.

Retrieving the Current Date

The current date is normally returned either to compare it to a stored date or to return the value of the current date as some sort of time stamp. The current date is ultimately stored on the host computer for the database and is called the *system date*. The database, which interfaces with the appropriate operating system, has the capability to retrieve the system date for its own purpose or to resolve database requests, such as queries.

Take a look at a couple methods of attaining the system date, based on commands from two different implementations.

Microsoft SQL Server uses a function called `GETDATE()` to return the system date. This function is used in a query as follows:

```
SELECT GETDATE()
2015-06-01 19:23:38.167
```

MySQL uses the `NOW` function to retrieve the current date and time. `NOW` is called a *pseudocolumn* because it acts as any other column in a table and can be selected from any table in the database; however, it is not actually part of the table's definition.

The following MySQL statement returns the output if today were June 1, 2015:

```
SELECT NOW ();
01-JUN-15 13:41:45
```

Oracle uses a function known as `SYSDATE` and looks like this if using the `DUAL` table, which is a dummy table in Oracle:

```
SELECT SYSDATE FROM DUAL;
01-JUN-15 13:41:45
```

The default date format is typically set by the database administrator upon database creation. Oracle's default date normally includes a 2-digit year. The following command used at the Oracle SQL prompt changes the date format for the current session for the sample database so that it includes the full 4-digit year, to avoid any confusion.

```
SQL> alter session set NLS_DATE_FORMAT='mm-dd-yyyy';

Session altered.
```

Because no date columns are stored in the current BIRDS database, the following PHOTOGRAPHERS table was created to include the photographer's date of birth and the date that a given photographer started photography. In Oracle, the datatype for a date is simply DATE. The PHOTOGRAPHERS table also has records inserted to include the two new date fields.

```
SQL> drop table photographers;

Table dropped.

SQL> create table photographers
  2  (p_id              number(3)      not null      primary key,
  3   photographer      varchar(30)    not null,
  4   mentor_p_id       number(3)      null,
  5   dob               date           not null,
  6   dt_start_photo    date           not null,
  7   constraint p_fk1 foreign key (mentor_p_id) references photographers (p_id));

Table created.


SQL> insert into photographers values ( 7, 'Ryan Notstephens' , null, '07-16-1975',
'07-16-1989');

1 row created.

SQL> insert into photographers values ( 8, 'Susan Willamson' , null, '12-03-1979',
'02-22-2016');

1 row created.

SQL> insert into photographers values ( 9, 'Mark Fife' , null, '01-31-1982',
'12-25-2000');

1 row created.

SQL> insert into photographers values ( 1, 'Shooter McGavin' , null, '02-24-2005',
'01-01-2019');

1 row created.

SQL> insert into photographers values ( 2, 'Jenny Forest' , 8, '08-15-1963',
'08-16-1983');

1 row created.
```

```
SQL> insert into photographers values ( 3, 'Steve Hamm' , null, '09-14-1969',
'01-01-2000');

1 row created.

SQL> insert into photographers values ( 4, 'Harry Henderson' , 9, '03-22-1985',
'05-16-2011');

1 row created.

SQL> insert into photographers values ( 5, 'Kelly Hairtrigger' , 8, '01-25-2001',
'02-01-2019');

1 row created.

SQL> insert into photographers values ( 6, 'Gordon Flash' , null, '09-14-1971',
'10-10-2010');

1 row created.

SQL> insert into photographers values ( 10, 'Kate Kapteur' , 7, '09-14-1969',
'11-07-1976');

1 row created.

SQL> commit;

Commit complete.
```

The current date is ultimately stored on the host computer for the database and is called the *system date*. The following query returns the system date from the DUAL table. As mentioned previously, this is a dummy table in Oracle from which any literal string can be submitted.

```
SQL> select sysdate from dual;

SYSDATE
----------
07-24-2021

1 row selected.
```

In the next example, you select the system date from every row of data in the PHOTOGRAPHERS table. This might not seem desirable, but it offers an illustration of how the system date can be compared to any value that is stored in a database column, just like any literal string.

```
SQL> select sysdate from photographers;
```

```
SYSDATE
----------
07-24-2021
07-24-2021
07-24-2021
07-24-2021
07-24-2021
07-24-2021
07-24-2021
07-24-2021
07-24-2021
07-24-2021

10 rows selected.
```

In practical use, you might use the system date to compare photographers' dates of birth or dates photographers started taking photos as a hobby or career.

Dealing with Time Zones

Time zones can be a factor when dealing with date and time information. For instance, a time of 6:00 p.m. in the central United States does not equate to the same time in Australia, although the actual point in time is the same. People who live within the daylight savings time zone are accustomed to adjusting their clocks twice a year. If time zones are considerations when maintaining data in your case, you might need to consider time zones and perform time conversions, if they are available with your SQL implementation.

The following table lists some common time zones and their abbreviations.

Abbreviation	Time Zone
AST, ADT	Atlantic Standard Time, Atlantic Daylight Time
BST, BDT	Bering Standard Time, Bering Daylight Time
CST, CDT	Central Standard Time, Central Daylight Time
EST, EDT	Eastern Standard Time, Eastern Daylight Time
GMT	Greenwich Mean Time
HST, HDT	Alaska/Hawaii Standard Time, Alaska/Hawaii Daylight Time
MST, MDT	Mountain Standard Time, Mountain Daylight Time
NST	Newfoundland Standard Time, Newfoundland Daylight Time
PST, PDT	Pacific Standard Time, Pacific Daylight Time
YST, YDT	Yukon Standard Time, Yukon Daylight Time

The following table shows examples of time zone differences based on a given time.

Time Zone	Time
AST	June 12, 2015, at 1:15 p.m.
BST	June 12, 2015, at 6:15 a.m.
CST	June 12, 2015, at 11:15 a.m.
EST	June 12, 2015, at 12:15 p.m.
GMT	June 12, 2015, at 5:15 p.m.
HST	June 12, 2015, at 7:15 a.m.
MST	June 12, 2015, at 10:15 a.m.
NST	June 12, 2015, at 1:45 p.m.
PST	June 12, 2015, at 9:15 a.m.
YST	June 12, 2015, at 8:15 a.m.

NOTE

Handling Time Zones

Some implementations have functions that enable you to deal with different time zones. However, not all implementations support the use of time zones. Be sure to verify the use of time zones in your particular implementation, as well as your database's need to deal with them.

Adding Time to Dates

You can add days, months, and other components of time to dates so that you can compare them or provide more specific conditions in the WHERE clause of a query.

The following example is a query from the PHOTOGRAPHERS table that shows the photographer's name and date of birth.

```
SQL> select photographer, dob
  2  from photographers;

PHOTOGRAPHER                   DOB
------------------------------ ----------
Ryan Notstephens               07-16-1975
Susan Willamson                12-03-1979
Mark Fife                      01-31-1982
Shooter McGavin                02-24-2005
Jenny Forest                   08-15-1963
Steve Hamm                     09-14-1969
Harry Henderson                03-22-1985
Kelly Hairtrigger              01-25-2001
```

```
Gordon Flash                   09-14-1971
Kate Kapteur                   09-14-1969

10 rows selected.
```

Now that you have a visual of the data stored in the PHOTOGRAPHERS table for the date of birth, you can perform the following query, which uses the Oracle ADD_MONTH function to add 12 months, or 1 year, to the photographer's date of birth. Remember that every implementation of SQL can have functions that vary in syntax, but conceptually, they are all similar as related to the SQL standard.

```
SQL> select photographer, dob, add_months(dob, 12) "FIRST BIRTHDAY"
  2  from photographers;

PHOTOGRAPHER                   DOB        FIRST BIRT
------------------------------ ---------- ----------
Ryan Notstephens               07-16-1975 07-16-1976
Susan Willamson                12-03-1979 12-03-1980
Mark Fife                      01-31-1982 01-31-1983
Shooter McGavin                02-24-2005 02-24-2006
Jenny Forest                   08-15-1963 08-15-1964
Steve Hamm                     09-14-1969 09-14-1970
Harry Henderson                03-22-1985 03-22-1986
Kelly Hairtrigger              01-25-2001 01-25-2002
Gordon Flash                   09-14-1971 09-14-1972
Kate Kapteur                   09-14-1969 09-14-1970

10 rows selected.
```

The following query is essentially the same as a previous query, except that you add 365 days instead of 12 months to the date of birth. Compare the results to the previous query.

```
SQL> select photographer, dob, dob + 365 "FIRST BIRTHDAY"
  2  from photographers;

PHOTOGRAPHER                   DOB        FIRST BIRT
------------------------------ ---------- ----------
Ryan Notstephens               07-16-1975 07-15-1976
Susan Willamson                12-03-1979 12-02-1980
Mark Fife                      01-31-1982 01-31-1983
Shooter McGavin                02-24-2005 02-24-2006
Jenny Forest                   08-15-1963 08-14-1964
Steve Hamm                     09-14-1969 09-14-1970
Harry Henderson                03-22-1985 03-22-1986
Kelly Hairtrigger              01-25-2001 01-25-2002
Gordon Flash                   09-14-1971 09-13-1972
Kate Kapteur                   09-14-1969 09-14-1970

10 rows selected.
```

NOTE

Variations Between Implementations

Remember that the date, formatting, and functions can vary among implementations. Although different RDBMS implementations might differ syntactically from the exact ANSI standard, they derive their results based on the same concept described by the SQL standard.

Subtracting Time

Not only can you add time to a date, but you also can subtract time and incorporate other arithmetic into your query using date values.

The following example selects the photographer's name and the date of birth, but it subtracts the date of birth from the system date (which is today's date) and divides the entire calculation by 365 days per year. This simple calculation derives the age of each photographer.

```
SQL> select photographer, (sysdate - dob)/365 "AGE"
  2  from photographers;

PHOTOGRAPHER                          AGE
------------------------------ ----------
Ryan Notstephens                46.0561876
Susan Willamson                 41.6698863
Mark Fife                       39.5055027
Shooter McGavin                 16.4233109
Jenny Forest                     57.982215
Steve Hamm                      51.8945438
Harry Henderson                 36.3657767
Kelly Hairtrigger               20.5082424
Gordon Flash                    49.8945438
Kate Kapteur                    51.8945438

10 rows selected.
```

In the previous query, notice that each photographer's age is expressed as a decimal. Of course, most people do not talk about age in decimal format. In this example, therefore, the date calculation is embedded within the ROUND function to round the age up or down accordingly. This is an example of combining arithmetic and other functions with date values to get the data that you need out of the database.

```
SQL> select photographer, round((sysdate - dob)/365) "AGE"
  2  from photographers;

PHOTOGRAPHER                          AGE
------------------------------ ----------
Ryan Notstephens                        46
Susan Willamson                         42
```

```
Mark Fife                              40
Shooter McGavin                        16
Jenny Forest                           58
Steve Hamm                             52
Harry Henderson                        36
Kelly Hairtrigger                      21
Gordon Flash                           50
Kate Kapteur                           52

10 rows selected.
```

In the following example, you want to create a query that shows the number of years of experience that Gordon Flash has. You thus eliminate all other records in the table using the `WHERE` clause, and instead of using the `DOB` column as in the previous examples, you subtract the date that Gordon started taking photos from the system date and divide by 365 days. This shows that Gordon Flash has approximately 11 years of experience in photography.

```
SQL> select photographer, round((sysdate - dt_start_photo)/365) "YEARS EXPERIENCE"
  2  from photographers
  3  where photographer = 'Gordon Flash';

PHOTOGRAPHER                   YEARS EXPERIENCE
------------------------------ ----------------
Gordon Flash                                 11

1 row selected.
```

Using Miscellaneous Date Functions

Table 16.2 shows some powerful date functions that are available in the implementations for SQL Server, Oracle, and MySQL.

TABLE 16.2 Date Functions, by Platform

Product	Date Function	Use
SQL Server	`DATEPART`	Returns the integer value of a `DATEPART` for a date
	`DATENAME`	Returns the text value of a `DATEPART` for a date
	`GETDATE()`	Returns the system date
	`DATEDIFF`	Returns the difference between two dates for specified date parts, such as days, minutes, and seconds

Product	Date Function	Use
Oracle	NEXT_DAY	Returns the next day of the week as specified (for example, FRIDAY) since a given date
	MONTHS_BETWEEN	Returns the number of months between two given dates
MySQL	DAYNAME(date)	Displays the day of the week
	DAYOFMONTH(date)	Displays the day of the month
	DAYOFWEEK(date)	Displays the day of the week
	DAYOFYEAR(date)	Displays the day of the year

Converting Dates

You might need to convert dates for a variety of reasons. Conversions are mainly done to alter the data type of values defined as a DATETIME value or any other valid data type of a particular implementation.

Typical reasons for date conversions are as follows:

- To compare date values of different data types
- To format a date value as a character string
- To convert a character string into a date format

The ANSI CAST operator converts data types into other data types. The basic syntax follows:

```
CAST ( EXPRESSION AS NEW_DATA_TYPE )
```

The following subsections illustrate specific syntax examples of some implementations and cover these tasks:

- Representing the parts of a DATETIME value
- Converting dates to character strings
- Converting character strings to dates

Using Date Pictures

A *date picture* consists of formatting elements used to extract date and time information from the database in a desired format. Date pictures might not be available in all SQL implementations.

Without the use of a date picture and some type of conversion function, the date and time information is retrieved from the database in a default format, such as the following:

```
2010-12-31
31-DEC-10
2010-12-31 23:59:01.11
...
```

Let's say you want the date to display like this:

```
December 31, 2010
```

You now have to convert the date from a DATETIME format into a character string format. You do so using implementation-specific functions for this purpose, as you see in the following sections.

Table 16.3 displays some of the common date parts used in various implementations. This helps you use the date picture in the following sections to extract the proper DATETIME information from the database.

TABLE 16.3 Date Parts, by SQL Implementation

Product	Syntax	Date Part
SQL Server	yy	Year
	qq	Quarter
	mm	Month
	dy	Day of the year
	wk	Week
	dw	Weekday
	hh	Hour
	mi	Minute
	ss	Second
	ms	Millisecond
Oracle	AD	Anno Domini
	AM	Ante meridian
	BC	Before Christ
	CC	Century
	D	Number of the day in the week
	DD	Number of the day in the month

Product	Syntax	Date Part
	DDD	Number of the day in the year
	DAY	The day spelled out (MONDAY)
	Day	The day spelled out (Monday)
	day	The day spelled out (monday)
	DY	The three-letter abbreviation of the day (MON)
	Dy	The three-letter abbreviation of the day (Mon)
	dy	The three-letter abbreviation of the day (mon)
	HH	Hour of the day
	HH12	Hour of the day
	HH24	Hour of the day for a 24-hour clock
	J	Julian days since 12-31-4713 B.C.
	MI	Minute of the hour
	MM	The number of the month
	MON	The three-letter abbreviation of the month (JAN)
	Mon	The three-letter abbreviation of the month (Jan)
	mon	The three-letter abbreviation of the month (jan)
	MONTH	The month spelled out (JANUARY)
	Month	The month spelled out (January)
	month	The month spelled out (january)
	PM	Post meridian
	Q	The number of the quarter
	RM	The Roman numeral for the month
	RR	The two digits of the year
	SS	The second of a minute
	SSSSS	The seconds since midnight
	SYYYY	The signed year; if B.C. 500, B.C. = –500
	W	The number of the week in a month

Product	Syntax	Date Part
Oracle	WW	The number of the week in a year
	Y	The last digit of the year
	YY	The last two digits of the year
	YYY	The last three digits of the year
	YYYY	The year
	YEAR	The year spelled out (TWO-THOUSAND-TEN)
	Year	The year spelled out (Two-Thousand-Ten)
	year	The year spelled out (two-thousand-ten)
MySQL	SECOND	Seconds
	MINUTE	Minutes
	HOUR	Hours
	DAY	Days
	MONTH	Months
	YEAR	Years
	MINUTE_SECOND	Minutes and seconds
	HOUR_MINUTE	Hours and minutes
	DAY_HOUR	Days and hours
	YEAR_MONTH	Years and months
	HOUR_SECOND	Hours, minutes, and seconds
	DAY_MINUTE	Days and minutes
	DAY_SECOND	Days and seconds

NOTE

Date Parts in Oracle

This section uses some of the most common date parts for Oracle. Other date parts might be available, depending on the version of Oracle.

Converting Dates to Character Strings

DATETIME values are converted to character strings to alter the appearance of output from a query. A conversion function achieves this. Two examples of converting date and time data into a character string as designated by a query follow.

SQL implementations provide a variety of formats for displaying a date value. In this next example, you select DOB for photographers and also perform a character conversion on the default date format that is stored in the database, to produce output that might be more readable or desirable for a given situation. Take a minute to study the results.

```
SQL> select photographer, dob, to_char(dob, 'Day Month dd, yyyy') "LONG DOB"
  2  from photographers;

PHOTOGRAPHER          DOB        LONG DOB
--------------------- ---------- ------------------------------
Ryan Notstephens      07-16-1975 Wednesday July      16, 1975
Susan Willamson       12-03-1979 Monday    December  03, 1979
Mark Fife             01-31-1982 Sunday    January   31, 1982
Shooter McGavin       02-24-2005 Thursday  February  24, 2005
Jenny Forest          08-15-1963 Thursday  August    15, 1963
Steve Hamm            09-14-1969 Sunday    September 14, 1969
Harry Henderson       03-22-1985 Friday    March     22, 1985
Kelly Hairtrigger     01-25-2001 Thursday  January   25, 2001
Gordon Flash          09-14-1971 Tuesday   September 14, 1971
Kate Kapteur          09-14-1969 Sunday    September 14, 1969

10 rows selected.
```

Converting Character Strings to Dates

You can also convert character strings to dates. The following query shows an example of converting a character string using the TO_DATE function into a date value based on a literal string that you provide in the query. You can see in the results that an error was returned because of a built-in constraint within the database. The day of the week that you provided conflicts with the actual day of the week for that date in time, which the database "knows."

```
SQL> select to_date('Tuesday January 6, 1999',
  2  'Day Month dd, yyyy') "New Date"
  3  from dual;
select to_date('Tuesday January 6, 1999',
               *
ERROR at line 1:
ORA-01835: day of week conflicts with Julian date
```

In this final example, the two DATE functions successfully convert a literal string into a date value.

```
SQL> select to_date('Sunday September 14, 1969',
  2  Day Month dd, yyyy') "New Date"
  3  from dual;

New Date
----------
09-14-1969

1 row selected.
```

Summary

You now should have an understanding of DATETIME values. ANSI provided a standard; however, as with many SQL elements, most implementations have deviated from the exact functions and syntax of standard SQL commands. Still, the concepts remain the same in terms of the basic representation and manipulation of date and time information. In Hour 15, "Restructuring the Appearance of Data," you saw that functions vary depending on each implementation. This hour, you saw some of the differences between date and time data types, functions, and operators. Keep in mind that not all examples discussed in this hour work with your particular implementation, but the concepts of dates and times are the same and should be applicable to any implementation.

Q&A

Q. Why do implementations choose to deviate from a single standard set of data types and functions?

A. Implementations differ in their representation of data types and functions mainly because of the way each vendor chooses to internally store data and provide the most efficient means of data retrieval. However, all implementations should provide the same means for storing date and time values based on the required elements prescribed by ANSI, such as the year, month, day, hour, minute, second, and so on.

Q. What if I want to store date and time information differently than what my implementation offers?

A. Dates can be stored in nearly any type of format if you choose to define the column for a date as a variable-length character. The main point to remember when comparing date values to one another is that you are usually required to first convert the character string representation of the date to a valid `DATETIME` format for your implementation—that is, if appropriate conversion functions are available.

Workshop

The following workshop consists of a series of quiz questions and practical exercises. The quiz questions are designed to test your overall understanding of the current material. The practical exercises give you the opportunity to apply the concepts discussed during the current hour, as well as build on the knowledge you acquired in previous hours of study. Be sure to complete the quiz questions and exercises before continuing to the next hour. Refer to Appendix C, "Answers to Quizzes and Exercises," for answers.

Quiz

1. Where are the system date and time normally derived from?
2. What are the standard internal elements of a `DATETIME` value?
3. What is a major factor for international organizations when representing and comparing date and time values?
4. Can a character string date value be compared to a date value defined as a valid `DATETIME` data type?
5. What do you use in SQL Server and Oracle to get the current date and time?

Exercises

1. Type the following SQL code into the `sql` prompt to display the current date from the database:

```
SELECT SYSDATE FROM DUAL;
```

2. Create the `PHOTOGRAPHERS` table and insert the data shown at the beginning of this hour for these exercises.
3. Write a query to display all the data in the `PHOTOGRAPHERS` table that you just created.
4. Calculate your own age in a query using the system date.
5. Display the day of the week only that each photographer was born.
6. What is the age of Harry Henderson (rounded, of course, unless you just need to know)?
7. Which photographer has been taking photos the longest?
8. Were any photographers born on the same day?
9. Which photographers might have started taking photos because of a New Year's resolution?
10. Write a query to determine today's Julian date (day of year).
11. What is the combined age of all the photographers in the database?
12. Which photographer started taking photos at the youngest age?
13. Have some fun and come up with some queries of your own on this database or simply using the system date.

HOUR 17
Summarizing Data Results from a Query

What You'll Learn in This Hour:

- Defining functions
- Using aggregate functions
- Summarizing data with aggregate functions
- Getting results from functions
- Understanding why you want to group data
- Grouping results with the GROUP BY clause
- Using group value functions
- Understanding group functions
- Grouping by columns
- Deciding between GROUP BY and ORDER BY
- Reducing groups with the HAVING clause

In this hour, you learn about the aggregate functions of SQL. You can perform a variety of useful functions with aggregate functions, such as getting the highest total of a sale or counting the number of orders processed on a given day. The real power of aggregate functions is discussed in the next hour when you tackle the `GROUP BY` clause. You have already learned how to query the database and return data in an organized way. You have also learned how to sort data from a query. During this hour, you learn how to return data from a query and break it into groups for improved readability.

Using Aggregate Functions

Functions are keywords in SQL that you use to manipulate values within columns for output purposes. A *function* is a command normally used with a column name or expression that processes the incoming data to produce a result. SQL contains several types of functions. This hour covers aggregate functions. An *aggregate function* provides summarization information for a SQL statement, such as counts, totals, and averages.

This basic set of aggregate functions is discussed in this hour:

- COUNT
- SUM
- MAX
- MIN
- AVG

In previous hours, you updated some of the data in the BIRDS database. For example, several records in the table were updated to place a NULL value in the WINGSPAN column. During this hour, you rerun the scripts to rebuild the tables and the data, to return the data to its original form. Remember that at any point, you can execute the script tables.sql to drop and rebuild your tables, and the script data.sql to insert the original data back into your tables. The following tables are used for examples during this hour:

- BIRDS
- MIGRATION, BIRDS_MIGRATION
- FOOD, BIRDS_FOOD
- PHOTOGRAPHERS (created during the previous hour)

Be sure to check your data and reset it, if necessary, so that your results match the results in the examples during this hour. For example, if there are null values in the WINGSPAN column of BIRDS, any aggregate functions will return different results than if numeric values existed in all rows of data for WINGSPAN . Remember that you can reset your example BIRDS database at any time by rerunning the provided scripts tables.sql and data.sql to rebuild your tables and insert fresh data back into your tables.

The COUNT Function

You use the COUNT function to count rows or values of a column that do not contain a NULL value. When used within a query, the COUNT function returns a numeric value. You can also use the COUNT function with the DISTINCT command to count only the distinct rows of a dataset. ALL (opposite of DISTINCT) is the default; including ALL in the syntax is not necessary. Duplicate rows are counted if DISTINCT is not specified. One other option with the COUNT function is to use it with an asterisk. COUNT(*) counts all the rows of a table, including duplicates, regardless of whether a column contains a NULL value.

NOTE

Use DISTINCT Only in Certain Circumstances

You cannot use the DISTINCT command with COUNT(*), only with COUNT(*column_name*). This is because DISTINCT is a function that looks for a unique value in a column, whereas (*) represents all columns in a table or a complete row of data.

The syntax for the COUNT function follows:

```
COUNT [ (*) | (DISTINCT | ALL) ] (COLUMN NAME)
```

CAUTION

COUNT(*) Differs from Other Count Variations

COUNT(*) produces slightly different calculations than other count variations. When the COUNT function is used with the asterisk, it counts the rows in the returned result set without regard for duplicates and NULL values. This is an important distinction. If you need your query to return a count of a particular field and include NULLs, you should use a function such as ISNULL to replace the NULL values.

The following example simply counts all rows of data in the BIRDS table. In other words, this example tells you how many types of birds are in the database.

```
SQL> select count(*) from birds;

  COUNT(*)
----------
        23

1 row selected.
```

Before looking at the next example of the COUNT function, select all the photographers and their associated mentor identifications from the PHOTOGRAPHERS table. Remember that this table is related to itself through the mentor identification and the photographer identification; this is an example of a self join, as you have already learned. Take a minute to study the results, and try to match up photographers with their corresponding mentors.

```
SQL> select p_id, photographer, mentor_p_id
  2  from photographers;

      P_ID PHOTOGRAPHER                   MENTOR_P_ID
---------- ------------------------------ -----------
         7 Ryan Notstephens
         8 Susan Willamson
         9 Mark Fife
         1 Shooter McGavin
```

```
         2 Jenny Forest                                  8
         3 Steve Hamm
         4 Harry Henderson                               9
         5 Kelly Hairtrigger                             8
         6 Gordon Flash
        10 Kate Kapteur                                  7

10 rows selected.
```

The following example counts every occurrence of a mentor photographer identification that is `NOT NULL`. This gives you the total number of photographers in the database that are mentored by another photographer.

```
SQL> select count(mentor_p_id) "TOTAL PHOTOGRAPHERS MENTORED"
  2  from photographers;

TOTAL PHOTOGRAPHERS MENTORED
----------------------------
                           4
```

This example is a query that provides a count of any distinct occurrences of the mentor photographer identification, which gives you a total count of the number of photographers that mentor other photographers in the database.

```
SQL> select count(distinct(mentor_p_id)) "TOTAL MENTORS"
  2  from photographers;

TOTAL MENTORS
-------------
            3

1 row selected.
```

NOTE

Data Types Do Not Use COUNT

Because the `COUNT` function counts the rows, data types do not play a part. The rows can contain columns with any data type. The only consideration that actually counts is whether the value is `NULL`.

The SUM Function

The `SUM` function returns a total on the values of a column for a group of rows. You can also use the `SUM` function with `DISTINCT`. When you use `SUM` with `DISTINCT`, only the distinct rows are totaled, which might not have much purpose. Your total is not accurate in that case because rows of data are omitted.

The syntax for the SUM function follows:

```
SUM ([ DISTINCT ] COLUMN NAME)
```

CAUTION

SUM Must Be Numeric

The value of an argument must be numeric to use the SUM function. You cannot use the SUM function on columns that have a data type other than numeric.

This example simply returns the sum of the wingspan stored for all birds in the database. This simplistic example is not very useful, but you build upon it during this hour.

```
SQL> select sum(wingspan) from birds;

SUM(WINGSPAN)
-------------
       1163.1

1 row selected.
```

This next example is a bit more useful: An arithmetic calculation is embedded within the SUM function. First you multiply the number of eggs that a bird lays times a number of broods per year; then you apply the SUM function on that value for every bird in the BIRDS table. This returns the total number of eggs laid by all birds in a season or year.

```
SQL> select sum(eggs * broods) "TOTAL EGGS LAYED BY ALL BIRDS IN A SEASON"
  2  from birds;

TOTAL EGGS LAYED BY ALL BIRDS IN A SEASON
-----------------------------------------
                                      127

1 row selected.
```

The AVG Function

The AVG function finds the average value for a given group of rows. When used with the DISTINCT command, the AVG function returns the average of the distinct rows. The syntax for the AVG function follows:

```
AVG ([ DISTINCT ] COLUMN NAME)
```

NOTE

AVG Must Be Numeric

The value of the argument must be numeric for the AVG function to work.

The average value for all values in the BIRDS table's WINGSPAN column is retrieved in the following example:

```
SQL> select avg(wingspan) from birds;

AVG(WINGSPAN)
-------------
   50.5695652

1 row selected.
```

CAUTION

Sometimes Your Data Is Truncated

In some implementations, the results of your query are truncated to the precision of the data type. Review your database system's documentation to ensure that you understand the normal precision for the various data types. This will prevent you from unnecessarily truncating data and possibly getting an unexpected result from improper precision.

The MAX Function

The MAX function returns the maximum value from the values of a column in a group of rows. NULL values are ignored when using the MAX function. Using MAX with the DISTINCT command is an option, but because the maximum value for all the rows is the same as the distinct maximum value, DISTINCT is useless.

The syntax for the MAX function follows:

```
MAX([ DISTINCT ] COLUMN NAME)
```

The following example returns the highest WINGSPAN in the BIRDS table:

```
SQL> select max(wingspan) from birds;

MAX(WINGSPAN)
-------------
         94.8

1 row selected.
```

You can also use aggregate functions such as MAX and MIN on character data. When using these values, collation of your database comes into play again. Most commonly, your database collation is set to a dictionary order, so the results are ranked according to that. For example, say that you perform a MAX operation on the BIRD_NAME column of the BIRDS table:

```
SQL> select max(bird_name)
  2  from birds;

MAX(BIRD_NAME)
------------------------------
Turkey Vulture

1 row selected.
```

In this instance, the function returns the largest value according to a dictionary ordering of the data in the column.

The MIN Function

The MIN function returns the minimum value of a column for a group of rows. NULL values are ignored when using the MIN function. Using MIN with the DISTINCT command is an option. However, because the minimum value for all rows is the same as the minimum value for distinct rows, DISTINCT is useless.

The syntax for the MIN function follows:

```
MIN([ DISTINCT ] COLUMN NAME)
```

The following example returns the lowest WINGSPAN in the BIRDS table:

```
SQL> select min(wingspan) from birds;

MIN(WINGSPAN)
-------------
          3.2

1 row selected.
```

NOTE

DISTINCT and Aggregate Functions Don't Always Mix

One important consideration when using aggregate functions with the DISTINCT command is that your query might not return the wanted results. The purpose of aggregate functions is to return summarized data based on all rows of data in a table. When DISTINCT is used, first it is applied to the results and then those results are passed on to the aggregate function, which can dramatically alter the results. Be sure you understand this when you use DISTINCT with aggregate functions.

As with the MAX function, the MIN function can work against character data. It returns the minimum value according to the dictionary ordering of the data.

```
SQL> select min(bird_name)
  2  from birds;

MIN(BIRD_NAME)
------------------------------
American Coot

1 row selected.
```

Grouping Data

Grouping data is the process of combining columns with duplicate values in a logical order. For example, a database might contain information about employees; many employees live in different cities, but some employees live in the same city. You might want to execute a query that shows employee information for each particular city. You can group employee information by city and create a summarized report.

Or perhaps you want to figure the average salary paid to employees, according to each city. You can do this by using the aggregate function AVG on the SALARY column, as you learned in the previous hour, and by using the GROUP BY clause to group the output by city.

Grouping data is accomplished by using the GROUP BY clause of a SELECT statement (query). In this lesson, you learn how to use aggregate functions with the GROUP BY clause to display results more effectively.

Using the GROUP BY Clause

The GROUP BY clause is used in collaboration with the SELECT statement to arrange identical data into groups. This clause follows the WHERE clause in a SELECT statement and precedes the ORDER BY clause.

The position of the GROUP BY clause in a query follows:

```
SELECT
FROM
WHERE
GROUP BY
ORDER BY
```

The following is the SELECT statement's syntax, including the GROUP BY clause:

```
SELECT COLUMN1, COLUMN2
FROM TABLE1, TABLE2
WHERE CONDITIONS
GROUP BY COLUMN1, COLUMN2
ORDER BY COLUMN1, COLUMN2
```

This ordering normally takes a little getting used to when writing your first queries with the GROUP BY clause; however, it is logical. The GROUP BY clause is normally a much more CPU-intensive operation, and if you do not constrain the rows provided to it, you are grouping unnecessary data that later is discarded. Thus, you intentionally reduce the data set with the WHERE clause so that you perform your grouping only on the rows you need.

You can use the ORDER BY clause, but normally the RDBMS also orders the results by the column ordering in the GROUP BY clause, which is discussed more in depth later in this hour, in the section "Understanding the Difference Between GROUP BY and ORDER BY." Unless you need to order the values in a different pattern than the GROUP BY clause, the ORDER BY clause is redundant. However, sometimes it is provided because you use aggregate functions in the SELECT statement that are not in the GROUP BY clause, or because your particular RDBMS functions slightly differently from the standard.

The following sections explain how to use the GROUP BY clause and provide examples of using it in a variety of situations.

Group Functions

Typical group functions—functions that the GROUP BY clause uses to arrange data in groups—include AVG, MAX, MIN, SUM, and COUNT. These are the aggregate functions that you learned about in Hour 17. Remember that the aggregate functions were used for single values in Hour 17; now you use the aggregate functions for group values.

Grouping Selected Data

Grouping data is simple. The selected columns (the column list following the SELECT keyword in a query) are the columns you can reference in the GROUP BY clause. If a column is not in the SELECT statement, you cannot use it in the GROUP BY clause. How can you group data on a report if the data is not displayed?

If the column name has been qualified, the qualified name must go into the GROUP BY clause. The column name can also be represented by a number. When grouping the data, the order of columns grouped does not have to match the column order in the SELECT clause.

Creating Groups and Using Aggregate Functions

The SELECT clause has conditions that must be met when using GROUP BY. Specifically, whatever columns are selected must appear in the GROUP BY clause, except for any aggregate values. If the columns in the SELECT clause are qualified, the qualified names of the columns must be used in the GROUP BY clause. Some examples of syntax for the GROUP BY clause are shown next.

The following SQL statement selects the MIGRATION_LOCATION and a count of all entries in the BIRD_ID column in the BIRDS_MIGRATION table. Remember that the BIRDS_MIGRATION table links the MIGRATION table to the BIRDS table, so every BIRD_ID in the BIRDS_MIGRATION table that corresponds with a MIGRATION_ID value indicates the number of birds that migrate to a specific location. The tables are joined appropriately, of course, and the query is grouped by the migration location. This gives you a total count of birds in the database that migrate to each individual location.

```
SQL> select migration.migration_location, count(birds_migration.bird_id) birds
  2  from migration, birds_migration
  3  where migration.migration_id = birds_migration.migration_id
  4  group by migration.migration_location;

MIGRATION_LOCATION                  BIRDS
------------------------------ ----------
Central America                        12
Mexico                                 14
No Significant Migration                5
Partial, Open Water                     1
South America                           6
Southern United States                 18

6 rows selected.
```

This next example query focuses on the different types of foods that birds eat. You select the food name and the average wingspan of birds and then apply the ROUND function on the average wingspan to get a whole number. You can see in the FROM clause that you are selecting from three tables and that you have joined those three tables appropriately in the WHERE clause. The results are grouped by the FOOD_NAME and ordered by the second column, which is the AVG(WINGSPAN), in descending order. This sort operation shows the food names with the largest average wingspan of birds first, all the way down to the least. This query gives you a list of all food items in the database and the average wingspan of birds that eat certain food items.

```
SQL> select food.food_name, round(avg(birds.wingspan)) avg_wingspan
  2  from food, birds, birds_food
  3  where food.food_id = birds_food.food_id
  4  and birds.bird_id = birds_food.bird_id
  5  group by food.food_name
  6  order by 2 desc;
```

```
FOOD_NAME                      AVG_WINGSPAN
------------------------------ ------------
Reptiles                                 90
Deer                                     90
Ducks                                    84
Frogs                                    73
Birds                                    69
Crayfish                                 67
Small Mammals                            65
Snakes                                   63
Insects                                  61
Carrion                                  53
Fish                                     52
Plants                                   49
Rodents                                  48
Aquatic Plants                           43
Crustaceans                              41
Fruit                                    40
Aquatic Insects                          40
Seeds                                    38
Corn                                      3

19 rows selected.
```

Understanding the Difference Between GROUP BY and ORDER BY

The GROUP BY clause works the same as the ORDER BY clause, in that both sort data. Specifically, you use the ORDER BY clause to sort data from a query. The GROUP BY clause also sorts data from a query to properly group the data.

However, some differences and disadvantages arise when you use GROUP BY instead of ORDER BY for sorting operations:

- All non-aggregate columns selected must be listed in the GROUP BY clause.
- The GROUP BY clause generally is not necessary unless you use aggregate functions.

Let's look at a few examples. In the following query, you select the migration location and wingspan for birds that migrate to either Central America or Mexico; the results are sorted by the migration location. This is an example of the sort operation performed by the ORDER BY clause.

```
SQL> select m.migration_location, b.wingspan
  2  from birds b,
  3    birds_migration bm,
  4    migration m
```

```
  5  where b.bird_id = bm.bird_id
  6    and m.migration_id = bm.migration_id
  7    and m.migration_location in ('Central America', 'Mexico')
  8  order by 1;

MIGRATION_LOCATION                WINGSPAN
------------------------------ ----------
Central America                         78
Central America                         54
Central America                         72
Central America                         23
Central America                        6.5
Central America                         29
Central America                         18
Central America                         54
Central America                         34
Central America                         72
Central America                       26.8
Central America                       67.2
Mexico                                  78
Mexico                                  54
Mexico                                  72
Mexico                                  23
Mexico                                 6.5
Mexico                                  29
Mexico                                  18
Mexico                                  50
Mexico                                  54
Mexico                                  34
Mexico                                  72
Mexico                                26.8
Mexico                                67.2
Mexico                                  42

26 rows selected.
```

The following example is essentially the same as the first, except that you are trying to improperly use the GROUP BY clause to sort the data in the place of an ORDER BY. The GROUP BY clause performs a sort operation for the purpose of grouping data to perform aggregate functions, but it is not the same as the ORDER BY clause. You can see that an error is returned in this example because, again, you have to group any non-aggregate functions in the query that are in the SELECT clause.

```
SQL> select m.migration_location, b.wingspan
  2  from birds b,
  3    birds_migration bm,
  4    migration m
```

```
  5  where b.bird_id = bm.bird_id
  6    and m.migration_id = bm.migration_id
  7    and m.migration_location in ('Central America', 'Mexico')
  8  group by migration_location;
select m.migration_location, b.wingspan
                              *
ERROR at line 1:
ORA-00979: not a GROUP BY expression
```

NOTE

Error Messages Differ

Different SQL implementations return errors in different formats.

Following is a proper and useful example of using the GROUP BY clause in the same query. Here you perform the AVG aggregate function on the WINGSPAN column and group by the MIGRATION_LOCATION, which is required in this query.

```
SQL> select m.migration_location, avg(b.wingspan) "AVG WINGSPAN"
  2  from birds b,
  3    birds_migration bm,
  4    migration m
  5  where b.bird_id = bm.bird_id
  6    and m.migration_id = bm.migration_id
  7  group by migration_location;

MIGRATION_LOCATION             AVG WINGSPAN
------------------------------ ------------
Partial, Open Water                    94.8
Southern United States           46.3166667
Mexico                                44.75
South America                          48.3
No Significant Migration              61.32
Central America                  44.5416667

6 rows selected.
```

Now say that you want to sort the same grouped results, but independent of the GROUP BY expression. You simply add the ORDER BY clause to the end of the SQL statement to perform a "final" sort by the AVG(WINGSPAN). This shows locations that have birds migrating there with the lowest collective value of AVG(WINGSPAN).

```
SQL> select m.migration_location, avg(b.wingspan) "AVG WINGSPAN"
  2  from birds b,
  3    birds_migration bm,
  4    migration m
```

```
  5  where b.bird_id = bm.bird_id
  6    and m.migration_id = bm.migration_id
  7  group by migration_location
  8  order by 2;

MIGRATION_LOCATION              AVG WINGSPAN
------------------------------ ------------
Central America                  44.5416667
Mexico                                44.75
Southern United States           46.3166667
South America                          48.3
No Significant Migration              61.32
Partial, Open Water                    94.8

6 rows selected.
```

Although GROUP BY and ORDER BY perform a similar function, they have one major difference: The GROUP BY clause is designed to group identical data, whereas the ORDER BY clause is designed merely to put data into a specific order. You can use GROUP BY and ORDER BY in the same SELECT statement, but you must follow a specific order.

Using CUBE and ROLLUP Expressions

Sometimes getting summary totals within a certain group is advantageous. For instance, you might want to see a breakdown of the SUM of sales per year, country, and product type, but you also want to see the totals in each year and country. The ANSI SQL standard provides for such functionality using the CUBE and ROLLUP expressions.

The ROLLUP expression is used to get subtotals, or what is commonly referred to as *super-aggregate* rows, along with a grand total row. The ANSI syntax follows:

```
GROUP BY ROLLUP(ordered column list of grouping sets)
```

The ROLLUP expression works in this way: For every change in the LAST column provided for the grouping set, an additional row is inserted into the result set with a NULL value for that column and the subtotal of the values in the set. In addition, a row is inserted at the end of the result set with NULL values for each of the group columns and a grand total for the aggregate information. Both Microsoft SQL Server and Oracle follow the ANSI-compliant format.

First, examine a result set of a simple GROUP BY statement in which you examine the average wingspan of birds by MIGRATION:

```
SQL> select m.migration_location, avg(b.wingspan) "AVG WINGSPAN"
  2  from migration m,
  3    birds b,
  4    birds_migration bm
```

```
  5 where m.migration_id = bm.migration_id
  6   and b.bird_id = bm.bird_id
  7 group by migration_location;

MIGRATION_LOCATION              AVG WINGSPAN
------------------------------ ------------
Partial, Open Water                    94.8
Southern United States           46.3166667
Mexico                                44.75
South America                          48.3
No Significant Migration              61.32
Central America                  44.5416667

6 rows selected.
```

The following is an example of using the ROLLUP expression to get subtotals of the average wingspan of each migration location:

```
SQL> select m.migration_location, avg(b.wingspan) "AVG WINGSPAN"
  2 from migration m,
  3   birds b,
  4   birds_migration bm
  5 where m.migration_id = bm.migration_id
  6   and b.bird_id = bm.bird_id
  7 group by rollup (migration_location);

MIGRATION_LOCATION              AVG WINGSPAN
------------------------------ ------------
Central America                  44.5416667
Mexico                                44.75
No Significant Migration              61.32
Partial, Open Water                    94.8
South America                          48.3
Southern United States           46.3166667
                                    47.9625

7 rows selected.
```

Notice that you now get an average super-aggregate row for each one of the migration locations and an overall average for the entire set as the last row.

The CUBE expression is different: It returns a single row of data with every combination of the columns in the column list, along with a row for the grand total of the whole set. Because of its unique nature, CUBE is often used to create crosstab reports. The syntax for the CUBE expression follows:

```
GROUP BY CUBE(column list of grouping sets)
```

For a useful illustration of CUBE, study the example that follows. Let's suppose a column has been added to the MIGRATION table called REGION.

The following SQL query selects the REGION, MIGRATION_LOCATION, and AVG(WINGSPAN) from the MIGRATIONS table, BIRDS table, and BIRDS_MIGRATION table. The average wingspan was already calculated based on the migration location, but the CUBE expression provides an overall average wingspan for each region, each migration location itself, and the data set returned as a whole.

```
SQL> select m.region, m.migration_location,
  2      avg(b.wingspan) "AVG WINGSPAN"
  3 from migration m,
  4   birds b,
  5   birds_migration bm
  6 where m.migration_id = bm.migration_id
  7   and b.bird_id = bm.bird_id
  8 group by cube(region, migration_location)
  9 order by 1;

REGION               MIGRATION_LOCATION             AVG WINGSPAN
-------------------- ------------------------------ ------------
Minimal Migration    No Significant Migration              61.32
Minimal Migration    Partial, Open Water                    94.8
Minimal Migration                                           66.9
North                Mexico                                44.75
North                Southern United States           46.3166667
North                                                   45.63125
South                Central America                  44.5416667
South                South America                          48.3
South                                                 45.7944444
                     Central America                  44.5416667
                     Mexico                                44.75
                     No Significant Migration              61.32
                     Partial, Open Water                    94.8
                     South America                          48.3
                     Southern United States           46.3166667
                                                         47.9625

16 rows selected.
```

You can see that, with the CUBE expression, there are even more rows because the statement needs to return each combination of columns within the column set that you provide. An aggregate (average, in this case) is returned for the region, each location, and the result set as a whole.

Using the HAVING Clause

When the HAVING clause is used with the GROUP BY clause in a SELECT statement, it tells GROUP BY which groups to include in the output. HAVING is to GROUP BY as WHERE is to SELECT. In other words, the WHERE clause places conditions on the selected columns, and the HAVING clause places conditions on groups created by the GROUP BY clause. Therefore, when you use the HAVING clause, you are effectively including (or excluding) whole groups of data from the query results.

The following shows the position of the HAVING clause in a query:

```
SELECT
FROM
WHERE
GROUP BY
HAVING
ORDER BY
```

This is the syntax of the SELECT statement that includes the HAVING clause:

```
SELECT COLUMN1, COLUMN2
FROM TABLE1, TABLE2
WHERE CONDITIONS
GROUP BY COLUMN1, COLUMN2
HAVING CONDITIONS
ORDER BY COLUMN1, COLUMN2
```

In this final example, you select the FOOD_NAME and calculate the average wingspan of birds related to each food item. The results are grouped by FOOD_NAME, which is a requirement in this query, and the HAVING clause is applied to show only the food names that are eaten by birds that have an average wingspan greater than 50 inches. Finally, you order the results by the second column, AVG(BIRDS.WINGSPAN), in descending order to show the food items that are eaten by birds with the greatest wingspan, all the way down to the food items eaten by birds with the smallest wingspan.

```
SQL> select food.food_name, round(avg(birds.wingspan)) avg_wingspan
  2  from food, birds, birds_food
  3  where food.food_id = birds_food.food_id
  4  and birds.bird_id = birds_food.bird_id
  5  group by food.food_name
  6  having avg(birds.wingspan) > 50
  7  order by 2 desc;

FOOD_NAME                      AVG_WINGSPAN
------------------------------ ------------
Deer                                     90
Reptiles                                 90
```

```
Ducks                                           84
Frogs                                           73
Birds                                           69
Crayfish                                        67
Small Mammals                                   65
Snakes                                          63
Insects                                         61
Carrion                                         53
Fish                                            52

11 rows selected.
```

Summary

Aggregate functions can be useful and are quite simple to use. In this hour, you learned how to count values in columns, count rows of data in a table, get the maximum and minimum values for a column, figure the sum of the values in a column, and figure the average value for values in a column. Remember that NULL values are not considered when using aggregate functions, except when using the COUNT function in the format COUNT(*). Aggregate functions are the first functions in SQL that you learned in this book, but more follow in the coming hours. You can also use aggregate functions for group values, which are discussed during the next hour. As you learn about other functions, you see that the syntaxes of most functions are similar to one another and that their concepts of use are relatively easy to understand.

You also learned in this hour how to group the results of a query using the GROUP BY clause. The GROUP BY clause is primarily used with aggregate SQL functions, such as SUM, AVG, MAX, MIN, and COUNT. The nature of GROUP BY is like that of ORDER BY, in that both sort query results. The GROUP BY clause must sort data to group results logically, but you can also use it exclusively to sort data. However, an ORDER BY clause is much simpler for this purpose. The HAVING clause, an extension to the GROUP BY clause, places conditions on the established groups of a query. The WHERE clause places conditions on a query's SELECT clause. During the next hour, you learn a new arsenal of functions that enable you to further manipulate query results.

Q&A

Q. Why are `NULL` values ignored when using the `MAX` or `MIN` functions?

A. A `NULL` value means that nothing is there, so no maximum or minimum value is possible.

Q. Why don't data types matter when using the `COUNT` function?

A. The `COUNT` function counts only rows.

Q. Does the data type matter when using the `SUM` or `AVG` functions?

A. Not exactly. If the data can be implicitly converted to numeric data, it will still work. The data type matters less than what data is stored in it.

Q. Am I limited to using only column names inside of aggregate functions?

A. No, you can use any type of calculation or formula, as long as the output corresponds to the proper type of data that the function is expecting to use.

Q. Is using the `ORDER BY` clause mandatory when using the `GROUP BY` clause in a `SELECT` statement?

A. No, using the `ORDER BY` clause is strictly optional, but it can be helpful when used with `GROUP BY`.

Q. Must a column appear in the `SELECT` statement to use a `GROUP BY` clause on it?

A. Yes, a column must be in the `SELECT` statement to use a `GROUP BY` clause on it.

Q. Must all columns that appear in the `SELECT` statement be used in the `GROUP BY` clause?

A. Yes, every column that appears in the `SELECT` statement (except for aggregate functions) must be used in the `GROUP BY` clause, to avoid getting an error.

Workshop

The following workshop consists of a series of quiz questions and practical exercises. The quiz questions are designed to test your overall understanding of the current material. The practical exercises give you the opportunity to apply the concepts discussed during the current hour, as well as build on the knowledge you acquired in previous hours of study. Be sure to complete the quiz questions and exercises before continuing to the next hour. Refer to Appendix C, "Answers to Quizzes and Exercises," for answers.

Quiz

1. True or false: The AVG function returns an average of all rows from a SELECT column, including any NULL values.
2. True or false: The SUM function adds column totals.
3. True or false: The COUNT(*) function counts all rows in a table.
4. True or false: The COUNT([column name]) function counts NULL values.
5. Do the following SELECT statements work? If not, what fixes the statements?

   a.
   ```
   SELECT COUNT *
   FROM BIRDS;
   ```
   b.
   ```
   SELECT COUNT(BIRD_ID), BIRD_NAME
   FROM BIRDS;
   ```
   c.
   ```
   SELECT MIN(WEIGHT), MAX(HEIGHT)
   FROM BIRDS
   WHERE WINGSPAN > 48;
   ```
   d.
   ```
   SELECT COUNT(DISTINCT BIRD_ID) FROM BIRDS;
   ```
   e.
   ```
   SELECT AVG(BIRD_NAME) FROM BIRDS;
   ```
6. What is the purpose of the HAVING clause, and which other clause is it closest to?
7. True or false: You must also use the GROUP BY clause when using the HAVING clause.
8. True or false: The columns selected must appear in the GROUP BY clause in the same order.
9. True or false: The HAVING clause tells the GROUP BY clause which groups to include.

Exercises

1. What is the average wingspan of birds?
2. What is the average wingspan of birds that eat fish?
3. How many different types of food does the Common Loon eat?
4. What is the average number of eggs per type of nest?
5. What is the lightest bird?
6. Generate a list of birds that are above average in all the following areas: height, weight, and wingspan.

7. Write a query to generate a list of all migration locations and their average wingspans, but only for locations of birds that have an average wingspan greater than 48 inches.
8. Write a query showing a list of all photographers and the number of photographers mentored by each photographer.
9. Experiment on your own using aggregate functions, along with other functions that you learned in previous hours.

HOUR 18
Using Subqueries to Define Unknown Data

What You'll Learn in This Hour:

- Defining a subquery
- Justifying the use of subqueries
- Understanding examples of subqueries in regular database queries
- Using subqueries with data manipulation commands
- Using correlated subqueries to make subqueries specific

In this hour, you look at the concept of subqueries, a means by which you can perform additional queries of information from within the same SQL statement. Using subqueries enables you to easily perform complex queries that might rely on complex subsets of data in your database.

Defining Subqueries

A *subquery*, also known as a *nested query*, is a query embedded within the WHERE clause of another query to further restrict data returned by the query. A subquery returns data that is used in the main query as a condition to further restrict the data to be retrieved. Subqueries are employed with the SELECT, INSERT, UPDATE, and DELETE statements.

In some cases, you can use a subquery in place of a join operation by indirectly linking data between the tables based on one or more conditions. When you have a subquery in a query, the subquery is resolved first and then the main query is resolved according to the condition(s) resolved by the subquery. The results of the subquery process expressions in the WHERE clause of the main query. You can use the subquery in either the WHERE clause or the HAVING clause of the main query. Additionally, you can use logical and relational operators such as =, >, <, <>,!=, IN, NOT IN, AND, OR, and so on within the subquery to evaluate a subquery in the WHERE or HAVING clause.

Subqueries must follow a few rules:

- Subqueries must be enclosed within parentheses.
- A subquery can have only one column in the SELECT clause, unless multiple columns exist in the main query for the subquery to compare its selected columns.

- You cannot use an ORDER BY clause in a subquery, although the main query can use an ORDER BY clause. You can use the GROUP BY clause to perform the same function as the ORDER BY clause in a subquery.
- You can use only subqueries that return more than one row with multiple value operators, such as the IN operator.
- The SELECT list cannot include references to values that evaluate to a BLOB, ARRAY, CLOB, or NCLOB.
- You cannot immediately enclose a subquery in a SET function.
- You cannot use the BETWEEN operator with a subquery; however, you can use the BETWEEN operator within the subquery.

NOTE

The Rules of Using Subqueries

The same rules that apply to standard queries also apply to subqueries. You can use join operations, functions, conversions, and other options within a subquery.

The basic syntax for a subquery follows:

```
SELECT COLUMN_NAME
FROM TABLE
WHERE COLUMN_NAME = (SELECT COLUMN_NAME
                           FROM TABLE
                           WHERE CONDITIONS);
```

The following examples show how you can and cannot use the BETWEEN operator with a subquery. Consider this example of the correct use of BETWEEN in the subquery:

```
SELECT COLUMN_NAME
FROM TABLE_A
WHERE COLUMN_NAME OPERATOR (SELECT COLUMN_NAME
                                   FROM TABLE_B)
                                    WHERE VALUE BETWEEN VALUE)
```

You cannot use BETWEEN as an operator outside the subquery. The following is an example of the illegal use of BETWEEN with a subquery:

```
SELECT COLUMN_NAME
FROM TABLE_A
WHERE COLUMN_NAME BETWEEN VALUE AND (SELECT COLUMN_NAME
                                              FROM TABLE_B)
```

As you soon see in this hour, subqueries produce either a single value or a list of values, just as a query does. When a subquery is embedded within the main query, the result set of the main query must logically make sense when compared to the data set that the subquery returns. The subquery is resolved first and the data returned is substituted into the main query.

Subqueries with the SELECT Statement

Subqueries are most frequently used with the SELECT statement, although you can use them within a data manipulation statement as well. When employed with the SELECT statement, the subquery retrieves data for the main query to use.

The basic syntax follows:

```
SELECT COLUMN_NAME [, COLUMN_NAME ]
FROM TABLE1 [, TABLE2 ]
WHERE COLUMN_NAME OPERATOR
                      (SELECT COLUMN_NAME [, COLUMN_NAME ]
                       FROM TABLE1 [, TABLE2 ]
                      [ WHERE ])
```

Consider an example. Let's say that you want to query the database to get a list of birds that have an above average wingspan. The WINGSPAN column is stored in the database, but the average wingspan is not stored. Therefore, you cannot know the value of the average wingspan without first querying for the average wingspan from the BIRDS table. However, even if you perform this query, the average wingspan is a dynamic data value, which means that it can change at any given point in time as new birds are inserted into the database or as the wingspan data is updated. Thus, not only do you not know the value that you need to supply to the query, but that value might change the next time the query is run.

First, you query for the average wingspan from the BIRDS table.

```
SQL> select avg(wingspan)
  2  from birds;

AVG(WINGSPAN)
-------------
   50.5695652

1 row selected.
```

Now that you have the current value for the average wingspan (which is only for comparison purposes in this example), you use the same SELECT statement and substitute that value into the WHERE clause of the query. This is a simple example of a subquery.

```
SQL> select bird_name "BIRD",
  2  wingspan "WINGSPAN ABOVE AVERAGE"
  3  from birds
```

```
  4  where wingspan >
  5        (select avg(wingspan) from birds)
  6  order by 2 desc;

BIRD                           WINGSPAN ABOVE AVERAGE
------------------------------ ----------------------
Mute Swan                                        94.8
Brown Pelican                                      90
Golden Eagle                                       90
Bald Eagle                                         84
Great Blue Heron                                   78
Osprey                                             72
Canadian Goose                                     72
Turkey Vulture                                     72
Great Egret                                      67.2
Common Loon                                        54
Double-crested Cormorant                           54

11 rows selected.
```

You can see here that output was generated showing the name of a bird and the wingspan of each bird, but only for birds that have an above average wingspan. Compare the value of the previous query of 50 inches to the output of this query.

TIP

Using Subqueries for Unknown Values

Subqueries are frequently used to place conditions on a query when the exact conditions are unknown. The salary for `3908` in the previous example was unknown, but the subquery was designed to do the footwork for you.

Following is an example of a subquery attempt using an operator such as `BETWEEN` that creates an illogical comparison. Notice that the Oracle database returns an error. This is because the average wingspan value that the subquery returns is a single value, and the `BETWEEN` operator is looking for exactly two values. Additionally, the `AND` operator is required when using `BETWEEN`, which cannot be done here in the subquery and simply does not make sense.

```
SQL> select bird_name "BIRD",
  2       wingspan "WINGSPAN ABOVE AVERAGE"
  3  from birds
  4  where wingspan between
  5   (select avg(wingspan) from birds)
  6  order by 2 desc;
order by 2 desc
*
ERROR at line 6:
ORA-00905: missing keyword
```

The following query is a more appropriate example with a subquery that returns multiple records that are substituted into the main query using the IN operator.

```
SQL> select bird_name "BIRD",
  2      wingspan "WINGSPAN ABOVE AVERAGE"
  3  from birds
  4  where wingspan in
  5   (select wingspan from birds
  6    where wingspan > 48)
  7  order by 2 desc;



BIRD                           WINGSPAN ABOVE AVERAGE
------------------------------ ----------------------
Mute Swan                                        94.8
Brown Pelican                                      90
Golden Eagle                                       90
Bald Eagle                                         84
Great Blue Heron                                   78
Canadian Goose                                     72
Turkey Vulture                                     72
Osprey                                             72
Great Egret                                      67.2
Double-crested Cormorant                           54
Common Loon                                        54
Ring-billed Gull                                   50

12 rows selected.
```

Subqueries with the CREATE TABLE Statement

You can also use subqueries with Data Definition Language (DDL) statements. The CREATE TABLE that follows uses a subquery to gather the appropriate data. A table called ABOVE_AVG_BIRDS is being created based on the original BIRDS table, but only for birds that have an above average wingspan, an above average height, *and* an above average weight. All three conditions that have subqueries must be true for data to be returned. For example, records are created in this new table, ABOVE_AVG_BIRDS, only where:

- A bird's wingspan is greater than the average wingspan of all birds (subquery 1) *and*
- A bird's height is greater than the average height of all birds (subquery 2) *and*
- A bird's weight is greater than the average weight of all birds (subquery 3)

```
SQL> create table above_avg_birds as
  2  select bird_id, bird_name, wingspan, height, weight
  3  from birds
  4  where wingspan > (select avg(wingspan) from birds)
  5    and height > (select avg(height) from birds)
  6    and weight > (select avg(weight) from birds);

Table created.
```

Study the following data within the new ABOVE_AVG_BIRDS table:

```
SQL> select *
  2  from above_avg_birds;

   BIRD_ID BIRD_NAME              WINGSPAN     HEIGHT     WEIGHT
---------- -------------------- ---------- ---------- ----------
         3 Common Loon                  54         36         18
         4 Bald Eagle                   84         37         14
         5 Golden Eagle                 90         40         15
         9 Canadian Goose               72         43         14
        19 Mute Swan                  94.8         60         26
        20 Brown Pelican                90         54        7.6

6 rows selected.
```

You do not know the current value of any of these averages, but using a subquery, you can easily get a real-time value for each and create a new table specifically based on those results.

Subqueries with the INSERT Statement

You can also use subqueries with Data Manipulation Language (DML) statements. The INSERT statement is the first instance you examine. It uses the data that the subquery returns and inserts it into another table. You can modify the selected data in the subquery with any of the character, date, or number functions.

NOTE

Always Remember to Save Your Transactions

Remember to use the COMMIT and ROLLBACK commands when using DML commands such as the INSERT statement.

The basic syntax follows:

```
INSERT INTO TABLE_NAME [ (COLUMN1 [, COLUMN2 ]) ]
SELECT [ *|COLUMN1 [, COLUMN2 ]
FROM TABLE1 [, TABLE2 ]
[ WHERE VALUE OPERATOR ]
```

Before proceeding, you first need to truncate the ABOVE_AVG_BIRDS table to remove any existing data from that table.

```
SQL> truncate table above_avg_birds;

Table truncated.
```

Now you select all records from the ABOVE_AVG_BIRDS table to verify that no data exists.

```
SQL> select *
  2  from above_avg_birds;

no rows selected
```

Next, you issue an INSERT statement into the ABOVE_AVG_BIRDS table, selecting data from the BIRDS table using a subquery. You can see that six new rows of data are created in the new table.

```
SQL> insert into above_avg_birds
  2  select bird_id, bird_name, wingspan, height, weight
  3  from birds
  4  where wingspan > (select avg(wingspan) from birds)
  5    and height > (select avg(height) from birds)
  6    and weight > (select avg(weight) from birds);

6 rows created.
```

Review the following results and study the data that was inserted into the new table.

```
SQL> select *
  2  from above_avg_birds;

   BIRD_ID BIRD_NAME              WINGSPAN     HEIGHT     WEIGHT
---------- -------------------- ---------- ---------- ----------
         3 Common Loon                  54         36         18
         4 Bald Eagle                   84         37         14
         5 Golden Eagle                 90         40         15
         9 Canadian Goose               72         43         14
        19 Mute Swan                  94.8         60         26
        20 Brown Pelican                90         54        7.6

6 rows selected.
```

This INSERT statement inserts the EMPLOYEEID, LASTNAME, FIRSTNAME, and SALARY into a table called RICH_EMPLOYEES for all records of employees who have a pay rate greater than the pay rate of the employee with identification 3908.

Subqueries with the UPDATE Statement

You can use subqueries with the UPDATE statement to update single or multiple columns in a table. The basic syntax follows:

```
UPDATE TABLE
SET COLUMN_NAME [, COLUMN_NAME) ] =
    (SELECT ]COLUMN_NAME [, COLUMN_NAME) ]
    FROM TABLE
    [ WHERE ]
```

Following is an example of an UPDATE statement that uses similar subqueries as the previous example to update the values in the WINGSPAN column for birds that are above average in three categories: wingspan, height, and weight.

```
SQL> update birds
  2  set wingspan = 99, height = 99, weight = 99
  3  where wingspan > (select avg(wingspan) from birds)
  4    and height > (select avg(height) from birds)
  5    and weight > (select avg(weight) from birds);

6 rows updated.
```

Now if you query the BIRDS table, you see that the values in the columns have been set to the number 99, based on the criteria used in the subqueries.

```
SQL> select bird_name, wingspan, height, weight
  2  from birds;

BIRD_NAME                        WINGSPAN     HEIGHT     WEIGHT
------------------------------ ---------- ---------- ----------
Great Blue Heron                       78         52        5.5
Mallard                               3.2         28        3.5
Common Loon                            99         99         99
Bald Eagle                             99         99         99
Golden Eagle                           99         99         99
Red Tailed Hawk                        48         25        2.4
Osprey                                 72         24          3
Belted Kingfisher                      23         13        .33
Canadian Goose                         99         99         99
Pied-billed Grebe                     6.5         13          1
American Coot                          29         16          1
Common Sea Gull                        18         18          1
Ring-billed Gull                       50         19        1.1
Double-crested Cormorant               54         33        5.5
Common Merganser                       34         27        3.2
Turkey Vulture                         72         32        3.3
American Crow                        39.6         18        1.4
Green Heron                          26.8         22         .4
```

```
Mute Swan                                  99         99         99
Brown Pelican                              99         99         99
Great Egret                              67.2         38        3.3
Anhinga                                    42         35        2.4
Black Skimmer                              15         20          1

23 rows selected.
```

Subqueries with the DELETE Statement

You can also use subqueries with the DELETE statement. The basic syntax follows:

```
DELETE FROM TABLE_NAME
[ WHERE OPERATOR [ VALUE ]
                (SELECT COLUMN_NAME
                FROM TABLE_NAME)
                [ WHERE) ]
```

Let's review the data in the ABOVE_AVG_BIRDS table.

```
SQL> select bird_name, wingspan, height, weight
  2  from above_avg_birds;

BIRD_NAME                        WINGSPAN     HEIGHT     WEIGHT
------------------------------ ---------- ---------- ----------
Common Loon                            54         36         18
Bald Eagle                             84         37         14
Golden Eagle                           90         40         15
Canadian Goose                         72         43         14
Mute Swan                            94.8         60         26
Brown Pelican                          90         54        7.6

6 rows selected.
```

You delete the rows of data from the ABOVE_AVG_BIRDS table for any birds that have either a wingspan equal to the maximum wingspan currently stored in the table or a height that is exactly the same as the minimum height value for any birds in the table.

```
SQL> delete from above_avg_birds
  2  where wingspan = (select max(wingspan) from above_avg_birds)
  3  or height = (select min(height) from above_avg_birds);

2 rows deleted.
```

Now if you select all records from the ABOVE_AVG_BIRDS table, you can see that two rows of data are deleted for the birds that meet the criteria in the subqueries of the DELETE statement.

```
SQL> select bird_name, wingspan, height, weight
  2  from above_avg_birds;
```

```
BIRD_NAME                        WINGSPAN     HEIGHT     WEIGHT
------------------------------ ---------- ---------- ----------
Bald Eagle                             84         37         14
Golden Eagle                           90         40         15
Canadian Goose                         72         43         14
Brown Pelican                          90         54        7.6

4 rows selected.
```

Embedded Subqueries

You can embed a subquery within another subquery, just as you can embed the subquery within a regular query. When a subquery is used, that subquery is resolved before the main query. Likewise, the lowest-level subquery is resolved first in embedded or nested subqueries, working out to the main query.

NOTE

Check the Limits of Your System

Check your particular implementation for limits on the number of subqueries, if any, that you can use in a single statement. This might differ between vendors.

The basic syntax for embedded subqueries follows:

```
SELECT COLUMN_NAME [, COLUMN_NAME ]
FROM TABLE1 [, TABLE2 ]
WHERE COLUMN_NAME OPERATOR (SELECT COLUMN_NAME
                            FROM TABLE
                            WHERE COLUMN_NAME OPERATOR
                                   (SELECT COLUMN_NAME
                                   FROM TABLE
                                  [ WHERE COLUMN_NAME OPERATOR VALUE ]))
```

In the following query, you are looking for a list of birds whose `BIRD_ID` is found in a list of `BIRD_ID`s for only birds that migrate to the location of Mexico. A simple subquery gathers this data.

```
SQL> select bird_name
  2  from birds
  3  where bird_id in (select bird_id
  4         from birds_migration bm,
  5       migration m
  6         where bm.migration_id = m.migration_id
  7    and m.migration_location = 'Mexico');
```

```
BIRD_NAME
------------------------------
Great Blue Heron
Common Loon
Osprey
Belted Kingfisher
Pied-billed Grebe
American Coot
Common Sea Gull
Ring-billed Gull
Double-crested Cormorant
Common Merganser
Turkey Vulture
Green Heron
Great Egret
Anhinga

14 rows selected.
```

The following query, which does not use a subquery, takes a different approach to verify the output of the previous query. The data results are the same.

```
SQL> select m.migration_location, b.bird_name
  2  from birds b,
  3    birds_migration bm,
  4    migration m
  5  where b.bird_id = bm.bird_id
  6    and bm.migration_id = m.migration_id
  7    and m.migration_location = 'Mexico';

MIGRATION_LOCATION             BIRD_NAME
------------------------------ ------------------------------
Mexico                         Great Blue Heron
Mexico                         Common Loon
Mexico                         Osprey
Mexico                         Belted Kingfisher
Mexico                         Pied-billed Grebe
Mexico                         American Coot
Mexico                         Common Sea Gull
Mexico                         Ring-billed Gull
Mexico                         Double-crested Cormorant
Mexico                         Common Merganser
Mexico                         Turkey Vulture
Mexico                         Green Heron
Mexico                         Great Egret
Mexico                         Anhinga

14 rows selected.
```

In this next example, embedded subqueries further break down data. Not only do you want to see a list of birds found in a list of birds that migrate to the location of Mexico, but you also want to see only birds within that location that eat fish. Study the results closely and compare them to the previous examples.

```
SQL> select bird_name
  2  from birds
  3  where bird_id in
  4    (select bird_id
  5     from birds_migration bm,
  6  migration m
  7     where bm.migration_id = m.migration_id
  8       and m.migration_location = 'Mexico'
  9       and bm.bird_id in
 10   (select bf.bird_id
 11    from birds_food bf,
 12         food f
 13    where bf.food_id = f.food_id
 14      and f.food_name = 'Fish'));

BIRD_NAME
------------------------------
Great Blue Heron
Common Loon
Osprey
Belted Kingfisher
Common Sea Gull
Ring-billed Gull
Double-crested Cormorant
Common Merganser
Green Heron
Great Egret
Anhinga

11 rows selected.
```

CAUTION

Subquery Performance

Subquery use can either improve or degrade query performance—it depends on how many tables exist, how the tables are joined, how many conditions exist, how many embedded subqueries are used, and many other factors (including indexes on tables). The use of multiple subqueries results in slower response time and can result in reduced accuracy of the results due to possible mistakes in the statement coding. Consider that a subquery must be evaluated before the main part of the query, so the time that it takes to execute the subquery has a direct effect on the time it takes for the main query to execute.

Using Correlated Subqueries

Correlated subqueries are common in many SQL implementations. The concept of correlated subqueries is discussed as an ANSI-standard SQL topic and is covered briefly in this hour. A correlated subquery is a subquery that is dependent on information in the main query. This means that tables in a subquery can be related to tables in the main query.

NOTE

Proper Use of Correlated Subqueries

For a correlated subquery, you must reference the table in the main query before you can resolve the subquery.

In the following example, you are looking for a list of only birds and their associated wingspan that have a nickname containing the word *eagle*. In this example, instead of joining the BIRDS and NICKNAME tables together in the main query, you join the NICKNAMES table found in the subquery with the BIRDS table found in the main query. In this case, the subquery is dependent on the main query to return data.

```
SQL> select bird_id, bird_name, wingspan
  2  from birds
  3  where bird_id in (select bird_id
  4         from nicknames
  5         where birds.bird_id = nicknames.bird_id
  6   and nicknames.nickname like '%Eagle%');

   BIRD_ID BIRD_NAME                        WINGSPAN
---------- ------------------------------ ----------
         4 Bald Eagle                             99
         5 Golden Eagle                           99

2 rows selected.
```

Summary

By simple definition and general concept, a subquery is a query that is performed within another query to place further conditions on a query. You can use a subquery in a SQL statement's WHERE clause or HAVING clause. Queries are typically used within other queries (Data Query Language), but you can also use them in the resolution of DML statements such as INSERT, UPDATE, and DELETE. All basic rules for DML apply when using subqueries with DML commands.

The subquery's syntax is virtually the same as that of a standalone query, with a few minor restrictions. One of these restrictions is that you cannot use the ORDER BY clause within a subquery; however, you can use a GROUP BY clause, which renders virtually the same effect. Subqueries are used to place conditions that are not necessarily known for a query, providing more power and flexibility with SQL.

Q&A

Q. Is there a limit on the number of embedded subqueries that can be used in a single query?

A. Limitations such as the number of embedded subqueries allowed and the number of tables joined in a query are specific to each implementation. Some implementations do not have limits, although using too many embedded subqueries can drastically hinder SQL statement performance. Most limitations are affected by the actual hardware, CPU speed, and system memory available, but many other considerations also come into play.

Q. It seems that debugging a query with subqueries can be confusing, especially with embedded subqueries. What is the best way to debug a query with subqueries?

A. The best way to debug a query with subqueries is to evaluate the query in sections. First, evaluate the lowest-level subquery and then work your way to the main query (the same way the database evaluates the query). When you evaluate each subquery individually, you can substitute the returned values for each subquery to check your main query's logic. An error with a subquery often results from the use of the operator that evaluates the subquery, such as `(=)`, `IN`, >, and <.

Workshop

The following workshop consists of a series of quiz questions and practical exercises. The quiz questions are designed to test your overall understanding of the current material. The practical exercises give you the opportunity to apply the concepts discussed during the current hour, as well as build on the knowledge you acquired in previous hours of study. Be sure to complete the quiz questions and exercises before continuing to the next hour. Refer to Appendix C, "Answers to Quizzes and Exercises," for answers.

Quiz

1. What is the function of a subquery when used with a `SELECT` statement?
2. Can you update more than one column when using the `UPDATE` statement with a subquery?
3. Can you embed subqueries within other subqueries?
4. What is a subquery called that has a column related to a column in the main query?
5. Can you embed subqueries within other subqueries?
6. What is an example of an operator that cannot be used when accessing a subquery?

Exercises

1. Write a query with a subquery to create a list of birds and their wingspans for birds that have a wingspan less than the average wingspan in the BIRDS table.
2. Produce a list of birds and their associated migration locations for only birds that migrate to locations that have birds migrating there with an above average wingspan.
3. Use a subquery to find any food items that are eaten by the shortest bird in the database.
4. Applying the concept of a subquery, create a new table called BIRD_APPETIZERS based on the following information: This new table should list the FOOD_ID and FOOD_NAME, but only for food items associated with birds that are in the bottom 25 percentile of height.

HOUR 19
Combining Multiple Queries into One

What You'll Learn in This Hour:

- Identifying the operators that combine queries
- Knowing when to use the commands to combine queries
- Using the GROUP BY clause with the compound operators
- Using the ORDER BY clause with the compound operators
- Retrieving accurate data

In this hour, you learn how to combine SQL queries using the UNION, UNION ALL, INTERSECT, and EXCEPT operators. Because SQL is meant to work on data in sets, you need to combine and compare various sets of query data. The UNION, INTERSECT, and EXCEPT operators enable you to work with different SELECT statements and then combine and compare the results in different ways. Again, check your particular implementation for any variations in the use of these operators.

Differentiating Single Queries and Compound Queries

A single query uses one SELECT statement, whereas a compound query includes two or more SELECT statements.

You form compound queries using some type of operator to join the two queries. The UNION operator in the following examples joins two queries.

A single SQL statement can be written as follows:

```
select bird_name
from birds ;
```

This is the same statement using the UNION operator:

```
select bird_name
from birds
where wingspan > 48
```

```
UNION
select bird_name
from birds
where wingspan <= 48 ;
```

The previous statements both return a complete list of birds from the BIRDS table. The first query simply selects all birds with no conditions. The second query has two components to the compound query: The first selects birds with a wingspan greater than 48 inches, and the second selects birds that have wingspan less than or equal to 48 inches.

Compound operators combine and restrict the results of two SELECT statements. You can use these operators to return or suppress the output of duplicate records. Compound operators can bring together similar data that is stored in different fields.

NOTE

How UNION Works

The UNION operator simply merges the results of one or more queries. When using the UNION operator, column headings are determined by column names or column aliases used in the first SELECT statement.

Compound queries enable you to combine the results of more than one query to return a single set of data. This type of query is often simpler to write than a single query with complex conditions. Compound queries also allow for more flexibility in the never-ending task of data retrieval.

Using Compound Query Operators

Compound query operators vary among database vendors. The ANSI standard includes the UNION, UNION ALL, EXCEPT, and INTERSECT operators, all of which are discussed in the following sections.

The UNION Operator

The UNION operator combines the results of two or more SELECT statements without returning duplicate rows. In other words, if a row of output exists in the results of one query, the same row is not returned even though it exists in the second query. To use the UNION operator, each SELECT statement must have the same number of columns selected, the same number of column expressions, the same data type, and the same order—but the SELECT statements do not have to be the same length.

The syntax follows:

```
SELECT COLUMN1 [, COLUMN2 ]
FROM TABLE1 [, TABLE2 ]
[ WHERE ]
```

```
UNION
SELECT COLUMN1 [, COLUMN2 ]
FROM TABLE1 [, TABLE2 ]
[ WHERE ]
```

Let's look at two queries individually. The first query returns the MIGRATION_LOCATION for every row of data in the MIGRATION table. The second query returns the BIRD_NAME from the BIG_BIRDS table created earlier, based on the BIRDS table.

```
SQL> select migration_location
  2  from migration;

MIGRATION_LOCATION
------------------------------
Central America
Mexico
No Significant Migration
Partial, Open Water
South America
Southern United States

6 rows selected.



SQL> select bird_name
  2  from big_birds;


BIRD_NAME
------------------------------
Great Blue Heron
Common Loon
Bald Eagle
Golden Eagle
Osprey
Canadian Goose
Ring-billed Gull
Double-crested Cormorant
Turkey Vulture
Mute Swan
Brown Pelican
Great Egret

12 rows selected.
```

Between the two previous queries, there are 18 rows of data. Now let's combine the following two queries using the UNION operator. The UNION operator merges the results but does not show duplicate records (which do not exist in this example).

```
SQL> select migration_location
  2  from migration
  3  UNION
  4  select bird_name
  5  from big_birds;

MIGRATION_LOCATION
------------------------------
Bald Eagle
Brown Pelican
Canadian Goose
Central America
Common Loon
Double-crested Cormorant
Golden Eagle
Great Blue Heron
Great Egret
Mexico
Mute Swan
No Significant Migration
Osprey
Partial, Open Water
Ring-billed Gull
South America
Southern United States
Turkey Vulture

18 rows selected.
```

The previous example is a simple one, to show you how the UNION operator works. You might think that the data that is returned, displayed in a single column, is not necessarily relevant to other data in the column. This is true. However, this example illustrates that the database returns whatever data you ask for. It's important when writing any SQL statement that relevant and inaccurate data is returned. This data is accurate but might not have met a purpose.

In the next example, the first query returns a list of bird names and the food items they eat, but only for birds that eat fish. The second query also returns a list of bird names and the food they eat, but only for birds that eat small mammals. These are two individual queries that are combined. Take a minute to study the results of the two individual queries; look for birds that exist in both lists.

```
SQL> select b.bird_name, f.food_name
  2  from birds b,
```

```
  3       birds_food bf,
  4       food f
  5  where b.bird_id = bf.bird_id
  6    and f.food_id = bf.food_id
  7    and f.food_name = 'Fish';

BIRD_NAME                      FOOD_NAME
------------------------------ ------------------------------
Great Blue Heron               Fish
Common Loon                    Fish
Bald Eagle                     Fish
Golden Eagle                   Fish
Osprey                         Fish
Belted Kingfisher              Fish
Common Sea Gull                Fish
Ring-billed Gull               Fish
Double-crested Cormorant       Fish
Common Merganser               Fish
American Crow                  Fish
Green Heron                    Fish
Brown Pelican                  Fish
Great Egret                    Fish
Anhinga                        Fish
Black Skimmer                  Fish

16 rows selected.
```

```
SQL> select b.bird_name, f.food_name
  2  from birds b,
  3       birds_food bf,
  4       food f
  5  where b.bird_id = bf.bird_id
  6    and f.food_id = bf.food_id
  7    and f.food_name = 'Small Mammals';

BIRD_NAME                      FOOD_NAME
------------------------------ ------------------------------
Golden Eagle                   Small Mammals
American Crow                  Small Mammals

2 rows selected.
```

In the following example, the UNION operator combines the results of both previous queries. In the result set that follows, 18 rows of data are returned and include everything in the previous two result sets.

```
SQL> select b.bird_name, f.food_name
SQL> select b.bird_name, f.food_name
  2  from birds b,
  3       birds_food bf,
  4       food f

  5  where b.bird_id = bf.bird_id
  6    and f.food_id = bf.food_id
  7    and f.food_name = 'Fish'
  8  UNION
  9  select b.bird_name, f.food_name
 10  from birds b,
 11       birds_food bf,
 12       food f
 13  where b.bird_id = bf.bird_id
 14    and f.food_id = bf.food_id
 15    and f.food_name = 'Small Mammals';

BIRD_NAME                      FOOD_NAME
------------------------------ ------------------------------
American Crow                  Fish
American Crow                  Small Mammals
Anhinga                        Fish
Bald Eagle                     Fish
Belted Kingfisher              Fish
Black Skimmer                  Fish
Brown Pelican                  Fish
Common Loon                    Fish
Common Merganser               Fish
Common Sea Gull                Fish
Double-crested Cormorant       Fish
Golden Eagle                   Fish
Golden Eagle                   Small Mammals
Great Blue Heron               Fish
Great Egret                    Fish
Green Heron                    Fish
Osprey                         Fish
Ring-billed Gull               Fish

18 rows selected.
```

The following example is a query that produces the same results, except that the OR operator is used in the WHERE clause instead of the UNION operator to combine two queries. Sometimes using a compound query to get the results that you seek is easier, and sometimes you can more easily join more tables and use other operators to return one result set.

```
SQL> select b.bird_name, f.food_name
  2  from birds b,
  3       birds_food bf,
  4       food f
  5  where b.bird_id = bf.bird_id
  6    and f.food_id = bf.food_id
  7    and (f.food_name = 'Fish' or f.food_name = 'Small Mammals');

BIRD_NAME                      FOOD_NAME
------------------------------ ------------------------------
Great Blue Heron               Fish
Common Loon                    Fish
Bald Eagle                     Fish
Golden Eagle                   Fish
Osprey                         Fish
Belted Kingfisher              Fish
Common Sea Gull                Fish
Ring-billed Gull               Fish
Double-crested Cormorant       Fish
Common Merganser               Fish
American Crow                  Fish
Green Heron                    Fish
Brown Pelican                  Fish
Great Egret                    Fish
Anhinga                        Fish
Black Skimmer                  Fish
Golden Eagle                   Small Mammals
American Crow                  Small Mammals

18 rows selected.
```

The UNION ALL Operator

You use the UNION ALL operator to combine the results of two SELECT statements, including duplicate rows. The same rules that apply to UNION apply to the UNION ALL operator. The UNION and UNION ALL operators are the same, although one returns duplicate rows of data and the other does not.

The syntax follows:

```
SELECT COLUMN1 [, COLUMN2 ]
FROM TABLE1 [, TABLE2 ]
[ WHERE ]
UNION ALL
```

```
SELECT COLUMN1 [, COLUMN2 ]
FROM TABLE1 [, TABLE2 ]
[ WHERE ]
```

Following is a similar example that lists only the bird names. In the first SELECT statement, only birds that eat fish are returned, and in the second SELECT statement, only the birds that eat small mammals are returned. The UNION operator combines the two result sets. Take a look at the output:

```
SQL>> select b.bird_name
  2  from birds b,
  3       birds_food bf,
  4       food f
  5  where b.bird_id = bf.bird_id
  6    and f.food_id = bf.food_id
  7    and f.food_name = 'Fish'
  8  UNION
  9  select b.bird_name
 10  from birds b,
 11       birds_food bf,
 12       food f
 13  where b.bird_id = bf.bird_id
 14    and f.food_id = bf.food_id
 15    and f.food_name = 'Small Mammals'
 16  order by 1;

BIRD_NAME
------------------------------
American Crow
Anhinga
Bald Eagle
Belted Kingfisher
Black Skimmer
Brown Pelican
Common Loon
Common Merganser
Common Sea Gull
Double-crested Cormorant
Golden Eagle
Great Blue Heron
Great Egret
Green Heron
Osprey
Ring-billed Gull

16 rows selected.
```

Notice that only 16 rows of data are returned in this example, compared to the 18 rows of data in the previous UNION example. This is because previous queries selected the bird's name and also the food item that the bird eats. Even though duplicate bird names existed, the entire row of data itself was never duplicated in the previous results. In these results, you select only the bird's name. Two birds appear twice in the results sets, so this result set does not repeat those duplicate bird names; instead, only 16 rows of data are returned. Remember that the UNION operator does not return duplicate records.

In the following example, you have the same query with the UNION ALL operator—it works the same as the UNION operator, except that it returns all values, including any duplicate records. The ORDER BY clause also sorts the result by the bird's name so that you can more easily see the bird names that are duplicated. Notice that this example returns all 18 rows of data.

```
SQL> select b.bird_name
  2  from birds b,
  3       birds_food bf,
  4       food f
  5  where b.bird_id = bf.bird_id
  6    and f.food_id = bf.food_id
  7    and f.food_name = 'Fish'
  8  UNION ALL
  9  select b.bird_name
 10  from birds b,
 11       birds_food bf,
 12       food f
 13  where b.bird_id = bf.bird_id
 14    and f.food_id = bf.food_id
 15    and f.food_name = 'Small Mammals'
 16  order by 1;


BIRD_NAME
------------------------------
American Crow
American Crow
Anhinga
Bald Eagle
Belted Kingfisher
Black Skimmer
Brown Pelican
Common Loon
Common Merganser
Common Sea Gull
Double-crested Cormorant
Golden Eagle
Golden Eagle
Great Blue Heron
```

```
Great Egret
Green Heron
Osprey
Ring-billed Gull

18 rows selected.
```

The INTERSECT Operator

You use the INTERSECT operator to combine two SELECT statements, but it returns only rows from the first SELECT statement that are identical to rows in the second SELECT statement. The same rules apply when using the INTERSECT operator as when using the UNION operator.

The syntax follows:

```
SELECT COLUMN1 [, COLUMN2 ]
FROM TABLE1 [, TABLE2 ]
[ WHERE ]
INTERSECT
SELECT COLUMN1 [, COLUMN2 ]
FROM TABLE1 [, TABLE2 ]
[ WHERE ]
```

The following SQL statement takes the same query as before and uses the INTERSECT operator instead of the UNION ALL operator. Study the results:

```
SQL> select b.bird_name
  2  from birds b,
  3       birds_food bf,
  4       food f
  5  where b.bird_id = bf.bird_id
  6    and f.food_id = bf.food_id
  7    and f.food_name = 'Fish'
  8  INTERSECT
  9  select b.bird_name
 10  from birds b,
 11       birds_food bf,
 12       food f
 13  where b.bird_id = bf.bird_id
 14    and f.food_id = bf.food_id
 15    and f.food_name = 'Small Mammals'
 16  order by 1;

BIRD_NAME
------------------------------
American Crow
Golden Eagle

2 rows selected.
```

Notice that only two rows are returned because only two rows were identical between the output of the two single queries. The only bird names that were duplicated in the `UNION ALL` example were the `American Crow` and the `Golden Eagle`.

The EXCEPT and MINUS Operators

The `EXCEPT` operator combines two `SELECT` statements and returns rows from the first `SELECT` statement that are not returned by the second `SELECT` statement. Again, the same rules that apply to the `UNION` operator also apply to the `EXCEPT` operator. In Oracle, the `EXCEPT` operator is referenced by using the term `MINUS`, but it performs the same functionality.

The syntax follows:

```
SELECT COLUMN1 [, COLUMN2 ]
FROM TABLE1 [, TABLE2 ]
[ WHERE ]
MINUS
SELECT COLUMN1 [, COLUMN2 ]
FROM TABLE1 [, TABLE2 ]
[ WHERE ]
```

The following example applies the `MINUS` operator to the SQL statement that you have been using, to combine the results of the two queries.

```
SQL> select b.bird_name
  2  from birds b,
  3       birds_food bf,
  4       food f
  5  where b.bird_id = bf.bird_id
  6    and f.food_id = bf.food_id
  7    and f.food_name = 'Fish'
  8  MINUS
  9  select b.bird_name
 10  from birds b,
 11       birds_food bf,
 12       food f
 13  where b.bird_id = bf.bird_id
 14    and f.food_id = bf.food_id
 15    and f.food_name = 'Small Mammals'
 16  order by 1;

BIRD_NAME
------------------------------
Anhinga
Bald Eagle
Belted Kingfisher
Black Skimmer
Brown Pelican
```

```
Common Loon
Common Merganser
Common Sea Gull
Double-crested Cormorant
Great Blue Heron
Great Egret
Green Heron
Osprey
Ring-billed Gull

14 rows selected.
```

As you can see, only 14 rows of data were selected. Remember that the first `SELECT` statement in this compound query returns 16 rows of data, and the second `SELECT` statement returns 2 rows of data. The two rows of data in a second `SELECT`, which consists of the birds `American Crow` and `Golden Eagle`, are eliminated from the final result set. This query returns all birds found in the first set that are not found in a second set. In other words, the bird names found in the second set are eliminated from the first set.

Using ORDER BY with a Compound Query

You can use the `ORDER BY` clause with a compound query. However, you can use the `ORDER BY` clause only to order the results of both queries. Therefore, a compound query can have only one `ORDER BY` clause, even though the compound query might consist of multiple individual queries or `SELECT` statements. The `ORDER BY` clause must reference the columns ordered by an alias or by the column number.

The syntax follows:

```
SELECT COLUMN1 [, COLUMN2 ]
FROM TABLE1 [, TABLE2 ]
[ WHERE ]
OPERATOR{UNION | EXCEPT | INTERSECT | UNION ALL}
SELECT COLUMN1 [, COLUMN2 ]
FROM TABLE1 [, TABLE2 ]
[ WHERE ]
[ ORDER BY ]
```

The following example shows the simple use of the `ORDER BY` that you previously saw in this hour. Here you are sorting by `1`, which is the first column and happens to be the only column selected in this case.

```
SQL> select b.bird_name
  2  from birds b,
  3       birds_food bf,
  4       food f
  5  where b.bird_id = bf.bird_id
```

```
  6    and f.food_id = bf.food_id
  7    and f.food_name = 'Fish'
  8  MINUS
  9  select b.bird_name
 10  from birds b,
 11       birds_food bf,
 12       food f
 13  where b.bird_id = bf.bird_id
 14    and f.food_id = bf.food_id
 15    and f.food_name = 'Small Mammals'
 16  order by 1;

BIRD_NAME
------------------------------
Anhinga
Bald Eagle
Belted Kingfisher
Black Skimmer
Brown Pelican
Common Loon
Common Merganser
Common Sea Gull
Double-crested Cormorant
Great Blue Heron
Great Egret
Green Heron
Osprey
Ring-billed Gull

14 rows selected.
```

The following example is the same, except that you explicitly state the name of the column in the ORDER BY clause instead of using the numeric position of the column in the SELECT clause.

```
SQL> select b.bird_name
  2  from birds b,
  3       birds_food bf,
  4       food f
  5  where b.bird_id = bf.bird_id
  6    and f.food_id = bf.food_id
  7    and f.food_name = 'Fish'
  8  MINUS
  9  select b.bird_name
 10  from birds b,
 11       birds_food bf,
 12       food f
 13  where b.bird_id = bf.bird_id
 14    and f.food_id = bf.food_id
```

```
 15    and f.food_name = 'Small Mammals'
 16  order by bird_name;

BIRD_NAME
------------------------------
Anhinga
Bald Eagle
Belted Kingfisher
Black Skimmer
Brown Pelican
Common Loon
Common Merganser
Common Sea Gull
Double-crested Cormorant
Great Blue Heron
Great Egret
Green Heron
Osprey
Ring-billed Gull

14 rows selected.
```

NOTE

Using Numbers in the ORDER BY Clause

The column in the ORDER BY clause is referenced by the number 1 instead of the actual column name. Sorting compound queries lets you easily recognize duplicate records.

Using GROUP BY with a Compound Query

Unlike ORDER BY, you can use GROUP BY in each SELECT statement of a compound query. You also can use it following all individual queries. In addition, you can use the HAVING clause (sometimes used with the GROUP BY clause) in each SELECT statement of a compound statement.

The syntax follows:

```
SELECT COLUMN1 [, COLUMN2 ]
FROM TABLE1 [, TABLE2 ]
[ WHERE ]
[ GROUP BY ]
[ HAVING ]
OPERATOR {UNION | EXCEPT | INTERSECT | UNION ALL}
SELECT COLUMN1 [, COLUMN2 ]
FROM TABLE1 [, TABLE2 ]
[ WHERE ]
```

```
[ GROUP BY ]
[ HAVING ]
[ ORDER BY ]
```

To best illustrate this example, several queries follow that select data about migration locations in the BIRDS database. The first query that follows shows the migration location and a count of birds that migrate to each specific migration location. Notice that six rows of data are returned because the database contains six migration locations and you have not placed any conditions on the data that this query returns.

```
SQL> select m.migration_location,
  2         count(bm.bird_id) "COUNT OF BIRDS"
  3  from migration m,
  4       birds_migration bm
  5  where m.migration_id = bm.migration_id
  6  group by m.migration_location;

MIGRATION_LOCATION              COUNT OF BIRDS
------------------------------ --------------
Southern United States                     18
Central America                            12
South America                               6
Mexico                                     14
No Significant Migration                    5
Partial, Open Water                         1

6 rows selected.
```

The next query is the same as the first, except that you use the HAVING clause to return only migration locations that have more than six types of birds that migrate to each specific location. Verify the following results against the previous output:

```
SQL> select m.migration_location,
  2         count(bm.bird_id) "COUNT OF BIRDS"
  3  from migration m,
  4       birds_migration bm
  5  where m.migration_id = bm.migration_id
  5  group by m.migration_location
  7  having count(bm.bird_id) > 6
  8  order by 1;

MIGRATION_LOCATION              COUNT OF BIRDS
------------------------------ --------------
Central America                            12
Mexico                                     14
Southern United States                     18

3 rows selected.
```

In the following query, the HAVING clause returns only migration locations that have six or fewer types of birds that migrate to each specific location. Verify the following results against the previous output:

```
SQL> select m.migration_location,
  2         count(bm.bird_id) "COUNT OF BIRDS"
  3  from migration m,
  4       birds_migration bm
  5  where m.migration_id = bm.migration_id
  6  group by m.migration_location
  7  having count(bm.bird_id) <= 6
  8  order by 1;

MIGRATION_LOCATION             COUNT OF BIRDS
------------------------------ --------------
No Significant Migration                    5
Partial, Open Water                         1
South America                               6

3 rows selected.
```

In this last example, you use the UNION operator to combine two of the previous queries. Each individual SELECT statement in this compound query uses the GROUP BY and HAVING clauses, as well as the aggregate function COUNT to summarize and group the data. The results are combined using the UNION operator, which essentially shows the original results of a single query shown in this section. You can also see that ORDER BY is used only one time in this example, to perform a final sort of the results by MIGRATION_LOCATION. Remember that GROUP BY and HAVING can be used in each individual SELECT statement in a compound query, whereas ORDER BY can be used only at the end of the compound query, to sort the entire data set.

```
SQL> select m.migration_location,
  2         count(bm.bird_id) "COUNT OF BIRDS"
  3  from migration m,
  4       birds_migration bm
  5  where m.migration_id = bm.migration_id
  6  group by m.migration_location
  7  having count(bm.bird_id) > 6
  8  UNION
  9  select m.migration_location,
            count(bm.bird_id) "COUNT OF BIRDS"
 10  from migration m,
 11       birds_migration bm
 12  where m.migration_id = bm.migration_id
 13  group by m.migration_location
 14  having count(bm.bird_id) <= 6
 15  order by 1;
```

```
MIGRATION_LOCATION             COUNT OF BIRDS
------------------------------ --------------
Central America                            12
Mexico                                     14
No Significant Migration                    5
Partial, Open Water                         1
South America                               6
Southern United States                     18

6 rows selected.
```

Retrieving Accurate Data

Be cautious when using compound operators. You can return incorrect or incomplete data if you use the `INTERSECT` operator and you use the wrong `SELECT` statement as the first individual query. In addition, consider whether you want duplicate records when using the `UNION` and `UNION ALL` operators. What about `EXCEPT` and `MINUS`? Do you need any of the rows that the second query did not return? As you can see, using the wrong compound query operator or the wrong order of individual queries in a compound query can easily return misleading data.

Summary

This hour introduced you to compound queries. All SQL statements discussed before this hour consisted of a single query. Compound queries enable you to use multiple individual queries together as a single query to achieve the data result set you want as output. The compound query operators discussed include `UNION`, `UNION ALL`, `INTERSECT`, and `EXCEPT` (`MINUS`). `UNION` returns the output of two single queries without displaying duplicate rows of data. `UNION ALL` displays all output of single queries, regardless of existing duplicate rows. `INTERSECT` returns identical rows between two queries. `EXCEPT` (`MINUS` in Oracle) returns the results of one query that do not exist in another query. Compound queries provide greater flexibility when trying to satisfy the requirements of various queries that, without the use of compound operators, can result in complex queries.

Q&A

Q. How are the columns referenced in the `GROUP BY` clause in a compound query?

A. The columns can be referenced by the actual column name or by the number of the column placement in the query if the column names are not identical in the two queries.

Q. I understand what the `EXCEPT` operator does, but would the outcome change if I reversed the `SELECT` statements?

A. Yes, the order of the individual queries is important when using the `EXCEPT` or `MINUS` operator. Remember that all rows are returned from the first query that are not returned by the second query. Changing the order of the two individual queries in the compound query can definitely affect the results.

Q. Must the data type and the length of columns in a compound query be the same in both queries?

A. No, only the data type must be the same; the length can differ.

Q. What determines the column names when using the `UNION` operator?

A. The first query set determines the column names for the data returned when using a UNION operator.

Workshop

The following workshop consists of a series of quiz questions and practical exercises. The quiz questions are designed to test your overall understanding of the current material. The practical exercises give you the opportunity to apply the concepts discussed during the current hour, as well as build on the knowledge you acquired in previous hours of study. Be sure to complete the quiz questions and exercises before continuing to the next hour. Refer to Appendix C, "Answers to Quizzes and Exercises," for answers.

Quiz

1. Match the correct operator to the following statements:

Statement	Operator
a. Show duplicates	`UNION`
b. Return only rows from the first query that match those in the second query	`INTERSECT`
c. Return no duplicates	`UNION ALL`
d. Return only rows from the first query that are not returned by the second	`EXCEPT`

2. How many times can ORDER BY be used in a compound query?
3. How many times can GROUP BY be used in a compound query?
4. How many times can HAVING be used in a compound query?
5. Consider a query that uses the EXCEPT (or MINUS) operator. Suppose that the first SELECT statement returns 10 rows of distinct rows, and the second SELECT statement returns 4 distinct rows of data. How many rows of data are returned in the final result set of the compound query?

Exercises

1. Create a table using the following SQL code; then write a query to select all records from the table.

```
SQL> create table birds_menu as
  2  select b.bird_id, b.bird_name,
  3         b.incubation + b.fledging parent_time,
  4         f.food_name
  5  from birds b,
  6       food f,
  7       birds_food bf
  8  where b.bird_id = bf.bird_id
  9    and bf.food_id = f.food_id
 10    and f.food_name in ('Crustaceans', 'Insects',
 11                        'Seeds', 'Snakes')
 12  order by 1;
```

2. Issue the following queries and study the results. The first query selects the bird's name from the new table for birds whose parenting time exceeds 85 days. The second query is for those birds in the new table whose parenting time is less than or equal to 85 days. The third query combines both queries using the UNION operator.

```
SQL> select bird_name
  2  from birds_menu
  3  where parent_time > 85
  4  order by 1;

SQL> select bird_name
  2  from birds_menu
  3  where parent_time <= 85
  4  order by 1;

SQL> select bird_name
  2  from birds_menu
  3  where parent_time > 85
  4  UNION
  5  select bird_name
```

```
  6  from birds_menu
  7  where parent_time <= 85
  8  order by 1;
```

3. Issue the following SQL statement to practice with the previous query using the UNION ALL operator, and compare the results to the previous result set.

```
SQL> select bird_name
  2  from birds_menu
  3  where parent_time > 85
  4  UNION ALL
  5  select bird_name
  6  from birds_menu
  7  where parent_time <= 85
  8  order by 1;
```

4. Issue the following SQL statement to practice with the INTERSECT operator, and compare the results to the base data in the BIRDS_MENU table.

```
SQL> select bird_name
  2  from birds_menu
  3  INTERSECT
  4  select bird_name
  5  from birds_menu
  6  where food_name in ('Insects', 'Snakes')
  7  order by 1;
```

5. Issue the following SQL statement to practice with the MINUS operator, and compare the results to the base data in the BIRDS_MENU table.

```
SQL> select bird_name
  2  from birds_menu
  3  MINUS
  4  select bird_name
  5  from birds_menu
  6  where food_name in ('Insects', 'Snakes')
  7  order by 1;
```

6. Issue the following SQL statement to return a count of the number of food items eaten by each bird in the BIRDS_MENU table.

```
SQL> select bird_name, count(food_name)
  2  from birds_menu
  3  group by bird_name;
```

7. Issue the following SQL statement to use aggregate functions in a query. Study the results closely.

```
SQL> select bird_name, count(food_name)
  2  from birds_menu
  3  where parent_time > 100
  4  group by bird_name
  5  UNION
  6  select bird_name, count(food_name)
  7  from birds_menu
  8  where parent_time < 80
  9  group by bird_name;
```

8. Experiment with some compound queries on your own using the new table you created during these exercises, or for any tables in the BIRDS database, or for any tables you have created thus far.

HOUR 20

Creating and Using Views and Synonyms

What You'll Learn in This Hour:

- Defining views and seeing how they are used
- Enhancing security with views
- Storing, creating, and joining views
- Manipulating data in a view
- Using nested views
- Managing synonyms

In this hour, you learn about performance, as well as how to create and drop views, how to use views for security, and how to provide simplicity in data retrieval for end users and reports. This hour also includes a discussion on synonyms.

Defining Views

A view is a virtual table. That is, a view looks like a table and acts like a table as far as a user is concerned, but it doesn't require physical storage. A view is actually a composition of a table in the form of a predefined query that is stored in the database. For example, you can create a view from `BIRDS` that contains only the `BIRD_NAME` and `WINGSPAN` columns instead of all the columns in `BIRDS`. A view can contain all rows of a table or only certain rows. You can create a view from one or many tables.

When you create a view, a `SELECT` statement is run against the database and defines the view. The `SELECT` statement that defines the view might simply contain column names from the table. Alternatively, it can be more explicitly written using various functions and calculations to manipulate or summarize the data that the user sees. Figure 20.1 shows an example view.

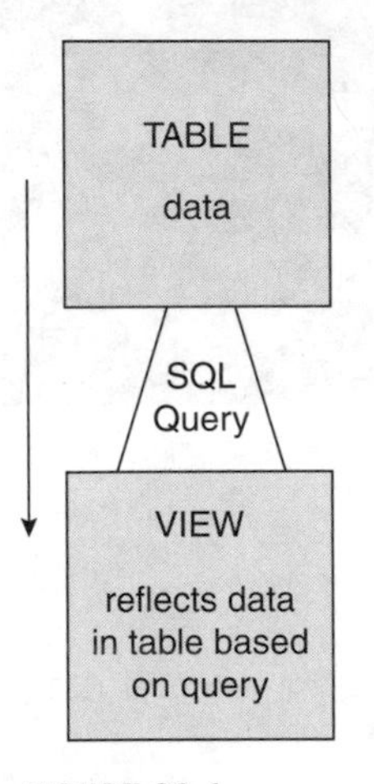

FIGURE 20.1
The view

A view is considered a database object, although it is stored in memory only. Unlike other database objects, it takes up no storage space (other than the space required to store the view definition). Either the view's creator or the schema owner owns the view. The view owner automatically has all applicable privileges on that view and, as with tables, can grant privileges on the view to other users. The `GRANT` command's `GRANT OPTION` privilege works the same as on a table. See Hour 21, "Managing Database Users and Security," for more information.

A view is used in the same manner that a table is used in the database, meaning that data can be selected from a view as it is from a table. Data can also be manipulated in a view, although some restrictions exist. The following sections discuss some common uses for views and how they are stored in the database.

CAUTION

Dropping Tables Used by Views

If a table that created a view is dropped, the view becomes inaccessible and you receive an error when trying to query against the view.

Using Views to Simplify Data Access

Sometimes your data might be contained in a table format that does not easily lend itself to querying by end users. This can happen through the process of normalizing your database or just as a process of database design. In this instance, you can create a series of views to make the data simpler for your end users to query. For example, your users might need to query the birds, the food they eat, and the migration location, but they might not totally understand how to create joins between BIRDS, FOODS, and MIGRATION. To bridge this gap, you can create a view that contains the join and gives the end users the right to select from the view.

Using Views As a Form of Security

Views can act as a form of security in the database. Say you have a table called BIRD_RESCUES_STAFF that contains a variety of information about individuals who work for and volunteer in bird rescue facilities, but it also includes pay information. You do not want all users to see the pay information for staff members. You can create a view based on BIRD_RESCUES_STAFF table that excludes the pay information and then give the appropriate users access to that view instead of having them access the base table.

TIP

Views Can Restrict Access to Columns

Views can restrict user access to particular columns or rows in a table that meet specific conditions as defined in the WHERE clause of the view definition.

Using Views to Maintain Summarized Data

Using a view with summarized data is beneficial if you have a summarized data report in which the data in the table (or tables) is updated often and the report is created often.

For example, suppose that you have a table containing information about individuals, such as city of residence, gender, salary, and age. You can create a view based on the table that shows summarized figures for individuals for each city, such as the average age, average salary, total number of males, and total number of females. To retrieve this information from the base table(s) after the view is created, you can simply query the view instead of composing a SELECT statement that might, in some cases, turn out to be complex.

The only difference in the syntax for creating a view with summarized data and the syntax for creating a view from a single table or multiple tables is the use of aggregate functions. Review Hour 17, "Summarizing Data Results from a Query," for the use of aggregate functions.

Creating Views

Views are created using the CREATE VIEW statement. You can create views from a single table, multiple tables, or another view. To create a view, a user must have the appropriate system privilege according to the specific implementation.

The basic CREATE VIEW syntax follows:

```
CREATE [RECURSIVE]VIEW VIEW_NAME
```

```
[COLUMN NAME [,COLUMN NAME]]
[OF UDT NAME [UNDER TABLE NAME]
[REF IS COLUMN NAME SYSTEM GENERATED |USER GENERATED | DERIVED]
[COLUMN NAME WITH OPTIONS SCOPE TABLE NAME]]
AS
{SELECT STATEMENT}
[WITH [CASCADED | LOCAL] CHECK OPTION]
```

The following subsections explore different methods for creating views using the CREATE VIEW statement.

TIP

ANSI SQL Has No ALTER VIEW Statement

ANSI SQL has no provision for an ALTER VIEW statement, although most database implementations do provide for that capability. For example, in older versions of MySQL, you use REPLACE VIEW to alter a current view. However, the newest versions of MySQL, SQL Server, and Oracle support the ALTER VIEW statement. Check with your specific database implementation's documentation to see what it supports.

Creating a View from a Single Table

You can create a view from a single table. The syntax follows:

```
CREATE VIEW VIEW_NAME AS
SELECT * | COLUMN1 [, COLUMN2 ]
FROM TABLE_NAME
[ WHERE EXPRESSION1 [, EXPRESSION2 ]]
[ WITH CHECK OPTION ]
[ GROUP BY ]
```

The simplest form for creating a view is based on the entire contents of a single table, as in the following example. First, you select bird names and their associated wingspans from the BIRDS table for birds with a wingspan greater than 48 inches. This is the base query that you use to create the view.

```
SQL> select bird_id, bird_name, wingspan
  2  from birds
  3  where wingspan > 48;

   BIRD_ID BIRD_NAME                         WINGSPAN
---------- ------------------------------ ----------
         1 Great Blue Heron                       78
         3 Common Loon                            99
```

```
         4 Bald Eagle                             99
         5 Golden Eagle                           99
         7 Osprey                                 72
         9 Canadian Goose                         99
        13 Ring-billed Gull                       50
        14 Double-crested Cormorant               54
        16 Turkey Vulture                         72
        19 Mute Swan                              99
        20 Brown Pelican                          99
        21 Great Egret                          67.2

12 rows selected.
```

Now you create a view using the previous query. The query is simply substituted into the `CREATE VIEW` statement and you can see that the view was created successfully.

```
SQL> create view big_birds_v as
  2  select bird_id, bird_name, wingspan
  3  from birds
  4  where wingspan > 48;

View created.
```

Now if you select all records from the view that was just created, the results are exactly the same as the standalone query that was executed before you created the view. This view is not a table; it is a virtual table. Remember that a view does not actually contain data; it is only a reflection of the data or a subset of data from one or more tables in the database.

```
SQL> select * from big_birds_v;

   BIRD_ID BIRD_NAME                        WINGSPAN
---------- ------------------------------ ----------
         1 Great Blue Heron                       78
         3 Common Loon                            99
         4 Bald Eagle                             99
         5 Golden Eagle                           99
         7 Osprey                                 72
         9 Canadian Goose                         99
        13 Ring-billed Gull                       50
        14 Double-crested Cormorant               54
        16 Turkey Vulture                         72
        19 Mute Swan                              99
        20 Brown Pelican                          99
        21 Great Egret                          67.2

12 rows selected.
```

Creating a View from Multiple Tables

You can create a view from multiple tables by using a JOIN in the SELECT statement. The syntax follows:

```
CREATE VIEW VIEW_NAME AS
SELECT * | COLUMN1 [, COLUMN2 ]
FROM TABLE_NAME1, TABLE_NAME2 [, TABLE_NAME3 ]
WHERE TABLE_NAME1 = TABLE_NAME2
[ AND TABLE_NAME1 = TABLE_NAME3 ]
[ EXPRESSION1 ][, EXPRESSION2 ]
[ WITH CHECK OPTION ]
[ GROUP BY ]
```

First, you query the BIRDS table. You can see that there are 23 rows of data in the table.

```
SQL> select bird_name
  2  from birds;

BIRD_NAME
------------------------------
American Coot
American Crow
Anhinga
Bald Eagle
Belted Kingfisher
Black Skimmer
Brown Pelican
Canadian Goose
Common Loon
Common Merganser
Common Sea Gull
Double-crested Cormorant
Golden Eagle
Great Blue Heron
Great Egret
Green Heron
Mallard
Mute Swan
Osprey
Pied-billed Grebe
Red Tailed Hawk
Ring-billed Gull
Turkey Vulture

23 rows selected.
```

The following query selects the bird's name and the food item that each bird eats. Three tables are joined together in the query. In this query, only birds that eat fish are returned in the result set.

```
SQL> select b.bird_id, b.bird_name, f.food_name
  2  from birds b,
  3        birds_food bf,
  4        food f
  5  where b.bird_id = bf.bird_id
  6    and f.food_id = bf.food_id
  7    and f.food_name = 'Fish';

   BIRD_ID BIRD_NAME                      FOOD_NAME
---------- ------------------------------ ------------------------
         1 Great Blue Heron               Fish
         3 Common Loon                    Fish
         4 Bald Eagle                     Fish
         5 Golden Eagle                   Fish
         7 Osprey                         Fish
         8 Belted Kingfisher              Fish
        12 Common Sea Gull                Fish
        13 Ring-billed Gull               Fish
        14 Double-crested Cormorant       Fish
        15 Common Merganser               Fish
        17 American Crow                  Fish
        18 Green Heron                    Fish
        20 Brown Pelican                  Fish
        21 Great Egret                    Fish
        22 Anhinga                        Fish
        23 Black Skimmer                  Fish

16 rows selected.
```

Now you use this query to create a view called FISH_EATERS. This view is a virtual table that contains data from the BIRDS table and the FOOD table for only birds that eat fish.

```
SQL> create view fish_eaters as
  2  select b.bird_id, b.bird_name
  3  from birds b,
  4       birds_food bf,
  5       food f
  6  where b.bird_id = bf.bird_id
  7    and f.food_id = bf.food_id
  8    and f.food_name = 'Fish';

View created.
```

If you select all the records from the FISH_EATERS view, you can see that only 16 rows of data are returned, not the original 23 records. This tells you that 16 birds in the database eat fish as part of their diet.

```
SQL> select *
  2  from fish_eaters;

   BIRD_ID BIRD_NAME
---------- ------------------------------
         1 Great Blue Heron
         3 Common Loon
         4 Bald Eagle
         5 Golden Eagle
         7 Osprey
         8 Belted Kingfisher
        12 Common Sea Gull
        13 Ring-billed Gull
        14 Double-crested Cormorant
        15 Common Merganser
        17 American Crow
        18 Green Heron
        20 Brown Pelican
        21 Great Egret
        22 Anhinga
        23 Black Skimmer

16 rows selected.
```

Suppose now that you want to return a list of migration locations and birds that migrate to those locations, but only for fish-eating birds. You can do this in several ways, but using a view is one of the simplest methods. You can also simply join all the appropriate tables together in a single query. Study the following output:

```
SQL> select m.migration_location, fe.bird_id, fe.bird_name
  2  from fish_eaters fe,
  3       birds_migration bm,
  4       migration m
  5  where fe.bird_id = bm.bird_id
  6    and bm.migration_id = m.migration_id
  7  order by 1;

MIGRATION_LOCATION                BIRD_ID BIRD_NAME
------------------------------ ---------- ------------------------------
Central America                         8 Belted Kingfisher
Central America                         7 Osprey
Central America                        18 Green Heron
Central America                        21 Great Egret
Central America                         3 Common Loon
```

```
Central America                    14 Double-crested Cormorant
Central America                    12 Common Sea Gull
Central America                    15 Common Merganser
Central America                     1 Great Blue Heron
Mexico                              7 Osprey
Mexico                             18 Green Heron
Mexico                             21 Great Egret
Mexico                              1 Great Blue Heron
Mexico                             14 Double-crested Cormorant
Mexico                             12 Common Sea Gull
Mexico                             15 Common Merganser
Mexico                              3 Common Loon
Mexico                              8 Belted Kingfisher
Mexico                             13 Ring-billed Gull
Mexico                             22 Anhinga
No Significant Migration           17 American Crow
No Significant Migration            5 Golden Eagle
No Significant Migration           20 Brown Pelican
No Significant Migration           23 Black Skimmer
South America                       8 Belted Kingfisher
South America                       7 Osprey
South America                      18 Green Heron
South America                       1 Great Blue Heron
South America                      12 Common Sea Gull
Southern United States             12 Common Sea Gull
Southern United States             14 Double-crested Cormorant
Southern United States              1 Great Blue Heron
Southern United States              7 Osprey
Southern United States             18 Green Heron
Southern United States             21 Great Egret
Southern United States             15 Common Merganser
Southern United States             13 Ring-billed Gull
Southern United States              8 Belted Kingfisher
Southern United States              4 Bald Eagle
Southern United States             22 Anhinga
Southern United States              3 Common Loon

41 rows selected.
```

You can see that the previous query returned 41 rows of data. You use the `ORDER BY` clause to sort the data so that you can easily see which values for migration locations and birds, if any within this data set, repeat. So many rows are returned because multiple birds migrate to multiple locations.

In the next query, you are essentially looking at the same information in a different way, but you return only the distinct value of each migration location that is associated with fish-eating birds. You achieve this by selecting the `MIGRATION_LOCATION` column only and using the `WHERE` clause to look for migration locations in a subquery that joins the BIRDS_MIGRATION table to the FISH_EATERS view. This is an example of using a view in a subquery and seeing how to use a view to drill down into the data you need.

```
SQL> select migration_location
  2  from migration
  3  where migration_id in (select bm.migration_id
  4                             from birds_migration bm,
  5                                  fish_eaters fe
  6                             where bm.bird_id = fe.bird_id);

MIGRATION_LOCATION
------------------------------
Southern United States
Mexico
Central America
South America
No Significant Migration

5 rows selected.
```

Remember that, when selecting data from multiple tables, the tables must be joined by common columns in the WHERE clause. A view is nothing more than a SELECT statement; therefore, tables are joined in a view definition the same as they are in a regular SELECT statement. Recall the use of table aliases to simplify the readability of a multiple-table query.

A view can also be joined with tables and other views. The same principles apply to joining views with tables and other views as when joining tables to other tables. Review Hour 14, "Joining Tables in Queries," for more information.

Creating a View from a View

You can create a view from another view using the following format:

```
CREATE VIEW2 AS
SELECT * FROM VIEW1
```

You can create a view from a view many layers deep (a view of a view of a view, and so on). How deep you can go is implementation specific. The only problem with creating views based on other views is their manageability. For example, suppose that you create VIEW2 based on VIEW1, and then create VIEW3 based on VIEW2. If VIEW1 is dropped, VIEW2 and VIEW3 are no good; the underlying information that supports these views no longer exists. Therefore, always maintain a good understanding of the views in the database and which other objects those views rely on (see Figure 20.2).

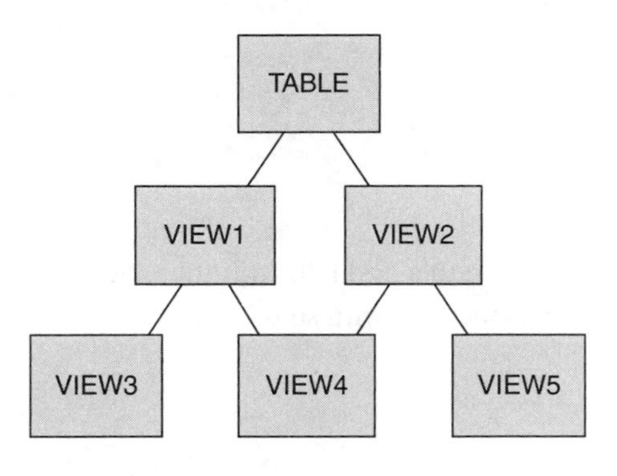

FIGURE 20.2
View dependencies

Figure 20.2 shows the relationship of views that are dependent not only on tables, but also on other views. VIEW1 and VIEW2 are dependent on the TABLE. VIEW3 is dependent on VIEW1. VIEW4 is dependent on both VIEW1 and VIEW2. VIEW5 is dependent on VIEW2. Based on these relationships, the following can be concluded:

- If VIEW1 is dropped, VIEW3 and VIEW4 are invalid.
- If VIEW2 is dropped, VIEW4 and VIEW5 are invalid.
- If the TABLE is dropped, none of the views is valid.

To set up the next example, take a look at all the rows of data in the view SMALL_BIRDS_V. This view has 13 birds that are considered small, according to the conditions provided in the view definition.

```
SQL> select * from small_birds_v;

   BIRD_ID BIRD_NAME                        WINGSPAN
---------- ------------------------------ ----------
         2 Mallard                               3.2
         6 Red Tailed Hawk                        48
         8 Belted Kingfisher                      23
        10 Pied-billed Grebe                     6.5
        11 American Coot                          29
        12 Common Sea Gull                        18
        13 Ring-billed Gull                       50
        14 Double-crested Cormorant               54
        15 Common Merganser                       34
        17 American Crow                        39.6
```

```
        18 Green Heron                         26.8
        22 Anhinga                               42
        23 Black Skimmer                         15

13 rows selected.
```

You can select the MIGRATION_LOCATION from the MIGRATION table and join with the SMALL_BIRDS_V view to return a list of migration locations that are associated with small birds.

```
SQL> select m.migration_location
  2  from migration m,
  3       birds_migration bm,
  4       small_birds_v sb
  5  where m.migration_id = bm.migration_id
  6    and bm.bird_id = sb.bird_id
  7  order by 1;

MIGRATION_LOCATION
------------------------------
Central America
Central America
Central America
Central America
Central America
Central America
Central America
Mexico
Mexico
Mexico
Mexico
Mexico
Mexico
Mexico
Mexico
Mexico
No Significant Migration
No Significant Migration
South America
South America
South America
Southern United States
Southern United States
Southern United States
Southern United States
Southern United States
Southern United States
Southern United States
Southern United States
```

```
Southern United States
Southern United States
Southern United States

32 rows selected.
```

The following query is the same as the previous query, except that the DISTINCT function has been applied to the MIGRATION_LOCATION column to show only distinct values of the migration location. In this case, you don't care how many birds migrate *to* each location; you just want a list of locations associated with small birds.

```
SQL> select distinct(m.migration_location) "MIGRATION LOCATION"
  2  from migration m,
  3       birds_migration bm,
  4       small_birds_v sb
  5  where m.migration_id = bm.migration_id
  6    and bm.bird_id = sb.bird_id;

MIGRATION LOCATION
------------------------------
Southern United States
Central America
South America
Mexico
No Significant Migration

5 rows selected.
```

Once again, let's look at the data in the SMALL_BIRDS_V view.

```
SQL> select * from small_birds_v;

   BIRD_ID BIRD_NAME                        WINGSPAN
---------- ------------------------------ ----------
         2 Mallard                               3.2
         6 Red Tailed Hawk                        48
         8 Belted Kingfisher                      23
        10 Pied-billed Grebe                     6.5
        11 American Coot                          29
        12 Common Sea Gull                        18
        13 Ring-billed Gull                       50
        14 Double-crested Cormorant               54
        15 Common Merganser                       34
        17 American Crow                        39.6
        18 Green Heron                          26.8
        22 Anhinga                                42
        23 Black Skimmer                          15

13 rows selected.
```

The following example shows a new view created called SMALLEST_BIRDS_V that is based on the data in the SMALL_BIRDS_V view, but only for birds that have a wingspan of less than the average wingspan in the SMALL_BIRDS table that was created earlier.

```
SQL> create view smallest_birds_v as
  2  select * from small_birds_v
  3  where wingspan < (select avg(wingspan)
  4                    from small_birds);

View created.
```

Now if you select data from the most recent view created, SMALLEST_BIRDS_V, you see that the view reflects five rows of data. These records represent the very smallest birds in the database, those that are below average even among the small birds that you defined earlier.

```
SQL> select * from smallest_birds_v;

   BIRD_ID BIRD_NAME                        WINGSPAN
---------- ------------------------------ ----------
         2 Mallard                               3.2
         8 Belted Kingfisher                      23
        10 Pied-billed Grebe                     6.5
        12 Common Sea Gull                        18
        23 Black Skimmer                          15

5 rows selected.
```

BY THE WAY

Choose Carefully How You Implement Your Views

If a view is as easy and efficient to create from the base table as from another view, give preference to the view created from the base table.

Creating a Table from a View

You can create a table from a view just as you can create a table from another table (or a view from another view) in Oracle: by using the CREATE TABLE AS SELECT syntax.

The syntax follows:

```
CREATE TABLE TABLE_NAME AS
SELECT {* | COLUMN1 [, COLUMN2 ]
FROM VIEW_NAME
[ WHERE CONDITION1 [, CONDITION2 ]
[ ORDER BY ]
```

BY THE WAY

Subtle Differences Between Tables and Views

Remember that the main difference between a table and a view is that a table contains actual data and consumes physical storage, whereas a view contains no data and requires no storage other than to store the view definition (the query). It's a subtle difference, yet not so subtle.

The following example creates a table called `SMALLEST_BIRDS` that is based on a query from the `SMALLEST_BIRDS_V` view that you just created.

```
SQL> create table smallest_birds as
  2  select * from smallest_birds_v;

Table created.

SQL>
SQL> select * from smallest_birds;

   BIRD_ID BIRD_NAME                        WINGSPAN
---------- ------------------------------ ----------
         2 Mallard                               3.2
         8 Belted Kingfisher                      23
        10 Pied-billed Grebe                     6.5
        12 Common Sea Gull                        18
        23 Black Skimmer                          15

5 rows selected.
```

Incorporating the ORDER BY Clause

Some implementations of SQL enable you to use the `ORDER BY` clause in the `CREATE VIEW` statement, whereas others do not. Following is an example of a `CREATE VIEW` statement that incorporates the `ORDER BY` clause.

```
SQL> create view small_birds2_v as
  2  select bird_id, bird_name
  3  from birds
  4  where wingspan < (select avg(wingspan) * .25
  5            from birds)
  6  order by bird_id, bird_name;

View created.

SQL> select * from small_birds2_v;
```

```
  BIRD_ID BIRD_NAME
---------- ------------------------------
         2 Mallard
        10 Pied-billed Grebe

2 rows selected.
```

TIP

Defer the Use of the GROUP BY Clause in Your Views

Using the ORDER BY clause in the SELECT statement that is querying the view is better and simpler than using the GROUP BY clause in the CREATE VIEW statement.

Updating Data Through a View

You can update the underlying data of a view under certain conditions:

- The view must not involve joins.
- The view must not contain a GROUP BY clause.
- The view must not contain a UNION statement.
- The view cannot contain a reference to the pseudocolumn ROWNUM.
- The view cannot contain group functions.
- The DISTINCT clause cannot be used.
- The WHERE clause cannot include a nested table expression that includes a reference to the same table as referenced in the FROM clause.
- The view can perform INSERTS, UPDATES, and DELETES as long as they honor these caveats.

Review Hour 10, “Manipulating Data,” for the UPDATE command’s syntax.

Once again, take a look at the data in the SMALL_BIRDS_V view.

```
SQL> select * from small_birds_v;

  BIRD_ID BIRD_NAME                        WINGSPAN
---------- ------------------------------ ----------
         2 Mallard                               3.2
         6 Red Tailed Hawk                        48
         8 Belted Kingfisher                      23
        10 Pied-billed Grebe                     6.5
```

```
        11 American Coot                                29
        12 Common Sea Gull                              18
        13 Ring-billed Gull                             50
        14 Double-crested Cormorant                     54
        15 Common Merganser                             34
        17 American Crow                              39.6
        18 Green Heron                                26.8
        22 Anhinga                                      42
        23 Black Skimmer                                15

13 rows selected.
```

The following `UPDATE` statement changes the bird's name to `Duck` for a bird identification of `2`.

```
SQL> update small_birds_v
  2  set bird_name = 'Duck'
  3  where bird_id = 2;

1 row updated.
```

Now if you select the data from the view, you can see that the bird name of `Mallard` shown in the previous output has been changed to `Duck`. The `ROLLBACK` command is issued because you do not want that change to remain in the database.

```
SQL> select * from small_birds_v;

   BIRD_ID BIRD_NAME                                WINGSPAN
---------- ------------------------------ ----------
         2 Duck                                        3.2
         6 Red Tailed Hawk                              48
         8 Belted Kingfisher                            23
        10 Pied-billed Grebe                           6.5
        11 American Coot                                29
        12 Common Sea Gull                              18
        13 Ring-billed Gull                             50
        14 Double-crested Cormorant                     54
        15 Common Merganser                             34
        17 American Crow                              39.6
        18 Green Heron                                26.8
        22 Anhinga                                      42
        23 Black Skimmer                                15

13 rows selected.

SQL> rollback;

Rollback complete.
```

In the following example, an UPDATE statement is attempting to set the height to a null value in the BIRDS table for birds with an identification of 2. An error is returned because, in the base table of BIRDS, the HEIGHT column is defined as a NOT NULL and is a mandatory column. Therefore, the following UPDATE statement violates a constraint that was previously defined in the database. Any data manipulation in a relational database, either directly using a DML command or indirectly through a view or any other type of object, must adhere to the constraints identified previously, to protect the integrity of the data.

```
SQL> update small_birds_v
  2  set height = ''
  3  where bird_id = 2;
set height = ''
    *
ERROR at line 2:
ORA-01407: cannot update ("RYAN2"."BIRDS"."HEIGHT") to NULL
```

Using the WITH CHECK Option to Control Data That a View Returns

The WITH CHECK option is a CREATE VIEW statement option. It ensures that all UPDATE and INSERT commands satisfy the condition(s) in the view definition. If the commands do not satisfy the condition(s), the UPDATE or INSERT returns an error. WITH CHECK enforces referential integrity by checking the view's definition to see that it is not violated.

Following is an example of creating a view with the WITH CHECK option. The small birds view is updated to set the wingspan equal to 72 when the bird name is Mallard. You can see that one row is updated.

```
SQL> update small_birds_v
  2  set wingspan = 72
  3  where bird_name = 'Mallard';

1 row updated.
```

Now if you issue a query from the SMALL_BIRDS_V view, you can see that the row of data for Mallard no longer exists. This is because you updated the WINGSPAN column to a value that is greater than the values that SMALL_BIRDS_V reflects in the view definition.

```
SQL> select * from small_birds_v;

   BIRD_ID BIRD_NAME                        WINGSPAN     HEIGHT
---------- ------------------------------ ---------- ----------
         6 Red Tailed Hawk                        48         25
         8 Belted Kingfisher                      23         13
        10 Pied-billed Grebe                     6.5         13
        11 American Coot                          29         16
        12 Common Sea Gull                        18         18
```

```
        13 Ring-billed Gull                              50         19
        14 Double-crested Cormorant                      54         33
        15 Common Merganser                              34         27
        17 American Crow                               39.6         18
        18 Green Heron                                 26.8         22
        22 Anhinga                                       42         35
        23 Black Skimmer                                 15         20

12 rows selected.
```

The following example sets the wingspan of the Red Tailed Hawk to 72 inches:

```
SQL> update small_birds_v
  2  set wingspan = 72
  3  where bird_name = 'Red Tailed Hawk';

1 row updated.
```

Once again, when you look at all the data in the SMALL_BIRDS_V view, you can see that Red Tailed Hawk no longer appears in the output and one fewer row of data is returned.

```
SQL> select * from small_birds_v;

   BIRD_ID BIRD_NAME                                WINGSPAN     HEIGHT
---------- ------------------------------ ---------- ----------
         8 Belted Kingfisher                              23         13
        10 Pied-billed Grebe                             6.5         13
        11 American Coot                                  29         16
        12 Common Sea Gull                                18         18
        13 Ring-billed Gull                               50         19
        14 Double-crested Cormorant                       54         33
        15 Common Merganser                               34         27
        17 American Crow                                39.6         18
        18 Green Heron                                  26.8         22
        22 Anhinga                                        42         35
        23 Black Skimmer                                  15         20

11 rows selected.
```

Now let's drop the view and then re-create the view using the WITH CHECK option. The ROLLBACK command places the record for Red Tailed Hawk back in the view (base table).

```
SQL> rollback;

Rollback complete.


SQL> drop view small_birds_v;

View dropped.
```

The next SQL statement creates the same view as before, but using the WITH CHECK option. The WITH CHECK option ensures that any changes to data associated with the view adhere to any criteria used to create the view, regardless of whether underlying constraints exist in the base table.

```
SQL>
SQL> create view small_birds_v as
  2  select bird_id, bird_name, wingspan
  3  from birds
  4  where wingspan < (select avg(wingspan)
  5               from birds)
  6  with check option;

View created.
```

Now that you have re-created the view using the WITH CHECK option, you can attempt to set the wingspan to 72 inches for the Red Tailed Hawk, just as you did before. However, you can see here that an error is returned. This is because a wingspan of 72 inches is greater than the definition of the view for the WINGSPAN column, which looks for wingspans less than the average wingspan of all birds. The value of 72 inches is greater than the average wingspan of all birds.

```
SQL> update small_birds_v
  2  set wingspan = 72
  3  where bird_name = 'Red Tailed Hawk';
update small_birds_v
       *
ERROR at line 1:
ORA-01402: view WITH CHECK OPTION where-clause violation



SQL> select * from small_birds_v;

   BIRD_ID BIRD_NAME                        WINGSPAN
---------- ------------------------------ ----------
         6 Red Tailed Hawk                        48
         8 Belted Kingfisher                      23
        10 Pied-billed Grebe                     6.5
        11 American Coot                          29
        12 Common Sea Gull                        18
        13 Ring-billed Gull                       50
        14 Double-crested Cormorant               54
        15 Common Merganser                       34
        17 American Crow                        39.6
        18 Green Heron                          26.8
        22 Anhinga                                42
        23 Black Skimmer                          15

12 rows selected.
```

When you choose to use the WITH CHECK option when creating a view from a view, you have two options: CASCADE and LOCAL. CASCADE is the default and is assumed if neither is specified. (CASCADED is the ANSI standard for the syntax; however, Microsoft SQL Server and Oracle use the slightly different keyword, CASCADE.) The CASCADE option checks all underlying views, all integrity constraints during an update for the base table, and all defining conditions in the second view. The LOCAL option checks only integrity constraints against both views and the defining conditions in the second view, not the underlying base table. Therefore, creating views is safer with the CASCADE option because it preserves the base table's referential integrity.

Dropping a View

You use the DROP VIEW command to drop a view from the database. The two options for the DROP VIEW command are RESTRICT and CASCADE. If a view is dropped with the RESTRICT option and other views are referenced in a constraint, the DROP VIEW errs. If the CASCADE option is used and another view or constraint is referenced, the DROP VIEW succeeds and the underlying view or constraint is dropped. An example follows:

```
SQL> drop view small_birds_v;

View dropped.
```

Understanding the Performance Impact of Nested Views

Views adhere to the same performance characteristics as tables when they are used in queries. As such, you need to be cognizant that embedding complex logic within a view does not negate that the data must be parsed and assembled by the system querying the underlying tables. However, the use of views can enhance performance by narrowing down data into smaller groups of data that can then be searched and joined with other tables or groups of data. Views must be treated as any other SQL statement for performance tuning. If the query that makes up your view is not performing well, the view itself experiences performance issues.

In addition, some users employ views to break down complex queries into multiple units of data, or views, that are created on top of other views. This might seem to be an excellent way to break down the logic into simpler steps, but it can present some performance degradation: The query engine must break down and translate each sublayer of view to determine what exactly it needs to do for the query request.

The more layers you have, the more the query engine has to work to come up with an execution plan. In fact, most query engines do not guarantee that you get the best overall plan; they merely give you a decent plan in the shortest amount of time. It is always best practice to keep the levels of code in your query as flat as possible and to test and tune the statements that make up your views.

Defining Synonyms

A *synonym* is another name for a table or a view. Synonyms are usually created so that a user can avoid having to qualify another user's table or view to access that table or view. Synonyms can be created as PUBLIC or PRIVATE. Any user of the database can use a PUBLIC synonym; only the owner of a database and any users that have been granted privileges can use a PRIVATE synonym.

Either a database administrator (or another designated individual) or individual users manage synonyms. Because two types of synonyms (PUBLIC and PRIVATE) are used, different system-level privileges might be required to create them. All users can generally create a PRIVATE synonym. Typically, only a DBA or a privileged database user can create a PUBLIC synonym. Refer to your specific implementation for the required privileges when creating synonyms.

BY THE WAY

Synonyms Are Not ANSI SQL Standard

Synonyms are not ANSI SQL standard; however, because several major implementations use synonyms, this hour discusses them briefly. Be sure to check your particular implementation for the exact use of synonyms, if available. Note that MySQL does not support synonyms; you can implement the same type of functionality using a view instead.

Creating Synonyms

The general syntax for creating a synonym follows:

```
CREATE [PUBLIC|PRIVATE] SYNONYM SYNONYM_NAME FOR TABLE|VIEW
```

Next, take a look at an example of a synonym called MY_BIRDS for the BIG_BIRDS table. This is simply another name that can be used to access the same table or view.

```
CREATE SYNONYM MY_BIRDS FOR BIG_BIRDS;
Synonym created.


SQL> select bird_id, bird_name
  2  from my_birds;

   BIRD_ID BIRD_NAME
---------- ------------------------------
         1 Great Blue Heron
         3 Common Loon
         4 Bald Eagle
         5 Golden Eagle
         7 Osprey
         9 Canadian Goose
        13 Ring-billed Gull
```

```
        14 Double-crested Cormorant
        16 Turkey Vulture
        19 Mute Swan
        20 Brown Pelican
        21 Great Egret

12 rows selected.
```

Table owners also commonly create a synonym for the table to which you have been granted access so that you do not have to qualify the table name by the name of the owner:

```
CREATE SYNONYM BIRDS FOR RYAN.BIRDS;
Synonym created.
```

Dropping Synonyms

Dropping synonyms works like dropping almost any other database object. The general syntax for dropping a synonym follows:

```
DROP [PUBLIC|PRIVATE] SYNONYM SYNONYM_NAME
```

Consider an example:

```
DROP SYNONYM MY_BIRDS;
Synonym dropped.
```

Summary

This hour discussed two important features in SQL: views and synonyms. In many cases, these features can aid in the overall functionality of relational database users. Views are defined as virtual table objects that look and act like tables but do not take up physical space as tables do. Views are actually defined by queries against tables and possible other views in the database. Administrators typically use views to restrict data that a user sees and to simplify and summarize data. You can create views from views, but take care not to embed views too deeply, to avoid losing control over their management. Various options are available when creating views; some are implementation specific.

Synonyms are objects in the database that represent other objects. They simplify the name of another object in the database, either by creating a synonym with a short name for an object with a long name or by creating a synonym on an object that another user owns and to which you have access. Two types of synonyms exist: `PUBLIC` and `PRIVATE`. A `PUBLIC` synonym is accessible to all database users, whereas a `PRIVATE` synonym is accessible to a single user. A DBA typically creates a `PUBLIC` synonym, whereas each user normally creates his or her own `PRIVATE` synonyms.

Q&A

Q. How can a view contain data but take up no storage space?

A. A view does not contain data; it is a virtual table or a stored query. The only space required for a view is for the actual view creation statement, called the view definition.

Q. What happens to the view if a table from which a view was created is dropped?

A. The view is invalid because the underlying data for the view no longer exists.

Q. What are the limits on naming the synonym when creating synonyms?

A. This is implementation specific. However, the naming convention for synonyms in most major implementations follows the same rules that apply to the tables and other objects in the database.

Workshop

The following workshop consists of a series of quiz questions and practical exercises. The quiz questions are designed to test your overall understanding of the current material. The practical exercises give you the opportunity to apply the concepts discussed during the current hour, as well as build on the knowledge you acquired in previous hours of study. Be sure to complete the quiz questions and exercises before continuing to the next hour. Refer to Appendix C, "Answers to Quizzes and Exercises," for answers.

Quiz

1. Can you delete a row of data from a view that you created from multiple tables?
2. When creating a table, the owner is automatically granted the appropriate privileges on that table. Is this true when creating a view?
3. Which clause orders data when creating a view?
4. Do Oracle and SQL Server handle the capability to order a view in the same way?
5. Which option can you use when creating a view from a view to check integrity constraints?
6. You try to drop a view and receive an error because of one or more underlying views. What must you do to drop the view?

Exercises

1. Write a SQL statement to create a view based on the total contents of the BIRDS table. Select all data from your view.
2. Write a SQL statement that creates a summarized view containing the average wingspan of birds in each migration location. Select all data from your view.
3. Query your view to return only the migration locations that are above average in the average wingspan category.
4. Drop your view.
5. Create a view called FISH_EATERS for only those birds that eat fish. Select all data from FISH_EATERS.
6. Write a query joining your FISH_EATERS view to the MIGRATION table, to return only migration locations for birds that eat fish.
7. Create a synonym for your FISH_EATERS view, and then write a query using the synonym.
8. Experiment with some views of your own. Try joining views and tables, and employ some SQL functions that you previously learned.

HOUR 21
Managing Database Users and Security

What You'll Learn in This Hour:

- Identifying types of users
- Managing users
- Identifying the user versus the schema
- Understanding the importance of user sessions
- Altering a user's attributes
- Dropping users from the database
- Maximizing tools utilized by users
- Defining database security
- Understanding security versus user management
- Assigning database system privileges
- Assigning database object privileges
- Granting privileges to users
- Revoking privileges from users
- Understanding security features in the database

In this hour, you learn about one of the most critical administration functions for any relational database: managing database users. Managing users ensures that your database is available to the required people and applications while keeping out external entities. Considering the amount of sensitive commercial and personal data that is stored in databases, this hour is definitely one that you should pay careful attention to.

You also learn the basics of implementing and managing security within a relational database using SQL and SQL-related commands. Each major implementation differs in syntax with its security commands, but the overall security for the relational database follows the same basic guidelines discussed in the ANSI standard. Check your particular implementation for syntax and any special guidelines for security.

Managing Users in the Database

Users are the reason for designing, creating, implementing, and maintaining any database. Their needs are considered when the database is designed, and the final goal in implementing a database is making the database available to users, who then utilize the database that you, and possibly many others, had a hand in developing.

Some people believe that if there were no users, nothing bad would ever happen to the database. Although this statement reeks with truth, the database was actually created to hold data so that users can function in their day-to-day jobs.

User management is often the database administrator's implicit task, but other individuals sometimes play a part in the user management process. User management is vital in the life of a relational database and is ultimately managed through the use of SQL concepts and commands, although they vary among vendors. The ultimate goal of the database administrator for user management is to strike a proper balance between giving users access to the data they need and maintaining the integrity of the data within the system.

NOTE

Roles Vary Widely

Titles, roles, and duties of users vary widely (and wildly) among workplaces, depending on the size of each organization and each organization's specific data processing needs. One organization's database administrator might be another organization's "computer guru."

Types of Users

Multiple types of database users exist, including these:

- Data entry clerks
- Programmers
- System engineers
- Database administrators
- System analysts
- Developers
- Testers
- Managers
- End users

- Functional users
- Customers and consumers
- Organizational stakeholders

Each type of user has a unique set of job functions (and problems), all of which are critical to the user's daily survival and job security. Furthermore, each type of user has different levels of authority and a special place in the database.

The Responsibility of Managing Users

A company's management staff is responsible for the day-to-day management of users; however, the *database administrator (DBA)* or other assigned individuals are ultimately responsible for managing users within the database.

The DBA usually handles creating the database user accounts, roles, privileges, and profiles, as well as dropping those user accounts from the database. Because this can become an overwhelming task in a large and active environment, some companies have a security officer who assists the DBA with the user management process.

The *security officer*, if one is assigned, is usually responsible for completing paperwork, relaying a user's job requirements to the DBA, and letting the DBA know when a user no longer requires access to the database.

The *system analyst*, or system administrator, is usually responsible for the operating system security, which entails creating users and assigning appropriate privileges. The security officer also might assist the system analyst in the same way he or she does the database administrator.

Maintaining an orderly way in which to assign and remove permissions, as well as document the changes, makes the process much easier to maintain. Documentation also results in a paper trail that points to when the security of the system needs to be audited, either internally or externally. This hour expands on the user management system.

NOTE

Follow a Systematic Approach to User Management

Organizations often have blurry lines between different types of users and administrators. Small organizations might have a one-man IT shop, whereas larger organizations might be equipped with a deep bench of IT professionals and backups, especially when 24×7 support is required.

The User's Place in the Database

Users should be given the roles and privileges necessary to accomplish their job. No user should have database access that extends beyond the scope of his or her job duties. Protecting the data is the entire reason for setting up user accounts and security. Data can be damaged or lost, even unintentionally, if the wrong user has access to the wrong data. When the user no longer requires database access, that user's account should be either removed from the database or disabled as quickly as possible.

All users have their place in the database, yet some have more responsibilities and duties than others. Database users are like parts of a human body: All work together in unison to accomplish some goal.

NOTE

Follow a Systematic Approach to User Management

User account management is vital to the protection and success of any database. When this process is not managed systematically, it often fails. User account management is one of the simplest database management tasks in theory, but it is often complicated by politics and communication problems.

How a User Differs from a Schema

A database's objects are associated with database user accounts, called schemas. A *schema* is a collection of database objects that a database user owns. This database user is called the *schema owner*. Often schemas logically group similar objects in a database and then assign them to a particular schema owner to manage. For example, all the personnel tables might be grouped under a schema called HR, for Human Resources. The difference between a regular database user and a schema owner is that a schema owner owns objects within the database, whereas most users do not own objects. Users generally are given database accounts to access data that is contained in other schemas. Because the schema owner actually owns these objects, that user has complete control over them.

Every database typically has a database creator or owner. The database owner has access to all schemas and objects within the database. Additionally, users with administrative access, such as database administrators, typically have access to every schema and object within the database so that they can effectively manage all users and objects.

Understanding the Management Process

A stable user management system is mandatory for data security in any database system. The user management system starts with the new user's immediate supervisor, who should initiate the access request and then go through the company's approval authorities. If management accepts the request, it is routed to the security officer or database administrator, who takes action. A good notification process is necessary; the supervisor and the user must be notified that the user account has been created and that access to the database has been granted. The user account password should be given only to the user, who should immediately change the password upon initial login to the database.

Creating Users

The creation of database users involves using SQL commands within the database. No single standard command works for creating database users in SQL; each implementation has a method for doing so. The basic concept is the same, regardless of the implementation. Several *graphical user interface (GUI)* tools on the market can be used for user management.

When the DBA or assigned security officer receives a user account request, the request should be analyzed for the necessary information. This information should include the company's particular requirements for establishing a user account.

Some items that should be included are the Social Security number, full name, address, phone number, office or department name, assigned database, and sometimes a suggested user account name.

NOTE

User Creation and Management Varies Between Systems

Check your particular implementation for details on how to create users. Also refer to company policies and procedures when creating and managing users. The following section compares the user creation processes in Oracle, MySQL, and Microsoft SQL Server to show some of the similarities and differences between implementations.

Creating Users in Oracle

Following are the steps for creating a user account in an Oracle database:

1. Create the database user account, with default settings.
2. Grant the appropriate privileges to the user account.

The following is the syntax for creating a user:

```
CREATE USER USER_ID
IDENTIFIED BY [PASSWORD | EXTERNALLY ]
[ DEFAULT TABLESPACE TABLESPACE_NAME ]
[ TEMPORARY TABLESPACE TABLESPACE_NAME ]
[ QUOTA (INTEGER (K | M) | UNLIMITED) ON TABLESPACE_NAME ]
```

```
[ PROFILE PROFILE_TYPE ]
[PASSWORD EXPIRE |ACCOUNT [LOCK | UNLOCK]
```

If you are not using Oracle, do not concern yourself with some of the options in this syntax. A *tablespace* is a logical area managed by the DBA that houses database objects, such as tables and indexes. The `DEFAULT TABLESPACE` is the tablespace in which objects created by the particular user reside. The `TEMPORARY TABLESPACE` is the tablespace used for sort operations (table joins, `ORDER BY`, `GROUP BY`) from queries the user executes. The `QUOTA` is the space limit placed on a particular tablespace to which the user has access. `PROFILE` is a particular database profile that has been assigned to the user.

The following is the syntax for granting privileges to the user account:

```
GRANT PRIV1 [ , PRIV2, ... ] TO USERNAME | ROLE [, USERNAME ]
```

NOTE

Implementation Differences for CREATE USER

MySQL does not support the `CREATE USER` command. Instead, users can be managed using the `mysqladmin` tool. After a local user account is set up on a Windows computer, a login is not required. However, in a multiuser environment, you should use `mysqladmin` to set up a user for each user that requires access to the database.

The `GRANT` statement can grant one or more privileges to one or more users in the same statement. The privilege(s) can also be granted to a role, which can then be granted to a user(s).

In MySQL, the `GRANT` command can grant users access to the current database on the local computer. For example:

```
GRANT USAGE ON *.* TO USER@LOCALHOST IDENTIFIED BY 'PASSWORD';
```

Additional privileges can be granted to a user as follows:

```
GRANT SELECT ON TABLENAME TO USER@LOCALHOST;
```

For the most part, multiuser setup and access for MySQL is required only in multiuser environments.

Creating Users in Microsoft SQL Server

The steps for creating a user account in a Microsoft SQL Server database follow:

1. Create the login user account for SQL Server and assign a password and a default database for the user.
2. Add the user to the appropriate database(s) so that a database user account is created.

3. Grant appropriate privileges to the database user account. This hour discusses privileges within a relational database.

Following is the syntax for creating the user account:

```
SP_ADDLOGIN USER_ID ,PASSWORD [, DEFAULT_DATABASE ]
```

This is the syntax for adding the user to a database:

```
SP_ADDUSER USER_ID [, NAME_IN_DB [, GRPNAME ] ]
```

As you can see, SQL Server distinguishes between a login account that is granted access to log into the SQL Server instance and a database user account that grants access to database objects. You can view this by looking at the security folders in SQL Server Management Studio after you create the login account, and then at the database level when you issue the `SP_ADDUSER` command. This is an important distinction with SQL Server because you can create a login account that does not have access to any of the databases on the instance.

A common error when creating accounts on SQL Server is forgetting to assign them access to their default database. So when you set up accounts, make sure that they have access to at least their default database, or you might be setting up the users to receive an error when logging into your system.

Following is the syntax for granting privileges to the user account:

```
GRANT PRIV1 [ , PRIV2, ... ] TO USER_ID
```

Creating Users in MySQL

The steps for creating a user account in MySQL follow:

1. Create the user account within the database.

2. Grant the appropriate privileges to the user account.

The syntax for creating the user account is similar to the syntax used in Oracle:

```
SELECT USER user [IDENTIFIED BY [PASSWORD] 'password']
```

The syntax for granting the user's privileges is also similar to the Oracle version:

```
GRANT priv_type [(column_list)] [, priv_type [(column_list)]] ...
    ON [object_type]
        {tbl_name | * | *.* | db_name.* | db_name.routine_name}
       TO user
```

Examples of Creating Users in the `BIRDS` Database

You might recall the following SQL code to create a username for yourself to get set up for this book. You can also find this in Hour 4, "Setting Up Your Database." To do this, you logged in as a system user in the database. Remember that, to create users in a database, you must have the appropriate administrative privileges, which vary between implementations.

```
SQL> alter session set "_ORACLE_SCRIPT"=true;

Session altered.

SQL> create user your_username
  2  identified by your_passwd;

User created.

SQL> grant dba to your_username;

Grant succeeded.

SQL> connect your_username
Connected.
SQL>
SQL> show user
USER is "YOUR_USERNAME"
SQL>
```

Next is an example for creating two additional user accounts in the database you are using. Keep in mind that this syntax is specific to Oracle.

```
SQL> create user bob_smith
  2  identified by new_password;

User created.

SQL> grant connect to bob_smith;

Grant succeeded.

SQL> create user bird_owner
  2  identified by new_password
  3  default tablespace users
  4  quota 10m on users;

User created.


SQL> grant connect, resource to bird_owner;

Grant succeeded.
```

You might notice the GRANT commands. The CONNECT role was granted to Bob Smith. The user BIRD_OWNER was set up with a default tablespace to create tables and was given a quota, or limit, of 10MB. This user was also granted the CONNECT and RESOURCE privileges, which bestow the ability to connect to the database and perform basic operations such as selects, and also allow a user to create objects such as tables within the database.

Creating Schemas

Schemas can be created via the CREATE SCHEMA statement for implementations that have this feature. Schemas can also be created by simply creating a user and granting the appropriate pivot privileges for that user to create objects in the database. Then the user connects to the database and simply creates objects. That is a schema also.

The syntax for CREATE SCHEMA follows:

```
CREATE SCHEMA [ SCHEMA_NAME ] [ USER_ID ]
                [ DEFAULT CHARACTER SET CHARACTER_SET ]
                [PATH SCHEMA NAME [,SCHEMA NAME] ]
                [ SCHEMA_ELEMENT_LIST ]
```

Following is an example:

```
CREATE SCHEMA USER1
CREATE TABLE TBL1
  (COLUMN1     DATATYPE     [NOT NULL],
   COLUMN2     DATATYPE     [NOT NULL]...)
CREATE TABLE TBL2
  (COLUMN1     DATATYPE     [NOT NULL],
   COLUMN2     DATATYPE     [NOT NULL]...)
GRANT SELECT ON TBL1 TO USER2
GRANT SELECT ON TBL2 TO USER2
[ OTHER DDL COMMANDS ... ]
```

Take a look at the application of the CREATE SCHEMA command in the example database using Oracle:

```
SQL> connect bird_owner/new_password;
Connected.

SQL> create schema authorization bird_owner
  2  create table new_birds
  3         (id   number            not null,
  4          bird varchar2(20)      not null)
  5  grant select on new_birds to bob_smith;

Schema created.
```

```
SQL> insert into new_birds
  2  values (1, 'Pterodactyl');

1 row created.

SQL> commit;

Commit complete.

SQL> disconnect;
Disconnected from Oracle Database 18c Express Edition Release 18.0.0.0.0 -
Production
Version 18.4.0.0.0
```

The schema was created with a table and a row of data, and access to the new table was granted to Bob Smith. The user then disconnected from the database. After this, you connected as Bob Smith and performed a select on the `NEW_BIRDS` table. Notice that Bob Smith had to qualify the name of the table by the owner of the table: `BIRD_OWNER.NEW_BIRDS`.

```
SQL> connect bob_smith/new_password;
Connected.

SQL> select * from bird_owner.new_birds;

        ID BIRD
---------- --------------------
         1 Pterodactyl

1 row selected.
```

The `AUTHORIZATION` keyword is added to the `CREATE SCHEMA` command. This example was performed in an Oracle database. You can see (as you have also seen in this book's previous examples) that vendor syntax for commands often varies among implementations.

Implementations that do support the creation of schemas often assign a default schema to a user. Most often this is aligned with the user's account. Therefore, a user with the account `BethA2` normally has a default schema of `BethA2`. This is important to remember because objects are created in the user's default schema unless otherwise directed by providing a schema name at the time of creation. If you issue the following `CREATE TABLE` statement using the account for `BethA2` account, it is created in the `BethA2` schema.

CAUTION

CREATE SCHEMA Is Not Always Supported

Some implementations might not support the CREATE SCHEMA command. However, schemas can be implicitly created when a user creates objects. The CREATE SCHEMA command is simply a method for accomplishing this task in a single step. After a user creates objects, the user can grant privileges to other users that allow access to the user's objects.

MySQL does not support the CREATE SCHEMA command; a schema in MySQL is considered to be a database. Thus, you use the CREATE DATABASE command to essentially create a schema to populate with objects.

Dropping a Schema

You can remove a schema from the database using the DROP SCHEMA statement. When dropping a schema, you must consider two options: RESTRICT and CASCADE. If RESTRICT is specified, an error occurs if objects currently exist in the schema. You must use the CASCADE option if any objects currently exist in the schema. Remember that when you drop a schema, you also drop all database objects associated with that schema.

The syntax follows:

```
DROP SCHEMA SCHEMA_NAME { RESTRICT | CASCADE }
```

Take a look at an example:

```
SQL> connect ryan/ryan;
Connected.

SQL> alter session set "_ORACLE_SCRIPT"=true;

Session altered.


SQL> drop user bird_owner cascade;

User dropped.
```

NOTE

Different Ways to Remove a Schema

A schema might have no objects because objects, such as tables, can be dropped using the DROP TABLE command. Some implementations have a procedure or command that drops a user and can also drop a schema. If the DROP SCHEMA command is not available in your implementation, you can remove a schema by removing the user who owns the schema objects.

Altering Users

An important part of managing users is the capability to alter a user's attributes after user creation. Life for the DBA would be a lot simpler if personnel with user accounts were never promoted or left the company, or if the new employees rarely joined the organization. In the real world, high personnel turnover and changes in users' responsibilities are a significant factor in user management. Nearly everyone changes jobs or job duties at some point. Therefore, user privileges in a database must be adjusted to fit a user's needs.

Following is an example of altering the current state of a user in Oracle:

```
ALTER USER USER_ID [ IDENTIFIED BY PASSWORD | EXTERNALLY |GLOBALLY AS 'CN=USER']
[ DEFAULT TABLESPACE TABLESPACE_NAME ]
[ TEMPORARY TABLESPACE TABLESPACE_NAME ]
[ QUOTA  INTEGER K|M |UNLIMITED ON TABLESPACE_NAME ]
[ PROFILE PROFILE_NAME ]
[ PASSWORD EXPIRE]
[ ACCOUNT [LOCK |UNLOCK]]
[ DEFAULT ROLE ROLE1 [, ROLE2 ] | ALL
[ EXCEPT ROLE1 [, ROLE2 | NONE ] ]
```

One of the most common applications of the `alter user` command is to reset a user's password, as shown in the following example:

```
SQL> alter user bob_smith
  2  identified by another_password;

User altered.
```

You can alter many of the user's attributes in this syntax. Unfortunately, not all implementations provide a simple command that allows the manipulation of database users. MySQL, for instance, offers several ways to modify the user account. For example, you use the following syntax to reset the user's password in MySQL:

```
UPDATE mysql.user SET Password=PASSWORD('new password')
WHERE user='username';
```

In addition, you might want to change the username for the user. You can accomplish this with the following syntax:

```
RENAME USER old_username TO new_username;
```

Some implementations also provide GUI tools that enable you to create, modify, and remove users.

Monitoring User Sessions

A user database *session* is the time between when a database user logs in and when the user logs out. During the user session, the user can perform various actions that have been granted, such as queries and transactions.

After establishing the connection and initiating the session, the user can start and perform any number of transactions until the connection is disconnected; at that time, the database user session terminates.

Users can explicitly connect and disconnect from the database, starting and terminating SQL sessions, using commands such as the following:

```
CONNECT TO DEFAULT | STRING1 [ AS STRING2 ] [ USER STRING3 ]
DISCONNECT DEFAULT | CURRENT | ALL | STRING
SET CONNECTION DEFAULT | STRING
```

User sessions can be—and often are—monitored by the DBA or other personnel that are interested in user activities. A user session is associated with a particular user account when a user is monitored. A database user session is ultimately represented as a process on the host operating system.

NOTE

Some Databases and Tools Obscure the Underlying Commands

Remember that syntax varies among implementations. In addition, most database users do not manually issue the commands to connect to or disconnect from the database. Most users access the database through a vendor-provided or third-party tool that prompts the user for a username and password, and then connects to the database and initiates a database user session.

Removing User Access

You can remove a user from the database or disallow a user's access using a couple of simple commands. Again, however, variations among implementations are numerous, so check your particular implementation for the syntax or tools to accomplish user removal or access revocation.

The following are methods for removing user database access:

- Change the user's password
- Drop the user account from the database
- Revoke appropriate previously granted privileges from the user

You can use the DROP command in some implementations to drop a user from the database:

```
DROP USER USER_ID [ CASCADE ]

SQL> drop user bob_smith cascade;

User dropped.
```

The REVOKE command is the counterpart of the GRANT command in many implementations, enabling you to revoke privileges that have been granted to a user. An example syntax for this command for SQL Server, Oracle, and MySQL follows:

```
REVOKE PRIV1 [ ,PRIV2, ... ] FROM USERNAME

SQL> revoke insert on new_birds from bob_smith;

Revoke succeeded.
```

Maximizing Tools Utilized by Database Users

Some people say that you do not need to know SQL to perform database queries. In a sense, they are correct; however, knowing SQL definitely helps when querying a database, even when using GUI tools. GUI tools work great when they are available, but understanding what happens behind the scenes is beneficial so that you can maximize the efficiency of these user-friendly tools.

Many GUI tools that aid the database user automatically generate SQL code by navigating through windows, responding to prompts, and selecting options. Reporting tools generate reports. Forms can be created for users to query, update, insert, or delete data from a database. Tools can convert data into graphs and charts. Certain database administration tools monitor database performance, and others allow remote connectivity to a database. Database vendors provide some of these tools, whereas other vendors offer them as third-party tools.

Understanding Database Security

Database security is simply the process of protecting the data from unauthorized usage. Unauthorized usage includes data access by database users who should have access to part of the database, but not all parts. This protection also includes policing against unauthorized connectivity and distributing privileges. Many user levels exist in a database, from the database creator, to individuals responsible for maintaining the database (such as the database administrator [DBA]), to database programmers, to end users. Although end users have the most limited access, they are the users for which the database exists. Users should be granted the fewest number of privileges needed to perform their particular jobs.

You might be wondering what the difference is between user management and database security. After all, the previous hour discussed user management, which seems to cover security. User management and database security are definitely related, but each has its own purpose. The two work together to achieve a secure database.

A well-planned and well-maintained user management program goes hand in hand with the overall security of a database. Users are assigned user accounts and passwords that give them general access to the database. The user accounts within the database should be stored with information such as the user's actual name, the office and department where the user works, a telephone number or extension, and the database name to which the user has access. Personal user information should be accessible only to the DBA. A DBA or security officer assigns an initial password for the database user; the user should change this password immediately. Remember that the DBA does not need to know, and should not want to know, the individual's password. This ensures a separation of duties and protects the DBA's integrity in case problems arise with a user's account.

If a user no longer requires certain privileges, those privileges should be revoked. If a user no longer requires access to the database, the user account should be dropped from the database.

Generally, user management is the process of creating user accounts, removing user accounts, and keeping track of users' actions within the database. Database security goes a step further by granting privileges for specific database access, revoking certain privileges from users, and taking measures to protect other parts of the database, such as the underlying database files.

Assigning Privileges

Privileges are authority levels used to access the database, access objects within the database, manipulate data in the database, and perform various administrative functions within the database. Privileges are issued using the `GRANT` command and are taken away using the `REVOKE` command.

Just because a user can connect to a database does not mean that the user can access data within a database. Access to data within the database is handled through these privileges. The two types of privileges are system privileges and object privileges.

NOTE

Database Security Involves More Than Just Privileges

Because this is a SQL book, not a database book, it focuses on database privileges. However, keep in mind that database security also involves other aspects, such as the protection of underlying database files; that duty is just as important as the distribution of database privileges. High-level database security can become complex and differs immensely among relational database implementations. If you would like to learn more about database security, you can find information on The Center for Internet Security's web page: www.cisecurity.org/.

System Privileges

System privileges enable database users to perform administrative actions within the database, such as creating a database, dropping a database, creating user accounts, dropping users, dropping and altering database objects, altering the state of objects, altering the state of the database, and other actions that can result in serious repercussions if they are not carefully used.

System privileges vary greatly among the different relational database vendors, so check your particular implementation for all the available system privileges and their correct use.

Following are some common system privileges in SQL Server:

- `CREATE DATABASE`—Create a new database
- `CREATE PROCEDURE`—Create stored procedures
- `CREATE VIEW`—Create views
- `BACKUP DATABASE`—Control backup of the database system
- `CREATE TABLE`—Create new tables
- `CREATE TRIGGER`—Create triggers on tables
- `EXECUTE`—Execute given stored procedures within the specific database

Following are some common system privileges in Oracle:

- `CREATE TABLE`—Create new tables in the specified schema
- `CREATE ANY TABLE`—Create tables in any schema
- `ALTER ANY TABLE`—Alter table structure in any schema
- `DROP TABLE`—Drop table objects in the specified schema
- `CREATE USER`—Create other user accounts
- `DROP USER`—Drop existing user accounts
- `ALTER USER`—Make alterations to existing user accounts
- `ALTER DATABASE`—Alter database properties
- `BACKUP ANY TABLE`—Back up data from any table in any schema
- `SELECT ANY TABLE`—Perform a select on any table from any schema

Object Privileges

Object privileges are authority levels on objects, meaning that you must have been granted the appropriate privileges to perform certain operations on database objects. For example, to select data from another user's table, the user must first grant you access to do so. Object privileges are granted to users in the database by the object's owner. Remember that this owner is also called the schema owner.

The ANSI standard for privileges includes the following object privileges:

- `USAGE`—Authorizes usage of a specific domain
- `SELECT`—Allows access to a specific table
- `INSERT(`*`column_name`*`)`—Inserts data into a specific column of a specified table
- `INSERT`—Inserts data into all columns of a specific table
- `UPDATE(`*`column_name`*`)`—Updates a specific column of a specified table
- `UPDATE`—Updates all columns of a specified table
- `REFERENCES(`*`column_name`*`)`—Allows a reference to a specified column of a specified table in integrity constraints; this privilege is required for all integrity constraints
- `REFERENCES`—Allows references to all columns of a specified table

TIP

Some Privileges Are Granted Automatically

The owner of an object is automatically granted all privileges that relate to the objects owned. These privileges are also granted with the `GRANT OPTION`, which is a nice feature available in some SQL implementations. This feature is discussed in the "`GRANT OPTION`" section, later this hour.

Most implementations of SQL adhere to the standard list of object privileges for controlling access to database objects.

You should use these object-level privileges to grant and restrict access to objects in a schema. These privileges can protect objects in one schema from database users who have access to another schema in the same database.

A variety of other object privileges are available among different implementations but are not listed in this section. The capability to delete data from another user's object is another common object privilege available in many implementations. Check your implementation documentation for all the available object-level privileges.

Authority to Grant and Revoke Privileges

The DBA is usually the one who issues the GRANT and REVOKE commands, although a security administrator, if one exists, might have the authority to do so. The authority to grant or revoke certain privileges comes from management and normally should be carefully tracked to ensure that only authorized individuals are given these types of permissions.

The owner of an object must grant privileges to other users in the database on the object. Even the DBA cannot grant database users privileges on objects that do not belong to the DBA (although there are ways to work around that).

Controlling User Access

User access is primarily controlled by a user account and password, but that is not enough to access the database in most major implementations. Creating a user account is only the first step in allowing and controlling access to the database.

After the user account has been created, the database administrator, security officer, or designated individual must assign appropriate system-level privileges to a user before that user can perform actual functions within the database, such as creating tables or selecting from tables. Furthermore, the schema owner usually needs to grant database users access to objects in the schema so that users can do their jobs.

Two commands in SQL allow database access control involving the assignment of privileges and the revocation of privileges. The GRANT and REVOKE commands distribute both system and object privileges in a relational database.

The GRANT Command

The GRANT command grants both system-level and object-level privileges to an existing database user account.

The syntax follows:

```
GRANT PRIVILEGE1 [, PRIVILEGE2 ][ ON OBJECT ]
TO USERNAME [ WITH GRANT OPTION | ADMIN OPTION]
```

This is the syntax for granting one privilege to a user:

```
SQL> grant select on new_birds to bob_smith;

Grant succeeded.
```

The syntax for granting multiple privileges to a user follows:

```
SQL> grant select, insert on new_birds to bob_smith;

Grant succeeded.
```

Notice that, when granting multiple privileges to a user in a single statement, each privilege is separated by a comma.

The syntax for granting privileges to multiple users follows:

```
SQL> grant select, insert on new_birds to bob_smith, ryan;

Grant succeeded.
```

NOTE

Be Sure to Understand the Feedback the System Gives You

Notice the phrase `Grant succeeded`, denoting the successful completion of each `GRANT` statement. This is the feedback that you receive when you issue these statements in the implementation used for the book examples (Oracle). Most implementations have some sort of feedback, although the phrase used might vary.

GRANT OPTION

`GRANT OPTION` is a powerful `GRANT` command option. When an object's owner grants privileges on an object to another user with `GRANT OPTION`, the new user can also grant privileges on that object to other users, even though the user does not actually own the object. An example follows:

```
SQL> grant select on new_birds to bob_smith with grant option;

Grant succeeded.
```

ADMIN OPTION

`ADMIN OPTION` is similar to `GRANT OPTION`, in that the user who has been granted the privileges also inherits the capability to grant those privileges to another user. `GRANT OPTION` is used for object-level privileges, whereas `ADMIN OPTION` is used for system-level privileges. When a user grants system privileges to another user with `ADMIN OPTION`, the new user can also grant the system-level privileges to any other user. An example follows:

```
GRANT CREATE TABLE TO USER1 WITH ADMIN OPTION;
Grant succeeded.
```

CAUTION

Dropping a User Can Drop Granted Privileges

When a user who has granted privileges using either GRANT OPTION or ADMIN OPTION has been dropped from the database, the privileges that the user granted are disassociated with the users to whom the privileges were granted.

The REVOKE Command

The REVOKE command removes privileges that have been granted to database users. The REVOKE command has two options: RESTRICT and CASCADE. When the RESTRICT option is used, REVOKE succeeds only if the privileges specified explicitly in the REVOKE statement leave no other users with abandoned privileges. The CASCADE option revokes any privileges that would otherwise be left with other users. In other words, if the owner of an object grants USER1 privileges with GRANT OPTION, USER1 grants USER2 privileges with GRANT OPTION, and then the owner revokes USER1's privileges. CASCADE also removes the privileges from USER2.

Abandoned privileges are privileges that are left with a user who was granted privileges with the GRANT OPTION from a user who has been dropped from the database or had those privileges revoked.

The syntax for REVOKE follows:

```
REVOKE PRIVILEGE1 [, PRIVILEGE2 ] [ GRANT OPTION FOR ] ON OBJECT
FROM USER { RESTRICT | CASCADE }
```

Following is an example:

```
SQL> revoke insert on new_birds from bob_smith;

Revoke succeeded.
```

Controlled Access on Individual Columns

Instead of granting object privileges (INSERT, UPDATE, or DELETE) on a table as a whole, you can grant privileges on specific columns in the table, to restrict user access. Consider the following example:

```
SQL> grant update (bird) on new_birds to bob_smith;

Grant succeeded.
```

The `PUBLIC` Database Account

The `PUBLIC` database user account is a database account that represents all users in the database. All users are part of the `PUBLIC` account. If a privilege is granted to the `PUBLIC` account, all database users have the privilege. Likewise, if a privilege is revoked from the `PUBLIC` account, the privilege is revoked from all database users, unless that privilege was explicitly granted to a specific user. Following is an example:

```
SQL> grant select on new_birds to public;

Grant succeeded.
```

CAUTION

PUBLIC Privileges Can Grant Unintended Access

Use extreme caution when granting privileges to `PUBLIC`; all database users acquire the privileges granted. Therefore, by granting permissions to `PUBLIC`, you might unintentionally give access to data to users who have no business accessing it. For example, giving `PUBLIC` access to `SELECT` from the employee salary table gives everyone who has access to the database the rights to see what everyone in the company is paid.

Groups of Privileges

Some implementations have groups of privileges in the database. These groups of permissions are referred to with different names. Having a group of privileges allows simplicity for granting and revoking common privileges to and from users. For example, if a group consists of 10 privileges, the group can be granted to a user instead of individually granting all 10 privileges.

NOTE

Database Privilege Groups Vary Among Systems

Each implementation differs in its use of groups of database privileges. If this feature is available, it should be used for ease of database security administration.

Oracle has groups of privileges that are called *roles*. Oracle includes the following groups of privileges with its implementations:

- `CONNECT`—Allows a user to connect to the database and perform operations on any database objects to which the user has access
- `RESOURCE`—Allows a user to create objects, drop objects he or she owns, grant privileges to objects he or she owns, and so on.

- DBA—Allows a user to perform any function within the database. The user can access any database object and perform any operation with this group.

Consider this example for granting a group of privileges to a user:

```
GRANT DBA TO USER1;
Grant succeeded.
```

SQL Server has several groups of permissions at the server level and the database level. Some of the database-level permission groups are listed here:

- DB_DDLADMIN—Allows the user to manipulate any of the objects within the database through any legal data definition language command
- DB_DATAREADER—Allows the user to select from any of the tables within the database from which it is assigned
- DB_DATAWRITER—Allows the user to perform any data manipulation syntax (INSERT, UPDATE, or DELETE) on any of the tables within the database

Controlling Privileges Through Roles

A *role* is an object created in the database that contains grouplike privileges. Roles can reduce security maintenance by not having to grant explicit privileges directly to a user. Group privilege management is much easier to handle with roles. A role's privileges can be changed, and such a change is transparent to the user.

If a user needs SELECT and UPDATE table privileges on a table at a specified time within an application, a role with those privileges can temporarily be assigned until the transaction is complete.

When a role is created, it has no real value other than being a role within a database. It can be granted to users or other roles. Say that a schema named BIRD_OWNER grants the SELECT table privilege to the PHOTOGRAPHER_SELECT role on the NEW_BIRDS table. Any user or role granted the PHOTOGRAPHER_SELECT role now has SELECT privileges on the NEW_BIRDS table.

Likewise, if BIRD_OWNER revokes the SELECT table privilege from the PHOTOGRAPHER_SELECT role on the NEW_BIRDS table, any user or role granted the PHOTOGRAPHER_SELECT role no longer has SELECT privileges on that table.

When assigning permissions in a database, ensure that you think through what permissions a user needs and whether other users need the same sets of permissions. For example, several members of an accounting team might need to access a set of accounting tables. In this case, unless they each need drastically different permissions to these tables, it is far easier to set up a role, assign the role the appropriate conditions, and then assign the users to the role.

If a new object is created and needs to have permissions granted to the accounting group, you can do it in one location instead of having to update each account. Likewise, if the accounting team brings on a new member or decides that someone else needs the same access to its tables, you must assign the role to only the new user; then you are good to go. Roles are an excellent tool to enable the DBA to work smarter, not harder, when dealing with complex database security protocols.

NOTE

Roles Are Not Supported in MySQL

MySQL does not support roles. The lack of role usage is a weakness in some implementations of SQL.

The CREATE ROLE Statement

A role is created with the `CREATE ROLE` statement:

```
CREATE ROLE role_name;
```

Granting privileges to roles works the same as granting privileges to a user, as shown in the following example:

```
SQL> create role photographers_select;

Role created.

SQL>
SQL> grant select on new_birds to photographers_select;

Grant succeeded.

SQL> grant photographers_select to bob_smith;

Grant succeeded.
```

The DROP ROLE Statement

A role is dropped using the `DROP_ROLE` statement:

```
DROP ROLE role_name;
```

Consider an example:

```
SQL> drop role photographers_select;

Role dropped.
```

The SET ROLE Statement

A role can be set for just the user's current SQL session using the SET_ROLE statement:

```
SET ROLE role_name;
```

The following is an example:

```
SQL> SET ROLE PHOTOGRAPHER_SELECT;

Role set.
```

You can set more than one role at once:

```
SQL> SET ROLE PHOTOGRAPHER_SELECT, PHOTOGRAPHER_UPDATE;

Role set.
```

NOTE

SET ROLE Is Not Always Used

In some implementations, such as Microsoft SQL Server and Oracle, all roles granted to a user are automatically default roles, which means they are set and available to the user as soon as the user logs into the database. The SET ROLE syntax here is shown so that you can understand the ANSI standard for setting a role

Summary

As you learned in this hour, all databases have users, whether one or thousands. The user is the reason for the database.

Managing users in the database involves three necessities. First, you must create database user accounts for the proper individuals and services. Second, you must grant privileges to the accounts to accommodate the tasks that must be performed within the database. Finally, you must either remove a user account from the database or revoke certain privileges within the database from an account.

This hour touched on some of the most common tasks of managing users; extraneous detail was avoided because most databases differ in how users are managed. However, it is important to discuss user management because of its relationship with SQL. The American National Standards Institute (ANSI) has not defined or discussed in detail many of the commands for managing users, but the concept remains the same.

This hour also showed you the basics of implementing security in a SQL database or a relational database. After a user is created, the user must be assigned certain privileges that give him or her access to specific parts of the database. ANSI allows the use of roles as discussed during this hour. Privileges can be granted to users or roles.

The two types of privileges are system and object privileges. System privileges allow the user to perform various tasks within the database, such as actually connecting to the database, creating tables, creating users, and altering the state of the database. Object privileges give a user access to specific objects within the database, such as granting the capability to select data or manipulate data in a specific table.

Two commands in SQL allow a user to grant privileges to and revoke privileges from other users or roles in the database: `GRANT` and `REVOKE`. These two commands control the overall administration of privileges in the database. Although many other considerations come into play when implementing security in a relational database, this hour discussed the basics that relate to SQL.

Q&A

Q. Is there a SQL standard for adding users to a database?

A. ANSI provides some commands and concepts, although each implementation and each company has its own commands, tools, and rules for creating or adding users to a database.

Q. Can user access be temporarily suspended without completely removing the user ID from the database?

A. Yes, you can temporarily suspend user access by simply changing the user's password or revoking privileges that allow the user to connect to the database. You can reinstate the functionality of the user account by changing and issuing the password to the user or by granting privileges to the user that might have been revoked.

Q. Can users change their own passwords?

A. Yes, in most major implementations. Upon user creation or addition to the database, a generic password is given to the user, who must change it as quickly as possible to a password of his or her choice. After the user changes the initial password, even the DBA does not know the new password.

Q. If users forget their passwords, what should they do to gain access to the database again?

A. Users should go to their immediate management or an available help desk. A help desk generally can reset a user's password. If not, the DBA or security officer can do so. The user should change the password to a new password as soon as the password is reset. Sometimes the DBA can affect this by setting a specific property that forces the user to change the password at the next login. Check your particular implementation's documentation for specifics.

Q. What can I do if I want to grant `CONNECT` to a user, but the user does not need all the privileges that are assigned to the `CONNECT` role?

A. You would simply not grant the full `CONNECT` role to the user, but only the privileges required. If you do grant `CONNECT` and the user no longer needs all the privileges that go with it, simply revoke `CONNECT` from the user and grant the specific privileges required.

Q. Why is it so important for the new user to change the password when received from whoever created the new user?

A. An initial password is assigned when the user ID is created. No one, not even the DBA or management, should know a user's password. The password should be kept a secret at all times, to prevent another user from logging on to the database under another user's account.

Workshop

The following workshop consists of a series of quiz questions and practical exercises. The quiz questions are designed to test your overall understanding of the current material. The practical exercises give you the opportunity to apply the concepts discussed during the current hour, as well as build on the knowledge you acquired in previous hours of study. Be sure to complete the quiz questions and exercises before continuing to the next hour. Refer to Appendix C, "Answers to Quizzes and Exercises," for answers.

Quiz

1. Which command establishes a session?
2. Which option drops a schema that still contains database objects?
3. Which statement removes a database privilege?
4. Which command creates a grouping or collection of tables, views, and privileges?
5. What option must a user have to grant another user privileges on an object that the user does not own?
6. When privileges are granted to `PUBLIC`, do all database users acquire the privileges or only specified users?
7. What privilege is required to look at data in a specific table?
8. What type of privilege is `SELECT`?
9. What option revokes a user's privilege to an object, as well as the other users that they might have granted privileges to, by use of the `GRANT` option?

Exercises

1. Describe how you would create the new user `John` in your `sample` database.
2. Explain the steps you would take to grant access to the `BIRDS` table to your new user, `John`.
3. Describe how you would assign permissions to all objects within the `BIRDS` database to `John`.
4. Describe how you would revoke the previous privileges from `John` and then remove his account.
5. Create a new database user as follows:

```
Username: Steve
Password: Steve123
```

6. Create a role for your new database user, `Steve`, from the previous exercise. Call the role `bird_query` and give the role `SELECT` on just the `BIRDS` table. Assign `Steve` to this role.
7. Connect as Steve and query the `BIRDS` table. Be sure to qualify the `BIRDS` table because Steve is not the owner (`owner.table_name`).
8. Connect back as your original user.
9. Now revoke `Steve`'s `SELECT` access from the other tables in the database. Now connect to the database as Steve and try to select from the `EMPLOYEES`, `AIRPORTS`, and `ROUTES` tables. What happened?
10. Connect to the database once again as Steve and try to query the `BIRDS` table.
11. Experiment on your own with your database.

HOUR 22
Using Indexes to Improve Performance

What You'll Learn in This Hour:

- How indexes work
- How to create an index
- The different types of indexes
- When to use indexes
- When not to use indexes

In this hour, you learn how to improve SQL statement performance by creating and using indexes. You begin with the `CREATE INDEX` command and learn how to use indexes that have been created on tables.

Defining an Index

An *index* is basically a pointer to data in a table. An index in a database is similar to an index in the back of a book. If you want to reference all the pages in a book that discuss a certain topic, you first refer to the index, which lists all topics alphabetically; the index then refers you to one or more specific page numbers. An index in a database works the same way: It points a query to the exact physical location of data in a table. You are actually directed to the data's location in an underlying file of the database, but as far as you are concerned, you are referring to a table.

Which works faster, looking through a book page by page for some information or searching the book's index and getting a page number? Of course, using the book's index is the most efficient method, especially if the book is large. If you have a smaller book with just a few pages, however, flipping through the chapters for the information might go faster than flipping back and forth between the index and the chapters. When a database does not use an index, it is performing a full table scan, the same as flipping through a book page by page. Hour 23, "Improving Database Performance," discusses full table scans.

An index is typically stored separately from the table for which the index was created. An index's main purpose is to improve the performance of data retrieval. Indexes can be created or dropped with no effect on the data. However, after an index is dropped, performance of data retrieval might slow. Indexes take up physical space and can often grow larger than the table. Therefore, you need to consider them when estimating your database storage needs.

Understanding How Indexes Work

When an index is created, it records the location of values in a table that are associated with the column that is indexed. Entries are added to the index when new data is added to the table. When a query is executed against the database and a condition is specified on a column in the `WHERE` clause that is indexed, the index is first searched for the values specified in the `WHERE` clause. If the value is found in the index, the index returns the exact location of the searched data in the table. Figure 22.1 illustrates the function of an index.

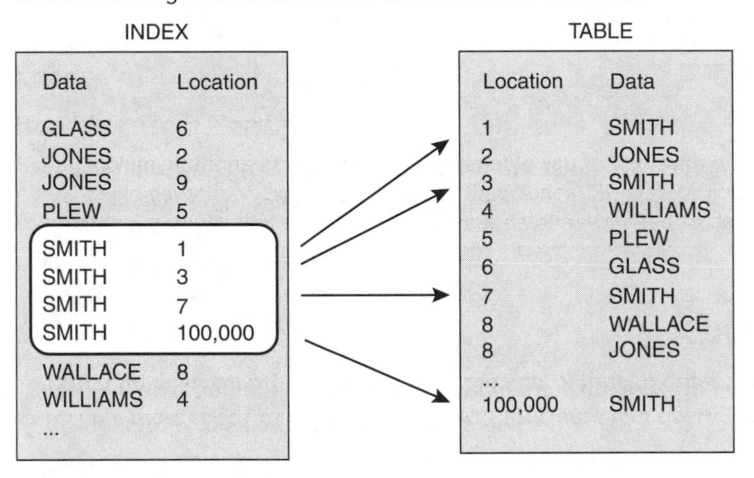

FIGURE 22.1
Table access using an index

Suppose the following query was issued:

```
SELECT *
FROM TABLE_NAME
WHERE NAME = 'SMITH';
```

As Figure 22.1 shows, the `NAME` index is referenced to resolve the location of all names equal to `SMITH`. After the location is determined, the data can quickly be retrieved from the table. The data—names, in this case—is alphabetized in the index.

NOTE

Variations of Index Creation

Indexes can be created during table creation in certain implementations. Most implementations accommodate a command, aside from the `CREATE TABLE` command, used to create indexes. Check your particular implementation for the exact syntax for the command, if any, that is available to create an index.

A full table scan occurs if there is no index on the table and the same query is executed. This means, then, that every row of data in the table is read to retrieve information pertaining to all individuals with the name `SMITH`.

An index works faster because it typically stores information in an orderly, treelike format. Say that you have a list of books upon which you place an index. The index has a root node, which is the beginning point of each query. Then it is split into branches. Maybe in this case the index has two branches, one for letters *A–L* and the other for letters *M–Z*. If you ask for a book with a name that starts with the letter *M*, you enter the index at the root node and immediately travel to the branch containing letters *M–Z*. This effectively shortens the time needed to find the book by eliminating nearly half of the possibilities.

Using the CREATE INDEX Command

As with many other statements in SQL, the `CREATE INDEX` statement, varies greatly among relational database vendors. This command is used to create the various types of indexes available for a table. Most relational database implementations use the `CREATE INDEX` statement:

```
CREATE INDEX INDEX_NAME ON TABLE_NAME
```

Some implementations allow the specification of a storage clause (as with the `CREATE TABLE` statement), ordering (`DESC||ASC`), and the use of clusters. Check your particular implementation for its correct syntax.

Identifying Types of Indexes

You can create different types of indexes on tables in a database, all of which serve the same goal: to improve database performance by expediting data retrieval. This hour discusses single-column indexes, composite indexes, and unique indexes.

Single-Column Indexes

Indexing on a single column of a table is the simplest and most common manifestation of an index. A *single-column index* is one that is created based on only one table column. The basic syntax follows:

```
CREATE INDEX INDEX_NAME_IDX
ON TABLE_NAME (COLUMN_NAME)
```

As you look at a few examples of creating indexes, you first create a table called `BIRDS_TRAVEL` that is based on birds and their migration habits. Following is the `CREATE` statement and a `SELECT` statement from the new table that returns 56 rows of data. Remember that even though the database contains only 23 birds in the database, many birds migrate to many different locations. This creates a situation of duplicate bird names and duplicate migration location names in a table. In this example, 56 rows is not a lot. However, in a real organization, tables can easily contain millions of rows of data. This is where indexing is necessary to maintain acceptable performance.

```
SQL> create table birds_travel as
  2  select b.bird_id, b.bird_name, b.wingspan, m.migration_location
  3  from birds b,
  4       migration m,
  5       birds_migration bm
  6  where b.bird_id = bm.bird_id
  7    and m.migration_id = bm.migration_id;

Table created.

SQL> select * from birds_travel;

   BIRD_ID BIRD_NAME                WINGSPAN MIGRATION_LOCATION
---------- -------------------- ---------- --------------------
         1 Great Blue Heron             78 Central America
         3 Common Loon                  99 Central America
         7 Osprey                       72 Central America
         8 Belted Kingfisher            23 Central America
        10 Pied-billed Grebe           6.5 Central America
        11 American Coot                29 Central America
        12 Common Sea Gull              18 Central America
        14 Double-crested Cormorant     54 Central America
        15 Common Merganser             34 Central America
        16 Turkey Vulture               72 Central America
        18 Green Heron                26.8 Central America
        21 Great Egret                67.2 Central America
         1 Great Blue Heron             78 Mexico
         3 Common Loon                  99 Mexico
         7 Osprey                       72 Mexico
```

```
  8 Belted Kingfisher              23 Mexico
 10 Pied-billed Grebe             6.5 Mexico
 11 American Coot                  29 Mexico
 12 Common Sea Gull                18 Mexico
 13 Ring-billed Gull               50 Mexico
 14 Double-crested Cormorant       54 Mexico
 15 Common Merganser               34 Mexico
 16 Turkey Vulture                 72 Mexico
 18 Green Heron                  26.8 Mexico
 21 Great Egret                  67.2 Mexico
 22 Anhinga                        42 Mexico
  5 Golden Eagle                   99 No Significant Migration
  9 Canadian Goose                 99 No Significant Migration
 17 American Crow                39.6 No Significant Migration
 20 Brown Pelican                  99 No Significant Migration
 23 Black Skimmer                  15 No Significant Migration
 19 Mute Swan                      99 Partial, Open Water
  1 Great Blue Heron               78 South America
  7 Osprey                         72 South America
  8 Belted Kingfisher              23 South America
 12 Common Sea Gull                18 South America
 16 Turkey Vulture                 72 South America
 18 Green Heron                  26.8 South America
  1 Great Blue Heron               78 Southern United States
  2 Mallard                        72 Southern United States
  3 Common Loon                    99 Southern United States
  4 Bald Eagle                     99 Southern United States
  6 Red Tailed Hawk                48 Southern United States
  7 Osprey                         72 Southern United States
  8 Belted Kingfisher              23 Southern United States
  9 Canadian Goose                 99 Southern United States
 10 Pied-billed Grebe             6.5 Southern United States
 11 American Coot                  29 Southern United States
 12 Common Sea Gull                18 Southern United States
 13 Ring-billed Gull               50 Southern United States
 14 Double-crested Cormorant       54 Southern United States
 15 Common Merganser               34 Southern United States
 16 Turkey Vulture                 72 Southern United States
 18 Green Heron                  26.8 Southern United States
 21 Great Egret                  67.2 Southern United States
 22 Anhinga                        42 Southern United States

56 rows selected.
```

The following focuses on creating a simple index on the BIRDS_TRAVEL table on the BIRD_NAME column. This column is being indexed because it would be typically used in a query to search for specific data within this table.

```
SQL> create index birds_travel_idx1
  2  on birds_travel (bird_name);

Index created.
```

TIP

Best Places for Single-Column Indexes

Single-column indexes are most effective when they are used on columns that are frequently used alone in the WHERE clause as query conditions. Good candidates for a single-column index are individual identification numbers, serial numbers, and system-assigned keys.

Unique Indexes

You use *unique indexes* for performance and data integrity. A unique index does not allow duplicate values to be inserted into the table. Otherwise, the unique index performs the same way a regular index performs. The syntax follows:

```
CREATE UNIQUE INDEX INDEX_NAME
ON TABLE_NAME (COLUMN_NAME)
```

The first example that follows attempts to create a unique index on the BIRD_NAME within the BIRDS_TRAVEL table. An error message is returned. A unique index cannot be created for this column because duplicate rows of data are already found in the table. Refer back to the previous output of the query. You can see duplicate values of bird names in the BIRDS_TRAVEL table because birds can migrate to many different locations.

```
SQL> create unique index birds_travel_idx2
  2  on birds_travel (bird_name);
on birds_travel (bird_name)
   *
ERROR at line 2:
ORA-01452: cannot CREATE UNIQUE INDEX; duplicate keys found
```

Next is a legitimate example. Here a unique index is created on the combination of the BIRD_NAME column in the MIGRATION_LOCATION column. Even though both birds and migration locations have duplicate entries in this table, the combination of a bird's name and the migration location should always be unique.

```
SQL> create unique index birds_travel_idx3
  2  on birds_travel (bird_name, migration_location);

Index created.
```

You might be wondering, what happens if a bird's identification number is the primary key for a table? An index is usually implicitly created when you define a primary key for a table, so normally you do not also have to create a unique index on the table.

When working with objects such as unique indexes, it is often beneficial to create the indexes on empty tables during the creation of the database structure. This ensures that the data going into the structure already meets the demand of the constraints you want to place on it. If you work with existing data, you want to analyze the impact of whether the data needs to be adjusted to properly apply the index.

TIP

Unique Index Constraints

You can create a unique index only on a column in a table whose values are unique. In other words, you cannot create a unique index on an existing table with data that already contains records on the indexed key that are not unique. Similarly, you cannot create a unique index on a column that allows for NULL values. If you attempt to create a unique index on a column that violates one of these principles, the statement fails.

Composite Indexes

A composite index is an index on two or more columns of a table. You should consider performance when creating a composite index because the order of columns in the index has a measurable effect on the data retrieval speed. Generally, the most restrictive value should be placed first for optimum performance. However, the columns that are always specified in your queries should be placed first. The syntax follows:

```
CREATE INDEX INDEX_NAME
ON TABLE_NAME (COLUMN1, COLUMN2)
```

An example of a composite index follows:

```
SQL> create index birds_travel_idx4
  2  on birds_travel (bird_name, wingspan);

Index created.
```

In this example, you create a composite index based on two columns in the BIRDS_TRAVEL table: BIRD_NAME and WINGSPAN. You might create a composite index here because of the assumption that these two columns are frequently used together as conditions in the WHERE clause of a query.

In deciding whether to create a single-column index or a composite index, consider the column(s) that you might use frequently in a query's WHERE clause as filter conditions. If only one column is used, choose a single-column index. If two or more columns are frequently used in the WHERE clause as filters, a composite index is the best choice.

Implicit Indexes

Implicit indexes are indexes that are automatically created by the database server when an object is created. Indexes are automatically created for primary key constraints and unique constraints.

Why are indexes automatically created for these constraints? Imagine a database server. Now say that a user adds a new product to the database. The product identification is the primary key on the table, which means that it must be a unique value. To efficiently make sure the new value is unique among hundreds or thousands of records, the product identifications in the table must be indexed. Therefore, when you create a primary key or a unique constraint, an index is automatically created for you.

Knowing When to Consider Using an Index

Unique indexes are implicitly used with a primary key for the primary key to work. Foreign keys are also excellent candidates for an index because you often use them to join the parent table. Most, if not all, columns used for table joins should be indexed.

Columns that you frequently reference in the `ORDER BY` and `GROUP BY` clauses should be considered for indexes. For example, if you are sorting on an individual's name, having an index on the name column is beneficial: It renders an automatic alphabetical order on every name, thus simplifying the actual sort operation and expediting the output results.

Furthermore, you should create indexes on columns with a high number of unique values, or columns that, when used as filter conditions in the `WHERE` clause, return a low percentage of rows of data from a table. This is where trial and error might come into play. Just as you should always test production code and database structures before implementing them into production, you should test indexes. Your testing should center on trying different combinations of indexes, no indexes, single-column indexes, and composite indexes; no cut-and-dried rule governs using indexes. The effective use of indexes requires a thorough knowledge of table relationships, query and transaction requirements, and the data itself.

NOTE

Plan for Indexing Accordingly

Be sure to plan your tables and indexes. Don't assume that because an index has been created, all performance issues are resolved. The index might not help at all—it might actually hinder performance and take up disk space.

Knowing When to Avoid Indexes

Although indexes are intended to enhance a database's performance, sometimes you should avoid them. The following guidelines indicate when to reconsider using an index:

- Avoid using indexes on small tables. Indexes have an overhead associated with them in terms of query time to access them. In the case of small tables, the query engine to do a quick scan over the table more quickly than it can look at an index first.
- Do not use indexes on columns that return a high percentage of data rows when used as a filter condition in a query's `WHERE` clause. For instance, you do not see entries for the words *the* or *and* in the index of a book.
- You can index tables that have a frequent, large batch update jobs run. However, the index considerably slows the batch job's performance. You can correct the conflict of having an index on a table that is frequently loaded or manipulated by a large batch process in this way: Drop the index before the batch job and then re-create the index after the job has completed. The indexes are also updated as the data is inserted, causing additional overhead.
- Do not use indexes on columns that contain a high number of `NULL` values. Indexes operate best on columns that have a higher uniqueness of data between rows. If a lot of `NULL` values exist, the index will skew toward the `NULL` values, which might affect performance.
- Avoid indexing columns that are frequently manipulated. Maintenance on the index can become excessive.

You can see in Figure 22.2 that an index on a column such as gender might not prove beneficial. For example, suppose the following query was submitted to the database:

```
SELECT *
FROM TABLE_NAME
WHERE GENDER = 'FEMALE';
```

Referring to Figure 22.2, which is based on the previous query, you can see constant activity between the table and its index. Because a high number of data rows is returned for `WHERE GENDER = 'FEMALE'` (or `'MALE'`), the database server constantly has to read the index, then the table, then the index, then the table, and so on. In this case, it might be more efficient to use a full table scan because a high percentage of the table must be read anyway.

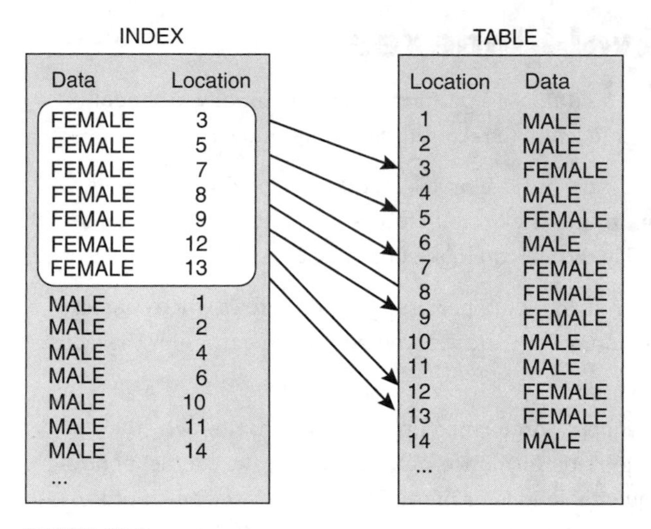

FIGURE 22.2
An example of an ineffective index

CAUTION

Indexes Can Sometimes Lead to Performance Problems

Use caution when creating indexes on a table's extremely long keys. Performance is inevitably slowed by high I/O costs.

As a general rule, do not use an index on a column used in a query's condition that returns a high percentage of data rows from the table. In other words, do not create an index on a column such as gender or any column that contains few distinct values. This is often referred to as a column's *cardinality,* or the uniqueness of the data. High cardinality refers to a very unique quality and describes information such as identification numbers. Low-cardinality values are not very unique and refer to columns such as gender.

Altering an Index

You can alter an index after it has been created using syntax that is similar to the `CREATE INDEX` syntax. The types of alterations that you can manage with the statement differ between implementations, but they handle all the basic variations of an index in terms of columns, ordering, and such. The syntax follows:

```
ALTER INDEX INDEX_NAME
```

Take care when altering an existing index on production systems. In most cases, the index is immediately rebuilt, which creates an overhead in terms of resources. In addition, on most basic implementations, while the index is being rebuilt, it cannot be utilized for queries. This further hinders system performance.

Dropping an Index

An index can be dropped rather simply. Check your particular implementation for the exact syntax, but most major implementations use the DROP command. Take care when dropping an index because it can drastically slow (or, conversely, improve) performance. The syntax follows:

```
DROP INDEX INDEX_NAME

SQL> drop index birds_travel_idx4;

Index dropped.
```

MySQL uses a slightly different syntax; you also specify the table name of the table that you are dropping the index from:

```
DROP INDEX INDEX_NAME ON TABLE_NAME
```

The most common reason for dropping an index is to improve performance. Remember that if you drop an index, you can re-create it later. You might need to rebuild an index to reduce fragmentation. Often you must experiment with indexes in a database to determine the route to best performance; this might involve creating an index, dropping it, and eventually re-creating it, with or without modifications.

Summary

In this hour, you learned that you can use indexes to improve the overall performance of queries and transactions performed within the database. As with the index of a book, database indexes enable specific data to be quickly referenced from a table. The most common method for creating indexes is to use the CREATE INDEX command. Different types of indexes are available among SQL implementations, including unique indexes, single-column indexes, and composite indexes. You need to consider many factors when deciding on the index type that best meets the needs of your database. The effective use of indexes often requires some experimentation, a thorough knowledge of table relationships and data, and a little patience—being patient when you create an index can save minutes, hours, or even days of work later.

Q&A

Q. Does an index actually take up space the way a table does?

A. Yes, an index takes up physical space in a database. In fact, an index can become much larger than the table for which the index was created.

Q. If you drop an index so that a batch job can complete faster, how long does it take to re-create the index?

A. Many factors are involved, such as the size of the index being dropped, the CPU usage, and the machine's power.

Q. Should all indexes be unique?

A. No, unique indexes allow no duplicate values. You might need to allow duplicate values in a table.

Workshop

The following workshop consists of a series of quiz questions and practical exercises. The quiz questions are designed to test your overall understanding of the current material. The practical exercises give you the opportunity to apply the concepts discussed during the current hour, as well as build on the knowledge you acquired in previous hours of study. Be sure to complete the quiz questions and exercises before continuing to the next hour. Refer to Appendix C, "Answers to Quizzes and Exercises," for answers.

Quiz

1. What are some major disadvantages of using indexes?
2. Why is the order of columns in a composite index important?
3. Should a column with a large percentage of `NULL` values be indexed?
4. Is the main purpose of an index to stop duplicate values in a table?
5. True or false: The main reason for a composite index is for aggregate function usage in an index.
6. What does cardinality refer to? What is considered a column of high cardinality?

Exercises

1. For the following situations, decide whether an index should be used and, if so, what type of index should be used:

   a. Several columns, but a small table

   b. Medium-size table, no duplicates allowed

   c. Several columns, very large table, several columns used as filters in the WHERE clause

   d. Large table, many columns, a lot of data manipulation

2. Write a SQL statement to create an index called FOOD_IDX in FOOD on the FOOD_NAME column.

3. Write a SQL statement to create an index called WINGSPAN_IDX in BIRDS on the WINGSPAN column.

4. Drop the indexes you created.

5. Study the tables used in this book. List some good candidates for indexed columns, based on how a user might search for data.

6. Create some additional indexes on your tables as you like. Think about how your data might be searched and where indexes can create efficiencies.

HOUR 23

Improving Database Performance

What You'll Learn in This Hour:

- Defining SQL statement tuning
- Comparing database tuning and SQL statement tuning
- Properly joining tables
- Understanding the problems of full table scans
- Invoking the use of indexes
- Avoiding the use of `OR` and `HAVING`
- Avoiding large sort operations

In this hour, you learn how to tune your SQL statement for maximum performance using some simple methods. Although so far this book has focused on how to write SQL, it is just as important to learn how to write efficient SQL that can help keep the database running optimally. This hour focuses on simple steps you can take when working with various queries to ensure that your SQL performs optimally.

Defining SQL Statement Tuning

SQL statement tuning is the process of optimally building SQL statements to achieve results in the most effective and efficient manner. SQL tuning begins with the basic arrangement of the elements in a query. Simple formatting can play a large role in optimizing a statement.

SQL statement tuning mainly involves tweaking a statement's `FROM` and `WHERE` clauses. The database server decides how to evaluate a query using mostly these two clauses. To this point, you have learned the basics of the `FROM` and `WHERE` clauses; now it is time to fine-tune them for better results and happier users.

Comparing Database Tuning and SQL Statement Tuning

Before learning about SQL statement tuning, you need to understand the difference between tuning a database and tuning the SQL statements that access the database.

Database tuning is the process of tuning the actual database, which encompasses the allocated memory, disk usage, CPU, I/O, and underlying database processes. Tuning a database also involves the management and manipulation of the database structure, such as the design and layout of tables and indexes. In addition, database tuning often involves modification of the database architecture to optimize the use of the hardware resources available. You need to take many other considerations into account when tuning a database, but the database administrator (DBA) and system administrator normally accomplish these tasks. The objective of database tuning is to ensure that the database has been designed in a way that best accommodates the expected activity within the database.

SQL tuning is the process of tuning the SQL statements that access the database. These SQL statements include database queries and transactional operations, such as inserts, updates, and deletes. The objective of SQL statement tuning is to formulate statements that most effectively access the database in its current state, taking advantage of database and system resources and indexes. The objective is to reduce the operational overhead of executing the query on the database.

NOTE

Tuning Is Not One-Dimensional

You must perform both database tuning and SQL statement tuning to achieve optimal results when accessing the database. A poorly tuned database might render your efforts in SQL tuning useless, and vice versa. Ideally, you should first tune the database, ensure that indexes exist where needed, and then tune the SQL code.

Formatting Your SQL Statement

Formatting your SQL statement sounds like an obvious task, but it is worth mentioning. A newcomer to SQL will probably neglect to address several considerations when building a SQL statement. The upcoming sections discuss the following points—some are common sense and others are not so obvious:

- The format of SQL statements for readability
- The order of tables in the `FROM` clause
- The placement of the most restrictive conditions in the `WHERE` clause
- The placement of join conditions in the `WHERE` clause

Formatting a Statement for Readability

Formatting a SQL statement for readability is fairly obvious, but many SQL statements are not written neatly. The neatness of a statement does not affect the actual performance (the database does not care how neat the statement appears), but careful formatting is the first step in tuning a statement. When you look at a SQL statement with tuning intentions, making the statement readable is always the first priority. How can you determine whether the statement is well written if it is difficult to read?

Consider some basic rules for making a statement readable:

- Always begin a new line with each clause in the statement. For example, place the `FROM` clause on a separate line from the `SELECT` clause. Then place the `WHERE` clause on a separate line from the `FROM` clause, and so on.
- Use tabs or spaces for indentation when arguments of a clause in the statement exceed one line.
- Use tabs and spaces consistently.
- Use table aliases when multiple tables are used in the statement. Using the full table name to qualify each column in the statement quickly clutters the statement and makes reading it difficult.
- Use remarks sparingly in SQL statements (if they are available within your specific implementation). Remarks are great for documentation, but too many of them clutter a statement.
- Begin a new line with each column name in the `SELECT` clause if many columns are selected.
- Begin a new line with each table name in the `FROM` clause if many tables are used.
- Begin a new line with each condition of the `WHERE` clause. You can easily see all conditions of the statement and the order in which they are used.

Following is an example of a statement that is hard to decipher:

```
SQL> select birds.bird_name,
  2  birds.incubation + birds.fledging "PARENTING",    food.food_name,
  3  migration.migration_location
  4  from birds, food, birds_food, migration, birds_migration
  5  where birds.bird_id = birds_food.bird_id
  6    and food.food_id = birds_food.food_id
  7    and birds.bird_id = birds_migration.bird_id
  8    and migration.migration_id = birds_migration.migration_id
  9    and birds.wingspan > 48
 10    and birds.incubation + birds.fledging > 60
```

```
 11     and migration.migration_location not in ('Mexico', 'Central America')
 12     and food.food_name = 'Fish'
 13     order by birds.bird_name;

BIRD_NAME                 PARENTING FOOD_NAME  MIGRATION_LOCATION
------------------- ---------- ---------- -----------------------
Bald Eagle                  126 Fish       Southern United States
Brown Pelican               107 Fish       No Significant Migration
Common Loon                 111 Fish       Southern United States
Double-crested Cormorant     71 Fish       Southern United States
Golden Eagle                125 Fish       No Significant Migration
Great Blue Heron             88 Fish       Southern United States
Great Blue Heron             88 Fish       South America
Great Egret                  75 Fish       Southern United States
Osprey                      100 Fish       Southern United States
Osprey                      100 Fish       South America
Ring-billed Gull             61 Fish       Southern United States

11 rows selected.
```

Here the statement has been reformatted for improved readability:

```
SQL> select b.bird_name,
  2         b.incubation + fledging "PARENTING",
  3         f.food_name,
  4         m.migration_location
  5  from birds b,
  6       food f,
  7       birds_food bf,
  8       migration m,
  9       birds_migration bm
 10  where b.bird_id = bf.bird_id
 11    and f.food_id = bf.food_id
 12    and b.bird_id = bm.bird_id
 13    and m.migration_id = bm.migration_id
 14    and b.wingspan > 48
 15    and b.incubation + b.fledging > 60
 16    and m.migration_location not in ('Mexico', 'Central America')
 17    and f.food_name = 'Fish'
 18  order by bird_name;
```

Both statements have the same content, but the second statement is much more readable. It has been greatly simplified through the use of table aliases, which have been defined in the query's FROM clause. In addition, the second statement aligns the elements of each clause, making each clause stand out.

Again, making a statement more readable does not directly improve its performance, but it assists you in making modifications and debugging a lengthy and otherwise complex statement. Now you can easily identify the columns selected, the tables used, the table joins performed, and the conditions placed on the query.

NOTE

Always Establish Standards

It is especially important to establish coding standards in a multiuser programming environment. If all code is consistently formatted, shared code and modifications to code are much easier to manage.

Arranging Tables in the FROM Clause

The arrangement or order of tables in the FROM clause can make a difference, depending on how the optimizer reads the SQL statement. For example, experienced users have found that listing the smaller tables first and the larger tables last is more efficient.

Take a look at an example of the FROM clause:

```
FROM SMALLEST TABLE,
     LARGEST TABLE
```

NOTE

Check for Performance When Using Multiple Tables

Check your particular implementation for performance tips, if any, when listing multiple tables in the FROM clause.

Ordering Join Conditions

As you learned in Hour 14, "Joining Tables in Queries," most joins use a base table to link tables that have one or more common columns on which to join. The base table is the main table that most or all tables are joined to in a query. The column from the base table is normally placed on the right side of a join operation in the WHERE clause. The tables joined to the base table are normally listed in order from smallest to largest, similar to the tables listed in the FROM clause.

If a base table does not exist, the tables should be listed from smallest to largest, with the largest tables on the right side of the join operation in the WHERE clause. The join conditions should be in the first position(s) of the WHERE clause, followed by the filter clause(s), as shown here:

```
FROM TABLE1,                              Smallest table
     TABLE2,                               to
     TABLE3                                Largest table, also base table
```

```
WHERE TABLE1.COLUMN = TABLE3.COLUMN       Join condition
  AND TABLE2.COLUMN = TABLE3.COLUMN       Join condition
[ AND CONDITION1 ]                           Filter condition
[ AND CONDITION2 ]                           Filter condition
```

CAUTION

Be Restrictive with Your Joins

Because joins typically return a high percentage of rows of data from the table(s), you should evaluate join conditions after more restrictive conditions.

In this example, TABLE3 is used as the base table. TABLE1 and TABLE2 are joined to TABLE3 for both simplicity and proven efficiency.

Identifying the Most Restrictive Condition

The most restrictive condition is typically the driving factor in achieving optimal performance for a SQL query. The most restrictive condition is the condition in the WHERE clause of a statement that returns the fewest rows of data. Conversely, the least restrictive condition is the condition in a statement that returns the most rows of data. This hour is concerned with the most restrictive condition simply because it does the most filtering of the data that is to be returned by the query.

Your goal is for the SQL optimizer to evaluate the most restrictive condition first because the condition returns a smaller subset of data, thus reducing the query's overhead. Effectively placing the most restrictive condition in the query requires knowing how the optimizer operates. In some cases, the optimizers seem to read from the bottom of the WHERE clause up. Therefore, you want to place the most restrictive condition last in the WHERE clause, which is the condition that the optimizer reads first. The following example shows how to structure the WHERE clause based on the restrictiveness of the conditions and the FROM clause based on the size of the tables:

```
FROM TABLE1,                                Smallest table
     TABLE2,                                 to
     TABLE3                                  Largest table, also base table
WHERE TABLE1.COLUMN = TABLE3.COLUMN      Join condition
  AND TABLE2.COLUMN = TABLE3.COLUMN      Join condition
[ AND CONDITION1 ]                          Least restrictive
[ AND CONDITION2 ]                          Most restrictive
```

CAUTION

Always Test Your WHERE Clauses

If you do not know how your particular implementation's SQL optimizer works, the DBA also does not know, or you do not have sufficient documentation, you can execute a large query that takes a while to run and then rearrange conditions in the WHERE clause. Be sure to record the time it takes the query to complete each time you make changes. You should have to run only a couple tests to figure out whether the optimizer reads the WHERE clause from the top to bottom or the bottom to top. Turn off database caching during the testing for more accurate results.

Following is an example using a phony table:

Table	TEST
Row Count	5,611
Conditions	WHERE LASTNAME = 'SMITH'
	returns 2,000 rows
	WHERE STATE = 'IN'
	returns 30,000 rows
Most Restrictive Condition	WHERE LASTNAME = 'SMITH'

Following is the first query:

```
SELECT COUNT(*)
FROM TEST
WHERE LASTNAME = 'SMITH'
  AND STATE = 'IN';

  COUNT(*)
----------
     1,024
```

This is the second query:

```
SELECT COUNT(*)
FROM TEST
WHERE STATE = 'IN'
  AND LASTNAME = 'SMITH';

  COUNT(*)
----------
     1,024
```

Suppose that the first query completed in 20 seconds, whereas the second query completed in 10 seconds. Because the second query returned faster results and the most restrictive condition was listed last in the WHERE clause, you can safely assume that the optimizer reads the WHERE clause from the bottom up.

NOTE

Try to Use Indexed Columns

Using an indexed column as the most restrictive condition in a query is a good practice. Indexes generally improve a query's performance.

Running Full Table Scans

A full table scan occurs when an index is not used by the query engine or no index is present for the table(s) being used. Full table scans usually return data much more slowly than when an index is used. The larger the table, the slower that data is returned when a full table scan is performed. The query optimizer decides whether to use an index when executing the SQL statement. In most cases, the index is used if it exists.

Some implementations have sophisticated query optimizers that can decide whether to use an index. Decisions such as this are based on statistics that are gathered on database objects, such as the size of an object and the estimated number of rows that are returned by a condition with an indexed column. Refer to your implementation documentation for specifics on the decision-making capabilities of your relational database's optimizer.

Avoid full table scans when reading large tables. For example, a full table scan is performed when a table that does not have an index is read, which usually takes considerably more time to return the data. For most larger tables, consider using an index. For small tables, as previously mentioned, the optimizer might choose the full table scan instead of the index if the table is indexed. For a small table with an index, consider dropping the index and reserving that space for other needy objects in the database.

TIP

Simple Ways to Avoid Table Scans

The easiest and most obvious way to avoid a full table scan—aside from ensuring that indexes exist on the table—is to use conditions in a query's `WHERE` clause to filter data to be returned.

This is a good time for a reminder of data that should be indexed. Consider, for example, a book written about the `BIRDS` database: You would never index words or data such as *and*, *the*, *bird*, a specific weight, wingspan, and so forth. Indexing columns that do not contain many unique values is not beneficial. Instead, you want to index columns that tend to have many unique values, especially those used to search for data:

- Columns used as primary keys
- Columns used as foreign keys

- Columns frequently used to join tables
- Columns frequently used as conditions in a query
- Columns that have a high percentage of unique values

TIP

Table Scans Are Not Always Bad

Sometimes full table scans are beneficial. You want to perform them on queries against small tables or queries whose conditions return a high percentage of rows. The easiest way to force a full table scan is to avoid creating an index on the table.

Identifying Other Performance Considerations

Other performance considerations come into play as well when tuning SQL statements. The next sections discuss the following concepts:

- Using the LIKE operator and wildcards
- Avoiding the OR operator
- Avoiding the HAVING clause
- Avoiding large sort operations
- Using stored procedures
- Disabling indexes during batch loads

Using the LIKE Operator and Wildcards

The LIKE operator is a useful tool that places conditions on a query in a flexible manner. Using wildcards in a query can eliminate many possibilities of data that should be retrieved. Wildcards are flexible for queries that search for similar data (data that is not equivalent to an exact value specified).

Suppose you want to write a query using the fictitious table EMPLOYEE_TBL and selecting the EMP_ID, LAST_NAME, FIRST_NAME, and STATE columns. You need to know the employee identification, name, and state for all the employees with the last name Stevens. Three SQL statements with different wildcard placements serve as examples.

Query 1 follows:

```
SELECT EMPLOYEEID, LASTNAME, FIRSTNAME, STATE
FROM EMPLOYEES
WHERE LASTNAME LIKE 'STEVENS';
```

Next is Query 2:

```
SELECT EMPLOYEEID, LASTNAME, FIRSTNAME, STATE
FROM EMPLOYEES
WHERE LASTNAME LIKE '%EVENS%';
```

The final query is Query 3:

```
SELECT EMPLOYEEID, LASTNAME, FIRSTNAME, STATE
FROM EMPLOYEES
WHERE LASTNAME LIKE 'ST%';
```

The SQL statements do not necessarily return the same results. More than likely, Query 1 returns fewer rows than the other two queries and takes advantage of indexing. Query 2 and Query 3 are less specific about the desired returned data, thus making them slower than Query 1. In addition, Query 3 is probably faster than Query 2 because it specifies the first letters of the string for which you are searching. (Additionally, the column `LASTNAME` is likely to be indexed.) Query 3 could thus potentially take advantage of an index.

With Query 1, you might retrieve all individuals with the last name Stevens—but Stevens can be spelled in different ways. Query 2 picks up all individuals with the last name Stevens and its various spellings. Query 3 also picks up any last name that starts with `ST`; this is the only way to ensure that you receive all the Stevens (or Stephens).

Avoiding the OR Operator

Rewriting the SQL statement using the `IN` predicate instead of the `OR` operator consistently and substantially improves data retrieval speed. Your implementation tells you about tools you can use to time or check the performance between the `OR` operator and the `IN` predicate. This section gives you an example of how to rewrite a SQL statement by removing the `OR` operator and replacing it with the `IN` predicate. Refer to Hour 13, "Using Operators to Categorize Data," for more on using the `OR` operator and the `IN` predicate.

The following query uses the `OR` operator:

```
SELECT EMPLOYEEID, LASTNAME, FIRSTNAME
FROM EMPLOYEES
WHERE CITY = 'INDIANAPOLIS IN'
   OR CITY = 'KOKOMO'
   OR CITY = 'TERRE HAUTE';
```

This is the same query using the IN operator:

```
SELECT EMPLOYEEID, LASTNAME, FIRSTNAME
FROM EMPLOYEES
WHERE CITY IN ('INDIANAPOLIS IN', 'KOKOMO',
              'TERRE HAUTE');
```

The SQL statements retrieve the same data. However, through testing and experience, you will find that the data retrieval is measurably faster by replacing OR conditions with the IN predicate, as in the second query.

Avoiding the HAVING Clause

The HAVING clause is useful for parsing the result of a GROUP BY clause; however, you can't use it without cost. Using the HAVING clause gives the SQL optimizer extra work, which results in extra time. The query must be concerned not only with grouping result sets, but also with parsing those result sets down through the restrictions of the HAVING clause. The queries performed in the BIRDS database are fairly simple and do not touch many rows of data. However, adding the HAVING clause in a larger database can introduce some overhead, especially when the HAVING clause has more complex logic and a higher number of groupings to be applied. If possible, write SQL statements without using the HAVING clause, or design the HAVING clause restrictions so that they are as simple as possible.

Avoiding Large Sort Operations

Large sort operations mean using the ORDER BY, GROUP BY, and HAVING clauses. Subsets of data must be stored in memory or to disk (if not enough space is available in allotted memory) whenever sort operations are performed. You must sort data often. The main point is that these sort operations affect a SQL statement's response time. Because you cannot always avoid large sort operations, it is best to schedule queries with large sorts as periodic batch processes during off-peak database usage; this ensures that the performance of most user processes is not affected.

Using Stored Procedures

You should create stored procedures for SQL statements that are executed on a regular basis—particularly large transactions or queries. Stored procedures are SQL statements that are compiled and permanently stored in the database in an executable format.

Normally, when a SQL statement is issued in the database, the database must check the syntax and convert the statement into an executable format within the database (called *parsing*). After it is parsed, the statement is stored in memory; however, it is not permanent. When other operations need memory, the statement might be ejected from memory. For stored procedures, the SQL statement is always available in an executable format and remains in the database until it is dropped like any other database object.

Using Views

Not everyone agrees on whether using views improves or degrades query performance. Mostly this depends on the situation. Consider using views to improve performance. It is easy to test a query with or without views, and quite often you might find a huge performance opportunity. If used under the right circumstances, views create a subset of data from base database tables using the indexes that have already been defined and then create a subset of data that is stored in memory on the server instead of hard disk space. Memory is much faster to access than physical disk space. With a view, you also end up querying a small percentage of the data that exists in the base database tables, which typically improves query performance.

Disabling Indexes During Batch Loads

When a user submits a transaction to the database (`INSERT`, `UPDATE`, or `DELETE`), an entry is made to both the database table and any indexes associated with the table being modified. This means that if the `EMPLOYEES` table has an index and a user updates the `EMPLOYEES` table, an update also occurs to the index associated with the `EMPLOYEES` table. In a transactional environment, having a write to an index occur every time a write to the table occurs is usually not an issue.

During batch loads, however, an index can cause serious performance degradation. A batch load might consist of hundreds, thousands, or millions of manipulation statements or transactions. Because of their volume, batch loads take a long time to complete and are normally scheduled during off-peak hours—usually during weekends or evenings. Sometimes, simply dropping the indexes on tables associated with batch loads can dramatically decrease the time it takes a batch load to complete. Of course, you would need to re-create the indexes on the tables after the batch load. When you drop the indexes, changes are written to the tables much faster, so the job completes more quickly. When the batch load is complete, you should rebuild the indexes. During the rebuild, the indexes are populated with all the appropriate data from the tables. Although it might take a while for an index to be created on a large table, the overall time expended is less if you drop the index and rebuild it.

Another advantage to rebuilding an index after a batch load completes is the reduction of fragmentation that is found in the index. When a database grows, records are added, removed, and updated. Fragmentation can then occur. For any database that experiences a lot of growth, it is a good idea to periodically drop and rebuild large indexes. When you rebuild an index, the number of physical extents that comprise the index decreases, less disk I/O is involved to read the index, the user gets results more quickly, and everyone is happy.

Using Cost-Based Optimization

Often you inherit a database that is in need of SQL statement tuning. These existing systems might have thousands of SQL statements executing at any given time. To optimize the amount of time spent on performance tuning, you need a way to determine what queries are most beneficial. This is where cost-based optimization comes into play. Cost-based optimization attempts to determine which queries are most costly in relation to the overall system resources spent. For instance, say you measure cost by execution duration and you have the following two queries with their corresponding run times:

```
SELECT * FROM EMPLOYEES
WHERE FIRSTNAME LIKE '%LE%'                 2 sec

SELECT * FROM EMPLOYEES
WHERE FIRSTNAME LIKE 'G%';                  1 sec
```

Initially, it might appear that the first statement is the one you need to concentrate your efforts on. However, what if the second statement is executed 1,000 times an hour but the first is performed only 10 times in the same hour? This makes a huge difference in how you allocate your time.

Cost-based optimization ranks SQL statements in order of total computational cost. Computational cost is easily determined based on some measure of query execution (duration, number of reads, and so on) multiplied by the number of executions over a given period:

Total Computational Cost = Execution Measure × (Number of Executions)

You get the most overall benefit by first tuning the queries with the most total computational cost. Looking at the previous example, if you cut each statement execution time in half, you can easily figure out the total computational savings:

Statement #1: 1 second × 10 executions = 10 seconds of computational savings

Statement #2: .5 second × 1000 executions = 500 seconds of computational savings

Now you can more easily understand why you should spend your valuable time on the second statement instead of the first. Not only have you worked to optimize your database, but you've optimized your time as well.

TIP

Performance Tools

Many relational databases have built-in tools that assist in SQL statement database performance tuning. For example, Oracle has a tool called `EXPLAIN PLAN` that shows the user the execution plan of a SQL statement. Another tool in Oracle that measures the actual elapsed time of a SQL statement is `TKPROF`. In SQL Server, the Query Analyzer has several options to give you an estimated execution plan or statistics from the executed query. Check with your DBA and implementation documentation for more information on available tools.

Summary

In this hour, you learned the meaning of tuning SQL statements in a relational database. You learned about two basic types of tuning: database tuning and SQL statement tuning—both of which are vital to the efficient operation of the database and the SQL statements within it. Each type of tuning is equally important and the overall performance of the database cannot be optimized without the other.

You read about methods for tuning a SQL statement, starting with a statement's actual readability, which does not directly improve performance but does aid the programmer in the development and management of statements. One of the main issues that arises in SQL statement performance involves the use of indexes. Sometimes you should use indexes; other times you should avoid them. For all measures taken to improve SQL statement performance, you need to understand the data itself, the database design and relationships, and the users' needs in accessing the database.

Q&A

Q. By following what I have learned about performance, what realistic performance gains can I expect to see in data retrieval time?

A. Realistically, you can see performance gains from fractions of a second to minutes, hours, or even days.

Q. How can I test my SQL statements for performance?

A. Each implementation should have a tool or system to check performance. Oracle7 was used to test the SQL statements in this book. Oracle offers several tools for checking performance, including the `EXPLAIN PLAN`, `TKPROF`, and `SET` commands. Check your particular implementation for tools that are similar to Oracle's.

Workshop

The following workshop consists of a series of quiz questions and practical exercises. The quiz questions are designed to test your overall understanding of the current material. The practical exercises give you the opportunity to apply the concepts discussed during the current hour, as well as build on the knowledge you acquired in previous hours of study. Be sure to complete the quiz questions and exercises before continuing to the next hour. Refer to Appendix C, "Answers to Quizzes and Exercises," for answers.

Quiz

1. Is using a unique index on a small table beneficial?
2. What happens when the optimizer chooses not to use an index on a table when a query has been executed?
3. Should the most restrictive clause(s) be placed before or after the join condition(s) in the `WHERE` clause?
4. When is the `LIKE` operator considered bad in terms of performance?
5. How can you optimize batch load operations in terms of indexes?
6. Which three clauses are the cause of sort operations that degrade performance?

Exercises

1. Rewrite the following SQL statements to improve their performance. Use the fictitious `EMPLOYEE_TBL` and `EMPLOYEE_PAY_TBL`, as described here:

```
EMPLOYEE_TBL
EMP_ID          VARCHAR(9)     NOT NULL     Primary key,
LAST_NAME       VARCHAR(15)    NOT NULL,
```

```
FIRST_NAME     VARCHAR(15)     NOT NULL,
MIDDLE_NAME    VARCHAR(15),
ADDRESS        VARCHAR(30)     NOT NULL,
CITY           VARCHAR(15)     NOT NULL,
STATE          VARCHAR(2)      NOT NULL,
ZIP            INTEGER(5)      NOT NULL,
PHONE          VARCHAR(10),
PAGER          VARCHAR(10),
CONSTRAINT EMP_PK PRIMARY KEY (EMP_ID)
EMPLOYEE_PAY_TBL
EMP_ID             VARCHAR(9)      NOT NULL      primary key,
POSITION           VARCHAR(15)     NOT NULL,
DATE_HIRE          DATETIME,
PAY_RATE           DECIMAL(4,2)    NOT NULL,
DATE_LAST_RAISE    DATETIME,
SALARY             DECIMAL(8,2),
BONUS              DECIMAL(8,2),
CONSTRAINT EMP_FK FOREIGN KEY (EMP_ID)
REFERENCES EMPLOYEE_TBL (EMP_ID)
```

a.
```
SELECT EMP_ID, LAST_NAME, FIRST_NAME,
          PHONE
      FROM EMPLOYEE_TBL
      WHERE SUBSTRING(PHONE, 1, 3) = '317' OR
          SUBSTRING(PHONE, 1, 3) = '812' OR
          SUBSTRING(PHONE, 1, 3) = '765';
```

b.
```
SELECT LAST_NAME, FIRST_NAME
      FROM EMPLOYEE_TBL
       WHERE LAST_NAME LIKE '%ALL%;
```

c.
```
SELECT E.EMP_ID, E.LAST_NAME, E.FIRST_NAME,
          EP.SALARY
      FROM EMPLOYEE_TBL E,
      EMPLOYEE_PAY_TBL EP
      WHERE LAST_NAME LIKE 'S%'
          AND E.EMP_ID = EP.EMP_ID;
```

2. Add another table called EMPLOYEE_PAYHIST_TBL that contains a large amount of pay history data. Use the following table to write a series of SQL statements to address the following problems. Be sure to ensure that the queries you write perform well.

```
EMPLOYEE_PAYHIST_TBL
PAYHIST_ID         VARCHAR(9)      NOT NULL      primary key,
EMP_ID             VARCHAR(9)      NOT NULL,
START_DATE         DATETIME        NOT NULL,
```

```
END_DATE            DATETIME,
PAY_RATE            DECIMAL(4,2)    NOT NULL,
SALARY              DECIMAL(8,2)    NOT NULL,
BONUS               DECIMAL(8,2)    NOT NULL,
CONSTRAINT EMP_FK FOREIGN KEY (EMP_ID)
REFERENCES EMPLOYEE_TBL (EMP_ID)
```

a. Find the SUM of the salaried versus nonsalaried employees, by the year in which their pay started.

b. Find the difference in the yearly pay of salaried employees versus nonsalaried employees, by the year in which their pay started. Consider the nonsalaried employees to be working full time during the year (PAY_RATE × 52 × 40).

c. Find the difference in what employees make now versus what they made when they started with the company. Again, consider the nonsalaried employees to be full time. Also consider that the employees' current pay is reflected in EMPLOYEE_PAY_TBL and also EMPLOYEE_PAYHIST_TBL. In the pay history table, the current pay is reflected as a row with the END_DATE for pay equal to NULL.

HOUR 24
Working with the System Catalog

What You'll Learn in This Hour:

- Defining the system catalog
- Creating the system catalog
- Understanding what data the system catalog contains
- Working with examples of system catalog tables
- Querying the system catalog
- Updating the system catalog

In this hour, you learn about the system catalog, commonly referred to as the data dictionary in some relational database implementations. By the end of this hour, you will understand the purpose and contents of the system catalog and will be able to query it to find information about the database based on commands that you have learned in previous hours. Each major implementation has some form of a system catalog that stores information about the database. This hour shows examples of the elements contained in a few of the different system catalogs for the implementations discussed in this book.

Defining the System Catalog

The *system catalog* is a collection of tables and views that contain important information about a database. A system catalog is available for each database. Information in the system catalog defines the structure of the database and information on the data contained therein. For example, the Data Definition Language (DDL) for all tables in the database is stored in the system catalog.

Figure 24.1 shows an example of the system catalog within the database. You can see that the system catalog for a database is actually part of the database. Within the database are objects, such as tables, indexes, and views. The system catalog is basically a group of objects that contain information that defines other objects in the database, the structure of the database, and various other significant information.

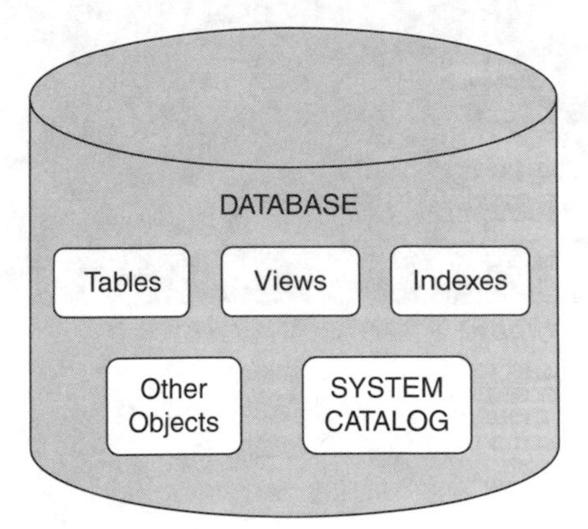

FIGURE 24.1
The system catalog

The system catalog for your implementation might be divided into logical groups of objects to provide tables that are accessible by the database administrator (DBA) and any other database user. For example, users might need to view the particular database privileges that they have been granted but don't care how this is internally structured in the database. Users typically query the system catalog to acquire information on their own objects and privileges, whereas the DBA needs to inquire about any structure or event within the database. In some implementations, system catalog objects are accessible only by the DBA.

The system catalog is crucial to the DBA or any other database user who needs to know about the database's structure and nature. It is especially important when the database user is not presented with a graphical user interface (GUI). The system catalog ensures that orders are kept not only by the DBA and users, but also by the database server.

TIP

Database System Catalogs Vary

Each implementation has its own naming conventions for the system catalog's tables and views. The naming is ***not*** important; however, learning what the system catalog does ***is*** important, as is knowing what it contains and how and where you can retrieve the information.

Creating the System Catalog

The system catalog is created either automatically with the creation of the database or by the DBA immediately following the creation of the database. For example, a set of predefined, vendor-provided SQL scripts in Oracle is executed, which builds all the database tables and views in the system catalog that are accessible to a database user.

The system catalog tables and views are system owned and are not specific to any one schema. In Oracle, for example, the system catalog owner is a user account called `SYS` that has full authority in the database. In Microsoft SQL Server, the system catalog for the SQL server is located in the `master` database. Check your specific vendor documentation to find where the system catalogs are stored.

Determining What Is Contained in the System Catalog

The system catalog contains a variety of information accessible to many users and is sometimes used for different specific purposes by each of those users.

The system catalog contains information such as the following:

- User accounts and default settings
- Privileges and other security information
- Performance statistics
- Object sizing
- Object growth
- Table structure and storage
- Index structure and storage
- Information on other database objects, such as views, synonyms, triggers, and stored procedures
- Table constraints and referential integrity information
- User sessions
- Auditing information
- Internal database settings
- Locations of database files

The database server maintains the system catalog. For example, when a table is created, the database server inserts the data into the appropriate system catalog table or view. When a table's structure is modified, appropriate objects in the data dictionary are updated. The following sections describe the types of data that the system catalog contains.

User Data

The system catalog stores all information about individual users: the system and object privileges a user has been granted, the objects a user owns, and the objects that the user does not own but can still access. The user tables and views are accessible for the individual to query for information. See your implementation documentation on the system catalog objects.

Security Information

The system catalog also stores security information, such as user identifications, encrypted passwords, and various privileges and groups of privileges that database users use to access the data. Audit tables exist in some implementations for tracking actions that occur within the database, as well as tracking by whom and when. Database user sessions can be closely monitored through the system catalog in many implementations.

Database Design Information

The system catalog contains information regarding the actual database. That information includes the database's creation date, name, object sizing, size and location of data files, referential integrity information, indexes that exist in the database, and specific column information and column attributes for each table in the database.

Performance Statistics

Performance statistics are typically maintained in the system catalog as well. Performance statistics include information concerning the performance of SQL statements, both elapsed time and the execution method of an SQL statement taken by the optimizer. Other information for performance concerns memory allocation and usage, free space in the database, and information that allows table and index fragmentation to be controlled within the database. You can use this performance information to properly tune the database, rearrange SQL queries, and redesign methods of access to data to achieve better overall performance and SQL query response time.

Identifying System Catalog Tables by Implementation

Each implementation has several tables and views that comprise the system catalog, some of which are categorized by user level, system level, and DBA level. For your particular implementation, you should query these tables and read your implementation's documentation for more information on system catalog tables. Table 24.1 has examples from the Oracle implementation, which is used for the examples in this book.

TABLE 24.1 Major Implementation System Catalog Objects

Oracle Table Name	Information On...
DBA_TABLES	All tables in the database
DBA_SEGMENTS	Segment storage
DBA_INDEXES	All indexes
DBA_USERS	All users of the database
DBA_ROLE_PRIVS	Roles granted
DBA_ROLES	Roles in the database
DBA_SYS_PRIVS	System privileges granted
DBA_FREE_SPACE	Database free space
V$DATABASE	The creation of the database
V$SESSION	Current sessions
ALL_TABLES	Tables accessible by a user
USER_TABLES	Tables owned by a user
ALL_TAB_COLUMNS	All columns in tables accessible by a user
USER_TAB_COLUMNS	All columns in tables owned by a user
ROLE_TAB_PRIVS	All table privileges granted to a role

These are just a few of the system catalog objects from the Oracle relational database implementations that have been used in the book for examples. Many system catalog objects are similar between implementations, but they do vary and a plethora of information is stored in the system catalog. This hour strives to provide a brief overview of the system catalog and show some examples of how you can use the system catalog to get information about the `BIRDS` database and your users. Just keep in mind that each implementation is specific to the organization of the system catalog's contents.

Querying the System Catalog

The system catalog tables or views are queried as any other table or view in the database using SQL. A user can usually query the user-related tables but might be denied access to various system tables that are accessible only by privileged database user accounts, such as the DBA.

The first example that follows uses the Oracle `show user` command to verify the current user account by which you are connected to the database. After that, a simple query is performed to select the name from the V$ database system catalog view. This confirms the name of the database in Oracle that you are connected to.

```
SQL> show user;
USER is "RYAN"


SQL> select name from v$database;

NAME
---------
XE

1 row selected.
```

The next example accesses the USER_TABLES system catalog table, which tells you information about any table that you own—in other words, any table that your user has created.

```
SQL> select table_name
  2  from user_tables
  3  where table_name not like 'DMRS_%';

TABLE_NAME
--------------------------------------------------
LOCATIONS2
MIGRATION_TEST_DELETE
BIG_BIRDS
SMALL_BIRDS
BIRDS_NESTS
MIGRATION
BIRDS_MIGRATION
PREDATORS
BIRDS_PREDATORS
PHOTO_STYLES
PHOTO_LEVELS
CAMERAS
PHOTOGRAPHERS
FAVORITE_BIRDS
PHOTOGRAPHER_STYLES
PHOTOGRAPHER_CAMERAS
OLD_CAMERAS
COLORS
BIRDS_COLORS
FORMER_PHOTOGRAPHERS
BIRDS
LOCATIONS
PHOTOS
FOOD
```

```
BIRDS_FOOD
NESTS
SHORT_BIRDS

27 rows selected.
```

NOTE

A Word About the Examples

These examples use the Oracle system catalog, simply because this implementation is used for the examples in this book.

The following query gets information from the ALL_TABLES system catalog table. ALL_TABLES returns not only any tables that you own, but also any tables to which you have been granted access. This query is actually the same as a previous query because you qualified the owner as the current connected user—in this case, RYAN.

```
SQL> select table_name
  2  from all_tables
  3  where table_name not like 'DMRS_%'
  4    and owner = 'RYAN';

TABLE_NAME
--------------------------------------------------
LOCATIONS2
MIGRATION_TEST_DELETE
BIG_BIRDS
SMALL_BIRDS
BIRDS_NESTS
MIGRATION
BIRDS_MIGRATION
PREDATORS
BIRDS_PREDATORS
PHOTO_STYLES
PHOTO_LEVELS
CAMERAS
PHOTOGRAPHERS
FAVORITE_BIRDS
PHOTOGRAPHER_STYLES
PHOTOGRAPHER_CAMERAS
OLD_CAMERAS
COLORS
BIRDS_COLORS
FORMER_PHOTOGRAPHERS
BIRDS
LOCATIONS
```

```
PHOTOS
FOOD
BIRDS_FOOD
NESTS
SHORT_BIRDS

27 rows selected.
```

CAUTION

Manipulating System Catalog Tables Can Be Dangerous

Never directly manipulate tables in the system catalog in any way. (Only the DBA has access to manipulate system catalog tables.) Doing so might compromise the database's integrity. Remember that information concerning the structure of the database, as well as all objects in the database, is maintained in the system catalog. The system catalog is typically isolated from all other data in the database. Some implementations, such as Microsoft SQL Server, do not allow the user to manipulate the system catalog directly, to maintain the integrity of the system.

The next query uses the COUNT aggregate function to return the total number of tables that the current user owns.

```
SQL> select count(table_name) "MY TABLES"
  2  from user_tables
  3  where table_name not like 'DMRS_%';

 MY TABLES
----------
        27

1 row selected.
```

The following two SQL statements are examples of a query against the USER_TAB_COLUMNS table. This table has information about all the columns in a given table.

```
SQL> select column_name
  2  from user_tab_columns
  3  where table_name = 'BIRDS';

COLUMN_NAME
------------------------
BIRD_ID
BIRD_NAME
HEIGHT
WEIGHT
WINGSPAN
```

```
EGGS
BROODS
INCUBATION
FLEDGING
NEST_BUILDER
BEAK_LENGTH

11 rows selected.


SQL> select data_type
  2  from user_tab_columns
  3  where table_name = 'BIRDS'
  4    and column_name = 'WINGSPAN';

DATA_TYPE
----------------
NUMBER

1 row selected.
```

In the following examples, you are creating a role called SEE_BIRDS. Study these SQL statements as the role is created, SELECT access is granted to the role on the BIRDS table, and then information about the role is selected from the table ROLE_TAB_PRIVS.

```
SQL> alter session set "_ORACLE_SCRIPT"=true;

Session altered.


SQL> drop role see_birds;

Role dropped.


SQL> create role see_birds;

Role created.


SQL> grant select on birds to see_birds;

Grant succeeded.


SQL> select role from role_tab_privs where owner = 'RYAN';
```

```
ROLE
---------------------
SEE_BIRDS

1 row selected.


SQL> select role, owner, table_name, privilege
  2  from role_tab_privs
  3  where role = 'SEE_BIRDS';


ROLE                 OWNER      TABLE_NAME       PRIVILEGE
-----------------    ---------  ---------------  -------------------
SEE_BIRDS            RYAN       BIRDS            SELECT


1 row selected.
```

NOTE

These Are Just a Few of the System Catalog Tables Available

The examples shown in this section represent a small sampling of the information that is available from any system catalog. You might find it extremely helpful to dump data dictionary information using queries to a file that you can print and use as a reference. Refer to your implementation documentation for specific system catalog tables and columns within those available tables.

Updating System Catalog Objects

The system catalog is used only for query operations—even when the DBA is using it. The database server makes updates to the system catalog automatically. For example, a table is created in the database when a database user issues a `CREATE TABLE` statement. The database server then places the DDL that created the table in the system catalog under the appropriate system catalog table.

You never need to manually update a table in the system catalog, even though you might have the power to do so. The database server for each implementation performs these updates according to actions that occur within the database, as Figure 24.2 shows.

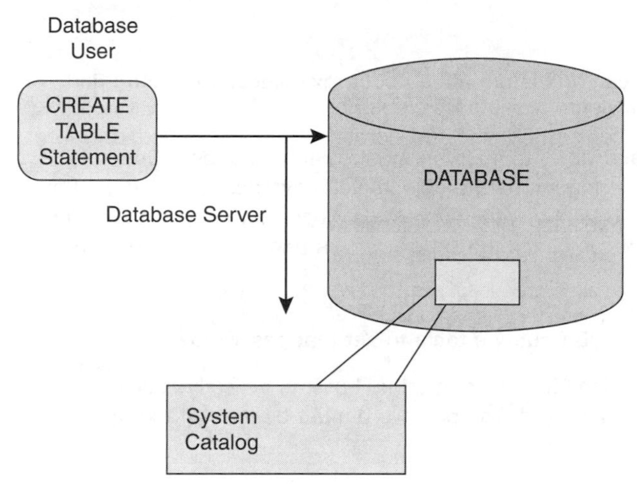

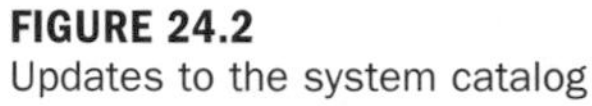
FIGURE 24.2
Updates to the system catalog

Summary

In this hour, you learned about the system catalog for a relational database. In a sense, the system catalog is a database within a database; it contains all the information about the database in which it resides. The system catalog serves as a way of maintaining the database's overall structure, tracking events and changes that occur within the database, and providing the vast pool of information necessary for overall database management. The system catalog is used only for query operations; database users should not make changes directly to system tables. However, changes are implicitly made each time a change is made to the database structure itself, such as during the creation of a table. The database server makes these entries in the system catalog automatically.

Q&A

Q. As a database user, I realize that I can find information about my objects. How can I find information about other users' objects?

A. Users can employ sets of tables and views to query in most system catalogs. One set of these tables and views includes information on the objects you have access to. To find out about other users' access, you need to check the system catalogs that contain that information. For example, in Oracle, you can check the `DBA_TABLES` and `DBA_USERS` system catalogs.

Q. If a user forgets a password, can the DBA query a table to get that password?

A. Yes and no. The password is maintained in a system table, but it is typically encrypted so that even the DBA cannot read the password. The password must be reset if the user forgets it, which the DBA can easily accomplish.

Q. How can I tell which columns are in a system catalog table?

A. You can query the system catalog tables as you query any other table. Simply query the table that holds that particular information.

Workshop

The following workshop consists of a series of quiz questions and practical exercises. The quiz questions are designed to test your overall understanding of the current material. The practical exercises give you the opportunity to apply the concepts discussed during the current hour, as well as build on the knowledge you acquired in previous hours of study. Be sure to complete the quiz questions and exercises before continuing to the next hour. Refer to Appendix C, "Answers to Quizzes and Exercises," for answers.

Quiz

1. What is the system catalog also known as in some implementations?
2. Can a regular user update the system catalog?
3. Who owns the system catalog?
4. What is the difference between the Oracle system objects `ALL_TABLES` and `DBA_TABLES`?
5. Who makes modifications to the system tables?

Exercises

1. At the prompt, type in queries to bring up each of the following:
   - Information on all your tables
   - Information on all columns in your tables
2. Show the name of the current database.
3. Show the name of the user by which you are connected to the database.
4. Create a role to update your `FOOD` table.
5. Select information about the role you created from the system catalog.
6. Explore the system catalog on your own. The information contained is nearly endless. Remember that, in Oracle, you can use the `DESCRIBE table_name` command to show the columns that comprise a table.

HOUR 25
Bonus Workshop for the Road

What You'll Learn in This Hour:

- Explore the expansion of the sample database used for examples and exercises
- Use SQL to define and modify new database objects
- Manage transactions within your database to create SQL queries and composite queries with multiple types of joins
- Use functions to dig deeper into information and group data sets
- Create more advanced queries with views and subqueries
- Use SQL to generate SQL code

In this hour, you expand upon the current BIRDS database and walk through numerous additional examples using the SQL knowledge you have learned in this book. Afterward, you perform a final set of exercises. The goal of this bonus hour is to bring everything together while applying the concepts of the SQL language from beginning to end with hands-on, real-world practice. This hour includes very little instruction—mostly you'll find examples to follow and opportunities to unleash what you have learned. Do not be intimidated by the length of this hands-on chapter; just follow along at your own pace—maybe 1 hour, maybe 10 hours, or maybe more as you explore at your leisure. Reflect on the investment you have made and your progress in learning SQL. Your knowledge of SQL has incubated and the fledging period is over—now it is time for you to fly. Let's have some fun!

The BIRDS Database

In this hour, you continue to work with the original BIRDS database, adding two data sets (on predators and photographers) that will be integrated with the database. Figure 25.1 is an ERD of the original BIRDS database, for a quick reference to the data and relationships. Refer back to Hour 3, "Getting to Know Your Data," to see a list of all the data in the BIRDS database. Remember that you can also simply query from each table at any time (SELECT * FROM TABLE_NAME) to view the data before you perform any queries.

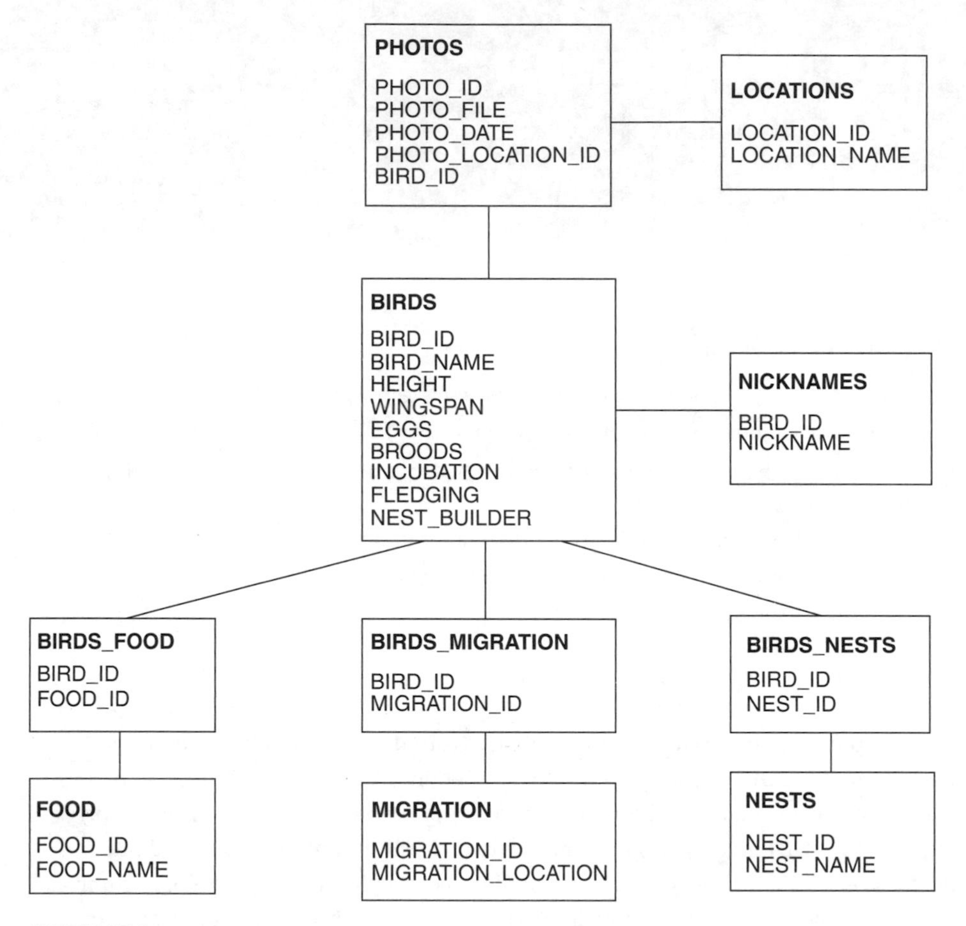

FIGURE 25.1
The BIRDS database

For your convenience during this hour, the following is a list of the bird identifications and the name of the birds from the BIRDS table.

```
SQL> select bird_id, bird_name
  2  from birds;

   BIRD_ID BIRD_NAME
---------- ------------------------------
         1 Great Blue Heron
         2 Mallard
         3 Common Loon
         4 Bald Eagle
         5 Golden Eagle
         6 Red Tailed Hawk
```

```
  7 Osprey
  8 Belted Kingfisher
  9 Canadian Goose
 10 Pied-billed Grebe
 11 American Coot
 12 Common Sea Gull
 13 Ring-billed Gull
 14 Double-crested Cormorant
 15 Common Merganser
 16 Turkey Vulture
 17 American Crow
 18 Green Heron
 19 Mute Swan
 20 Brown Pelican
 21 Great Egret
 22 Anhinga
 23 Black Skimmer

23 rows selected.
```

Predators of Birds

The first of the two data sets that will be integrated into the BIRDS database is data about predators of birds. Figure 25.2 provides an ERD for the two tables that will be related to the BIRDS database. As you can see by the relationships in the ERD, a bird can have many predators. Likewise, a predator might prey on many different types of birds. The BIRDS_PREDATORS table is a base table that is used to join the BIRDS table with the PREDATORS table. If you want, you can take this a step further and keep track of the predators that are also eaten by birds. We have not taken the data to this extent at this point, but you can consider what that might look like and try it on your own.

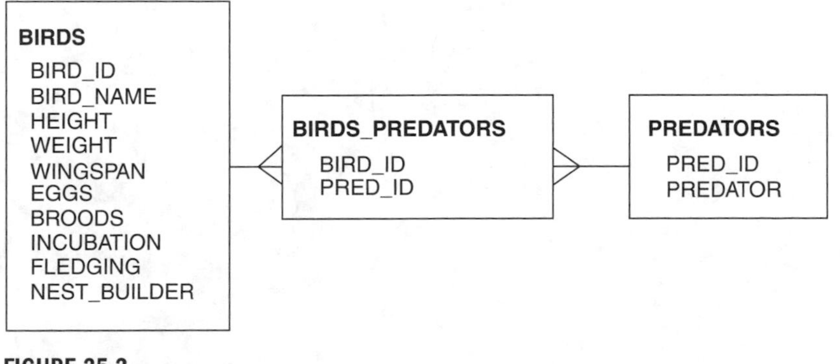

FIGURE 25.2
Predators of birds

Following is the data in both of the predators tables. You can see that the database has 106 rows of data in the database; this is only a subset of the data in the table, to give you an idea of how the data is stored. Take a few minutes to study the output and even make manual comparisons between these new tables and the BIRDS table. For example, what are the predators of the Great Blue Heron?

```
SQL> select * from birds_predators;

   BIRD_ID    PRED_ID
---------- ----------
         1          1
         1          4
         1         17
         1         18
         2          1
         2          2
         2          4
         2          5
         2          7
         2          9
         2         11
         2         14
         2         17
         2         19
         2         20
         3          4
         ...........
         ...........
         ...........

106 rows selected.

SQL> select * from predators;

   PRED_ID PREDATOR
---------- ------------------------------
         1 Humans
         2 Cats
         3 Chipmunks
         4 Other Birds
         5 Snakes
         6 Frogs
         7 Dogs
         8 Deer
         9 Coyotes
        10 Reptiles
```

```
        11 Weasels
        12 Foxes
        13 Carnivorous Plants
        14 Predatory Fish
        15 Seals
        16 Insects
        17 Racoons
        18 Bears
        19 Skunks
        20 Turtles
        21 Wolves
        22 Cougars
        23 Bobcats
        24 Alligators
        25 Minks
        26 Rats
        27 Squirrels
        28 Opposums
        29 Crocodiles

29 rows selected.
```

Photographers of Birds

The second set of data that will be integrated into the BIRDS database is information about photographers of birds. Figure 25.3 provides an ERD to illustrate the data, relationships, and how everything ties into the BIRDS database through the BIRDS table. Take a few minutes to study Figure 25.3.

Notice the different types of relationships in Figure 25.3. For example, the PHOTOGRAPHERS table has a recursive relationship with itself. This was previously discussed by example in this book: Photographers might mentor other photographers, and photographers might be mentored by other photographers. Remember that a self join is used to relate data in a table to itself.

Following is a list of data in each of the new photographer-related tables. Study the data and make sure you understand how it relates to the BIRDS database and how it might be used. Perform a few manual queries. For example, what is the favorite bird of Steve Hamm? How many different cameras does Gordon Flash use? What photographer mentors Jenny Forest?

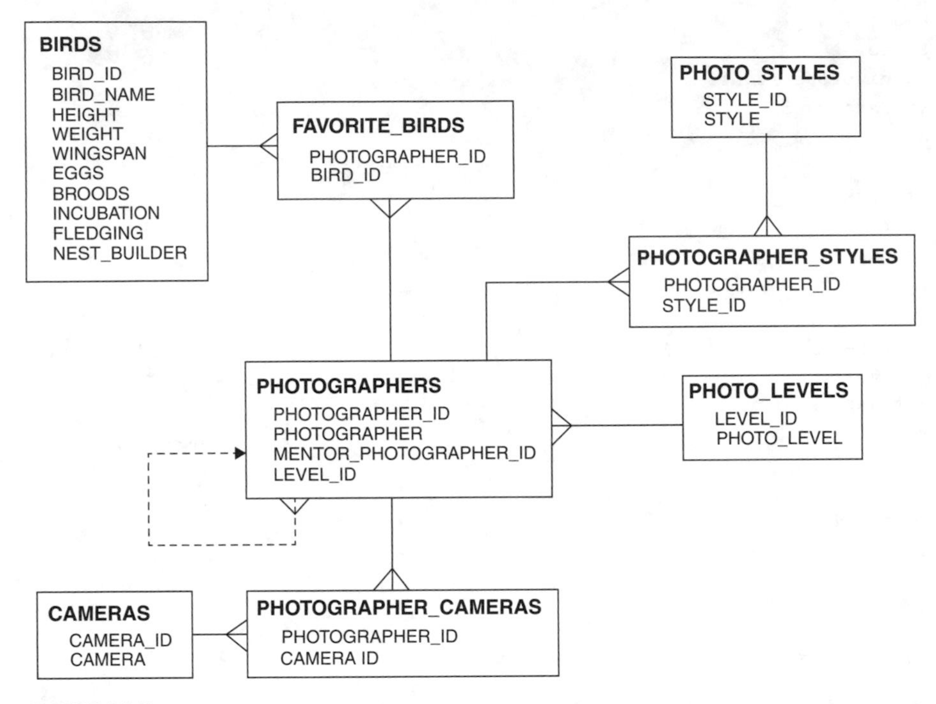

FIGURE 25.3
Photographers of birds

In addition to the previous questions, manually answer the following questions just by looking at the lists of data:

- Which photographers use a Canon camera?
- Which photographers do not use a Canon camera?
- Which photographers have the highest photo level?
- What equipment does Gordon Flash use?
- Which photographer has a favorite bird that is preyed upon by coyotes?
- Which photographer has the most diverse styles of photography?
- Does any photographer like to take still photographs of the Bald Eagle as a favorite bird?

NOTE

Explore Your New Data

Use your imagination to ask and answer some of your own questions about the data. Think about how that data might be used in the real world.

```
SQL> select * from photographers;

PHOTOGRAPHER_ID PHOTOGRAPHER         MENTOR_PHOTOGRAPHER_ID   LEVEL_ID
--------------- -------------------- ---------------------- ----------
              7 Ryan Notstephens                                     7
              8 Susan Willamson                                      6
              9 Mark Fife                                            6
              1 Shooter McGavin                                      1
              2 Jenny Forest                              8          3
              3 Steve Hamm                                           4
              4 Harry Henderson                           9          5
              5 Kelly Hairtrigger                         8          2
              6 Gordon Flash                                         1
             10 Kate Kapteur                              7          4

10 rows selected.

SQL> select * from favorite_birds;

PHOTOGRAPHER_ID    BIRD_ID
--------------- ----------
              1          3
              1          4
              1          7
              2         19
              2         20
              2         23
              3          1
              3          3
              4          4
              5          8
              6         18
              7         11
              7         16
              7         22
              8         14
              9          4
              9          5
             10          2
             10          6
             10         17
             10         21

21 rows selected.
```

```
SQL> select * from photographer_cameras;

PHOTOGRAPHER_ID  CAMERA_ID
--------------- ----------
              1          1
              2          1
              2          8
              3          2
              3          9
              4          3
              5          4
              6          7
              7          1
              7          5
              7          9
              8          2
              8          8
              9          6
              9          9
             10          8

16 rows selected.

SQL> select * from cameras;

 CAMERA_ID CAMERA
---------- ------------------------------
         1 Canon
         2 Nikon
         3 Sony
         4 Olympus
         5 GoPro
         6 Fujifilm
         7 Polaroid
         8 Apple iPhone
         9 Samsung Galaxy

9 rows selected.

SQL> select * from photo_levels;

  LEVEL_ID PHOTO_LEVEL
---------- ------------------------------
         1 Beginner
         2 Novice
         3 Hobbyist
```

```
         4 Competent
         5 Skilled
         6 Artist
         7 World-class

7 rows selected.
```

SQL> select * from photographer_styles;

```
PHOTOGRAPHER_ID   STYLE_ID
--------------- ----------
              1          3
              1          8
              2          1
              3          2
              4          5
              4          8
              5          3
              5          5
              5          7
              6          2
              6          6
              7          1
              8          5
              8          8
              9          3
              9          4
             10          6
             10          8

18 rows selected.
```

SQL> select * from photo_styles;

```
  STYLE_ID STYLE
---------- ------------------------------
         1 Action
         2 Portrait
         3 Landscape
         4 Sunset
         5 Artistic
         6 Close-up
         7 Underwater
         8 Still

8 rows selected.
```

Creating the New Tables

This section walks through the process of creating the new tables for predators and photographers that will be integrated into the existing `BIRDS` database. To give you a clean start, you execute the following scripts that have been provided with this book. It is recommended that you create a new user so that any previous work that you performed is still saved under your original schema; you can then execute the provided scripts without error. Log in to SQL and perform the following steps.

Create the new user (schema owner):

```
SQL> alter session set "_ORACLE_SCRIPT"=true;
```

Session altered.

```
SQL> create user your_new_username
  2  identified by your_new_passwd;
```

User created.

```
SQL> grant dba to your_new_username;
```

Grant succeeded.

NOTE

Follow Along

Follow along with all the examples in this hour as the new user that you are creating. You will have the opportunity to perform exercises on your own, without any guidance.

Connect to the database as the new user:

```
SQL> connect your_new_username
Connected.

SQL> show user
USER is "YOUR_USERNAME"
```

Execute the provided script called `bonus_tables.sql` to create the table for this hour.

```
SQL> start c:\sqlbook\bonus_tables.sql
drop table birds_food
           *
ERROR at line 1:
ORA-00942: table or view does not exist


drop table birds_nests
           *
```

```
ERROR at line 1:
ORA-00942: table or view does not exist


drop table birds_migration
           *
ERROR at line 1:
ORA-00942: table or view does not exist


drop table migration
           *
ERROR at line 1:
ORA-00942: table or view does not exist
```

In the previous output, notice that errors were received when attempting to drop tables. This is because the first time you run this script, the tables do not exist—and you cannot drop a table that does not exist. The following output is the second half of the output from executing the `bonus_tables.sql` script, where the tables are actually created. The output, or feedback, confirms the results of any SQL statement that you issue at the `SQL>` prompt.

```
Table created.


Table created.


Table created.


Table created.


Table created.
```

Execute the provided script called `bonus_data.sql` to insert data into the new tables for this chapter:

```
SQL> start c:\sqlbook\bonus_data.sql

0 rows deleted.


0 rows deleted.


0 rows deleted.
```

```
0 rows deleted.


0 rows deleted.


0 rows deleted.


0 rows deleted.
```

In the previous output, you can see that zero rows were deleted from the new tables that you just created. This is because no data currently exists in those tables. If you run this script in the future, you will see that rows are deleted and then reinserted into the new tables. In the following second half of the output from the `bonus_data.sql` script, you can see feedback for every row that is created.

```
1 row created.


1 row created.


1 row created.


1 row created.


1 row created.


1 row created.
```

Workshop: Describing Your Tables

Use the `DESC` command to study the structure of each new table during this hour that was incorporated into the `BIRDS` database.

```
SQL> desc birds;

 Name                          Null?    Type
 ----------------------------- -------- --------------------------
 BIRD_ID                       NOT NULL NUMBER(3)
 BIRD_NAME                     NOT NULL VARCHAR2(30)
```

```
 HEIGHT                      NOT NULL NUMBER(4,2)
 WEIGHT                      NOT NULL NUMBER(4,2)
 WINGSPAN                             NUMBER(4,2)
 EGGS                        NOT NULL NUMBER(2)
 BROODS                               NUMBER(1)
 INCUBATION                  NOT NULL NUMBER(2)
 FLEDGING                    NOT NULL NUMBER(3)
 NEST_BUILDER                NOT NULL CHAR(1)
```

Workshop: Basic Queries

Issue some basic `SELECT` statements to explore the data within the new tables.

```
SQL> select * from cameras;

 CAMERA_ID CAMERA
---------- ------------------------------
         1 Canon
         2 Nikon
         3 Sony
         4 Olympus
         5 GoPro
         6 Fujifilm
         7 Polaroid
         8 Apple iPhone
         9 Samsung Galaxy

9 rows selected.
```

Workshop: Adding Tables

Use the `CREATE TABLE` command to create the following new tables that are related to bird habitats.

```
SQL> create table habitats
  2  (habitat_id      number(3)        not null       primary key,
  3   habitat         varchar(30)      not null);

Table created.

SQL> create table birds_habitats
  2  (habitat_id      number(3)      not null      primary key,
  3   bird_id         number(3)      not null);

Table created.
```

```
SQL> create table habitat_types
  2  (habitat_type_id      number(3)        not null      primary key,
  3   habitat_type         varchar(30)      not null);

Table created.
```

Workshop: Manipulating Data

Follow along with the next series of SQL statements to manipulate data within the new tables using Data Manipulation Language and transactional control commands. Study the results between each SQL statement.

```
SQL> select * from photographers;

PHOTOGRAPHER_ID PHOTOGRAPHER              MENTOR_PHOTOGRAPHER_ID   LEVEL_ID
--------------- ------------------------- ---------------------- ----------
              7 Ryan Notstephens                                          7
              8 Susan Willamson                                           6
              9 Mark Fife                                                 6
              1 Shooter McGavin                                           1
              2 Jenny Forest                                   8          3
              3 Steve Hamm                                                4
              4 Harry Henderson                                9          5
              5 Kelly Hairtrigger                              8          2
              6 Gordon Flash                                              1
             10 Kate Kapteur                                   7          4

10 rows selected.

SQL> insert into photographers
  2  values (11, 'Sam Song', null, 4);

1 row created.

SQL> commit;

Commit complete.

SQL> select * from photographers;

PHOTOGRAPHER_ID PHOTOGRAPHER              MENTOR_PHOTOGRAPHER_ID   LEVEL_ID
--------------- ------------------------- ---------------------- ----------
              7 Ryan Notstephens                                          7
              8 Susan Willamson                                           6
              9 Mark Fife                                                 6
              1 Shooter McGavin                                           1
```

```
              2 Jenny Forest                                      8          3
              3 Steve Hamm                                                   4
              4 Harry Henderson                                   9          5
              5 Kelly Hairtrigger                                 8          2
              6 Gordon Flash                                                 1
             10 Kate Kapteur                                      7          4
             11 Sam Song                                                     4

11 rows selected.

SQL> update photographers set level_id = 5
  2  where photographer_id = 11;

1 row updated.

SQL> select * from photographers;

PHOTOGRAPHER_ID PHOTOGRAPHER              MENTOR_PHOTOGRAPHER_ID   LEVEL_ID
--------------- ------------------------- ---------------------- ----------
              7 Ryan Notstephens                                         7
              8 Susan Willamson                                          6
              9 Mark Fife                                                6
              1 Shooter McGavin                                          1
              2 Jenny Forest                                      8          3
              3 Steve Hamm                                                   4
              4 Harry Henderson                                   9          5
              5 Kelly Hairtrigger                                 8          2
              6 Gordon Flash                                                 1
             10 Kate Kapteur                                      7          4
             11 Sam Song                                                     5

11 rows selected.

SQL> rollback;

Rollback complete.

SQL> select * from photographers;

PHOTOGRAPHER_ID PHOTOGRAPHER              MENTOR_PHOTOGRAPHER_ID   LEVEL_ID
--------------- ------------------------- ---------------------- ----------
              7 Ryan Notstephens                                         7
              8 Susan Willamson                                          6
              9 Mark Fife                                                6
              1 Shooter McGavin                                          1
              2 Jenny Forest                                      8          3
              3 Steve Hamm                                                   4
              4 Harry Henderson                                   9          5
```

```
              5 Kelly Hairtrigger                                  8          2
              6 Gordon Flash                                                  1
             10 Kate Kapteur                                       7          4
             11 Sam Song                                                      4

11 rows selected.

SQL> delete from photographers
  2  where photographer_id = 11;

1 row deleted.

SQL> commit;

Commit complete.

SQL> select * from photographers;

PHOTOGRAPHER_ID PHOTOGRAPHER              MENTOR_PHOTOGRAPHER_ID   LEVEL_ID
--------------- ------------------------- ---------------------- ----------
              7 Ryan Notstephens                                          7
              8 Susan Willamson                                           6
              9 Mark Fife                                                 6
              1 Shooter McGavin                                           1
              2 Jenny Forest                                   8          3
              3 Steve Hamm                                                4
              4 Harry Henderson                                9          5
              5 Kelly Hairtrigger                              8          2
              6 Gordon Flash                                              1
             10 Kate Kapteur                                   7          4

10 rows selected.
```

Workshop: Joining Tables

Issue the following SQL statements to join three tables in a query. Notice that the table names are fully qualified in the first query and aliases are not used. The second query uses aliases when joining the tables.

```
SQL> select photographers.photographer, cameras.camera
  2  from photographers, cameras, photographer_cameras
  3  where photographers.photographer_id = photographer_cameras.camera_id
  4    and cameras.camera_id = photographer_cameras.camera_id
  5  order by photographer;
```

```
PHOTOGRAPHER                   CAMERA
------------------------------ ------------------------------
Gordon Flash                   Fujifilm
Harry Henderson                Olympus
Jenny Forest                   Nikon
Jenny Forest                   Nikon
Kelly Hairtrigger              GoPro
Mark Fife                      Samsung Galaxy
Mark Fife                      Samsung Galaxy
Mark Fife                      Samsung Galaxy
Ryan Notstephens               Polaroid
Shooter McGavin                Canon
Shooter McGavin                Canon
Shooter McGavin                Canon
Steve Hamm                     Sony
Susan Willamson                Apple iPhone
Susan Willamson                Apple iPhone
Susan Willamson                Apple iPhone

16 rows selected.

SQL> select p.photographer, c.camera
  2  from photographers p,
  3       cameras c,
  4       photographer_cameras pc
  5  where p.photographer_id = pc.photographer_id
  6    and c.camera_id = pc.camera_id
  7  order by 1;

PHOTOGRAPHER                   CAMERA
------------------------------ ------------------------------
Gordon Flash                   Polaroid
Harry Henderson                Sony
Jenny Forest                   Apple iPhone
Jenny Forest                   Canon
Kate Kapteur                   Apple iPhone
Kelly Hairtrigger              Olympus
Mark Fife                      Fujifilm
Mark Fife                      Samsung Galaxy
Ryan Notstephens               Samsung Galaxy
Ryan Notstephens               Canon
Ryan Notstephens               GoPro
Shooter McGavin                Canon
Steve Hamm                     Samsung Galaxy
Steve Hamm                     Nikon
Susan Willamson                Apple iPhone
Susan Willamson                Nikon

16 rows selected.
```

Following is an example of a self join. This example joins the PHOTOGRAPHERS table to itself to get information about photographers that mentor other photographers. This is also an example that was previously used.

```
SQL> select p1.photographer photographer,
  2        p2.photographer mentor
  3  from photographers p1,
  4    photographers p2
  5  where p2.photographer_id = p1.mentor_photographer_id
  6  order by 1;

PHOTOGRAPHER                   MENTOR
------------------------------ ------------------------------
Harry Henderson                Mark Fife
Jenny Forest                   Susan Willamson
Kate Kapteur                   Ryan Notstephens
Kelly Hairtrigger              Susan Willamson

4 rows selected.
```

The following SQL statements demonstrate the concept of an outer join in a query.

```
SQL> select * from photographers;

PHOTOGRAPHER_ID PHOTOGRAPHER              MENTOR_PHOTOGRAPHER_ID   LEVEL_ID
--------------- ------------------------- ---------------------- ----------
              7 Ryan Notstephens                                          7
              8 Susan Willamson                                           6
              9 Mark Fife                                                 6
              1 Shooter McGavin                                           1
              2 Jenny Forest                                     8          3
              3 Steve Hamm                                                4
              4 Harry Henderson                                  9          5
              5 Kelly Hairtrigger                                8          2
              6 Gordon Flash                                              1
             10 Kate Kapteur                                     7          4

10 rows selected.

SQL> select p1.photographer photographer, p2.photographer mentor
  2  from photographers p1, photographers p2
  3  where p2.photographer_id(+) = p1.mentor_photographer_id
  4  order by 1;

PHOTOGRAPHER                   MENTOR
------------------------------ ------------------------------
Gordon Flash
Harry Henderson                Mark Fife
```

```
Jenny Forest                    Susan Willamson
Kate Kapteur                    Ryan Notstephens
Kelly Hairtrigger               Susan Willamson
Mark Fife
Ryan Notstephens
Shooter McGavin
Steve Hamm
Susan Willamson

10 rows selected.
```

Workshop: Comparison Operators

Follow along with the next examples to refresh your memory on comparison operators.

```
SQL> select bird_name from birds
  2  where bird_name = 'Bald Eagle';

BIRD_NAME
------------------------------
Bald Eagle

1 row selected.

SQL> select * from cameras
  2  where camera != 'Canon';

 CAMERA_ID CAMERA
---------- ----------------------------
         2 Nikon
         3 Sony
         4 Olympus
         5 GoPro
         6 Fujifilm
         7 Polaroid
         8 Apple iPhone
         9 Samsung Galaxy

8 rows selected.

SQL> select bird_id, bird_name, wingspan
  2  from birds
  3  where wingspan > 48;

   BIRD_ID BIRD_NAME                        WINGSPAN
---------- ------------------------------ ----------
         1 Great Blue Heron                       78
         3 Common Loon                            54
```

```
         4 Bald Eagle                             84
         5 Golden Eagle                           90
         7 Osprey                                 72
         9 Canadian Goose                         72
        13 Ring-billed Gull                       50
        14 Double-crested Cormorant               54
        16 Turkey Vulture                         72
        19 Mute Swan                            94.8
        20 Brown Pelican                          90
        21 Great Egret                          67.2

12 rows selected.

SQL> select bird_id, bird_name, wingspan
  2  from birds
  3  where wingspan <= 20;

   BIRD_ID BIRD_NAME                        WINGSPAN
---------- ------------------------------ ----------
         2 Mallard                               3.2
        10 Pied-billed Grebe                     6.5
        12 Common Sea Gull                        18
        23 Black Skimmer                          15

4 rows selected.
```

Workshop: Logical Operators

The following examples use logical operators in queries to test the data that is returned.

```
SQL> select *
  2  from photographers
  3  where mentor_photographer_id is null;

PHOTOGRAPHER_ID PHOTOGRAPHER               MENTOR_PHOTOGRAPHER_ID   LEVEL_ID
--------------- ------------------------- ---------------------- ----------
              7 Ryan Notstephens                                          7
              8 Susan Willamson                                           6
              9 Mark Fife                                                 6
              1 Shooter McGavin                                           1
              3 Steve Hamm                                                4
              6 Gordon Flash                                              1

6 rows selected.

SQL> select *
  2  from photographers
  3  where mentor_photographer_id is not null;
```

```
PHOTOGRAPHER_ID PHOTOGRAPHER              MENTOR_PHOTOGRAPHER_ID   LEVEL_ID
--------------- ------------------------- ---------------------- ----------
              2 Jenny Forest                                   8          3
              4 Harry Henderson                                9          5
              5 Kelly Hairtrigger                              8          2
             10 Kate Kapteur                                   7          4

4 rows selected.
```

```
SQL> select bird_id, bird_name, wingspan
  2  from birds
  3  where wingspan between 30 and 65;

   BIRD_ID BIRD_NAME                        WINGSPAN
---------- ------------------------------ ----------
         3 Common Loon                            54
         6 Red Tailed Hawk                        48
        13 Ring-billed Gull                       50
        14 Double-crested Cormorant               54
        15 Common Merganser                       34
        17 American Crow                        39.6
        22 Anhinga                                42

7 rows selected.
```

```
SQL> select *
  2  from migration
  3  where migration_location in ('Central America', 'South America');

MIGRATION_ID MIGRATION_LOCATION
------------ ------------------------------
           3 Central America
           4 South America

2 rows selected.
```

```
SQL> select bird_name
  2  from birds
  3  where bird_name like '%Eagle%';

BIRD_NAME
------------------------------
Bald Eagle
Golden Eagle

2 rows selected.
```

```
SQL> select bird_name
  2  from birds
  3  where bird_name like '%Eagle';

BIRD_NAME
------------------------------
Bald Eagle
Golden Eagle

2 rows selected.
```

Workshop: Conjunctive Operators

The following queries are examples of using conjunctive operators, which consist of the AND and OR operators. Remember that, with the AND operator, both conditions on each side of the operator must be true for data to be returned. With the OR operator, either condition on surrounding the OR operator must be true for data to be returned by the query.

```
SQL> select * from predators
  2  where predator = 'Crocodiles'
  3    and predator = 'Snakes';

no rows selected

SQL> select * from predators
  2  where predator = 'Crocodiles'
  3     or predator = 'Snakes';


   PRED_ID PREDATOR
---------- ------------------------------
         5 Snakes
        29 Crocodiles

2 rows selected.
```

Workshop: Arithmetic Operators

The following example refreshes your memory on the use of arithmetic operators in a query. This is a simple and useful concept, but make sure that your math is correct; otherwise, the query might return incorrect data.

```
SQL> select bird_name, eggs * broods "EGGS PER SEASON"
  2  from birds
  3  where wingspan > 48
  4  order by 2 desc;
```

```
BIRD_NAME                      EGGS PER SEASON
------------------------------ ---------------
Canadian Goose                              10
Mute Swan                                    8
Great Blue Heron                             5
Ring-billed Gull                             4
Brown Pelican                                4
Double-crested Cormorant                     4
Osprey                                       4
Great Egret                                  3
Golden Eagle                                 3
Common Loon                                  2
Bald Eagle                                   2
Turkey Vulture                               2

12 rows selected.
```

Workshop: Character Functions

Character functions are useful in changing the way data appears in the output of a query. They can also be used to change the way data is viewed by a query while searching the data. Following are several examples. Take time to carefully study the results; refer back to previous hours of instruction, if necessary.

```
SQL> select 'Bald Eagle'
  2  from photographers;

'BALDEAGLE
----------
Bald Eagle
Bald Eagle
Bald Eagle
Bald Eagle
Bald Eagle
Bald Eagle
Bald Eagle
Bald Eagle
Bald Eagle
Bald Eagle

10 rows selected.

SQL> select 'Bald Eagle'
  2  from birds
  3  where bird_name = 'Great Blue Heron';
```

```
'BALDEAGLE
----------
Bald Eagle

1 row selected.

SQL> select p2.photographer || ' mentors ' ||
  2         p1.photographer || '.' "MENTORS"
  3  from photographers p1, photographers p2
  4  where p1.mentor_photographer_id = p2.photographer_id;


MENTORS
------------------------------------------------------------
Ryan Notstephens mentors Kate Kapteur.
Susan Willamson mentors Jenny Forest.
Susan Willamson mentors Kelly Hairtrigger.
Mark Fife mentors Harry Henderson.

4 rows selected.


SQL> select photographer,
  2         decode(mentor_photographer_id, null, 'None',
  3                mentor_photographer_id) "MENTOR"
  4  from photographers;


PHOTOGRAPHER                   MENTOR
------------------------------ ------------------------
Ryan Notstephens               None
Susan Willamson                None
Mark Fife                      None
Shooter McGavin                None
Jenny Forest                   8
Steve Hamm                     None
Harry Henderson                9
Kelly Hairtrigger              8
Gordon Flash                   None
Kate Kapteur                   7

10 rows selected.

SQL> select bird_name,
  2         decode(nest_builder, 'M', 'Male', 'F', 'Female', 'B', 'Both',
  3                'Neither') "NESTER"
```

```
  4  from birds
  5  where nest_builder != 'B';

BIRD_NAME                      NESTER
------------------------------ -------
Mallard                        Female
Canadian Goose                 Female
Common Merganser               Female
Turkey Vulture                 Neither
American Crow                  Female
Brown Pelican                  Female

6 rows selected.

SQL> select * from cameras;

 CAMERA_ID CAMERA
---------- ------------------------------
         1 Canon
         2 Nikon
         3 Sony
         4 Olympus
         5 GoPro
         6 Fujifilm
         7 Polaroid
         8 Apple iPhone
         9 Samsung Galaxy

9 rows selected.

SQL> select upper(substr(camera, 1, 3)) ABBR
  2  from cameras;

ABBR
------------
CAN
NIK
SON
OLY
GOP
FUJ
POL
APP
SAM

9 rows selected.
```

```
SQL> select substr(photographer, 1, instr(photographer, ' ', 1, 1))
  2               first_name
  3  from photographers;


FIRST_NAME
------------------------------------------
Ryan
Susan
Mark
Shooter
Jenny
Steve
Harry
Kelly
Gordon
Kate

10 rows selected.

SQL> select substr(photographer, instr(photographer, ' ', 1, 1) +1) last_name
  2  from photographers;

LAST_NAME
------------------------------------------
Notstephens
Willamson
Fife
McGavin
Forest
Hamm
Henderson
Hairtrigger
Flash
Kapteur

10 rows selected.
```

Workshop: Aggregating Data

The capability to aggregate data is an important feature when constructing SQL queries. Follow along with the simple examples here. Study the results before you move on to the next section, which groups data output from aggregate functions.

```
SQL> select p1.photographer, p2.photographer "MENTOR"
  2  from photographers p1, photographers p2
  3  where p1.mentor_photographer_id = p2.photographer_id;
```

```
PHOTOGRAPHER                   MENTOR
------------------------------ ------------------------------
Kate Kapteur                   Ryan Notstephens
Jenny Forest                   Susan Willamson
Kelly Hairtrigger              Susan Willamson
Harry Henderson                Mark Fife

4 rows selected.

SQL> select count(mentor_photographer_id) "TOTAL PHOTOGRAPHERS MENTORED"
  2  from photographers;

TOTAL PHOTOGRAPHERS MENTORED
----------------------------
                           4

1 row selected.

SQL> select count(distinct(mentor_photographer_id)) "TOTAL MENTORS"
  2  from photographers;

TOTAL MENTORS
-------------
            3

1 row selected.

SQL> select sum(eggs * broods) "TOTAL EGGS LAYED BY ALL BIRDS IN A SEASON"
  2  from birds;

TOTAL EGGS LAYED BY ALL BIRDS IN A SEASON
-----------------------------------------
                                      127

1 row selected.

SQL> select max(wingspan)
  2  from birds;

MAX(WINGSPAN)
-------------
         94.8

1 row selected.

SQL> select avg(wingspan)
  2  from birds;
```

```
AVG(WINGSPAN)
-------------
   50.5695652

1 row selected.
```

Workshop: GROUP BY and HAVING

These examples use the GROUP BY and HAVING clauses in SQL queries to further massage the output of aggregate functions before the final result set is returned.

```
SQL> select photo_levels.photo_level,
  2       count(photographers.photographer_id) "NUMBER OF PHOTOGRAPHERS"
  3  from photo_levels, photographers
  4  where photo_levels.level_id = photographers.level_id
  5  group by photo_levels.photo_level;

PHOTO_LEVEL                    NUMBER OF PHOTOGRAPHERS
------------------------------ -----------------------
Artist                                               2
World-class                                          1
Beginner                                             2
Competent                                            2
Novice                                               1
Skilled                                              1
Hobbyist                                             1

7 rows selected.
```

```
SQL> select photo_levels.photo_level,
  2       count(photographers.photographer_id) "NUMBER OF PHOTOGRAPHERS"
  3  from photo_levels, photographers
  4  where photo_levels.level_id = photographers.level_id
  5  group by photo_levels.photo_level
  6  having count(photographers.photographer_id) > 1;

PHOTO_LEVEL                    NUMBER OF PHOTOGRAPHERS
------------------------------ -----------------------
Artist                                               2
Beginner                                             2
Competent                                            2

3 rows selected.
```

Workshop: Composite Queries

Composite queries combine the result sets of two or more queries. Several examples follow.

```
SQL> select bird_name from birds
  2  UNION
  3  select predator from predators;

BIRD_NAME
------------------------------
Alligators
American Coot
American Crow
Anhinga
Bald Eagle
Bears
Belted Kingfisher
Black Skimmer
Bobcats
Brown Pelican
Canadian Goose
Carnivorous Plants
Cats
Chipmunks
Common Loon
Common Merganser
Common Sea Gull
Cougars
Coyotes
Crocodiles
Deer
Dogs
Double-crested Cormorant
Foxes
Frogs
Golden Eagle
Great Blue Heron
Great Egret
Green Heron
Humans
Insects
Mallard
Minks
Mute Swan
Opposums
Osprey
Other Birds
Pied-billed Grebe
```

```
Predatory Fish
Racoons
Rats
Red Tailed Hawk
Reptiles
Ring-billed Gull
Seals
Skunks
Snakes
Squirrels
Turkey Vulture
Turtles
Weasels
Wolves

52 rows selected.

SQL> select photographer,
2         decode(mentor_photographer_id, null, 'Not Mentored',
3                'Mentored')     "MENTORED?"
  4  from photographers
  5  UNION
  6  select photographer,
  7         decode(mentor_photographer_id, null, 'Mentored',
  8                'Mentored') "MENTORED?"
  9  from photographers
 10  where mentor_photographer_id is not null;




PHOTOGRAPHER                   MENTORED?
------------------------------ ------------
Gordon Flash                   Not Mentored
Harry Henderson                Mentored
Jenny Forest                   Mentored
Kate Kapteur                   Mentored
Kelly Hairtrigger              Mentored
Mark Fife                      Not Mentored
Ryan Notstephens               Not Mentored
Shooter McGavin                Not Mentored
Steve Hamm                     Not Mentored
Susan Willamson                Not Mentored

10 rows selected.
```

```
SQL> select photographer,
2          decode(mentor_photographer_id, null, 'Not Mentored',
3                'Mentored') "MENTORED?"
  4  from photographers
  5  UNION
  6  select photographer,
  7          decode(mentor_photographer_id, null, 'Mentored',
  8                'Mentored') "MENTORED?"
  9  from photographers
 10  where mentor_photographer_id is not null;

PHOTOGRAPHER                   MENTORED?
------------------------------ ------------
Gordon Flash                   Not Mentored
Harry Henderson                Mentored
Jenny Forest                   Mentored
Kate Kapteur                   Mentored
Kelly Hairtrigger              Mentored
Mark Fife                      Not Mentored
Ryan Notstephens               Not Mentored
Shooter McGavin                Not Mentored
Steve Hamm                     Not Mentored
Susan Willamson                Not Mentored

10 rows selected.

SQL> select photographer
  2  from photographers
  3  where level_id > 4
  4  INTERSECT
  5  select photographer
  6  from photographers, photographer_cameras, cameras
  7  where photographers.photographer_id =
  8        photographer_cameras.photographer_id
  9    and photographer_cameras.camera_id = cameras.camera_id
 10    and camera not in ('Apple iPhone', 'Samsung Galaxy');

PHOTOGRAPHER
------------------------------
Harry Henderson
Mark Fife
Ryan Notstephens
```

```
Susan Willamson

4 rows selected.

SQL> select photographer
  2  from photographers
  3  where level_id > 4
  4  MINUS
  5  select photographer
  6  from photographers, photographer_cameras, cameras
  7  where photographers.photographer_id =
  8        photographer_cameras.photographer_id
  9    and photographer_cameras.camera_id = cameras.camera_id
 10    and camera not in ('Apple iPhone', 'Samsung Galaxy');


no rows selected
```

Workshop: Creating Tables from Existing Tables

The results of a query can easily be used to create a new table that is based on a result set from one or more existing tables. Try the following example.

```
SQL> create table old_cameras as
  2  select * from cameras;

Table created.

SQL> select * from old_cameras;

 CAMERA_ID CAMERA
---------- ------------------------------
         1 Canon
         2 Nikon
         3 Sony
         4 Olympus
         5 GoPro
         6 Fujifilm
         7 Polaroid
         8 Apple iPhone
         9 Samsung Galaxy

9 rows selected.
```

Workshop: Inserting Data into a Table from Another Table

The next example walks through truncating the new table that was just created to remove the data and then inserting data into that table based on the results of a query. This is similar to the previous example that used the CREATE TABLE statement; the concept is the same.

```
SQL> truncate table old_cameras;

Table truncated.

SQL> select * from old_cameras;

no rows selected

SQL> insert into old_cameras
  2  select * from cameras;

9 rows created.

SQL> select * from old_cameras;

 CAMERA_ID CAMERA
---------- ------------------------------
         1 Canon
         2 Nikon
         3 Sony
         4 Olympus
         5 GoPro
         6 Fujifilm
         7 Polaroid
         8 Apple iPhone
         9 Samsung Galaxy

9 rows selected.
```

Workshop: Creating Views

Views are arguably one of the most powerful features of SQL when querying the database, especially with complex data sets. Follow along with these examples and create some views of your own. Remember that a view is a virtual table and does not actually store data. The results of a view are just like a query. The data set is stored temporarily in memory, not written physically to the database.

```
SQL> create or replace view fish_eaters as
  2  select b.bird_id, b.bird_name
```

```
  3  from birds b,
  4       birds_food bf,
  5       food f
  6  where b.bird_id = bf.bird_id
  7    and bf.food_id = f.food_id
  8    and f.food_name = 'Fish';


View created.

SQL> select * from fish_eaters;

   BIRD_ID BIRD_NAME
---------- ------------------------------
         1 Great Blue Heron
         3 Common Loon
         4 Bald Eagle
         5 Golden Eagle
         7 Osprey
         8 Belted Kingfisher
        12 Common Sea Gull
        13 Ring-billed Gull
        14 Double-crested Cormorant
        15 Common Merganser
        17 American Crow
        18 Green Heron
        20 Brown Pelican
        21 Great Egret
        22 Anhinga
        23 Black Skimmer

16 rows selected.

SQL> create or replace view predators_of_big_birds as
  2  select distinct(p.predator)
  3  from predators p,
  4       birds_predators bp,
  5       birds b
  6  where p.pred_id = bp.pred_id
  7    and b.bird_id = bp.bird_id
  8    and b.wingspan > 48;


View created.

SQL> select * from predators_of_big_birds;
```

```
PREDATOR
------------------------------
Humans
Other Birds
Predatory Fish
Seals
Coyotes
Weasels
Cougars
Bobcats
Opposums
Bears
Skunks
Wolves
Foxes
Racoons

14 rows selected.
```

Workshop: Embedding Subqueries

The concept of a subquery is powerful as well. A subquery is simply a query that is embedded within another query. Remember that the innermost subquery is always resolved first in an SQL statement. Try this one:

```
SQL> select *
  2  from photographers
  3  where level_id >
  4       (select avg(level_id)
  5        from photo_levels);


PHOTOGRAPHER_ID PHOTOGRAPHER              MENTOR_PHOTOGRAPHER_ID   LEVEL_ID
--------------- ------------------------- ---------------------- ----------
              7 Ryan Notstephens                                          7
              8 Susan Willamson                                           6
              9 Mark Fife                                                 6
              4 Harry Henderson                                9          5

4 rows selected.
```

Workshop: Creating Views from Subqueries

Following is an example of creating a view based on a subquery. Then a query is written to join the view to other database tables.

```
SQL> select avg(level_id)
  2  from photo_levels;

AVG(LEVEL_ID)
-------------
            4

1 row selected.


SQL> create or replace view top_photographers as
  2  select *
  3  from photographers
  4  where level_id >
  5       (select avg(level_id)
  6        from photo_levels);


View created.


SQL> select distinct(ps2.style)
  2  from photographer_styles ps,
  3       top_photographers tp,
  4       photo_styles ps2
  5  where ps.photographer_id = tp.photographer_id
  6    and ps.style_id = ps2.style_id
  7  order by 1;

STYLE
------------------------------
Action
Artistic
Landscape
Still
Sunset

5 rows selected.
```

Workshop: Generating SQL Code from a SQL Statement

Let's say that you want to create a new user account for every photographer in the database. This is a simple example of why you might need to generate SQL statements automatically. Only 10 photographers are included here, but what if the database listed 1,000 photographers? A query such as the following can be written using a combination of literal strings and character functions to generate output that corresponds to the syntax of the CREATE USER command. Try this one, and see if you can think of other situations when it might be useful to generate SQL code from a SQL statement.

```
SQL> select 'CREATE USER ' ||
  2      substr(photographer, 1, instr(photographer, ' ', 1, 1) -1) ||
  3      '_' ||
  4      substr(photographer, instr(photographer, ' ', 1, 1) +1) ||
  5      ' IDENTIFIED BY NEW_PASSWORD_1;' "SQL CODE TO CREATE NEW USERS"
  6  from photographers;

SQL CODE TO CREATE NEW USERS
---------------------------------------------------------------
CREATE USER Ryan_Notstephens IDENTIFIED BY NEW_PASSWORD_1;
CREATE USER Susan_Willamson IDENTIFIED BY NEW_PASSWORD_1;
CREATE USER Mark_Fife IDENTIFIED BY NEW_PASSWORD_1;
CREATE USER Shooter_McGavin IDENTIFIED BY NEW_PASSWORD_1;
CREATE USER Jenny_Forest IDENTIFIED BY NEW_PASSWORD_1;
CREATE USER Steve_Hamm IDENTIFIED BY NEW_PASSWORD_1;
CREATE USER Harry_Henderson IDENTIFIED BY NEW_PASSWORD_1;
CREATE USER Kelly_Hairtrigger IDENTIFIED BY NEW_PASSWORD_1;
CREATE USER Gordon_Flash IDENTIFIED BY NEW_PASSWORD_1;
CREATE USER Kate_Kapteur IDENTIFIED BY NEW_PASSWORD_1;

10 rows selected.
```

Summary

In this hour, you walked through numerous examples touching on most of the SQL topics you covered in this book. Hopefully this has been an enjoyable journey. Of course, you will have so much more to learn as you get more practice with SQL. Thank you for taking the time to start learning SQL using this book. The information technology world offers many opportunities for those who truly understand relational databases and know how to utilize data for business intelligence. With SQL, you can be much more effective in your daily job and help make your organization more competitive in today's global market. Enjoy this final batch of exercises.

Workshop

The following workshop consists of only an assortment of exercises during this hour, since this hour is a workshop itself. Refer to Appendix C, "Answers to Quizzes and Exercises," for answers.

Exercises

1. Select data from your tables to explore your data, starting with the following:
    - Select all the data from the `BIRDS` table.
    - Select all the data from the `PHOTOGRAPHERS` table.
    - What are the predators of the Bald Eagle?
2. When looking at the ERD for this database, you can see that a relationship is missing between the `PHOTOGRAPHERS` and `PHOTOS` tables.
    - What kind of relationship should be added?
    - Use SQL to define a relationship between these two tables in your database. (*Hint:* add any necessary foreign key constraints.)
3. Add a table called `COLORS` for colors that each bird might have and create any other necessary tables and relationships (primary and foreign keys) to create a relationship between `BIRDS` and `COLORS`. If you want, you can save your `CREATE TABLE` statements in a file to easily regenerate at a later time, or you can add them to your main `tables.sql` script. If you add these statements to the main `tables.sql` script, be sure that the `DROP` and `CREATE TABLE` statements are in the proper order in relation to the other tables in your database, based on primary/foreign key relationships (for example, you must drop child tables before parent tables, and you must create parent tables before child tables).
4. Insert a few rows of data into the `COLORS` table and any other tables you may have created.
5. Add the following bird to your database: Easter Kingbird, 9 inches, .2 pounds, 15-inch wingspan, 5 eggs, up to 4 broods per season, incubation period of 17 days, fledging period of 17 days, both participate with the nest.
6. Add the following photographer to your database: Margaret Hatcher, mentored by Susan Williamson, hobbyist level.
7. Make sure you have saved your recent transactions. If you want, you can save the previous `INSERT` statements to a file so that you can regenerate this data later if you need to, or you can add them to the main data.sql script.
8. Generate a simple list of all photographers, skill levels, and styles. Then sort the results, showing the photographers with the highest skill levels first in your results.
9. Generate a list of photographers and their protégés (the photographers they mentor). List only the photographers that are mentors.

10. Re-create the same list of photographers and their protégés, but show all photographers, regardless of whether they mentor anyone, and sort the results by the photographer with the highest skill levels first.

11. Using UNION to combine the results of multiple queries, show a list of all animals in your database (for example, birds and predators).

12. Create a table called FORMER_PHOTOGRAPHERS that is based on the PHOTOGRAPHERS table.

13. Truncate the table FORMER_PHOTOGRAPHERS.

14. Insert all data from the PHOTOGRAPHERS table into the FORMER_PHOTOGRAPHERS table.

15. Can you think of any views that can be created to make the exercises from the previous section easier, or more easily repeatable, for similar future queries?

16. Create at least one view that you can imagine.

17. Write a query that produces a list of the most versatile photographers in your database. For example, the query might contain one or more of the following subqueries:

    - Photographers that have a skill level greater than the average skill level of all photographers
    - Photographers whose count of birds of interest is more than the average of all photographers
    - Photographers who have more styles than the average photographer

18. Create a view called Versatile_Photographers that is based on the subqueries you used earlier.

19. Suppose that each photographer needs a database user account to access information in the database about birds and other photographers. Generate a SQL script that creates database user accounts for each photographer with the following syntax:

    ```
    CREATE USER MARGARET_HATCHER IDENTIFIED BY NEW_PASSWORD_1;
    ```

20. What are the predators of each bird?

21. Which birds have the most predators?

22. Which predators eat the most birds in your database?

23. Which predators eat only fish-eating birds?

24. Which types of nests attract the most predators?

25. Which photographers are most likely to see a crocodile when capturing an image of a bird?

26. Which predators are most likely to be in a landscape-style photograph?

27. What birds have a diet more diverse than the average bird in the database?

28. What cameras are used by these photographers:

- Photographers that mentor others
- Photographers with a skill level above average

APPENDIX A
Common SQL Commands

This appendix details some of the most common SQL commands. As stated throughout the book, be sure to check your database documentation: Some of the statements vary, depending on your implementation.

SQL Statements

ALTER TABLE

```
ALTER TABLE TABLE_NAME
[MODIFY | ADD | DROP]
  [COLUMN COLUMN_NAME][DATATYPE|NULL NOT NULL] [RESTRICT|CASCADE]
[ADD | DROP]  CONSTRAINT CONSTRAINT_NAME]
```

Description: Alters a table's columns

ALTER USER

```
ALTER USER USERNAME IDENTIFIED BY NEW_PASSWORD;
```

Description: Resets a given user's password

COMMIT

```
COMMIT [ TRANSACTION ]
```

Description: Saves a transaction to the database

CREATE INDEX

```
CREATE INDEX INDEX_NAME
ON TABLE_NAME (COLUMN_NAME)
```

Description: Creates an index on a table

CREATE ROLE

```
CREATE ROLE ROLE NAME
[ WITH ADMIN [CURRENT_USER | CURRENT_ROLE]]
```

Description: Creates a database role to which system and object privileges can be granted

CREATE TABLE

```
CREATE TABLE TABLE_NAME
( COLUMN1     DATA_TYPE     [NULL|NOT NULL],
  COLUMN2     DATA_TYPE     [NULL|NOT NULL])
```

Description: Creates a database table

CREATE TABLE AS

```
CREATE TABLE TABLE_NAME AS
SELECT COLUMN1, COLUMN2,...
FROM TABLE_NAME
[ WHERE CONDITIONS ]
[ GROUP BY COLUMN1, COLUMN2,...]
[ HAVING CONDITIONS ]
```

Description: Creates a database table based on another table

CREATE TYPE

```
CREATE TYPE typename AS OBJECT
( COLUMN1     DATA_TYPE     [NULL|NOT NULL],
  COLUMN2     DATA_TYPE     [NULL|NOT NULL])
```

Description: Creates a user-defined type that can define columns in a table

CREATE USER

```
CREATE USER username IDENTIFIED BY password
```

Description: Creates a user account in the database

CREATE VIEW

```
CREATE VIEW AS
SELECT COLUMN1, COLUMN2,...
FROM TABLE_NAME
[ WHERE CONDITIONS ]
```

```
[ GROUP BY COLUMN1, COLUMN2,... ]
[ HAVING CONDITIONS ]
```

Description: Creates a view of a table

DELETE

```
DELETE
FROM TABLE_NAME
[ WHERE CONDITIONS ]
```

Description: Deletes rows of data from a table

DROP INDEX

```
DROP INDEX INDEX_NAME
```

Description: Drops an index on a table

DROP TABLE

```
DROP TABLE TABLE_NAME
```

Description: Drops a table from the database

DROP USER

```
DROP USER user1 [, user2, ...]
```

Description: Drops a user account from the database

DROP VIEW

```
DROP VIEW VIEW_NAME
```

Description: Drops a view of a table

GRANT

```
GRANT PRIVILEGE1, PRIVILEGE2, ... TO USER_NAME
```

Description: Grants privileges to a user

INSERT

```
INSERT INTO TABLE_NAME [ (COLUMN1, COLUMN2,...]
VALUES ('VALUE1','VALUE2',...)
```

Description: Inserts new rows of data into a table

INSERT...SELECT

```
INSERT INTO TABLE_NAME
SELECT COLUMN1, COLUMN2
FROM TABLE_NAME
[ WHERE CONDITIONS ]
```

Description: Inserts new rows of data into a table, based on data in another table

REVOKE

```
REVOKE PRIVILEGE1, PRIVILEGE2, ... FROM USER_NAME
```

Description: Revokes privileges from a user

ROLLBACK

```
ROLLBACK [ TO SAVEPOINT_NAME ]
```

Description: Undoes a database transaction

SAVEPOINT

```
SAVEPOINT SAVEPOINT_NAME
```

Description: Creates transaction savepoints to roll back to, if necessary

SELECT

```
SELECT [ DISTINCT ] COLUMN1, COLUMN2,...
FROM TABLE1, TABLE2,...
[ WHERE CONDITIONS ]
[ GROUP BY COLUMN1, COLUMN2,...]
[ HAVING CONDITIONS ]
[ ORDER BY COLUMN1, COLUMN2,...]
```

Description: Returns data from one or more database tables; used to create queries

UPDATE

```
UPDATE TABLE_NAME
SET COLUMN1 = 'VALUE1',
    COLUMN2 = 'VALUE2',...
[ WHERE CONDITIONS ]
```

Description: Updates existing data in a table

SQL Query Clauses

SELECT

```
SELECT *
SELECT COLUMN1, COLUMN2,...
SELECT DISTINCT (COLUMN1)
SELECT COUNT(*)
```

Description: Defines columns to display as part of query output

FROM

```
FROM TABLE1, TABLE2, TABLE3,...
```

Description: Defines tables from which to retrieve data

WHERE

```
WHERE COLUMN1 = 'VALUE1'
  AND COLUMN2 = 'VALUE2'
...
WHERE COLUMN1 = 'VALUE1'
   OR COLUMN2 = 'VALUE2'
...
WHERE COLUMN IN ('VALUE1' [, 'VALUE2'] )
```

Description: Defines conditions (criteria) placed on a query for data to be returned

GROUP BY

```
GROUP BY GROUP_COLUMN1, GROUP_COLUMN2,...
```

Description: Divides output into logical groups; a form of sorting operation

HAVING

```
HAVING GROUP_COLUMN1 = 'VALUE1'
   AND GROUP_COLUMN2 = 'VALUE2'
...
```

Description: Places conditions on the `GROUP BY` clause; similar to the `WHERE` clause

ORDER BY

```
ORDER BY COLUMN1, COLUMN2,...
ORDER BY 1,2,...
```

Description: Sorts a query's results

APPENDIX B
Popular Vendor RDBMS Implementations

The relational database is offered in so many implementations by so many vendors that this book cannot show all the examples and syntax from even the top implementations. This book uses Oracle in its exercises, but the examples stay as close to the SQL standard as possible so that they can easily be adapted to other database implementations. The following list highlights some of the most popular implementations available as of publication, along with websites where you can access their database software. Many software products are available for free download or are freely distributed for personal, development, and educational purposes.

Oracle Database XE	www.oracle.com
Oracle Live SQL	livesql.oracle.com
Microsoft SQL Server	www.microsoft.com
MySQL	www.mysql.com
PostgreSQL	www.postgresql.org
MariaDB	www.mariadb.org
SQLite	www.sqlite.org
Firebirdsql	www.firebirdsql.org
InterBase	www.ermbarcadero.com
DB2 Express-C	www.ibm.com
CUBRID	www.cubrid.org

NOTE

RDBMS Recommendation for This Book

Oracle is the recommended database management system to use for this book—not because the author thinks Oracle is the right database for you or your organization, but because it facilitates a seamless transition for you when working through the examples and hands-on exercises. The examples and exercises in this book are simple and as compliant with the SQL standard as possible; any code used in this book should be portable to most relational database management systems, with minor adjustments to vendor-specific SQL syntax.

Installing the Oracle Database Software Used for Examples and Hands-On Exercises

Hour 3, "Getting to Know Your Data," covers the steps for downloading and installing Oracle, as well as the process of creating the tables and data that comprise the `Bird` database used throughout this book.

Hour 3 also walks through the instructions for installing Oracle for the Windows operating system and covers the process of creating the tables and data that make up the sample database. Oracle is the database used for both the examples and the hands-on exercises in this book. Oracle is available on other operating systems as well, including macOS and Linux. These instructions are accurate as of the date this book was written. Neither the author nor Sams Publishing places any warranties on the software or the software support. For any installation problems, or to inquire about software support, refer to the particular implementation's documentation or contact customer support for the implementation.

APPENDIX C
Answers to Quizzes and Exercises

Hour 1, “Understanding the Relational Database and SQL”

Quiz

1. What does the acronym SQL stand for?

   Answer: Structured Query Language

2. What is a schema? Give an example.

   Answer: A schema is a collection of database objects owned by a single database user that can be made available to other users in the database. The tables in the BIRDS database are an example of a schema.

3. How do logical and physical components within a relational database differ? How are they related?

   Answer: Logical components are used to conceive and model a database (entities and attributes). Physical components are the actual objects, such as tables, that are created based on the database design.

4. What keys are used to define and enforce referential integrity in a relational database?

   Answer: Primary and foreign keys

5. What is the most basic type of object in a relational database?

   Answer: Table

6. What elements comprise this object?

   Answer: Columns

7. Must primary key column values be unique?

   Answer: Yes

8. Must foreign key column values be unique?

   Answer: No

Exercises

For the following exercises, refer to Figure 1.6 in Hour 1.

1. Who are Mary Smith's dependents?

   Answer: John and Mary Ann

2. How many employees do not have dependents?

   Answer: One, Bob Jones

3. How many duplicate foreign key values exist in the `DEPENDENTS` table?

   Answer: Three

4. Who is Tim's parent or guardian?

   Answer: Ron Burk

5. Which employee can be deleted without first having to delete any dependent records?

   Answer: Bob Jones

Hour 2, "Exploring the Components of the SQL Language"

Quiz

1. What are the six main categories of SQL commands?

   Answer: Data Definition Language (DDL)

   Data Manipulation Language (DML)

   Data Query Language (DQL)

   Data Control Language (DCL)

   Data administration commands (DAC)

   Transactional control commands (TCC)

2. What is the difference between data administration commands and database administration?

   Answer: Data administration commands enable a user to perform audit-type functions on data within the database, whereas database administration involves the overall management of the database and related resources as a whole.

3. What are some benefits to a SQL standard?

   Answer: A standard encourages consistency between different vendor-specific implementations of SQL. This enables you to apply your SQL knowledge to various implementations, and data is more portable between different implementations. A standard ensures that core fundamentals exist within a technology. The SQL language itself is not specific to any one implementation.

Exercises

1. Identify the categories for the following SQL commands:

   ```
   CREATE TABLE
   DELETE
   SELECT
   INSERT
   ALTER TABLE
   UPDATE
   ```

   Answer: `CREATE TABLE`—Data Definition Language (DDL)

   `DELETE`—Data Manipulation Language (DML)

   `SELECT`—Data Query Language (DQL)

   `INSERT`—Data Manipulation Language (DML)

   `ALTER TABLE`—Data Definition Language (DDL)

   `UPDATE`—Data Manipulation Language (DML)

2. List the basic SQL statements to manipulate data.

   Answer: `INSERT, UPDATE, and DELETE`

3. List the SQL statement that is used to query a relational database.

   Answer: `SELECT`

4. Which transactional control command is used to save a transaction?

   Answer: `COMMIT`

5. Which transactional control command is used to undo a transaction?

   Answer: `ROLLBACK`

Hour 3, "Getting to Know Your Data"

Quiz

1. What is the difference between entities and tables?

   Answer: An entity is a logical object that is used to represent a table when designing a database. A table is the physical object that an entity becomes—that is, a physical object that contains data.

2. What is the purpose of the BIRD_FOOD entity?

   Answer: It is a base table that facilitates a relationship between BIRDS and FOOD.

3. How might photograph locations somehow be related to the food that birds eat?

   Answer: Some birds are more likely to be found in certain locations and more likely to be photographed where certain food items exist.

4. What does the abbreviation ERD stand for?

   Answer: Entity Relationship Diagram

5. How many direct relationships exist between entities in the Bird database?

   Answer: Nine

6. What is another name for a naming standard?

   Answer: Naming convention

Exercises

1. Give an example of an entity or attributes that might be added to this database.

   Answer: Predators of birds might be added, listing the predator identification and information about the predator itself. A base table might also be required to facilitate a relationship between this entity and BIRDS.

2. Give some examples of candidates for primary keys, based on Figure 1.2.

   Answer: BIRD_ID, FOOD_ID, MIGRATION_ID, LOCATION_ID

3. Give some examples of candidates for foreign keys, based on Figure 1.2.

   Answer: BIRD_ID in the base tables, FOOD_ID in the base table, and so on

Hour 4, "Setting Up Your Database"

Quiz

Refer to the data for the BIRDS database that was listed during this hour.

1. Why is the BIRDS table split into two separate output sets?

   Answer: This was done simply for readability so that data did not wrap.

2. Why do errors occur the first time you execute the file tables.sql?

   Answer: The first time you run the scripts, no tables or data exist, so the DROP TABLE statements in the scripts are not applicable.

3. Why are zero rows deleted the first time you execute the file data.sql?

   Answer: The first time you run this script, no data exists in the database tables.

4. What must an administrative user do after creating a user before that user can create and manage objects in the database?

   Answer: An administrative user must grant the appropriate privileges to the user to create and manage database objects. Those privileges vary among SQL implementations.

5. How many tables are in the BIRDS database?

   Answer: Ten, so far.

Exercises

Refer to the data for the BIRDS database that was listed during this hour.

1. Give some examples of parent tables in the BIRDS database.

   Answer: BIRDS, FOOD, MIGRATION

2. Give some examples of child tables in the BIRDS database.

   Answer: BIRDS_FOOD, NICKNAMES

3. How many unique types of birds are in the database?

   Answer: 23

4. What foods does the Bald Eagle eat?

   Answer: Fish, carrion, ducks

5. Who builds the most nests, male or female, or both?

   Answer: Female

6. How many birds migrate to Central America?

   Answer: 12

7. Which bird spends the most time raising its young?

   Answer: Mute swan, 190 days

8. Which birds have the term *eagle* in their nickname?

   Answer: Bald Eagle, Golden Eagle

9. What is the most popular migration location for birds in the database?

   Answer: Southern United States

10. Which bird(s) has/have the most diverse diet?

    Answer: American Crow, Golden Eagle

11. What is the average wingspan of birds that eat fish?

    Answer: 52.35 inches

Hour 5, "Understanding the Basics of Relational (SQL) Database Design"

Quiz

1. How is database design related to SQL?

   Answer: It is important to understand at least the basics of relational database design so that you can fully unlock the potential of using SQL to understand your data, see how it is related to other data in the database, and know how to effectively work with the data.

2. What diagram is used to model data and relationships for a database? What are fields also called in a physical database?

   Answer: Entity relationship diagram (ERD); columns

3. During database design, groups of data (also referred to as entities) become what type of object in the physical database?

   Answer: Tables

4. What is the difference between logical and physical design?

   Answer: Logical design deals with the initial modeling of data into entities, attributes, and relationships. Physical design takes the logical design to the next step by finalizing referential integrity, defining data structures, and converting entities to tables.

5. What are the three most common database environments that accommodate the database life cycle?

   Answer: Development, test, and production

Exercises

1. During the next few hours, you will be designing a database about wildlife photographers who take pictures of birds. This database should be designed so that it can eventually be integrated with the existing BIRDS database. Take a minute and review the ERD for the BIRDS database. These exercises have no right or wrong solutions; what's important is the way you interpret the information and envision the data coming together into a database model. Also review the examples during this hour on adding entities to the BIRDS database about bird rescues.

   Answer: No answer.

2. Read and analyze the following information about photographer data that you will be adding to the BIRDS database. Consider what the database is about, the purpose of the database, the anticipated users, the potential customers, and so on.

   All photographers have names, addresses, and education information. They might have received awards and maintain various websites or social media sites. Each photographer also likely has a particular passion, an artistic approach, photographic style, preferred bird targets, and so on. Additionally, photographers use various cameras and lenses and might produce media in a variety of formats using editing software. They have different types of clients, often are published in certain products, and contribute images to publications. Photographers also might be mentors or volunteers for bird rescue groups or other nonprofit organizations. They definitely have varying skill levels—beginner, novice, hobbyist, competent photographer, skilled, artist, and world class. In addition, photographers might market and sell various products, whether they are self-employed or work for an organization.

   The equipment photographers use includes cameras, lenses, and editing software. Cameras have a make and model, sensor type (full frame or crop sensor), megapixels, frames per second, ISO range, and cost. Lenses have a make, lens type, aperture range, and cost.

   Answer: No answer.

3. Make a list of all the basic entities, or groups of data, of wildlife photographers. This is then your basis for entities, and that eventually becomes your ERD.

   Answer: All answers vary, based on how you perceive the information.

4. Draw a basic data model based on the lists that you derived in the previous exercises. Draw lines between the entities in your diagram to depict relationships. This is the starting point for your ERD.

   Answer: All answers vary, based on how you perceive the information.

5. Make a list of all the basic attributes within each entity that you defined in the previous exercises, or fields, of wildlife photographers. This is the basis for your entities, and that eventually becomes your ERD.

   Answer: All answers vary, based on how you perceive the information.

Hour 6, "Defining Entities and Relationships"

Quiz

1. What are the four basic types of relationships between entities in a relational database?

   Answer: One-to-one, one-to-many, many-to-many, and recursive.

2. In which relationship does an attribute relate to another attribute in the same table?

   Answer: A recursive relationship

3. What constraints, or keys, are used to enforce referential integrity in a relational database?

   Answer: Primary key and foreign key constraints

4. If a primary key represents a parent record, what represents a child record in a relational database?

   Answer: A foreign key represents a child record

Exercises

1. Suppose that you came up with a group of data and lists of fields similar to the following for the information on photographers that will be integrated into the `BIRDS` database. This baseline data is provided for your convenience so that you can build on it during the next few hours. However, feel free to use any list that you already have derived, or you can combine your list of data with this example. Keep in mind that the solutions that you come up with might vary from the example solutions provided. You will also find throughout this book that although many of your solutions might vary from the book solutions, they still yield the same results, similar results, or even better results, based on how you interpret the data. Also keep in mind that the following data is merely a subset of the data that can be derived from the description provided in Hour 5. Figure 6.12 hints at where you might find a recursive relationship. Complete the other relationships as you see fit.

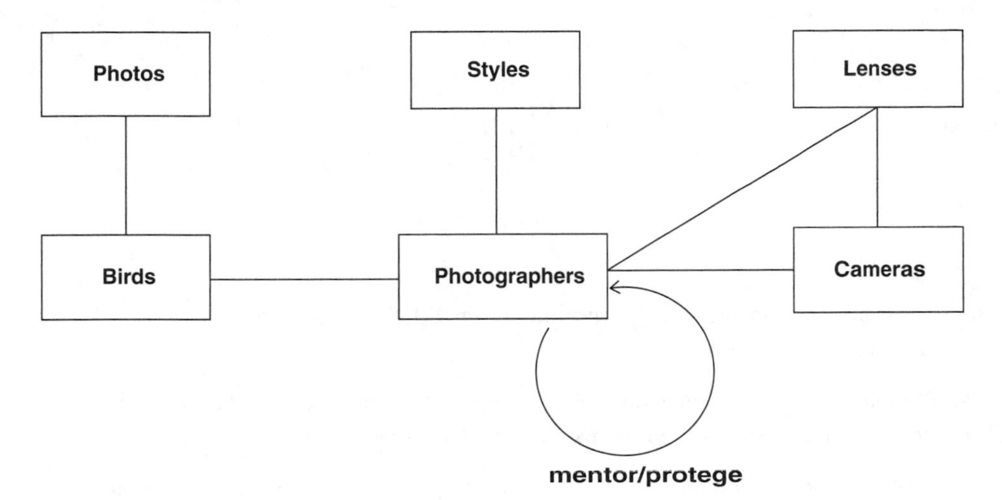

FIGURE 6.12
Example basic ERD for photographers

Answer: Sample limited lists of fields for photographer data might include the following:

```
PHOTOGRAPHERS

    Photographer_Id
    Photographer_Name
    Photographer_Contact_Info
    Education
    Website
    Mentor

STYLES

    Style_Id
    Style

CAMERAS

    Camera_Id
    Camera_Make
    Camera_Model
    Sensor_Type
    Megapixels
    Frames_Per_Second
    ISO_Range
    Cost
```

LENSES

Lens_Id

Lens_Make

Lens_Type

Aperature_Range

Cost

2. List some possible relationships for the information provided for photographers that will be integrated into the BIRDS database.

   Answer: Photographers might have multiple cameras, lenses might be compatible with multiple cameras, and cameras might have multiple lenses available.

3. List the attributes that you anticipate will comprise the primary keys for the entities that you have defined for the photographers.

   Answer: PHOTOGRAPHER_ID, STYLE_ID, CAMERA_ID, LENSE_ID

4. List the attributes that you anticipate will comprise the foreign keys for the entities that you have defined for the photographers.

   Answer: Any attributes in base entities that you define that are used to join other entities together, such as PHOTOGRAPHERS and CAMERAS.

5. Draw a basic ERD depicting the entities and the relationships between those entities that you envision at this point for the photographer data.

   Answer: Solutions will vary, based on how you perceive the information.

6. Using words, describe the two-way relationships between your entities. The types of relationships should already be represented on your ERD from question 5 using the symbols introduced during this hour.

   Answer: A photographer might have many cameras, a camera might be used by many photographers, and so on.

7. Refer to Figure 6.4 to answer the remaining questions in this exercise. Some of these questions might seem too simple, but these are the same types of questions you will be asking of the database using SQL commands. Remember that a major goal of this book is to get you to think the way that SQL does.

   A. What are the nicknames of the Great Blue Heron?

      Answer: Big Cranky, Blue Crane

B. What are the nicknames of the Mallard?

Answer: Green Head, Green Cap

C. Which birds have the word *green* in their nickname?

Answer: Green Head, Green Cap

D. Which birds have a nickname that starts with the letter *B*?

Answer: Great Blue Heron

E. Which birds do not have a nickname listed in the example?

Answer: Common Loon, Bald Eagle

F. How many unique birds are listed in this example?

Answer: 4

G. What is the average number of nicknames per bird in this example?

Answer: 1

H. Which birds do not have a nickname listed in the example?

Answer: Common Loon, Bald Eagle

I. Can any birds be deleted from the `BIRDS` table without first having to delete nicknames from the `NICKNAMES` table?

Answer: Yes. The Common Loon and Bald Eagle can be deleted because they do not have any child records in this example.

J. Which birds have child records in the `NICKNAMES` table?

Answer: Great Blue Heron, Mallard

K. Does any duplicate data exist in either table besides the `BIRD_ID` itself?

Answer: No.

Hour 7, "Normalizing Your Database"

Quiz

1. True or false: Normalization is the process of grouping data into logical related groups.

Answer: True

2. True or false: Having no duplicate data or redundant data in a database, and having everything in the database normalized, is always the best way to go.

   Answer: False. Generally, a normalized database is the best way to go, but levels of normalization vary, based on the data itself and how it is used.

3. True or false: If data is in the third normal form, it is automatically in the first and second normal forms.

   Answer: True

4. What is a major advantage of a denormalized database versus a normalized database?

   Answer: Performance

5. What are some major disadvantages of denormalization?

   Answer: A denormalized database has redundant data, so it is more difficult to enforce referential integrity and even make changes to the database as it evolves.

6. How do you determine whether data needs to be moved to a separate table when normalizing your database?

   Answer: If data is not fully dependent on the primary key in a table, it is normally better to move that data into its own entity with its own attributes.

7. What are the disadvantages of overnormalizing your database design?

   Answer: Performance degradation

8. Why is it important to eliminate redundant data?

   Answer: To protect the integrity of data

9. What is the most common level of normalization?

   Answer: Third normal form (TNF)

Exercises

1. Assuming that you came up with a similar configuration to the entities shown in Figure 7.11 for the photographer data set that is to be incorporated into the `BIRDS` database, take a minute to compare this example to yours. Feel free to use this example as a baseline for these exercises, use your own, or combine the two as you see fit. Also review Figure 6.12 in Hour 6, "Defining Entities and Relationships," to envision how this data might be integrated into the original `BIRDS` database.

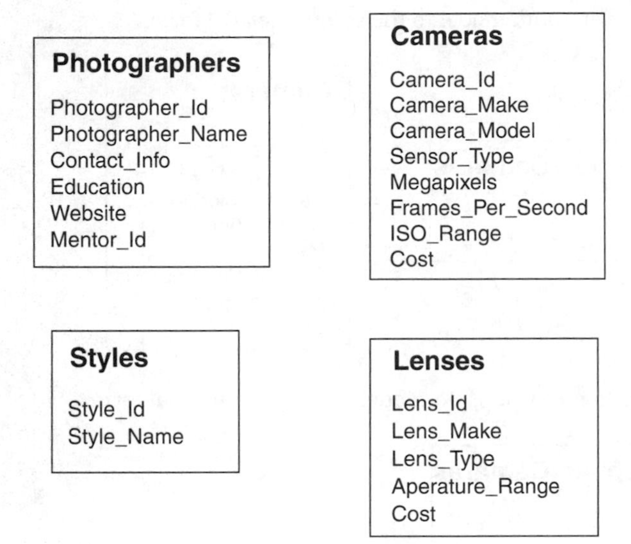

FIGURE 7.11
Example entities and attributes for photographer data

2. List some of the redundant data that you see in this example and the ERD you modeled.

   Answer: The most potential for redundant data occurs with cameras, styles, and lenses. Each photographer might have many of each of those items, and each of those items could be associated with multiple photographers.

3. Use the guidelines of the first normal form to model your database appropriately.

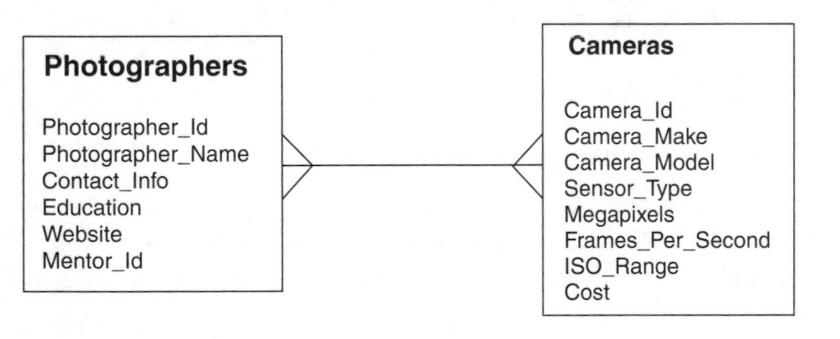

4. Use the guidelines in this hour to take your data model to the second normal form.

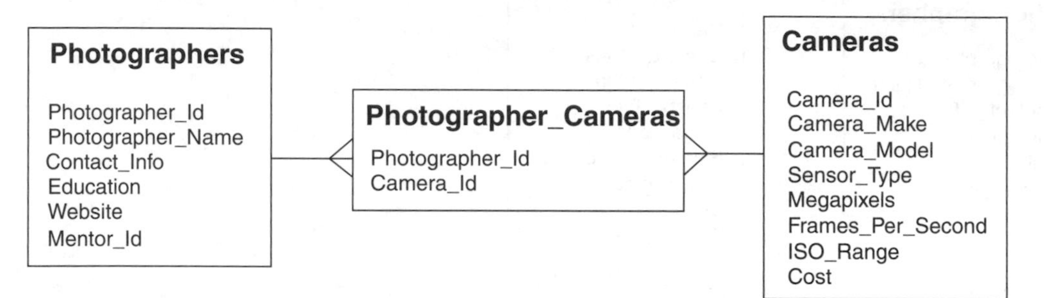

5. Finally, use the guidelines in this hour to take your data model to the third normal form.

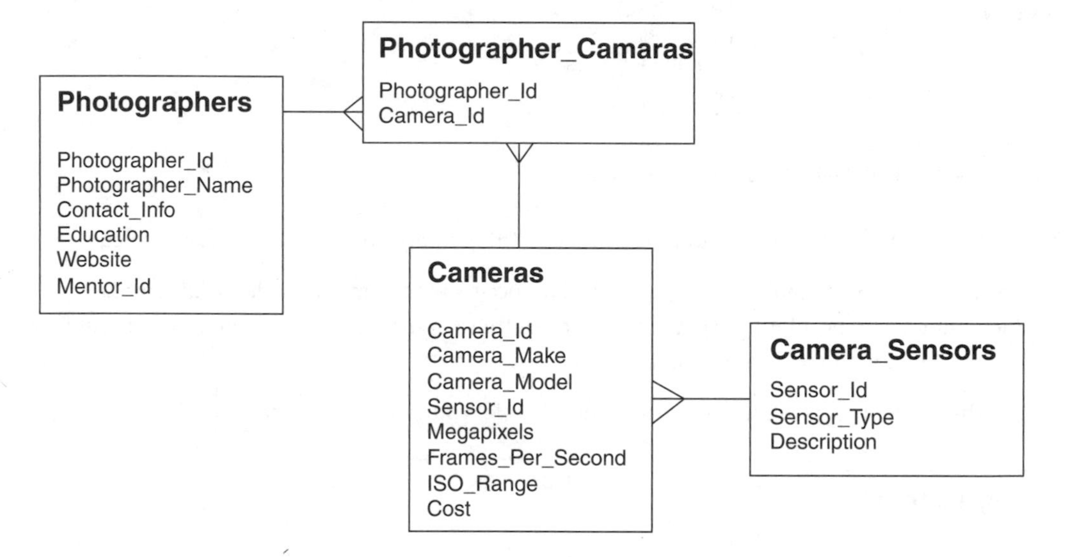

6. Verbally describe all relationships in your third normal form model.

   Answer: Each photographer might use many different cameras. Each type of camera might be used by many different photographers. Cameras have sensors such as full frame or crop sensor. Each sensor type might be used on many different types of cameras. However, each camera has only one sensor.

7. List all primary and foreign keys from your third normal form model.

   Answer: Primary keys: `PHOTOGRAPHERS.PHOTOGRAPHER_ID`, `PHOTOGRAPHER_ID`, and `CAMERA_ID` together comprise a composite primary key in `PHOTOGRAPHER_CAMERAS`, `CAMERAS.CAMERA_ID`, `CAMERA_SENSORS.SENSOR_ID`.

   Foreign keys: `PHOTOGRAPHER_ID` in `PHOTOGRAPHER_CAMERAS` references `PHOTOGRAPHER_ID` in `PHOTOGRAPHERS`; `CAMERA_ID` in `PHOTOGRAPHER_CAMERAS` references CAMERA_ID in CAMERAS; SENSOR_ID in CAMERAS references SENSOR_ID in CAMERA_SENSORS.

8. Can you envision any other data that could be added to your ERD?

   Answer: Solutions will vary, based on how you interpret the information.

Hour 8, "Defining Data Structures"

Quiz

1. What are the three most basic categories of data types?

   Answer: Character, numeric, date

2. True or false: An individual's Social Security number, entered in the format '111111111', can be any of the following data types: constant-length character, varying-length character, or numeric.

   Answer: True

3. True or false: The scale of a numeric value is the total length allowed for values.

   Answer: False

4. Do all implementations use the same data types?

   Answer: No, but most are similar and follow the same basic rules.

5. What are the precision and scale of the following?

```
DECIMAL(4,2)
DECIMAL(10,2)
DECIMAL(14,1)
```

   Answer: Precision of 4 and scale of 2 (99.99 maximum value), precision of 10 and scale of 2 (99999999.99), precision of 14 and scale of 1 (9999999999999.9)

6. Which numbers can be inserted into a column whose data type is DECIMAL(4,1)?

   A. 16.2

   B. 116.2

   C. 16.21

   D. 1116.2

   E. 1116.21

   Answer: A and B

Exercises

1. Assign the following column titles to a data type, decide on the proper length, and give an example of the data you would enter into that column:

   A. `ssn`

   B. `state`

   C. `city`

   D. `phone_number`

   E. `zip`

   F. `last_name`

   G. `first_name`

   H. `middle_name`

   I. `salary`

   J. `hourly_pay_rate`

   K. `date_hired`

   Answer: Solutions vary, based on your interpretation.

2. Using the same column titles, decide whether they should be `NULL` or `NOT NULL`. Be sure to realize that, for some columns that would normally be `NOT NULL`, the column could be `NULL`, or vice versa, depending on the application.

   A. `ssn`

   B. `state`

   C. `city`

   D. `phone_number`

   E. `zip`

   F. `last_name`

   G. `first_name`

   H. `middle_name`

   I. `salary`

   J. `hourly_pay_rate`

   K. `date_hired`

   Answer: Solutions vary, based on your interpretation.

3. Based on the birds rescue data from previous hours, assign data types and nullability as you see fit.

   Answer: Solutions vary, based on your interpretation.

4. Based on the photographer data you have modeled, assign data types and nullability as you see fit.

   Answer: Solutions vary, based on your interpretation.

Hour 9, "Creating and Managing Database Objects"

Quiz

1. What is the most common object created in a database to store data?

   Answer: A table

2. Can you drop a column from a table?

   Answer: Yes, but you cannot drop a column or any table element if the drop violates any predefined data rules or constraints.

3. What statement do you issue to create a primary key constraint on the preceding BIRDS table?

   Answer: ALTER TABLE

4. What statement do you issue on the preceding BIRDS table to allow the WINGSPAN column to accept NULL values?

   Answer: ALTER TABLE modify WINGSPAN null;

5. What statement do you use to restrict the birds added into the preceding MIGRATION table to migrate only to certain migration locations?

   Answer:

```
ALTER TABLE MIGRATION ADD CONSTRAINT CHK_LOC CHECK (MIGRATION_LOCATION IN
('LOCATION1', 'LOCATION2');
```

6. What statement do you use to add an autoincrementing column called BIRD_ID to the preceding BIRDS table using both the MySQL and SQL Server syntax?

   Answer:

```
CREATE TABLE BIRDS
 (BIRD_ID      SERIAL,
 BIRD_NAME     VARCHAR(30));
```

7. What SQL statement can be used to create a copy of an existing table?

   Answer: `CREATE TABLE AS SELECT`...

8. Can you drop a column from a table?

   Answer: Yes, but you cannot drop a column or any table element if the drop violates any predefined data rules or constraints.

Exercises

In this exercise, refer to the examples in the previous hours for the `BIRDS` database, as well as the information provided for rescues and photographers that are integrated into the `BIRDS` database. At this point, you have been designing entities for photographer data that will be integrated into the `BIRDS` database. Review what you have come up with so far and use that information for the following exercises.

1. Using the SQL commands that you've learned during this hour, create a physical database based on the photographer data that you previously modeled that will be integrated with the `BIRDS` database.

   Answer: Solutions vary by individual.

2. Think about any columns in your tables that can be altered in any way. Use the `ALTER TABLE` command as an example to change the way one of your tables is defined.

   Answer: Solutions vary by individual.

3. Have you used SQL and the `CREATE TABLE` statements to define all primary key and foreign key constraints? If not, use the `ALTER TABLE` statement to define at least one.

   Answer: Solutions vary by individual.

4. Can you think of any check constraints that you can add to the photographer data? If so, use the `ALTER TABLE` statement to add the appropriate constraints.

   Answer: Solutions vary by individual.

Hour 10, "Manipulating Data"

Quiz

1. Do you always need to supply a column list for the table that you use an `INSERT` statement on?

   Answer: You do not have to specify a column list if you are inserting data into all columns in the order in which the columns are listed in the table.

2. What can you do if you do not want to enter a value for one particular column?

   Answer: Insert a `NULL` value by using the keyword `NULL` or by inserting `''` (two single quotations with no value between them).

3. Why is it important to use a `WHERE` clause with `UPDATE` and `DELETE`?

   Answer: If you do not specify criteria with the `WHERE` clause, the SQL statement attempts to update or delete all data in the table.

4. What is an easy way to check that an `UPDATE` or `DELETE` will affect the rows that you want?

   Answer: Perform a simple `SELECT` statement before the `UPDATE` or `DELETE` using the same criteria in the `WHERE` clause.

Exercises

1. Review the table structures in the `BIRDS` database, particularly the data in the `BIRDS` table itself. You will use this data to perform the exercises.

   Answer: No solution.

2. Use the `SELECT` statement to display all the data currently in the `BIRDS` table.

   Answer: SELECT * FROM BIRDS;

3. Create a new table called `TALL_BIRDS` that is based on the `BIRDS` table itself, with the following columns: `BIRD_ID`, `BIRD_NAME`, and `WINGSPAN`.

   Answer:

```
CREATE TABLE TALL_BIRDS AS
SELECT BIRD_ID, BIRD_NAME, WINGSPAN
FROM BIRDS;
```

4. Insert data from the `BIRDS` table into the `TALL_BIRDS` table for birds taller than 30 inches.

   Answer:

```
INSERT INTO TALL_BIRDS
SELECT BIRD_ID, BIRD_NAME, WINGSPAN
FROM BIRDS
WHERE HEIGHT > 30;
```

5. Use the `SELECT` statement to display all the new data in the `TALL_BIRDS` table.

   Answer: `SELECT * FROM TALL_BIRDS;`

6. Insert the following data into the TALL_BIRDS table:

   BIRD_NAME = Great Egret

   HEIGHT = 40

   WINGSPAN = 66

   Answer: INSERT INTO TALL_BIRDS VALUES (24, 'Great Egret', 66);

7. Update every data value in the BIRDS table for the bird name column to read Bird. Was this command successful? Why or why not?

   Answer:

   ```
   UPDATED TALL_BIRDS
   SET BIRD_NAME = 'Bird';
   ```

8. Update the wingspan of every bird in the TALL_BIRDS table to a NULL value.

   Answer:

   ```
   UPDATE TALL_BIRDS
   SET WINGSPAN = null;
   ```

9. Delete the record for Great Egret from the TALL_BIRDS table.

   Answer:

   ```
   DELETE FROM TALL_BIRDS
   WHERE BIRD_ID = 24;
   ```

10. Delete every remaining row of data from the TALL_BIRDS table.

    Answer:

    ```
    DELETE FROM TALL_BIRDS;
    ```

11. Drop the TALL_BIRDS table.

    Answer:

    ```
    DROP TABLE TALL_BIRDS;
    ```

Hour 11, "Managing Database Transactions"

Quiz

1. True or false: If you have committed several transactions, you have several more transactions that have not been committed, and you issue a `ROLLBACK` command, all your transactions for the same session are undone.

   Answer: False. Only the transactions since the last `COMMIT` or `ROLLBACK` command are undone.

2. True or false: A `SAVEPOINT` or `SAVE TRANSACTION` command saves transactions after a specified number of transactions have executed.

   Answer: False. A `SAVEPOINT` is only a marker within transactions to provide logical points for a `COMMIT` or `ROLLBACK`.

3. Briefly describe the purpose of each one of the following commands: `COMMIT`, `ROLLBACK`, and `SAVEPOINT`.

   Answer: `COMMIT` saves work to the database since the last `COMMIT` or `ROLLBACK`. `ROLLBACK` undoes any transactions since the last `COMMIT` or `ROLLBACK`. `SAVEPOINT` creates logical or periodic markers within transactions.

4. What are some differences in the implementation of transactions in Microsoft SQL Server?

   Answer: Minor differences in syntax exist, but the concepts are the same.

5. What are some performance implications when using transactions?

   Answer: Poor transactional control can hurt database performance and even bring the database to a halt. Repeated poor database performance might result from a lack of transactional control during large inserts, updates, or deletes. Large batch processes also cause temporary storage for rollback information to grow until either a `COMMIT` or a `ROLLBACK` command is issued.

6. When using several `SAVEPOINT` or `SAVE TRANSACTION` commands, can you roll back more than one?

   Answer: Yes, you can roll back to previous `SAVEPOINT` locations.

Exercises

1. For the following exercises, create the following tables based on the BIRDS database:

   A. Use the SQL statement CREATE TABLE *table_name* AS SELECT... to create a table called BIG_BIRDS that is based on the original BIRDS table. Include only the following columns in the BIG_BIRDS table: BIRD_ID, BIRD_NAME, HEIGHT, WEIGHT, and WINGSPAN. Use the WHERE clause to include only records for birds that have a wingspan greater than 48 inches.

   ```
   CREATE TABLE BIG_BIRDS AS
   SELECT BIRD_ID, BIRD_NAME, HEIGHT, WEIGHT, WINGSPAN
   FROM BIRDS
   WHERE WINGSPAN > 48;
   ```

   B. Create a table called LOCATIONS2 that is based on the original LOCATIONS table.

   ```
   CREATE TABLE LOCATIONS2 AS SELECT * FROM LOCATIONS;
   ```

2. Write a simple query to display all records in the BIG_BIRDS table, to familiarize yourself with the data.

   Answer:

   ```
   SELECT * FROM BIG_BIRDS;
   ```

3. Write a simple query to display all records in the LOCATIONS2 table, to familiarize yourself with the data.

   Answer:

   ```
   SELECT * FROM LOCATIONS2;
   ```

4. Modify the BIG_BIRDS table to change the name of the column WINGSPAN to AVG_WINGSPAN.

   Answer:

   ```
   DROP TABLE BIG_BIRDS;

   CREATE TABLE BIG_BIRDS AS
   SELECT BIRD_ID, BIRD_NAME, HEIGHT, WEIGHT, WINGSPAN "AVG_WINGSPAN"
   FROM BIRDS
   WHERE WINGSPAN > 48;
   ```

5. Manually compute the average wingspan of birds in the BIG_BIRDS table, and use the UPDATE statement to update the value of all birds' wingspans to the average wingspan value that you calculated.

   Answer:

   ```
   SELECT AVG(WINGSPAN) FROM BIG_BIRDS;

   UPDATE BIG_BIRDS
   SET AVG_WINGSPAN = 73;
   ```

6. Issue the ROLLBACK command.

   Answer:

   ```
   ROLLBACK;
   ```

7. Query all data in the BIG_BIRDS table using the SELECT statement. You should see in the output from the query that all the values for WINGSPAN have been restored to their original values; however, the name of the column is still the updated value of AVG_WINGSPAN.

   Answer:

   ```
   SELECT * FROM BIG_BIRDS;
   ```

8. Why did the ROLLBACK negate the update to data values in the AVG_WINGSPAN column, but not the UPDATE TABLE statement to rename the WINGSPAN column?

   Answer: Because a previous COMMIT was not performed

9. Insert a new row of data into the LOCATIONS2 table for a location called Lake Tahoe.

   Answer:

   ```
   INSERT INTO LOCATIONS2 VALUES (7, 'Lake Tahoe');
   ```

10. Issue the COMMIT command.

    Answer:

    ```
    COMMIT;
    ```

11. Query the LOCATIONS2 table to verify the changes you made.

    Answer:

    ```
    SELECT * FROM LOCATIONS;
    ```

12. Insert another new row of data into the LOCATIONS2 table for a location of Atlantic Ocean.

Answer:

```
INSERT INTO LOCATIONS2 VALUES (8, 'Atlantic Ocean');
```

13. Create a SAVEPOINT called SP1.

Answer:

```
SAVEPOINT SP1;
```

14. Update the value of Atlantic Ocean to Pacific Ocean.

Answer:

```
UPDATE LOCATIONS2
SET LOCATION_NAME = 'Pacific Ocean'
WHERE LOCATION_NAME = 'Atlantic Ocean';
```

15. Create a SAVEPOINT called SP2.

Answer:

```
SAVEPOINT SP2;
```

16. Update the value of Lake Tahoe that you previously added to Lake Erie.

Answer:

```
UPDATE LOCATIONS2
SET LOCATION_NAME = 'Lake Erie
WHERE LOCATION_NAME = 'Lake Tahoe;
```

17. Create a SAVEPOINT called SP3.

Answer:

```
SAVEPOINT SP3;
```

18. Issue the ROLLBACK command back to SAVEPOINT SP2.

Answer:

```
ROLLBACK;
```

19. Query the LOCATIONS2 table and study the behavior of the ROLLBACK command to SAVEPOINT.

Answer:

```
SELECT * FROM LOCATIONS2;
```

20. Get creative with some transactions of your own on these two tables. Remember that these tables are copies of the original tables, so anything you do should not affect the original data. Also remember that, at any point during your progression through this book, you can rerun the scripts provided called `tables.sql` and, subsequently, `data.sql` to restore your tables and the data for the `BIRDS` database back to its original state.

    Answer: No solution

Hour 12, "Introduction to Database Queries"

Quiz

1. Name the required parts for any `SELECT` statement.

   Answer: `SELECT` and `FROM`

2. In the `WHERE` clause, are single quotation marks required for all the data?

   Answer: Single quotation marks are not required for numeric data.

3. Can multiple conditions be used in the `WHERE` clause?

   Answer: Yes

4. Is the `DISTINCT` option applied before or after the `WHERE` clause?

   Answer: After

5. Is the `ALL` option required?

   Answer: No

6. How are numeric characters treated when ordering based on a character field?

   Answer: From 0 to 9

7. How does Oracle handle its default case sensitivity differently from Microsoft SQL Server?

   Answer: By default, Oracle is case sensitive when testing data, whereas Microsoft SQL Server is not, by default.

8. How is the ordering of the fields in the `ORDER BY` clause important?

   Answer: The `ORDER BY` clause provides a final sort for the data that a query returns.

9. How is the ordering determined in the `ORDER BY` clause when you use numbers instead of column names?

   Answer: Numbers in the `ORDER BY` clause are shorthand for the position of columns in the `SELECT` clause.

Exercises

1. Write a query that tells you how many birds are stored in the database.

   Answer:

   ```
   select count(*)
   from birds;
   ```

2. How many types of nest builders exist in the database?

   Answer:

   ```
   select count(distinct(nest_builder))
   from birds;
   ```

3. Which birds lay more than seven eggs?

   Answer:

   ```
   select bird_name
   from birds
   where eggs > 7;
   ```

4. Which birds have more than one brood per year?

   Answer:

   ```
   select bird_name
   from birds
   where broods > 1;
   ```

5. Write a query from the BIRDS table showing only the bird's name, the number of eggs the bird typically lays, and the incubation period.

   Answer:

   ```
   select bird_name, eggs, incubation
   from birds;
   ```

6. Modify the previous query in exercise 5 to show only the birds that have a wingspan greater than 48 inches.

   Answer:

   ```
   select bird_name, eggs, incubation
   from birds
   where wingspan > 48;
   ```

7. Sort the previous query by `WINGSPAN` in ascending order.

   Answer:

```
select bird_name, eggs, incubation
from birds
where wingspan > 48
order by wingspan;
```

8. Sort the previous query by `WINGSPAN` in descending order, to show the biggest birds first.

   Answer:

```
select bird_name, eggs, incubation
from birds
where wingspan > 48
order by wingspan desc;
```

9. How many nicknames are stored in the database?

   Answer:

```
select count(*)
from nicknames;
```

10. How many different food items are stored in the database?

    Answer:

```
select count(*)
from food;
```

11. Using the manual process described in this hour, determine which food items the Bald Eagle consumes.

    Answer:

```
FOOD_NAME
----------
Fish
Carrion
Ducks
```

12. Bonus exercise: Using a manual process and simple SQL queries, provide a list of birds that eat fish.

    Answer:

```
BIRD_NAME
------------------------------
Great Blue Heron
```

```
Common Loon
Bald Eagle
Golden Eagle
Osprey
Belted Kingfisher
Common Sea Gull
Ring-billed Gull
Double-crested Cormorant
Common Merganser
American Crow
Green Heron
Brown Pelican
Great Egret
Anhinga
Black Skimmer
```

Hour 13, "Using Operators to Categorize Data"

Quiz

1. True or false: When using the `OR` operator, both conditions must be `TRUE` for data to be returned.

   Answer: False

2. True or false: All specified values must match when using the `IN` operator for data to be returned.

   Answer: False

3. True or false: The `AND` operator can be used in the `SELECT` and the `WHERE` clauses.

   Answer: False

4. True or false: The `ANY` operator can accept an expression list.

   Answer: True

5. What is the logical negation of the `IN` operator?

   Answer: `NOT IN`

6. What is the logical negation of the `ANY` and `ALL` operators?

   Answer: `<> ANY`, `<> ALL`

Exercises

1. Use the original BIRDS database for these exercises. Write a SELECT statement from the BIRDS table to return all rows of data, to familiarize yourself with the data. Then write the appropriate SELECT statements using the operators you learned in this chapter for the remaining exercises.

   Answer:

   ```
   select * from birds;
   ```

2. Which birds have more than two broods per year?

   Answer:

   ```
   select bird_name
   from birds
   where broods > 2;
   ```

3. Show all records in the MIGRATIONS table in which the MIGRATION_LOCATION is not Mexico.

   Answer:

   ```
   select *
   from migration
   where migration_location != 'Mexico';
   ```

4. List all birds that have a wingspan less than 48 inches.

   Answer:

   ```
   select bird_name, wingspan
   from birds
   where wingspan < 48;
   ```

5. List all birds that have a wingspan greater than or equal to 72 inches.

   Answer:

   ```
   select bird_name, wingspan
   from birds
   where wingspan >= 72;
   ```

6. Write a query to return the BIRD_NAME and WINGSPAN of birds that have a wingspan between 30 and 70 inches.

   Answer:

   ```
   select bird_name,wingspan
   from birds
   where wingspan between 30 and 70;
   ```

7. Select all migration locations that are in Central America and South America.

Answer:

```
select migration_location
from migration
where migration_location in ('Central America', 'South America');
```

8. List all birds by name that have the word *green* in their name.

Answer:

```
select bird_name
from birds
where bird_name like '%Green%';
```

9. List all birds that begin with the word *bald*.

Answer:

```
select bird_name
from birds
where bird_name like 'Bald%';
```

10. Do any birds have a wingspan less than 20 inches or a height shorter than 12 inches?

Answer:

```
select bird_name
from birds
where wingspan < 20
    or height < 12;
```

11. Do any birds have a weight more than 5 pounds and a height shorter than 36 inches?

Answer:

```
select bird_name
from birds
where weight > 5
  and height < 36;
```

12. List all bird names that do not have the word *green* in their name.

Answer:

```
select bird_name
from birds
where bird_name not like '%Green%';
```

13. List all bird names that have one of the three primary colors in their name.

    Answer:

```
select bird_name
from birds
where bird_name like '%Red%'
   or bird_name like '%Blue%'
   or bird_name like '%Yellow%';
```

14. How many birds spend more than 75 days total with their young?

    Answer:

```
select bird_name, incubation + fledging
from birds
where incubation + fledging > 75;
```

15. Experiment with some of your own queries using the operators you learned in this chapter.

Hour 14, “Joining Tables in Queries”

Quiz

1. What type of join do you use to return records from one table, regardless of the existence of associated records in the related table?

   Answer: Outer join

2. The `JOIN` conditions are located in which parts of the SQL statement?

   Answer: The `WHERE` clause

3. What type of `JOIN` do you use to evaluate equality among rows of related tables?

   Answer: Equijoin

4. What happens if you select from two different tables but fail to join the tables?

   Answer: All possible combinations of rows of data are joined between all tables, which is called a Cartesian product.

Exercises

1. Type the following code into the database and study the result set (Cartesian product):

   Answer:

```
select bird_name, migration_location
from birds, migration;
```

2. Now modify the previous query with a proper table join to return useful data and avoid the Cartesian product. You might have to review the ERD for the BIRDS database in Hour 3 to refresh your memory on how these two tables are related to one another.

   Answer:

```
select bird_name, migration_location
from birds,
     migration,
     birds_migration
where birds.bird_id = birds_migration.bird_id
  and migration.migration_id = birds_migration.migration_id;
```

3. Generate a list of the food items eaten by the Great Blue Heron.

   Answer:

```
select b.bird_name, f.food_name
from birds b,
     birds_food bf,
     food f
where b.bird_id = bf.bird_id
  and bf.food_id = f.food_id
  and b.bird_name = 'Great Blue Heron';
```

4. Which birds in the database eat fish?

   Answer:

```
select b.bird_name, f.food_name
from birds b,
     birds_food bf,
     food f
where b.bird_id = bf.bird_id
  and bf.food_id = f.food_id
  and f.food_name = 'Fish';
```

5. Create a report showing the BIRD_NAME and MIGRATION_LOCATION for birds that migrate to South America.

   Answer:

```
select b.bird_name, m.migration_location
from birds b,
     birds_migration bm,
     migration m
where b.bird_id = bm.bird_id
  and bm.migration_id = m.migration_id
  and m.migration_location = 'South America';
```

6. Do any birds have a wingspan less than 30 inches and also eat fish?

   Answer:

```
select b.bird_name, b.wingspan, f.food_name
from birds b,
     birds_food bf,
     food f
where b.bird_id = bf.bird_id
  and bf.food_id = f.food_id
  and f.food_name = 'Fish'
  and b.wingspan < 30;
```

7. Write a query to display the following results: the BIRD_NAME, FOOD_NAME, and NEST_TYPE for any birds that eat fish or build a platform nest.

   Answer:

```
select b.bird_name, f.food_name, n.nest_name
from birds b,
     birds_food bf,
     food f,
     birds_nests bn,
     nests n
where b.bird_id = bf.bird_id
  and bf.food_id = f.food_id
  and b.bird_id = bn.bird_id
  and bn.nest_id = n.nest_id
  and (f.food_name = 'Fish' or n.nest_name = 'Platform');
```

8. Ask some questions you would anticipate database users, photographers, bird rescues, and so forth might inquire about the BIRDS database. Experiment with some of your own queries using table joins.

Hour 15, "Restructuring the Appearance of Data"

Quiz

1. Match the descriptions with the possible functions.

   Answer:

Description	Function
a. Selects a portion of a character string	SUBSTR
b. Trims characters from either the right or the left of a string	LTRIM/RTRIM
c. Changes all letters to lower case	LOWER
d. Finds the length of a string	LENGTH
e. Combines strings	||

2. True or false: Using functions in a SELECT statement to restructure the appearance of data in output also affects the way the data is stored in the database.

   Answer: False

3. True or false: The outermost function is always resolved first when functions are embedded within other functions in a query.

   Answer: False. The innermost function is always resolved first when embedding functions within one another.

Exercises

1. Write a query to select (display) the word Somewhere for every MIGRATION_LOCATION in the MIGRATION_LOCATIONS table.

   Answer:

```
select 'Somewhere'
from migration;
```

2. Write a query to produce results for every bird in the BIRDS table that looks like the following:

```
The Bald Eagle eats Fish.
The Bald Eagle eats Mammals.
Etc.
```

Answer:

```
select 'The ' || b.bird_name || ' eats ' || f.food_name ||'.'
from birds b,
     birds_food bf,
     food f
where b.bird_id = bf.bird_id
  and bf.food_id = f.food_id
order by b.bird_name;
```

3. Write a query to convert all nicknames to upper case.

Answer:

```
select upper(nickname)
from nicknames;
```

4. Use the REPLACE function to replace the occurrence of every MIGRATION_LOCATION that has the word United States in it with US.

Answer:

```
select replace(migration_location, 'United States', 'US')
from migration;
```

5. Write a query using the RPAD function to produce output to display every numeric column in the BIRDS table as a character, or left-justify.

Answer:

```
select bird_name,
       rpad(height, 6, ' ') height,
       rpad(weight, 6, ' ') weight,
       rpad(wingspan, 8, ' ') wingspan,
       rpad(eggs, 4, ' ') eggs,
       rpad(broods, 6, ' ') broods,
       rpad(incubation, 10, ' ') incubation,
       rpad(fledging, 8, ' ') fledging
from birds;
```

6. Write a query to produce the following results for types of herons in the BIRDS table.

Answer:

```
BIRD_NAME                      TYPE OF HERON
------------------------------ -----------------------
Great Blue Heron               Great Blue
Green Heron                    Green

2 rows selected.
```

```
select bird_name,
       ltrim(bird_name, ' ') "TYPE OF HERON"
from birds
where bird_name like '%Heron%';
```

7. Experiment with the functions in this hour on your own. Trial and error is a good way to learn with queries because you do not affect any data that is actually stored in the database.

Hour 16, "Understanding Dates and Times"

Quiz

1. Where are the system date and time normally derived from?

   Answer: The system date and time are derived from the current date and time of the operating system on the host machine.

2. What are the standard internal elements of a DATETIME value?

   Answer: Year, month, day, time of day, day of week, and so forth

3. What is a major factor for international organizations when representing and comparing date and time values?

   Answer: The time zone

4. Can a character string date value be compared to a date value defined as a valid DATETIME data type?

   Answer: Yes, if a TO_DATE conversion function is used

5. What do you use in SQL Server and Oracle to get the current date and time?

   Answer: The system date, such as: `SELECT SYSDATE FROM DUAL;` (Oracle)

Exercises

1. Type the following SQL code into the sql prompt to display the current date from the database:

   ```
   SELECT SYSDATE FROM DUAL;
   ```

2. Create the PHOTOGRAPHERS table and insert the data shown at the beginning of this hour for these exercises.

Answer:

```
create table photographers2
(p_id           number(3)     not null       primary key,
photographer    varchar(30)   not null,
mentor_p_id     number(3)     null,
dob             date          not null,
dt_start_photo date           not null,
constraint p2_fk1 foreign key (mentor_p_id) references photographers2 (p_id));


insert into photographers2 values
( 7, 'Ryan Notstephens' , null, '07-16-1975', '07-16-1989');

insert into photographers2 values
( 8, 'Susan Willamson' , null, '12-03-1979', '02-22-2016');

insert into photographers2 values
( 9, 'Mark Fife' , null, '01-31-1982', '12-25-2000');

insert into photographers2 values
( 1, 'Shooter McGavin' , null, '02-24-2005', '01-01-2019');

insert into photographers2 values
( 2, 'Jenny Forest' , 8, '08-15-1963', '08-16-1983');

insert into photographers2 values
( 3, 'Steve Hamm' , null, '09-14-1969', '01-01-2000');

insert into photographers2 values
( 4, 'Harry Henderson' , 9, '03-22-1985', '05-16-2011');

insert into photographers2 values
( 5, 'Kelly Hairtrigger' , 8, '01-25-2001', '02-01-2019');

insert into photographers2 values
( 6, 'Gordon Flash' , null, '09-14-1971', '10-10-2010');

insert into photographers2 values
( 10, 'Kate Kapteur' , 7, '09-14-1969', '11-07-1976');

commit;
```

3. Write a query to display all the data in the PHOTOGRAPHERS table that you just created.

Answer:

```
select * from photographers2;
```

4. Calculate your own age in a query using the system date.

Answer:

```
select round((sysdate - to_date('09-14-1969','mm-dd-yyyy'))/365) age
from dual;
```

5. Display the day of the week only that each photographer was born.

Answer:

```
select photographer, to_char(dob, 'Day') "DAY OF BIRTH"
from photographers2;
```

6. What is the age of Harry Henderson (rounded, of course, unless you just need to know)?

Answer:

```
select round((sysdate - dob)/365) age
from photographers2
where photographer = 'Harry Henderson';
```

7. Which photographer has been taking photos the longest?

Answer:

```
select photographer,
       round((sysdate - dt_start_photo)/365) "YEARS TAKING PHOTOS"
from photographers2
order by 2 desc;
```

8. Were any photographers born on the same day?

Answer:

```
select photographer, to_char(dob, 'Day') "DAY OF BIRTH"
from photographers2
order by 2;
```

9. Which photographers might have started taking photos because of a New Year's resolution?

Answer:

```
select photographer
from photographers2
where to_char(dt_start_photo, 'Mon dd') = 'Jan 01';
```

10. Write a query to determine today's Julian date (day of year).

Answer:

```
select to_char(sysdate, 'DDD')
from dual;
```

11. What is the combined age of all the photographers in the database?

Answer:

```
select round(sum((sysdate - dob)/365)) "COMBINED AGES OF ALL PHOTOGRAPHERS"
from photographers2;
```

12. Which photographer started taking photos at the youngest age?

Answer:

```
select photographer,
       round((dt_start_photo - dob)/365) "AGE STARTED TAKING PHOTOS"
from photographers2
order by 2;
```

13. Have some fun and come up with some queries of your own on this database or simply using the system date.

Hour 17, "Summarizing Data Results from a Query"

Quiz

1. True or false: The `AVG` function returns an average of all rows from a `SELECT` column, including any `NULL` values.

   Answer: False. Columns with `NULL` values are not evaluated.

2. True or false: The `SUM` function adds column totals.

   Answer: True

3. True or false: The `COUNT(*)` function counts all rows in a table.

   Answer: True

4. True or false: The `COUNT([column name])` function counts `NULL` values.

   Answer: False. A count of non-`NULL` values found in a column is returned.

5. Do the following SELECT statements work? If not, what fixes the statements?

   a. SELECT COUNT *

      FROM BIRDS;

      No; parentheses must enclose the *:

      SELECT COUNT(*)

      FROM BIRDS;

   b. SELECT COUNT(BIRD_ID), BIRD_NAME

      FROM BIRDS;

      Yes

   c. SELECT MIN(WEIGHT), MAX(HEIGHT)

      FROM BIRDS

      WHERE WINGSPAN > 48;

      Yes

   d. SELECT COUNT(DISTINCT BIRD_ID) FROM BIRDS;

      No; another set of parentheses must enclose BIRD_ID:

      SELECT COUNT(DISTINCT(BIRD_ID)) FROM BIRDS;

   e. SELECT AVG(BIRD_NAME) FROM BIRDS;

      No; you cannot calculate an average on a non-numeric column.

6. What is the purpose of the HAVING clause, and which other clause is it closest to?

   Answer: The HAVING clause places criteria for data returned from groups as defined in the GROUP BY clause. HAVING has a function similar to the WHERE BY clause.

7. True or false: You must also use the GROUP BY clause when using the HAVING clause.

   Answer: True. The HAVING clause is applied to data returned by the GROUP BY clause.

8. True or false: The columns selected must appear in the GROUP BY clause in the same order.

   Answer: True

9. True or false: The HAVING clause tells the GROUP BY clause which groups to include.

   Answer: True

Exercises

1. What is the average wingspan of birds?

   Answer:

```
select avg(wingspan)
from birds;
```

2. What is the average wingspan of birds that eat fish?

   Answer:

```
select avg(b.wingspan)
from birds b,
     birds_food bf,
     food f
where b.bird_id = bf.bird_id
  and bf.food_id = f.food_id
  and f.food_name = 'Fish';
```

3. How many different types of food does the Common Loon eat?

   Answer:

```
select count(bf.food_id)
from birds b,
     birds_food bf
where b.bird_id = bf.bird_id
   and b.bird_name = 'Common Loon';
```

4. What is the average number of eggs per type of nest?

   Answer:

```
select n.nest_name, avg(b.eggs)
from birds b,
     birds_nests bn,
     nests n
where b.bird_id = bn.bird_id
  and bn.nest_id = n.nest_id
group by n.nest_name;
```

5. What is the lightest bird?

   Answer:

```
select min(weight)
from birds;
```

```
select bird_name
from birds
where weight = "weight from previous query";
```

6. Generate a list of birds that are above average in all the following areas: height, weight, and wingspan.

   Answer:

```
select avg(wingspan) from birds;
select avg(height) from birds;
select avg(weight) from birds;

select bird_name
from birds
where wingspan > "value from previous query"
  and height > "value from previous query"
  and weight > "value from previous query";
```

7. Write a query to generate a list of all migration locations and their average wingspans, but only for locations of birds that have an average wingspan greater than 48 inches.

   Answer:

```
select m.migration_location, avg(b.wingspan)
from migration m,
     birds_migration bm,
     birds b
where m.migration_id = bm.migration_id
  and bm.bird_id = b.bird_id
group by m.migration_location
having avg(b.wingspan) > 48;
```

8. Write a query showing a list of all photographers and the number of photographers mentored by each photographer.

   Answer:

```
select p2b.photographer, count(p2a.photographer)
from photographers2 p2a,
     photographers2 p2b
where p2a.mentor_p_id(+) = p2b.p_id
group by p2b.photographer;
```

9. Experiment on your own using aggregate functions, along with other functions that you learned in previous hours.

Hour 18, "Using Subqueries to Define Unknown Data"

Quiz

1. What is the function of a subquery when used with a SELECT statement?

   Answer: A subquery returns a set of values that are substituted into the WHERE clause of a query.

2. Can you update more than one column when using the UPDATE statement with a subquery?

   Answer: Yes

3. Can you embed subqueries within other subqueries?

   Answer: Yes

4. What is a subquery called that has a column related to a column in the main query?

   Answer: Correlated subquery

5. Can you embed subqueries within other subqueries?

   Answer: Yes

6. What is an example of an operator that cannot be used when accessing a subquery?

   Answer: BETWEEN

Exercises

1. Write a query with a subquery to create a list of birds and their wingspans for birds that have a wingspan less than the average wingspan in the BIRDS table.

   Answer:

```
select bird_name, wingspan
from birds
where wingspan < (select avg(wingspan)
                  from birds);
```

2. Produce a list of birds and their associated migration locations for only birds that migrate to locations that have birds migrating there with an above average wingspan.

   Answer:

```
select b.bird_name, m.migration_location
from birds b,
     birds_migration bm,
     migration m
```

```
where b.bird_id = bm.bird_id
  and bm.migration_id = m.migration_id
  and b.wingspan > (select avg(wingspan)
                    from birds);
```

3. Use a subquery to find any food items that are eaten by the shortest bird in the database.

   Answer:

```
select b.bird_name, f.food_name
from birds b,
     birds_food bf,
     food f
where b.bird_id = bf.bird_id
  and bf.food_id = f.food_id
  and b.height = (select min(height) from birds);
```

4. Applying the concept of a subquery, create a new table called BIRD_APPETIZERS based on the following information: This new table should list the FOOD_ID and FOOD_NAME, but only for food items associated with birds that are in the bottom 25 percentile of height.

   Answer:

```
create table bird_appetizers as
select food_id, food_name
from food
where food_id in (select bf.food_id
                  from birds_food bf,
                       birds b
                  where bf.bird_id = b.bird_id
                    and b.height < (select avg(height) * .5
                                    from birds));


select * from bird_appetizers;
```

Hour 19, "Combining Multiple Queries into One"

Quiz

1. Match the correct operator to the following statements:

Statement	Operator
a. Show duplicates	UNION
b. Return only rows from the first query that match those in the second query	INTERSECT
c. Return no duplicates	UNION ALL
d. Return only rows from the first query not returned by the second	EXCEPT

Answer:

a. UNION ALL

b. INTERSECT

c. UNION

d. EXCEPT (and MINUS)

2. How many times can ORDER BY be used in a compound query?

Answer: Once

3. How many times can GROUP BY be used in a compound query?

Answer: Once for each SELECT in the compound query

4. How many times can HAVING be used in a compound query?

Answer: Once for each SELECT in the compound query

5. Consider a query that uses the EXCEPT (or MINUS) operator. Suppose that the first SELECT statement returns 10 rows of distinct rows, and the second SELECT statement returns 4 distinct rows of data. How many rows of data are returned in the final result set of the compound query?

Answer: 6 rows

Exercises

1. Create a table using the following SQL code; then write a query to select all records from the table.

```
SQL> create table birds_menu as
  2  select b.bird_id, b.bird_name,
  3      b.incubation + b.fledging parent_time,
  4      f.food_name
  5  from birds b,
  6    food f,
  7    birds_food bf
  8  where b.bird_id = bf.bird_id
  9    and bf.food_id = f.food_id
 10    and f.food_name in ('Crustaceans', 'Insects', 'Seeds', 'Snakes')
 11  order by 1;
```

Answer:

```
select * from birds_menu;
```

2. Issue the following queries and study the results. The first query selects the bird's name from the new table for birds whose parenting time exceeds 85 days. The second query is for those birds in the new table whose parenting time is less than or equal to 85 days. The third query combines both queries using the `UNION` operator.

```
SQL> select bird_name
  2  from birds_menu
  3  where parent_time > 85
  4  order by 1;

SQL> select bird_name
  2  from birds_menu
  3  where parent_time <= 85
  4  order by 1;

SQL> select bird_name
  2  from birds_menu
  3  where parent_time > 85
  4  UNION
  5  select bird_name
  6  from birds_menu
  7  where parent_time <= 85
  8  order by 1;
```

3. Issue the following SQL statement to practice with the previous query using the `UNION ALL` operator, and compare the results to the previous result set.

```
SQL> select bird_name
  2  from birds_menu
  3  where parent_time > 85
  4  UNION ALL
  5  select bird_name
  6  from birds_menu
  7  where parent_time <= 85
  8  order by 1;
```

4. Issue the following SQL statement to practice with the `INTERSECT` operator, and compare the results to the base data In the `BIRDS_MENU` table.

```
SQL> select bird_name
  2  from birds_menu
  3  INTERSECT
  4  select bird_name
  5  from birds_menu
  6  where food_name in ('Insects', 'Snakes')
  7  order by 1;
```

5. Issue the following SQL statement to practice with the `MINUS` operator, and compare the results to the base data in the `BIRDS_MENU` table.

```
SQL> select bird_name
  2  from birds_menu
  3  MINUS
  4  select bird_name
  5  from birds_menu
  6  where food_name in ('Insects', 'Snakes')
  7  order by 1;
```

6. Issue the following SQL statement to return a count of the number of food items eaten by each bird in the `BIRDS_MENU` table.

```
SQL> select bird_name, count(food_name)
  2  from birds_menu
  3  group by bird_name;
```

7. Issue the following SQL statement to using aggregate functions in a compound query. Study the results closely.

```
SQL> select bird_name, count(food_name)
  2  from birds_menu
  3  where parent_time > 100
  4  group by bird_name
  5  UNION
```

```
6  select bird_name, count(food_name)
7  from birds_menu
8  where parent_time < 80
9  group by bird_name;
```

8. Experiment with some compound queries on your own using the new table you created during these exercises, or for any tables in the BIRDS database, or for any tables you have created thus far.

Hour 20, "Creating and Using Views and Synonyms"

Quiz

1. Can you delete a row of data from a view that you created from multiple tables?

   Answer: No

2. When creating a table, the owner is automatically granted the appropriate privileges on that table. Is this true when creating a view?

   Answer: Yes

3. Which clause orders data when creating a view?

   Answer: GROUP BY and, in some implementations, ORDER BY

4. Do Oracle and SQL Server handle the capability to order a view in the same way?

   Answer: They both can achieve a sort with GROUP BY, but Oracle does not allow the use of ORDER BY.

5. Which option can you use when creating a view from a view to check integrity constraints?

   Answer: WITH CHECK OPTION

6. You try to drop a view and receive an error because of one or more underlying views. What must you do to drop the view?

   Answer: Drop the underlying views or any dependencies

Exercises

1. Write a SQL statement to create a view based on the total contents of the `BIRDS` table. Select all data from your view.

   Answer:

   ```
   create or replace view more_birds as
   select * from birds;

   select * from more_birds;
   ```

2. Write a SQL statement that creates a summarized view containing the average wingspan of birds in each migration location. Select all data from your view.

   Answer:

   ```
   create or replace view migration_view as
   select m.migration_location, avg(b.wingspan) avg_wingspan
   from migration m,
        birds_migration bm,
        birds b
   where m.migration_id = bm.migration_id
     and bm.bird_id = b.bird_id
   group by m.migration_location;

   select * from migration_view;
   ```

3. Query your view to return only the migration locations that are above average in the average wingspan category.

   Answer:

   ```
   select *
   from migration_view
   where avg_wingspan > (select avg(avg_wingspan)
                         from migration_view);
   ```

4. Drop your view.

   Answer:

   ```
   drop view migration_view;
   ```

5. Create a view called `FISH_EATERS` for only those birds that eat fish. Select all data from `FISH_EATERS`.

   Answer:

   ```
   create or replace view fish_eaters as
   select b.bird_id, b.bird_name
   ```

```
from birds b,
     birds_food bf,
     food f
where b.bird_id = bf.bird_id
  and bf.food_id = f.food_id
  and f.food_name = 'Fish';

select * from fish_eaters;
```

6. Write a query joining your FISH_EATERS view to the MIGRATION table, to return only migration locations for birds that eat fish.

   Answer:

```
select m.migration_location
from migration m,
     birds_migration bm,
     fish_eaters f
where m.migration_id = bm.migration_id
  and bm.bird_id = f.bird_id;
```

7. Create a synonym for your FISH_EATERS view, and then write a query using the synonym.

   Answer:

```
create synonym eat_fish for fish_eaters;

select * from eat_fish;
```

8. Experiment with some views of your own. Try joining views and tables, and employ some SQL functions that you previously learned.

Hour 21, "Managing Database Users and Security"

Quiz

1. Which command establishes a session?

   Answer: CONNECT

2. Which option drops a schema that still contains database objects?

   Answer: DROP SCHEMA with the CASCADE option

3. Which statement removes a database privilege?

   Answer: REVOKE

4. Which command creates a grouping or collection of tables, views, and privileges?

   Answer: CREATE SCHEMA (or CREATE USER), with the appropriate privileges, creates a user that can create objects in a database, which is a schema.

5. What option must a user have to grant another user privileges on an object that the user does not own?

   Answer: WITH GRANT OPTION

6. When privileges are granted to PUBLIC, do all database users acquire the privileges or only specified users?

   Answer: PUBLIC applies to all database users.

7. What privilege is required to look at data in a specific table?

   Answer: SELECT

8. What type of privilege is SELECT?

   Answer: The capability to query data from a database object. It is an object-level privilege.

9. What option revokes a user's privilege to an object, as well as the other users that they might have granted privileges to, by use of the GRANT option?

   Answer: The CASCADE option

Exercises

1. Describe how you would create the new user John in your sample database.

   Answer: Use the CREATE USER command

2. Explain the steps you would take to grant access to the BIRDS table to your new user, John.

   Answer: Use the GRANT command.

3. Describe how you would assign permissions to all objects within the BIRDS database to John.

   Answer: Use the GRANT command

4. Describe how you would revoke the previous privileges from John and then remove his account.

   Answer: Use the REVOKE command.

5. Create a new database user as follows:

```
Username: Steve
Password: Steve123
```

Answer: `CREATE USER STEVE IDENTIFIED BY STEVE123;`

6. Create a role for your new database user, `Steve`, from the previous exercise. Call the role `bird_query` and give the role `SELECT` on just the `BIRDS` table. Assign `Steve` to this role.

Answer:

```
CREATE ROLE BIRD_QUERY;
GRANT SELCT TO BIRD_QUERY ON BIRDS;
GRANT BIRD_QUERY TO STEVE;
```

7. Connect as Steve and query the `BIRDS` table. Be sure to qualify the `BIRDS` table because Steve is not the owner (`owner.table_name`).

Answer:

```
CONNECT STEVE
SELECT * FROM RYAN.BIRDS;
```

8. Connect back as your original user.

Answer:

```
CONNECT RYAN
```

9. Now revoke Steve's `SELECT` access from the other tables in the database. Connect to the database as Steve, and try to select from the `EMPLOYEES`, `AIRPORTS`, and `ROUTES` tables. What happened?

Answer:

```
revoke select on birds from steve;
```

10. Connect to the database once again as Steve and try to query the `BIRDS` table.

Answer:

```
connect steve
select * from ryan.birds;
```

11. Experiment on your own with your database.

Hour 22, "Using Indexes to Improve Performance"

Quiz

1. What are some major disadvantages of using indexes?

   Answer: Major disadvantages of an index include slowed batch jobs, storage space on the disk, and maintenance upkeep on the index.

2. Why is the order of columns in a composite index important?

   Answer: Because query performance is improved by putting the column with the most restrictive values first

3. Should a column with a large percentage of `NULL` values be indexed?

   Answer: No. A column with a large percentage of `NULL` values should not be indexed because the speed of accessing these rows degrades when the value of a large percentage of rows is the same.

4. Is the main purpose of an index to stop duplicate values in a table?

   Answer: No. The main purpose of an index is to enhance data retrieval speed; although a unique index stops duplicate values in a table.

5. True or false: The main reason for a composite index is for aggregate function usage in an index.

   Answer: False. The main reason for composite indexes is for two or more columns in the same table to be indexed.

6. What does cardinality refer to? What is considered a column of high cardinality?

   Answer: Cardinality refers to the uniqueness of the data within a column. The `SSN` column is an example of such a column.

Exercises

1. For the following situations, decide whether an index should be used and, if so, what type of index should be used:

   a. Several columns, but a rather small table.

      Answer: No

   b. Medium-sized table, no duplicates allowed

      Answer: No

c. Several columns, very large table, several columns used as filters in the WHERE clause

   Answer: Yes

d. Large table, many columns, a lot of data manipulation

   Answer: No

2. Write a SQL statement to create an index called FOOD_IDX in FOOD on the FOOD_NAME column.

   Answer:

```
create index food_idx
on food (food_name);
```

3. Write a SQL statement to create an index called WINGSPAN_IDX in BIRDS on the WINGSPAN column.

   Answer:

```
create index wingspan_idx
on birds (wingspan);
```

4. Drop the indexes you created.

   Answer:

```
drop index food_idx;

drop index wingspan_idx;
```

5. Study the tables used in this book. List some good candidates for indexed columns, based on how a user might search for data.

6. Create some additional indexes on your tables as you like. Think about how your data might be searched and where indexes can create efficiencies.

Hour 23, "Improving Database Performance"

Quiz

1. Is using a unique index on a small table beneficial?

   Answer: The index might not be of any use for performance issues, but the unique index keeps referential integrity intact. Referential integrity is discussed in Hour 3.

2. What happens when the optimizer chooses not to use an index on a table when a query has been executed?

   Answer: A full table scan occurs.

3. Should the most restrictive clause(s) be placed before or after the join condition(s) in the `WHERE` clause?

   Answer: The most restrictive clause(s) should be evaluated before the join condition(s) because join conditions normally return a large number of rows.

4. When is the `LIKE` operator considered bad in terms of performance?

   Answer: When the use of `LIKE` disables the use of indexes that exist on the target tables

5. How can you optimize batch load operations in terms of indexes?

   Answer: You can remove indexes prior to a batch load and re-create them afterward. It is beneficial to performance to rebuild indexes periodically anyhow.

6. Which three clauses are the cause of sort operations that degrade performance?

   Answer: `ORDER BY`, `GROUP BY`, and `HAVING`.

Exercises

1. Rewrite the following SQL statements to improve their performance. Use the fictitious `EMPLOYEE_TBL` and `EMPLOYEE_PAY_TBL`, as described here:

```
EMPLOYEE_TBL
EMP_ID          VARCHAR(9)     NOT NULL      Primary key
LAST_NAME       VARCHAR(15)    NOT NULL,
FIRST_NAME      VARCHAR(15)    NOT NULL,
MIDDLE_NAME     VARCHAR(15),
ADDRESS         VARCHAR(30)    NOT NULL,
CITY            VARCHAR(15)    NOT NULL,
STATE           VARCHAR(2)     NOT NULL,
ZIP             INTEGER(5)     NOT NULL,
PHONE           VARCHAR(10),
PAGER           VARCHAR(10),
EMPLOYEE_PAY_TBL
EMP_ID             VARCHAR(9)      NOT NULL  primary key
POSITION           VARCHAR(15)     NOT NULL,
DATE_HIRE          DATETIME,
PAY_RATE           DECIMAL(4,2)    NOT NULL,
DATE_LAST_RAISE    DATETIME,
SALARY             DECIMAL(8,2),
BONUS              DECIMAL(8,2),
```

a.

```
SELECT EMP_ID, LAST_NAME, FIRST_NAME,
       PHONE
FROM EMPLOYEE_TBL
   WHERE SUBSTRING(PHONE, 1, 3) = '317' OR
         SUBSTRING(PHONE, 1, 3) = '812' OR
         SUBSTRING(PHONE, 1, 3) = '765';
```

Answer:

```
SELECT EMP_ID, LAST_NAME, FIRST_NAME,
       PHONE
FROM EMPLOYEE_TBL
WHERE SUBSTRING(PHONE, 1, 3) IN ('317', '812', '765');
```

Typically, convert multiple OR conditions to an IN list works better.

b.

```
SELECT LAST_NAME, FIRST_NAME
FROM EMPLOYEE_TBL
WHERE LAST_NAME LIKE '%ALL%';
```

Answer:

```
SELECT LAST_NAME, FIRST_NAME
FROM EMPLOYEE_TBL
WHERE LAST_NAME LIKE 'WAL%';
```

You cannot take advantage of an index if you do not include the first character in a condition's value.

c.

```
SELECT E.EMP_ID, E.LAST_NAME, E.FIRST_NAME,
       EP.SALARY
FROM EMPLOYEE_TBL E,
EMPLOYEE_PAY_TBL EP
WHERE LAST_NAME LIKE 'S%'
AND E.EMP_ID = EP.EMP_ID;
```

Answer:

```
SELECT E.EMP_ID, E.LAST_NAME, E.FIRST_NAME,
       EP.SALARY
FROM EMPLOYEE_TBL E,
EMPLOYEE_PAY_TBL EP
WHERE E.EMP_ID = EP.EMP_ID
AND LAST_NAME LIKE 'S%';
```

2. Add another table called EMPLOYEE_PAYHIST_TBL that contains a large amount of pay history data. Use the following table to write a series of SQL statements to address the following problems. Be sure to ensure that the queries you write perform well.

```
EMPLOYEE_PAYHIST_TBL
PAYHIST_ID          VARCHAR(9)       NOT NULL      primary key,
EMP_ID              VARCHAR(9)       NOT NULL,
START_DATE          DATETIME         NOT NULL,
END_DATE            DATETIME,
PAY_RATE            DECIMAL(4,2)     NOT NULL,
SALARY              DECIMAL(8,2)     NOT NULL,
BONUS               DECIMAL(8,2)     NOT NULL,
CONSTRAINT EMP_FK FOREIGN KEY (EMP_ID)
REFERENCES EMPLOYEE_TBL (EMP_ID)
```

a. Find the SUM of the salaried versus nonsalaried employees, by the year in which their pay started.

Answer:

```
SELECT START_YEAR,SUM(SALARIED) AS SALARIED,SUM(HOURLY) AS
HOURLY
    FROM
    (SELECT YEAR(E.START_DATE) AS START_YEAR,COUNT(E.EMP_ID)     AS
SALARIED,0 AS HOURLY
    FROM EMPLOYEE_PAYHIST_TBL E INNER JOIN
    ( SELECT MIN(START_DATE) START_DATE,EMP_ID
     FROM EMPLOYEE_PAYHIST_TBL
    GROUP BY EMP_ID) F ON E.EMP_ID=F.EMP_ID AND
E.START_DATE=F.START_DATE
    WHERE E.SALARY > 0.00
    GROUP BY YEAR(E.START_DATE)
    UNION
SELECT YEAR(E.START_DATE) AS START_YEAR,0 AS SALARIED,
    COUNT(E.EMP_ID)  AS HOURLY
    FROM EMPLOYEE_PAYHIST_TBL E INNER JOIN
    ( SELECT MIN(START_DATE) START_DATE,EMP_ID
    FROM EMPLOYEE_PAYHIST_TBL
    GROUP BY EMP_ID) F ON E.EMP_ID=F.EMP_ID AND
E.START_DATE=F.START_DATE
    WHERE E.PAY_RATE > 0.00
    GROUP BY YEAR(E.START_DATE)
    ) A
    GROUP BY START_YEAR
    ORDER BY START_YEAR
```

b. Find the difference in the yearly pay of salaried employees versus nonsalaried employees, by the year in which their pay started. Consider the nonsalaried employees to be working full time during the year (PAY_RATE × 52 × 40).

Answer:

```
SELECT START_YEAR,SALARIED AS SALARIED,HOURLY AS HOURLY,
    (SALARIED - HOURLY) AS PAY_DIFFERENCE
    FROM
    (SELECT YEAR(E.START_DATE) AS START_YEAR,AVG(E.SALARY) AS
SALARIED,
    0 AS HOURLY
    FROM EMPLOYEE_PAYHIST_TBL E INNER JOIN
    ( SELECT MIN(START_DATE) START_DATE,EMP_ID
    FROM EMPLOYEE_PAYHIST_TBL
    GROUP BY EMP_ID) F ON E.EMP_ID=F.EMP_ID AND
E.START_DATE=F.START_DATE
    WHERE E.SALARY > 0.00
    GROUP BY YEAR(E.START_DATE)
    UNION
SELECT YEAR(E.START_DATE) AS START_YEAR,0 AS SALARIED,
    AVG(E.PAY_RATE * 52 * 40 ) AS HOURLY
    FROM EMPLOYEE_PAYHIST_TBL E INNER JOIN
    ( SELECT MIN(START_DATE) START_DATE,EMP_ID
     FROM EMPLOYEE_PAYHIST_TBL
    GROUP BY EMP_ID) F ON E.EMP_ID=F.EMP_ID AND
E.START_DATE=F.START_DATE
    WHERE E.PAY_RATE > 0.00
    GROUP BY YEAR(E.START_DATE)
    ) A
    GROUP BY START_YEAR
    ORDER BY START_YEAR
```

c. Find the difference in what employees make now versus what they made when they started with the company. Again, consider the nonsalaried employees to be full time. Also consider that the employees' current pay is reflected in EMPLOYEE_PAY_TBL and also EMPLOYEE_PAYHIST_TBL. In the pay history table, the current pay is reflected as a row with the END_DATE for pay equal to NULL.

Answer:

```
SELECT CURRENTPAY.EMP_ID,STARTING_ANNUAL_PAY,CURRENT_
ANNUAL_PAY,
CURRENT_ANNUAL_PAY - STARTING_ANNUAL_PAY AS PAY_DIFFERENCE
FROM
(SELECT EMP_ID,(SALARY + (PAY_RATE * 52 * 40)) AS
CURRENT_ANNUAL_PAY
  FROM EMPLOYEE_PAYHIST_TBL
```

```
  WHERE END_DATE IS NULL) CURRENTPAY
INNER JOIN
(SELECT E.EMP_ID,(SALARY + (PAY_RATE * 52 * 40)) AS
STARTING_ANNUAL_PAY
  FROM EMPLOYEE_PAYHIST_TBL E
  ( SELECT MIN(START_DATE) START_DATE,EMP_ID
           FROM EMPLOYEE_PAYHIST_TBL
           GROUP BY EMP_ID) F ON E.EMP_ID=F.EMP_ID AND
E.START_DATE=F.START_DATE
  ) STARTINGPAY ON
  CURRENTPAY.EMP_ID = STARTINGPAY.EMP_ID
```

Hour 24, "Working with the System Catalog"

Quiz

1. What is the system catalog also known as in some implementations?

   Answer: The data dictionary

2. Can a regular user update the system catalog?

   Answer: No

3. Who owns the system catalog?

   Answer: The database itself, the owner of the database, or the system user

4. What is the difference between the Oracle system objects `ALL_TABLES` and `DBA_TABLES`?

   Answer: `ALL_TABLES` shows information about all tables that a specific user can access, whereas `DBA_TABLES` contains information about all tables that exist in the database as a whole.

5. Who makes modifications to the system tables?

   Answer: The database itself makes modifications to the system tables, based on the activity in the database.

Exercises

1. At the prompt, type in queries to bring up each of the following:

    - Information on all your tables
    - Information on all columns in your tables

    Answer:

```
select table_name
from user_tables
where table_name not like 'DMRS_%';

select *
from user_tab_columns
order by table_name;
```

2. Show the name of the current database.

    Answer:

```
select * from v$database;
```

3. Show the name of the user by which you are connected to the database.

    Answer:

```
show user;
```

4. Create a role to update your FOOD table.

    Answer:

```
alter session set "_ORACLE_SCRIPT"=true;



create role updatefoodinfo_role;



grant update on updatefoodinfo_role to "username";



select role from role_tab_privs where owner = 'RYAN';
```

5. Select information about the role you created from the system catalog.

   Answer:

```
SQL> select role, owner, table_name, privilege
  2  from role_tab_privs
  3  where role = 'SEE_BIRDS';
```

6. Explore the system catalog on your own. The information contained is nearly endless. Remember that, in Oracle, you can use the `DESCRIBE table_name` command to show the columns that comprise a table.

Hour 25, "Bonus Workshop for the Road"

Exercises

1. Select data from your tables to explore your data, starting with the following:

   - Select all the data from the `BIRDS` table.
   - Select all the data from the `PHOTOGRAPHERS` table.
   - What are the predators of the Bald Eagle?

   Answer:

```
select * from birds;

select * from photographers;

select p.predator
from predators p,
     birds_predators bp,
     birds b
where p.pred_id = bp.pred_id
  and b.bird_id = bp.bird_id
  and b.bird_name = 'Bald Eagle';
```

2. When looking at the ERD for this database, you can see that a relationship is missing between the `PHOTOGRAPHERS` and `PHOTOS` tables.

   - What kind of relationship should be added?
   - Use SQL to define a relationship between these two tables in your database. (*Hint:* add any necessary foreign key constraints.)

   Answer: A photographer might take many photographs. `PHOTOGRAPHERS` and `PHOTOS` should have a common column to join the two tables.

3. Add a table called COLORS for colors that each bird might have and create any other necessary tables and relationships (primary and foreign keys) to create a relationship between BIRDS and COLORS. If you want, you can save your CREATE TABLE statements in a file to easily regenerate at a later time, or you can add them to your main tables.sql script. If you add these statements to the main tables.sql script, be sure that the DROP and CREATE TABLE statements are in the proper order in relation to the other tables in your database, based on primary/foreign key relationships (for example, you must drop child tables before parent tables, and you must create parent tables before child tables).

   Answer:

```
create table colors
(color_id    number(2)       not null      primary key,
 color       varchar2(20)    not null);

create table birds_colors
(bird_id     number(3)       not null,
 color_id    number(2)       not null,
 constraint birds_colors_pk1 primary key (bird_id, color_id),
 constraint birds_colors_fk1 foreign key (bird_id) references birds(bird_id),
 constraint birds_colors_fk2 foreign key(color_id) references colors(color_
id));
```

4. Insert a few rows of data into the COLORS table and any other tables you may have created.

   Answer:

```
insert into colors values (1, 'Blue');
insert into colors values (2, 'Green');
insert into colors values (3, 'Black');
insert into colors values (4, 'White');
insert into colors values (5, 'Brown');
insert into colors values (6, 'Gray');
insert into colors values (7, 'Yellow');
insert into colors values (8, 'Purple');
```

5. Add the following bird to your database: Easter Kingbird, 9 inches, .2 pounds, 15-inch wingspan, 5 eggs, up to 4 broods per season, incubation period of 17 days, fledging period of 17 days, both participate with the nest.

   Answer:

```
insert into birds values
(24, 'Eastern Kingbird', 9, .2, 15, 5, 4, 17, 17, 'B');
```

6. Add the following photographer to your database: Margaret Hatcher, mentored by Susan Williamson, hobbyist level.

   Answer:

```
insert into photographers values
(12, 'Margaret Hatcher', 8, 3);
```

7. Make sure you have saved your recent transactions. If you want, you can save the previous `INSERT` statements to a file so that you can regenerate this data later if you need to, or you can add them to the main data.sql script.

   Answer:

```
Commit;
```

8. Generate a simple list of all photographers, skill levels, and styles. Then sort the results, showing the photographers with the highest skill levels first in your results.

   Answer:

```
select p.photographer, pl.photo_level, s.style
from photographers p,
     photo_levels pl,
     photographer_styles ps,
     photo_styles s
where p.level_id = pl.level_id
  and p.photographer_id = ps.photographer_id
  and ps.style_id = s.style_id
order by 3 desc;
```

9. Generate a list of photographers and their protégés (the photographers they mentor). List only the photographers that are mentors.

   Answer:

```
select mentors.photographer mentor,
       proteges.photographer protege
from photographers mentors,
     photographers proteges
where mentors.photographer_id = proteges.mentor_photographer_id
order by 1;
```

10. Re-create the same list of photographers and their protégés, but show all photographers, regardless of whether they mentor anyone, and sort the results by the photographer with the highest skill levels first.

Answer:

```
select mentors.photographer mentor,
       proteges.photographer protege, pl.photo_level
from photographers mentors,
     photographers proteges,
     photo_levels pl
where mentors.photographer_id(+) = proteges.mentor_photographer_id
  and proteges.level_id = pl.level_id
order by 1;
```

11. Using UNION to combine the results of multiple queries, show a list of all animals in your database (for example, birds and predators).

Answer:

```
select bird_name from birds
union
select predator from predators;
```

12. Create a table called FORMER_PHOTOGRAPHERS that is based on the PHOTOGRAPHERS table.

Answer:

```
create table former_photographers as
select * from photographers;
```

13. Truncate the table FORMER_PHOTOGRAPHERS.

Answer:

```
truncate table former_photographers;
```

14. Insert all data from the PHOTOGRAPHERS table into the FORMER_PHOTOGRAPHERS table.

Answer:

```
insert into former_photographers
select * from photographers;
```

15. Can you think of any views that can be created to make the exercises from the previous section easier, or more easily repeatable, for similar future queries?

Answer: Solutions will vary.

16. Create at least one view that you can imagine.

Answer: Solutions will vary.

17. Write a query that produces a list of the most versatile photographers in your database. For example, the query might contain one or more of the following subqueries:

- Photographers that have a skill level greater than the average skill level of all photographers
- Photographers whose count of birds of interest is more than the average of all photographers
- Photographers who have more styles than the average photographer

Answer:

```
select p.photographer, pl.photo_level,
       count(fb.photographer_id) birds,
       count(ps.photographer_id) styles
from photographers p,
     photo_levels pl,
     favorite_birds fb,
     photographer_styles ps,
     photo_styles s
where p.level_id = pl.level_id
  and p.photographer_id = fb.photographer_id
  and p.photographer_id = ps.photographer_id
  and s.style_id = ps.style_id
  and pl.level_id > (select avg(level_id) from photographers)
group by p.photographer, pl.photo_level
having count(fb.photographer_id) > (select avg(count(f.bird_id))
                                    from favorite_birds f,
                                         photographers p
                                    where p.photographer_id = f.photographer_id
                                    group by p.photographer_id)
  and count(ps.photographer_id) > (select avg(count(ps.style_id))
                                   from photographer_styles ps,
                                        photographers p
                                   where ps.photographer_id = p.photographer_id
                                   group by p.photographer_id);
```

18. Create a view called `Versatile_Photographers` that is based on the subqueries you used earlier.

Answer:

```
create view versatile_photographers as
select p.photographer, pl.photo_level,
       count(fb.photographer_id) birds,
       count(ps.photographer_id) styles
from photographers p,
     photo_levels pl,
     favorite_birds fb,
     photographer_styles ps,
     photo_styles s
where p.level_id = pl.level_id
  and p.photographer_id = fb.photographer_id
  and p.photographer_id = ps.photographer_id
  and s.style_id = ps.style_id
  and pl.level_id > (select avg(level_id) from photographers)
group by p.photographer, pl.photo_level
having count(fb.photographer_id) > (select avg(count(f.bird_id))
                                    from favorite_birds f,
                                         photographers p
                                    where p.photographer_id = f.photographer_id
                                    group by p.photographer_id)
  and count(ps.photographer_id) > (select avg(count(ps.style_id))
                                   from photographer_styles ps,
                                        photographers p
                                   where ps.photographer_id = p.photographer_id
                                   group by p.photographer_id);

select * from versatile_photographers;
```

19. Suppose that each photographer needs a database user account to access information in the database about birds and other photographers. Generate a SQL script that creates database user accounts for each photographer with the following syntax:

`CREATE USER MARGARET_HATCHER IDENTIFIED BY NEW_PASSWORD_1;`

Answer:

```
select 'CREATE USER ' ||
        substr(photographer, 1, instr(photographer, ' ', 1, 1) -1) ||
        '_' ||
        substr(photographer, instr(photographer, ' ', 1, 1) +1) ||
        ' IDENTIFIED BY NEW_PASSWORD_1;' "SQL CODE TO CREATE NEW USERS"
from photographers;
```

20. What are the predators of each bird?

Answer:

```
select b.bird_name, p.predator
from birds b,
     birds_predators bp,
     predators p
where b.bird_id = bp.bird_id
  and bp.pred_id = p.pred_id
order by 1;
```

21. Which birds have the most predators?

Answer:

```
select b.bird_name, count(bp.pred_id)
from birds b,
     birds_predators bp
where b.bird_id = bp.bird_id
group by b.bird_name
order by 2 desc;
```

22. Which predators eat the most birds in your database?

Answer:

```
select p.predator, count(bp.bird_id) "BIRD DIET"
from birds b,
     predators p,
     birds_predators bp
where b.bird_id = bp.bird_id
  and p.pred_id = bp.pred_id
group by p.predator
order by 2 desc;
```

23. Which predators eat only fish-eating birds?

Answer:

```
select distinct(p.predator) predators
from predators p,
     birds_predators bp,
     fish_eaters fe
where p.pred_id = bp.pred_id
  and fe.bird_id = bp.bird_id;
```

24. Which types of nests attract the most predators?

Answer:

```
select n.nest_name, count(distinct(bp.pred_id)) predators
from nests n,
     birds_nests bn,
     birds b,
     birds_predators bp
where n.nest_id = bn.nest_id
  and bn.bird_id = b.bird_id
  and b.bird_id = bp.bird_id
group by n.nest_name
order by 2 desc;
```

25. Which photographers are most likely to see a crocodile when capturing an image of a bird?

Answer:

```
select p.photographer, b.bird_name "FAVORITE BIRDS", pr.predator
from photographers p,
     favorite_birds fb,
     birds b,
     birds_predators bp,
     predators pr
where p.photographer_id = fb.photographer_id
  and fb.bird_id = b.bird_id
  and b.bird_id = bp.bird_id
  and bp.pred_id = pr.pred_id
  and pr.predator = 'Crocodile';

select p.photographer, b.bird_name "FAVORITE BIRDS", pr.predator
from photographers p,
     favorite_birds fb,
     birds b,
     birds_predators bp,
     predators pr
where p.photographer_id = fb.photographer_id
  and fb.bird_id = b.bird_id
  and b.bird_id = bp.bird_id
  and bp.pred_id = pr.pred_id
  and pr.predator = 'Other Birds';
```

26. Which predators are most likely to be in a landscape-style photograph?

Answer:

```
select distinct(pr.predator)
from photographers p,
     favorite_birds fb,
```

```
     birds b,
     birds_predators bp,
     predators pr,
     photographer_styles ps,
     photo_styles s
where p.photographer_id = fb.photographer_id
  and fb.bird_id = b.bird_id
  and b.bird_id = bp.bird_id
  and bp.pred_id = pr.pred_id
  and ps.photographer_id = p.photographer_id
  and s.style_id = ps.style_id
  and s.style = 'Landscape';
```

27. What birds have a diet more diverse than the average bird in the database?

Answer:

```
select b.bird_name, count(bf.bird_id) "FOOD ITEMS"
from birds b,
     birds_food bf
where b.bird_id = bf.food_id
group by b.bird_name
having count(bf.bird_id) > (select avg(count(bf.bird_id))
                            from birds b, birds_food bf
                            where b.bird_id = bf.bird_id
                            group by b.bird_id);
```

28. What cameras are used by these photographers?

Photographers that mentor others

Photographers with a skill level above average

Answer:

```
select c.camera
from cameras c,
     photographer_cameras pc,
     photographers p
where c.camera_id = pc.camera_id
  and pc.photographer_id = p.photographer_id
  and p.level_id > (select avg(level_id)
                    from photographers)
  and p.photographer_id in (select p.photographer_id
                            from photographers p,
                                 photographers m
                            where m.mentor_photographer_id = p.photographer_
id);
```

Index

SYMBOLS

A

B

C

D

E

F

G

K

L

M

O

Q

R

S

T

U

V

W

Y